I Guess I Just Wasn't Thinking

Part Two:
The French Riviera, Leo, June, and Big Trouble

W.K. "Jake" Wehrell

*This series is dedicated to my four savvy kids,
who in spite of my flagrant and prolonged absence,
have grown up to be loving and capable parents,
unremittingly supportive of each other, and exceptionally
successful professionals. I would have to say,
all credit to their great mom.*

himself pitifully out of touch with all that surrounds him. After a series of endeavors—including a nausea-provoking "pyramid sales" scheme, he retreats to more familiar activities. You will accompany him on ten-hour Atlantic crossings and all-night flights across the Sahara—the sole pilot in small (puddle jumper) single-engine aircraft that were in no way designed for either. Have a cup of tea with Judy Garland; experience a UFO engagement over the Caspian Sea, live through jungle crashes and Roger's capture, and his attempted vision-saving surgery at the Clinica Barraquer in Barcelona (where he happens a private dinner with John and Yoko)! Sadly, these exploits do not mask the deficiency that has subjugated his being. Struggling in an ill-fitting world, he continues to seek that one magic but historically fated-to-failure union. Ashamed and embarrassed he sincerely and apologetically strives to explain to you his life-altering condition and his otherwise inexplicable behavior. Readers will be surprised and gratified; unable not to leap to their feet and applaud an entirely unexpected but spectacular turn of events at the end of this part.

Part Four: At the End of the Rainbow. Now, as a result of the no less than miraculous occurrence at the end of Part Three—his long-awaited, wholly unanticipated mastery of the unapproachable and eminent femme fatale in Dakar, he is a changed being, emboldened and empowered, having at long last found that one woman! However, he is now faced with a daunting challenge—one for which there could be no solution: he has to come up with some way to construct a life with Mireille—in France, the states, or somewhere. During this quest we observe Roger in drudgery-immersed positions, and a real "first" for him: reeling in the disgrace of being "outplaced for management convenience." (Fired.) We cannot expect Roger to "change his spots" and we again find ourselves screaming instructions at him as he retreats to more familiar territory, engaging in a string of dangerous, disjointed and sometimes illicit activities (one of which ends up having him rescuing a friend from a dirt-floored cell in Colombia). The unfolding of events in this part see Roger having the highest hopes and then enduring the gravest disappointments, and finally the surprising, startling consequences of past events. Having slogged alongside Roger for the first three parts, you will not want to miss the shocking finality of his story.

Chapter One
JUNE 1964 – GOING TO SEA

Casting Off

Our final period of dry land carrier-qualification training was over. Weeks of herding several tons of buffeting aluminum through the air, down to a painted rectangle the size of your living room rug, was finally finished. The scores of each of our hundreds of precision landing attempts were tallied and compared. The much awaited meeting was held and a list of the top fifteen pilots who had made it—who would be "going to sea," was announced. For the anointed few it was a real macho celebration that night I can tell you. Lots of high fives, trash talking and back slapping going on. The *Armed Forces Times* article had been pinned up all over the base. "Marine Attack Squadron 331 had completed Final Phase training and was Combat Ready, about to put to sea on board the USS *Forrestal*." Yup, we were going to go tactical, cruise the Mediterranean, be part of the awesome Fleet Marine Force. Finally going to do what we had spent one year training for. But I for one had felt some very mixed emotions, and key among them was an unsettling "not-for-the-best" premonition.

Now—still in port, about to cast off, standing high and alone on the non-skid deck of this ocean splitting behemoth, I had a strong suspicion I'd have been better off if I'd never seen it. Just *miss* the damned cruise— be transferred to another squadron and stay in the states. Play with the kids, watch Sara cooking supper, weed the yard and clean the carport for the next ten months. It was summer but there was a leaden sky and an annoying wind that continued to buffet my pressed khaki trousers and flip my tie into my face. I was in an unfamiliar world, just one separated figure in an old black and white photo—charcoal water, pewter ship, and lead gray sky. Nothing much I could have done to avoid this. Never really had a respectable option. And too late now, we were doing it. All around me people who should have been here and knew what they were doing, were carrying out their critical casting off duties with speed and conviction; had to give them credit for that.

This was a big operation and I could see that every last "hand" knew exactly what he was supposed to be doing. Apparently no one felt as misplaced as I did. Within the hour we would be under way, heading towards the Atlantic—into the open water outside the Chesapeake Bay Bridge, with Norfolk sinking over the horizon (along with my heart). The week before driving up to Norfolk had been a quiet and comfortable time, except for the cloud of impending separation. I knew the kids didn't understand. How could they? Time and distance are not things that little kids compute. They know when they're on your lap. They know when their mom and dad are being silly, or supper is on the stove. They know those things. It had only been forty-five minutes and already I was having a hard time visualizing their faces in as much detail as I would have liked. No problem visualizing Sara's face, that was easy—holding back tears. And she wasn't the only one. I was feeling a sadness, a heaviness I may have never felt before; numbed by the coming separation.

Though I have to admit—shamefully, for the first five years of my marriage I'd lived in constant fear of having way too soon "closed the book" on my life; that I'd foolishly allowed something to happen—the permanency and restrictions of which I had never stopped to consider. I was sadly (in spite of a wonderful wife) constantly weighted down and distracted by a feeling of having consigned myself to a course that would forever exclude any other avenues. I don't know why, I just did. But recently (at long last and gratefully) I think I finally shed that mindset. I had begun to find a strange new contentment being with my family and in our own home. At last not feeling left out to be attending a school play, raking the leaves, or just sitting on the couch watching TV; not at all the yet undefined but adventuresome life I thought I could be destined for. Thankfully it recently began to seem right: Sara and I. The kids. Us! I was pretty sure I had finally accepted my situation and knew where I belonged, *and now I wasn't going to be there.*

Like the final scene in a movie—just before the credits start rolling down. From high above I had watched our Ford station wagon turn out of the pier parking lot and blend into the metal patchwork of the other retreating vehicles. I saw Donna (our oldest—five), waving out her front window—not well, but I had seen her. Mark (two years younger) would be on the front seat in the center, legs straight out, head erect. Little guy—always trying to do things just right. Then the two youngest ones—Stacy and Kevin. I'd have to just imagine them in their car seats in the back, their tiny heads too low to see. Plus it was too far now, too much reflection in the tinted glass. It would be a very long time before I would see them again. *Damn ten month cruise.* Could be worse I guess. What will they be like? Kids change a lot in a year. God it was high up here. I could see forever, but no longer my car. It was gone. They were gone and I was part of this now.

The activity was becoming almost frenzied now. I retreated a bit to watch from a safer distance as members of the ship's company turned to. From stem to stern, one after another, time-critical tasks were being undertaken by obedient young sailors responding to the hoarse commands of the flush-faced senior petty officers. As a Marine it's traditional to poke fun at the Navy, and particularly the "black shoe" (non-aviation) component. This carrier cruise would put a stop to any of that joking as far as I was concerned. I would discover operations at sea to be a huge, demanding, precise and unforgiving campaign, run by a group of dedicated professionals (albeit they were sailors).

Uh oh, it was happening—right on time. I felt our seventy-five-thousand-ton gray monster begin to creak and lean. Great thundering vibrations erupted from deep within as she strained to move. Mammoth brass screws at the stern pounded the water into froth. Tiny tugs with scurrying crews crouched then lunged with bows down into wet and shivering lines. But the ship was a slumbering giant, appearing to ignore these efforts in favor of one last effort of her own. A final shudder and we were away from the dock. Swirling dark pools filled the gap between the concrete pier and the straight steel hull. For better or for worse, I was on my way. No chance of a last minute reprieve. This was it.

As best I could tell the entire squadron was now up on the flight deck, and no horseplay or joking going on that I could see. Every man silent—left with his own thoughts, feeling the tremors up through his feet and beginning to sense the permanency of this irreversible event. Far forward and alone on the port catwalk I gripped the railing and took a deep breath, determined to hang onto the sight of the Norfolk skyline as long as possible. I couldn't keep back the tears. But no one could see, and I suspect I wasn't the only one. In fifteen minutes we were past the last rock breakwaters. No more small boats. Just a handful of guys on deck now.

I GUESS I JUST WASN'T THINKING

I tried to imagine where Sara and the kids might be now, visualizing our car stopped at a light, going through the tunnel, or on the freeway. Could hardly believe this was happening. Another thirty minutes and we were into open water. Only the bay bridge itself and some tall loading cranes broke the horizon. Before too long I was completely alone. All the other officers had gone below to begin exploring the maze of passageways and compartments we would get to know so well in the months ahead. As if in defiance of the unavoidable fate awaiting, I swung around and blinked into the wind, staring eastward. 2800 miles towards the Azores. Despite the chill I stayed on deck alone. We continued to plow ahead determinedly, bashing the dark water to either side, leaving the continental states further and further behind us.

For the cruise, with only twelve aircraft deployed, the squadron had leaned itself to fifteen pilots. The selected few. As I said already, for me—from the beginning I had a sickening feeling about the separation from my wife and family that would ensue, and could easily have been talked out of going. Gotta admit I'm not the world's hottest aviator and there were a couple carrier qualification periods where I did so poorly I could have been cut from this prestigious team, irrespective of my wishes. This eventuality caused me to consider possibly not trying quite so hard—*actually fail to qualify on purpose*, but Jim Stremlow—our LSO (Landing Signal Officer) running the show, would not have understood. He and I were the two junior captains in the squadron and close friends since flight training, and boy was he Gung-Ho—the unquestioned team leader. An Alpha male if ever there was one. Never quite arrived at the point of verbalizing my reservations to him. Darker than dusk. Stars out now. Noticed I was shivering. Rubbed my arms and decided it was time to go below. Surrender.

Chapter Two

THE CROSSING

The Anatomy of a Marine Squadron

We forged across the Atlantic in a fearless manner, devouring mile after mile of helpless waves. The ocean was no match for the ship. The water ran over itself trying to get out of our way. Lots of flying fish. If you've never seen them, they're a sight to behold. You read how they beat their tail fins on the surface to propel themselves great distances out of the water. After watching them, I think the damn fish *do* fly. They go further and higher than the tail-beating theory supports.

Of course we weren't alone on the ship. There were six tactical squadrons on board: two Navy fighter squadrons, two Navy attack squadrons, a Marine attack squadron (us), and a Navy electro-countermeasures (sub-hunter) squadron. In case you never really understood the difference: "Fighter" aircraft have air-to-air weaponry—to shoot down other aircraft. "Attack" aircraft have air-to-ground weaponry—to destroy targets on the ground. In addition to these tactical aviation units there was the "Ship's Company"—the hundreds of departments and thousands of "hands" (Navy commissioned officers, chiefs, and enlisted men) that weren't going to do the annihilating, just keep the ship itself up and running—which is no small job. They do their stuff and we do ours.

Our Commanding Officer (from now on called the "Skipper") was Lieutenant Colonel Cunningham. An alright guy. Big—well over six-foot and bald-headed. (Looked just like *Mr Clean.*) He had been a tank commander in Korea and hadn't earned his wings until midpoint in his career—which is difficult and rarely attempted. (Flying is one of those things it's best to tackle before life's experiences have taught you much about caution.)

I GUESS I JUST WASN'T THINKING

The second-in-command is called the Executive Officer, and we had a good one—Major Keith Johnson. He was one of those few senior officers who could do anything the hot shot lieutenants could. Besides him we only one other major deployed with us—Major Burnham, the Maintenance Officer. He was okay I guess; wanted to be thought of as "one of the guys." However, while his comments were usually offered in an apparently jovial manner, they were not up for discussion. Major Johnson could have been one of the guys without trying. Major Burnham for some reason, would never quite make the bond (though I give him all credit for trying).

Besides me there were three captains, two of whom you'll meet later. The other—Jim Stremlow, mentioned previously, would be my roommate for the cruise. Long and angular, from Amarillo, Texas, he appeared to have been assembled out of pressure-treated-pine 2x4s, with big hands (a couple of concrete blocks) and large square wrists. He had close cropped sandy hair, steely eyes and a square jaw, and was serious about the Marine Corps and Texas. (Anyone doubting this would get to see those cold eyes get even colder, and suddenly discover Jim could appear real threatening.) In all the time I'd known him I had never seen him in doubt about anything for more than ten seconds. And (some guys have all the luck) not only was he big and tough, he was smart as hell. We had met during Preflight Training in Pensacola. He and I had represented our cadet battalions in the boxing competitions. He—because he was raw-boned and fearless. Me? That's a good question. Trying to win my own approval I guess, by forcing myself to engage in an unnatural and physically demanding encounter. (Something I wouldn't have had to do if I would have been born big to start with.)

The lieutenants were the cream of the crop. They were all cool-looking athletic guys, mostly still bachelors, and surprisingly well read. I envied them somewhat—not being able to recollect ever having had a similar phase in my own life. It seemed every one of them had owned a Corvette before we deployed, subscribed to *Playboy* and *Forbes,* and came from good families in Boston or South Hampton. The world was their oyster and as a captain in this outfit, I knew I had my work cut out for me. No slouching would go unnoticed (particularly when it came to Bob Harmon or Don Goft).

Thankfully, at least now during the crossing (if I didn't think of how long it was going to be) it seemed like the cruise might not be too bad. And since we were only renting space from the Navy we didn't have the facility-upkeep concerns of our previous landbase. The Skipper said all we had to do during the crossing was just make damn sure we would be 100% operational and ready to go when we got over there. Stay in close touch with our enlisted men, answer their questions and keep the rumors from flying. The rumor mill (from now on referred to as "scuttlebutt") was that when we got to the Med, the routine would be ten days at sea and then four or five days in port. During the at-sea periods, each pilot could plan on getting at least six days of flying. And perhaps one of the reasons I was feeling okay for the moment was—*no flying at all during this crossing.* And that's because conducting air operations when you're more than 400 miles from land is just tempting fate. If you broke a hook trying to land that would be the end of it for a shipboard recovery, and you'd not have enough fuel to make it to a land base. You would just have to fly alongside the ship, eject, and hope the rescue helicopter got you before you drowned.

To occupy our non-flying time we were all assigned collateral duties. These positions were most commonly as an Assistant Officer-in-Charge (or an Assistant, Assistant Officer-in-Charge) in one of the squadron's four departments: Administration, Intelligence, Operations, or Maintenance and Supply. (Known in the Marine Corps as S1, S2, S3, and S4.) The assigned junior officer's time and duties would be at the discretion of the more senior Officer-in-Charge (OIC), and he'd frequently finding himself directed to head up a hopefully necessary but not too glamorous project. Or if none were hot, supervise (or at least provide a sympathetic shoulder for) the enlisted personnel (the privates, corporals, and buck sergeants) within that department.

Perhaps the most vital department in the squadron was the Aviation Maintenance Department—responsible for the condition of all our aircraft. Major Burnham was the OIC of the Maintenance Department. And yup I was assigned as his assistant. Within this department were a variety of "shops:" The Engine Shop which rebuilt the engine, fuel controls, turbines, etc.; the Electric (or Avionics) shop which repaired and replaced the generators, wiring, flight instruments, gyros and radios; the Metal Shop that did all the repairs on the aircraft structure; the Hydraulic Shop which took care of the pumps and filters and lines that provided power to the landing gear, flaps and brakes; and the Flight Equipment Shop where they issued and maintained all the parachutes, life vests, rafts, and survival kits. My job would be to devote an hour or so to each shop each day, ascertaining that there were no work-order hangups, no shortage of parts, and that none of the men had any questions or personal problems. I looked forward to that part—being able to help some of these young guys. In spite of the above we junior officers still had a lot of time on our hands, and I was intending to use a good share of mine writing letters to Sara.

The Infamous "Ready Room"

Each day during the crossing (and the rest of the cruise) started with an 0800 *All Pilots Meeting* in the squadron Ready Room. This was a place designed for flight briefings and official squadron meetings, but more often serving as a hangout for any pilots not on the flight schedule. It was an olive-drab cross between an all metal schoolroom and a pool hall. Eight rows of steel-framed chairs (cockpit seats removed from retired transport aircraft) were bolted to the floor (from now on referred to as the "deck."), a few pieces of Naugahyde furniture against the walls (from now on referred to as "bulkheads"), and a raised platform with a podium and blackboard up front. Not well lit. Had some charm.

The key attraction here was a closed-circuit TV mounted high on one bulkhead, where pilots could watch one another attempt landings. The camera recording this hair-raising footage was embedded in the flight deck near the desired touchdown point (arresting wire number three), and aimed back up the final approach. Stenciled on the screen was a cross-hairs (gun sight) which—if the aircraft was in it, meant the pilot was on the ideal glidepath for landing. I say this is where the aircraft *should* be seen on its approach for landing. Since it's no small task guiding ten tons of metal at 140 knots to a spot the size of a kitchen table, few pilots would be in the cross-hairs the whole time. They'd be either above it (high) or below it (low).

If you were above it you weren't going to catch the desired "three wire"—had to hope for the "four wire." Miss that one (called a "bolter") and you'd be cursing the gods and adding full power to go around for another try. If you were a little below the desired trajectory you might catch the "two wire" (hopefully). Or lower yet—the "one wire" (please God). Or short of this, the aircraft landing gear would catch the aft end of deck *and you'd cartwheel down it in a disintegrating fiery ball.* Obviously being high meant you would have to try again. Being low could mean you would never have to try anything again. One did not walk away from these low approach encounters with the "spud locker" (the nickname for the aft end of the ship).

As you might imagine, sitting in front of the TV in the Ready Room would become a popular pastime, provoking loud and well-animated commentaries (interspersed with a fair share of "Holy Shits"). After each landing session (from now on called "recovery"), the pilots who had just landed would come down to the Ready Room and watch a replay of their own approach and touchdown. Entering the Ready Room, pressure suit hose swinging, smelling of sweat, hair plastered to your forehead, helmet in hand, and hearing what your buddies had to say about your landing, well that could be a humbling experience. Besides the oft filled Ready Room, we had our own squadron work areas (the shops), and our sleeping quarters (staterooms). A person could be in any of these three known areas, or a hundred other nifty hiding places on board. You could be present without being present. For sure you weren't AWOL (Absent Without Leave).

What was I doing in my spare time?

To make the best of my at-sea time and finally add some size to my slight frame, I had lugged a set of barbells onboard and found a neat hideaway for them in a rarely-visited cranny of the upper forecastle deck. (The "foc'sle" on the old sailing ships was a platform forward of the mast that archers stood on to shoot down on enemy vessels.) It became my own secret place. Unfortunately, being on a sloping upper deck , any listing or pitching was exaggerated and raised havoc with overhead lifts. One day complaining about this problem to Bob Harmon, he told me there might be a gym on board. Looking down through a grate in a passageway near our Ready Room, he had seen a guy lifting weights.

I decided to check it out and after descending a narrow ladder (stairs on a ship are called "ladders") into a lower deck radio room, I discovered some Navy guys had a pretty good set up. I met Dale Hornsby, a Navy lieutenant from the only propeller squadron (sub-hunters) on the carrier. He was a dedicated body-builder, an LSU graduate, and one good-looking son of a gun, with wavy black hair, dark brown eyes and a flashing smile. (The way I wished I was born, instead with my too-fine mousey brown hair and small chin.) Dale was a real Cajun from the bayou country who was loaded with charm and loved the ladies. I suspected if a guy went out with him and they only found one girl, he'd be in big trouble. By the same token if there were two girls, he was at least gonna get the "other" one. Dale and I became workout partners and would later share some times ashore together. His area was level and being lower in the ship reduced the adverse effect of the swells and listing. It was also more convenient.

Whenever I wasn't touring my shops, in my stateroom, or trying to lift weights, I was on the flight deck. It was my solace—sixty-five feet above the racing water. The expanse of the horizon was inspiring. The warm sun piqued my skin and the air was so fresh and clean I could actually smell its sweetness. (Made you wonder how those O2 molecules got all the way from the rain forest to my nostrils here in the middle of the ocean.) In light of my exhilaration, I could imagine how the old sailors must have felt and why they put to sea for a lifetime. If it was this inspiring atop this noisy, vaporous steel factory, I wondered what it must have been like a hundred years ago, standing on parched decks, hefting a wood wheel and listening to the snapping canvas above.

Arriving in the Med

Lo and Behold, on the eighth day. Gibraltar! We'd made it across. It looked just like the logo for the insurance ad. Would've looked better except it was overcast—not what I was envisioning for the Mediterranean. Fortunately this would be one of the few gray days I would see. The ship was bustling. Lots of questions now. *Were we going to try a launch before putting into port? What was our first port going to be? What would we do on our first hops?* Even the old hands seemed at a loss. In any case there sure was an increase in activity, and once again it seemed as if I was the only one for whom this was a first trip. The squadron and all the ship's company were somehow acting like they arrived here every six weeks. We would be replacing the *Saratoga*—another carrier on its way back to the states after its ten-month tour over here. There would be a big change of command ceremony tomorrow afternoon, on the north side of the island of Majorca (Pollensa Bay). The captain of the *Saratoga* would be relieved of duties, our ship's captain would receive his orders, and then when the *Saratoga* steamed westward we would be the new "good guys" in the Med. Now it'd be us cruising around, flexing, just waiting for the order to devastate the command and control centers (or whatever else for miles around we might accidentally destroy) in some small Eastern Bloc country. *Dirty no good Communists!*

1300 hours, 22 June. Pollensa Bay: Now *this* was what I was imagining. We sailed through a fjord-like cut into an emerald green bay and dropped anchor (which process I discovered emitted a bone jarring steel rattling that could wake the dead). Chalk-stained charcoal cliffs surrounded us, rising steeply upwards from the waters edge. And I can tell you it wasn't overcast today. Unlike Norfolk, the sky was cloudless and the golden sun was doing its job. Nestled on the beach directly in front of us was a dazzling white village. Luxury yachts and sleek speed boats began to hurry out to investigate this huge visitor. Each one as it entered our monstrous shadow would throttle back and settle in the water, apparently awed by the immensity of this strange hobbled giant. One by one as they gained their composure, they'd rev their engines and begin to circle the ship or race back and forth alongside. The well-tanned beautiful people reclining on their glistening teak decks pointed up at us and waved with great enthusiasm. I was flattered and felt a welcomed encouragement at this reception. Maybe this cruise and we Americans on it would be something special over here. At last I was feeling a little better. And this was only Pollensa Bay, still not the Mediterranean's main attraction. Everyone whose duties would allow (which appeared to be everybody) was topside gaping in awe.

The change of command ceremony, held on the *Saratoga*, was complete by 1600. Our captain had just been piped back onboard after the short passage in his private boat (although not looking like one, was referred to as the "Admiral's Barge"). We watched the *Saratoga* pull colors and grind out of the bay—homeward bound. The *Forrestal* was taking over. It would be us now. We were it and we were anxious. Tomorrow would be the first day of hunting season!

Chapter Three
MY FIRST LAUNCH

Everyone was a little surprised and disappointed. In view of the eight-day trip coming over, we thought we would put into port somewhere *before* commencing flight operations—give us a little time to get up our nerve. We had made it across and were hoping for a few days shore leave (referred to in the Navy as "Liberty") before putting our nose to the grindstone. Everyone onboard, from the ship's company and from the tactical units, was already assigned to either the "port" or "starboard" duty section. While docked, one section would be required to stay on board while the other was free to "hit the beach." Coming across the rumors had been rampant—maybe Cannes, maybe Barcelona. But no, we were told there would be a one week at-sea flying period before putting into Naples, and that flying was starting today.

We had spent our first day in the Med somewhere east of Menorca (which along with Majorca and Ibiza comprised the Spanish-owned Balearic Islands). There we ran alongside two tankers, taking on fuel and water and a bunch of other supplies. Besides the thick black hoses spanning the distance, there were multiple cables stretched between the ships, with gurneys hanging from them. In spite of a strong wind and rough seas which made them rock precariously, these gurneys continued to run back and forth all day, carrying supplies (and sometimes even people)! That completed we steamed south all night for today's flight ops. Based on the observed demeanor this morning, I think we all were a little apprehensive about starting flying (though no one was saying as much). We'd just recently qualified and had never done it for real, but I was about to.

1030 hours and not exactly feeling dauntless, in fact more than a little uneasy. The very first day of flight operations and Bob Harmon (the Crew Scheduler) has me assigned to be a Division Leader, which meant I would be in charge of a flight of four for the second launch. (I *did* know there was going to have to be a first time.) The Ready Room was air conditioned, but the back of my flight suit was soaked against the Naugahyde backrest. Only another half hour and I'd be leading my guys up to the flight deck. Not sure how this cruise is going to go. Having a hard time imagining ten straight months of mornings like this (at least the way my stomach feels right now). And the word is, flight ops are going to be scheduled six days a week. Only Sundays off. Although (thank God) we'd discover that once in a while they'd be canceled because of the sea state. During those days of high swells, the flight deck (our runway) could rise and fall over thirty feet!

The first launch (all Navy guys) had been shot into the air at 10:00 for a standard "1.5-er" (an hour and a half flight). They were already up there somewhere, milling around, practicing whatever (and I'll bet, dreading 11:30—their scheduled recovery time). We had been in the Ready Room, three decks down, when they went. And wow! Those catapults are something else. Raw power. Their heart-stopping explosive jarring made you wonder how long the ship was going to stay glued together. There was such inertia to them, each time they fired they seemed to yank the whole ship back and forth. If you were nearer the tracks (like up in the forecastle) the noise would make you fear for your life. They weren't going to be tamed and I'd just have to try to learn to ignore them.

Thought I noticed a minimum of wise-cracking this morning, especially among the guys scheduled to fly. Would've bet I wasn't the only one feeling a little queasy. Led my guys to a dim corner of the Ready Room, next to the furthest chalkboard (where—because I was concerned about the quality of my briefing, I wouldn't be overheard by the Skipper or Major Burnham). Began to brief my flight. You have to have a plan, a mission—some worthwhile training objective. Though I didn't state it in my briefing, I had an objective: *get out and get back safe.* Just get one under my belt. So I outlined a profile for a basic navigation drill without the use of electronic navigational aids. A nice safe kind of first try. No daring exploits. No exotic maneuvers. Just see if we could get off, go to one or two designated coordinates, turn around, come back, and find the friggin ship.

Navigating by just flying headings and times (with no electronic or satellite positioning guidance) is called "Dead Reckoning." I'd seen it written as *Dead* Reckoning for years before I learned we'd misunderstood the British. In eighteenth century sailing—with no technology, they plotted their position by Deductive Reckoning, which they abbreviated as *"Ded"* Reckoning. Our scenario today would be that sort of drill, in case one day either our aircraft's or the ship's navigational devices failed, and we were forced to go back to the basics. I guess you could say I *look* like a pilot and *talk* like one, but in all truthfulness (my little secret), I wasn't one of those guys who "could fly the box it came in" (like Jim Stremlow or Bob Harmon, and especially—Don Goft). I had to pay attention the whole time, and had my hands full with whatever flight maneuver I was doing. I really wasn't that keen on looping it or rolling it, or demonstrating any hammerhead stalls. I was just a "gentleman" flyer, content to do things safely and as briefed—methodically and within the envelope. So for sure there'd be no dogfights or other shenanigans today. We'd just fly the profile I'd designed: a big triangle with three 180 mile legs. We'd have to compute where the ship (continuing on its course) should be in an hour and a half, then fly each of those legs at a specific IAS (Indicated Airspeed), for a calculated time (which would vary based on our headwind or tailwind component), and at computed headings to achieve the necessary drift corrections (for the crosswind components), and hopefully at the end of the third leg, spy the ship.

600 miles at 450 knots ground airspeed—counting climb and descent, would take us an hour and eighteen minutes. We'd be back about 12:20, ten minutes before our "Recovery Time." Our launch—the second launch, would be a four squadron launch, three Navy squadrons and us. The first launch was three squadrons—twelve planes. (Maybe they should've just tried it with one flight of four first, to see if it worked.) I was already concerned about the potential confusion when sixteen birds came home to roost at the same time—in a damned small nest.

"Roger, which squadrons launch first? What's the order going to be?" I was brought back to the task at hand by Brad, one of my wingmen for the forthcoming flight. He was the only second lieutenant (the military's most junior commissioned rank) in the squadron, and youngest member of the outfit—who would unwittingly spend the next ten months driving the Colonel nuts.

"The fighters go first. They're our cover, they always go first. Then we'll share the "cats" with VA 81. You'll be able to tell your turn by where you're parked. Watch for the signalman."

11:10. Knew it was going to happen. Over the squawk box came the unmistakable call: "Gentlemen, man your aircraft."

The looks exchanged in that instant left no doubt that none of us were carrying an excess of confidence. Larry and Tripp who were usually quite vocal, were now as quiet as mice. Rising unsuredly and looking as nonchalant as we could, we picked up our helmets and kneeboards, and were—for better or for worse, on our way. We got a little boost from the round of cheers and thumbs-up from the lucky guys whose names did not appear on the flight schedule, and were now strewn around the Ready Room in various casual poses. They knew as soon as our second launch was airborne and the deck was clear—in fact, exactly thirty seconds after the last plane was launched, the first plane from the ten o'clock launch would be starting his approach. The second show—the one I was worried about, would be at 13:00 when *we* came back. For sure, every last one of our squadron mates would be in the Ready Room, parked in front of the closed-circuit TV for *that* display. Glued there, amongst gasps and slaps to the forehead they'd observe and critique our landings. The TV was irrefutable evidence of a good approach (or a porpoising, skidding, slipping, lunging, diving, *Thank God for small favors* excuse for a landing).

We were out of the Ready Room and on our way, beginning our trip up to the flight deck. Had to remember to step high enough through each "hatch" (doorway on a ship) to clear the ten-inch steel lip above the sill. (These were known as "shin splitters" to those who failed to lift their leg high enough.) The Ready Room was two decks down, along with a multitude of other shops and offices. Hundreds of them (called "spaces"). No daylight ever gets to this mid deck. The bulkheads are heavily coated with a pea soup-colored enamel, and poorly illuminated by not closely spaced, protectively caged incandescent 40-watt bulbs. (Not great surroundings when you're already a little nauseous.) The mid deck is the level used most frequently to travel fore and aft (from bow to stern), or left to right (port to starboard) across the ship. And let me tell you, the maze of passageways make one of these journeys no easy trip. In our ten month cruise, with a hundred trips to the flight deck, I don't think I ever took the same itinerary twice.

I hoped I was leading the guys along a proper route, but you could never be sure. You could be traipsing right along—no sweat, on a great path you had discovered the day before, yank open a hatch and step through it into the dead end confines of a hot and steamy, slick-floored galley, or into the sheeted jungle of some unit's bunk area. Now you're either face to face with a big silver-toothed Filipino cook with a huge skillet, eyeing you askance, or if the other intrusion, a pale-skinned, tattooed guy wearing only baggy undershorts, scratching his tousled hair and yawning—trying to figure if you're real or still part of a dream. *Oops, took a wrong turn somewhere.* A sheepish "Good Morning," a U-turn and you'd be on your way again.

We straggled through several ship's company areas, full of faces and uniforms we didn't recognize. Each tactical squadron on board and each department of the ship's company had their own work areas, eating areas, recreation areas, and sleeping quarters. The enlisted ranks sleep in large, barracks-like areas, in side-by-side, three-tiered bunks. The officers sleep in private staterooms—two to a room. The ship was like a county full of small towns, connected by narrow, winding, unmarked roads. Once you got your paths established, you could avoid the aforementioned surprise arrivals. If you were lucky, you could go for days without bumping into anybody other than your squadron-mates traveling the same dedicated routes. So far we were doing okay. No embarrassments yet. I stayed the course, only making lefts and rights where absolutely necessary (trying to keep the compass in my head from spinning). You could be on the starboard side of the ship, trying to go forward towards the bow, only to somewhere have made an unregistered turn, and end up unknowingly migrating across to the port side of the ship, going aft. What a surprise when you'd scamper up a ladder into daylight, fully expecting to see the bow of the ship, and find yourself peering over the "spud locker" at the aft end of the ship. *Oh well, let's try again.*

Success! Only three turns and two ladders later—*Bingo,* we emerged onto the hangar deck (one deck above the Ready Room, and one deck below the flight deck), where all the airplanes that aren't "topside," are tied down or undergoing repairs. It's a crowded dangerous place—a real obstacle course. On the starboard side of the hangar deck are two elevators—fifty-foot by fifty-foot steel platforms protruding out just over the treacherous water. Aircraft, after having been worked on are towed onto these elevators, to be raised to the flight deck. Almost every cruise, something or someone goes over the side off one of these elevators, never to be seen again.

This would be a first. I'd never buckled-in off dry land. When we qualified back in Beaufort we had just flown a hundred miles out to sea where the carrier *Enterprise* was waiting, made our "traps" and flown back to terra firma. Never set foot on the deck. This would be my first launch. (No wonder my knees were shaking.) Hugging the port side of the hangar deck, away from most the confusion, I found the ladder which would take us topside to the infamous flight deck. It was for launches and recoveries; pure flying business, nothing else. It's either abandoned or a furious pulpit of screaming, steaming, lashing, cable-slapping activity. Forget the *flying* part, a guy could get killed real quick just by standing in the wrong place. Objects of horrendous tonnage would be hurtling by just yards away. Seemingly chaotic but urgent activities were being carried out on all sides.

Understood by me but not sufficiently anticipated, was the fact that the carrier was steaming at 18 knots into a 15 knot wind—resulting in 33 knots of wind across the deck. When I popped out of the last hatch and onto the flight deck, I wasn't prepared for the elements. A gale force wind not only stopped me in my tracks, but were I not to have quickly put one foot back, would have blown me over. Eyes watering, cheeks buffeting and spit being sucked out of my mouth, I scanned the gaggle of aircraft trying to locate where our Marine A-4's were stationed. All three of my guys were out of earshot, but one of them had a hand raised and was making a pointing motion somewhere ahead. Squinting forward I recognized the shape of our Skyhawk rudders, all but masked by the taller tails of the Crusaders. We split and chose our own routes. In 30-plus knots of wind a man has a hard time standing up, and here we are carrying all our stuff, weaving our way around stacks of equipment and moving vehicles—taking giant steps and little hops to avoid the steel mooring cables. Almost every aircraft had two or three of these cables stretching out at weird low angles, seemingly put there to snag a foot and send you sprawling.

And if you didn't trip, you had a real good chance of being run over. Worst of all—the most dangerous thing to look for, were all the eighteen-year-old Mario Andretti's driving the tow tractors. These low flat tugs were screeching everywhere, popping in and out of gear, surging ahead or rearward—full speed. All I could think of was your Highway Patrol message, *Speed kills!* Their job was to hook up to an aircraft and push it or pull it to its pre-launch position. And besides these tugs and going just as fast, there were at least a half dozen motorized, Volkswagen-sized mobile power units zipping all over the deck. (Airplanes don't have batteries big enough to start their own engines.) Like a humming bird going from blossom to blossom, they would zoom up to and away from each launch aircraft, plugging in their big power cable to provide the high amps necessary to start a jet engine. Thirty seconds there and then scurry to the next waiting aluminum monster. Later in the cruise after a night launch, a Navy pilot would be hit by one of these power carts, breaking both of his legs. The flight deck is not for the faint of heart.

Kha-wham! The first test shot on the number two cat went and my heart almost came out of my mouth. The piston tracks were only a foot below the surface of the flight deck, and I had been walking right on top of number two. Like a drop of water off a scalding grill, I jumped two feet in the air and was now trying to hover there, to avoid the bone and cartilage damage that would surely result when the soles of my feet returned to the deck. If the sounds and vibrations were frightening way down in the Ready Room, you can imagine what it was like up here, standing right on top of them. When I was sure my heart was going to return to my chest, I continued towards my assigned aircraft (which was doing its impression of a young sapling in the wind). I could see it shifting and leaning as the ship listed and pitched. The steady gale was trying to thrash the flight control surfaces and succeeding in twisting the fuselage—so much so that the skin on the side of the aircraft was actually wrinkling. And the small open cockpit ten feet up, didn't look like a safe place even here, not yet airborne.

Standing by the side of the aircraft and awaiting my arrival was Sgt Parker—the assigned "Plane Captain" for this aircraft. He was the mechanic who would be responsible for giving this machine the necessary care and grooming, as well as assist the pilots in and out of the cockpit for the next ten months. Once assigned to an aircraft, that aircraft is his and his alone. By the end of the cruise it has usually developed into a serious love-hate relationship. He greeted me, apparently not noticing my preoccupation and doubt. *That's good.* No reason for him to know how scared I was. The next and never to be omitted ritual: the "Exterior Pre Flight Inspection," a quick, crouching, kneeling, neck-craning examination of the aircraft struts, tires, brakes, hydraulic lines and fittings, any visible cables or connectors, hinges, flight control surfaces, fluid levels and pressures, and general overall condition. Today they were all just fine—*no reason not to accept the aircraft.*

Up the rickety ladder. Whole plane rocking now. Standing on the top rung, and the last requirement before getting in: I checked the ejection seat for *two* "safety" pins, and pulled out *one*. (With one pin remaining in, the seat could not be fired, and I couldn't accidentally eject myself while strapping in.) Over the canopy rail and into the seat. *Whoaa*—I saw most of the canopies already closed, I was a little behind. *Gotta hurry.* Into the cockpit. Seat belt. Parachute harness. Shoulder straps. Sgt Parker was handing me items, helping me adjust and tighten them. "Thanks Scott." He's handing me my helmet. It's on. *It's off.* Damned inside top pad not sticking—came loose again. Pressed it back in. Helmet back on. "Where's my gloves? Thanks Scott." He took care of the final step: removing the remaining seat pin. *Seat's armed now, gotta be careful.* The canopy's coming down. It's down. Lever forward, lock it. This is it.

Geez. *Take it easy Scott.* He was shoving the power unit jack into the side of the plane with such force, the whole airplane was rocking. It's in. There's the indication. Got the voltage. Got the start clearance from Air Ops. Light-off. It's winding up. EGT (exhaust gas temperature) okay. Stabilized. Good. Radios on. Listen for the sequence. The first two aircraft, Navy Crusaders, were being towed onto the number one and two cats. Two more behind them. Larry and Tripp were somewhere behind me, couldn't tell for sure, they weren't in the mirrors. Searched ahead for my signal guy. The windscreen is an inch thick and has a fair amount of distortion (which isn't too bad now, but can be real dangerous when taxiing at night).

The ship's company flight deck personnel were responsible for a variety of critically important, rapidly occurring, sequential steps during the launch. They worked in highly specialized, well-coordinated teams, and to indicate their specific task and identify themselves to the pilots, each team wore like-colored vests. Beneath, in front and to the sides of me were fast moving patches of green (catapult and arresting gear handlers) and yellow (the aircraft directors)—the signalmen we searched for, obeyed, and hoped were directing us appropriately. No red today, that's what the ordnance crews (bomb and rocket loaders) wore. From the cockpit it was a coded blur of color as the various crews scurried here and there, unhooking cables, waving signals, shouting, hauling away tow bars, and finally—attaching the catapult halters to the aircraft. *What an operation.*

Brad was two back for the number three cat. There goes the first F-8. *Wow.* Now the second. Clouds of white steam and hot oil vapor poofed skyward, and then blew back over the waiting aircraft (smearing Scott's meticulously cleaned windscreen). Two more fighters were being pulled up. I was trying to do my post-start instrument and engine checks (in my opinion even more important than that exterior inspection I had done a few minutes ago), but found my eyes outside the cockpit taking in the action. *Inside! Stay inside—you've got your own things to do.* Checked the gauges for the critical "go, no-go" readings. Everything okay.

Suddenly had the feeling people were trying to get my attention. Lifted my eyes back up outside and into focus. Scanned ahead, and yeah, yeah, there's a yellow vest waving at me—in fact frantically. Didn't see him before. Don't think he was there before. I was unchocked. Got the signal. Tug's on me. Tug's on me, towing me to the number four cat. Going to the number four cat. Got that. Can see that. Wow! The whole plane shook. What the hell was that? They pulled me over something big. *Bang! Klunk!* Felt like the struts were going to buckle. On the cat. *I'm on the cat.* Christ, I'll bet I'm not five feet from the edge of the deck. Could look almost straight down at the water. If the ship lists, would I start sliding? If so, in just a few feet I would be over the side. *Geez!*

I could hear the noises and feel the vibrations up through the rudder pedals as the unseen crew beneath me in green sweaters was attaching the halter to the nose gear (the device that connects your plane to the catapult). *Holy Shit.* Only a matter of seconds now. The launch officer was out there. Saw him. He was looking forward. Back to me now. Looking forward again. Arm up. Waving it. Faster. Tight circles. Giving me the turn up signal. I'm doing it. All the way up. At full power. The engine was roaring, the plane was shuddering, the radio was blaring, my eyes were watering. There he goes! He dropped to one knee, twisting his torso towards the bow and throwing one hand forward.

Whoaa! Neck snapped back, helmet pinned against the headrest, hand half off the stick—*hang on with the fingers*, edge of the visor cutting the bridge of my nose. *Ride er' out!* I saw the end of the angle deck racing towards me, saw my airspeed, 110 knots, fifty feet to go. Need another 20 knots. *Thunk!* The halter's away. On my own. Over water. Sinking—losing altitude. Nose up! *More.* Get ten degrees nose up. Hold it. Wings level. Looks good. *We're flying!* Vertical speed indicator showing a 500 FPM (foot per minute) rate of climb. We're accelerating. *I did it!* I'm airborne. We're flying. *Jesus Christ, we're flying!* I think I'm gonna be able to do this. I think I'm gonna *like* it.

Chapter Four

NAPLES

The Chaplain's Tour

We pulled into the port of Naples about midnight Sunday. (Remember the Dean Martin song, "That's Amore." *Napoli ...When the moon hits your eye like a big pizza pie*.) Our first in-port stay—where we would put our feet on European soil for the first time. A bunch of us stayed on the flight deck to observe the city lights brightening and hear the unforgettable sound of a ten ton anchor dragging out chain links as big as 55-gallon drums. The sound we'd grow to love (meaning no more harrowing flights for a week and time to recreate ashore). Except in this case, prior to arrival the old hands had warned us not to expect too much here. According to them Naples was *not* going to be the highlight reel of our cruise. (Sophia Loren was Naples' sole claim to fame.) Jim Stremlow and I opted to take the veterans at their word and had our own plan for this in port stay. While the other guys were going to be stuck here, tomorrow morning we were going to take advantage of a three-day Chaplain's Tour of Rome.

0800 hours Monday morning: Jim and I were with the rest of the tour group, on the first liberty boat to shore. The carrier always moored a half mile out—in the deep water, and so the only way to get to the docks was by using these liberty boats. While in port they would run 18 hours a day, bringing the wild-eyed expectant reveler to shore, and the boasting but weary, out-of-money souls back to the ship. And these boats were open, so lots of wind and salt spray. Just rows of benches, no protected area, carried about fifty guys and offered a usually soaking and always bumpy ride. On the way in—viewing our surroundings, I could see why the old hands had said what they did. The scene coming ashore was not uplifting, not what I had conjured up. Instead, debris-strewn water, rusty tankers, dilapidated piers, and fume-spewing trucks chugging up and down the wharves. But then again we weren't arriving by a route the Chamber of Commerce would have recommended and I guess any port city has similarly depressing vantage points.

The bus trip to Rome was *not* a great ride. Hot and humid. Bad roads and bad shocks in the bus. In spite of this Jim and I enjoyed ourselves. We passed some time jawing about our pre-flight training days, and in particular the cadet battalion boxing "smokers" in which Jim had fought. For three months before Jim's arrival our battalion had entered an awesome heavyweight named Barry Stremlow, who had consistently come out, taken charge and won decisively. Now when Jim's battalion called out "Stremlow" (meaning Jim) none of the competing battalions volunteered a challenger. Realizing the reason there were no takers, our rep made the announcement that this was a *new* Stremlow; not the Barry guy. He'd been transferred to Whiting Field for Primary Training. *Oh, different story. No problem now.* One hand, then another, several more and now a lot of brave ones. Each of these would rue the day he had volunteered, as Jim racked up a murderous first round KO every single fight.

I never did see much of Naples so I may not have given it a fair shot, but as far as I was concerned, Rome was *something else!* Unfortunately the Navy had booked us into bargain accommodations—an unpainted concrete block hotel, way outside the city (that looked like it took a month to build and was just finished last week). I knew Jim wouldn't have understood if I tried to drag him to a better hotel in a more exciting looking area, especially since this one was part of the tour arrangement. Monday afternoon and most of Tuesday we availed ourselves of the scheduled tours: Trevi Fontana (the fountain from the famous movie *Three Coins in a Fountain*), the Coliseum, the Forum and the Catacombs. Ancient history was right now. Ten miles outside the city on some dusty road, one could easily imagine that the twelve disciples or a Roman legion were just around the next line of cypress trees. At long last the text book pages I'd turned were coming to life. And when we weren't on a tour? Well modern Rome, with its flamboyant and elegantly dressed citizenry, gave Jim and I another pastime: people watching. We spent a stupefied hour at a sidewalk table on the main drag—the Via Veneto, watching a stream of shapes and colors parading by us. All sorts—from divas to gigolos. It didn't take us long to realize that growing up in a USA *Happy Days* sort of town, there was quite a bit we did not see (nor imagine existed).

Like everyone else we were not only impressed by the beauty of the still standing early Roman infrastructure, but by its evidently advanced engineering. In front of us was a five hundred year old building full of government offices and bustling workers, *still 100 percent occupied.* And just down the street, the 2000-year-old coliseum. A million tons of marble on one city block. This place wasn't constructed of half inch plywood and aluminum siding. No question about it, the locals had something to be proud of. Made me kind of wish I had a city like this to live in and brag about as my birthplace.

Making our way through downtown Rome was a real adventure. The traffic was non-stop, high-speed gridlock. Sirens all the time. When it wasn't a police car screeching around a corner or knifing past cars (in the wrong lane), it was an ambulance careening through a four way intersection. While it was mostly harmless, there was an atmosphere of confusion and near calamity everywhere, and it was being sampled by a thousand sweltering sightseers per block. This was my first exposure to a live, world-class tourist attraction. I had never seen so many buses, so many lines, so many guides with signs, so many groups of yelling, sweating, van-boarding, camera-toting, sandwich-munching, posing, brochure-examining, strange-looking people.

For Jim and I, our jumping-off spot, the most well-marked place on our map, was the Piazza Republica. (Piazza, plaza, square—same thing.) It was right in front of the main bus station and only two blocks from the main railway station (Stazione Termini). At its center was a congested circle, where unimpressed local motorists herded their vehicles around a massive circular stone fountain. On one side was a small park with a few trees and benches. Every shady spot had its own souvenir vendor, newspaper kiosk, peanut roaster or ice cream stand. Skirting the other side of the circle was a curving, half-block-wide, old stone building. Its ground floor was a nicely shaded arcing promenade. Behind its huge pillars were a string of fashionable boutiques. These small and exclusive shops displayed some of the neatest sterling, leather and crystal items I'd ever seen. Propped up on the walkway outside one art gallery were (to my eyes) incredibly good but inexpensive oils by young Italian artists. It wasn't the Via Veneto, but we certainly saw our share of classy middle-aged businessmen and women, smartly dressed in well tailored wools and cashmeres. Lots of sophisticated matching outfits. For the guys, navy blue blazers and beige trousers seemed to be the "in" thing. Occasionally we'd catch a glimpse of one or two of the younger gentry strutting through the promenade. They were a different breed, sporting bright red, yellow and even orange *Alta Moda* shirts and even trousers (making them look like a flock of tropical birds flitting by).

Feared we were going to end up doing it and we did. We rented a motor scooter! For you Honda and Suzuki fans, the birthplace of two wheeled motorized travel was not in Japan, it was in Italy—home of the Vespa and Lambretta motor scooters. It seemed every other vehicle was one of these. But they must've only come in one color. I saw a million of them and they were all a pale, grayish green. They had a short wheel base and a very small front wheel, so they weren't very stable. If you turned too sharply, over the handle bars you went (as many of our young sailors discovered). They lacked power and a good clutch. With Jim on the back it was difficult to start up from a standstill without either stalling or jerking out from under him. One time while rounding that big fountain at Piazza Republica, I gave a burst of power to accelerate ahead of a wall of onrushing vehicles. When I had miraculously made it safely out the other side of the circle, I discovered I was solo. *Jim was not on board!* I looked back to see him lunging this way and that, trying to escape being engulfed by a sea of surging metal; like a matador without a cape trying to dodge a ring full of motorized bulls. Evidently I had driven the scooter right out from under him without having felt him leave. He made it okay, and fortunately for me—saw the humor in it.

An Unexpected Diversion

Wednesday—our next to last day, we visited the Vatican. I'd heard about it that's for sure, seen hundreds of photos, but had no idea it encompassed so much area—had such sanctity about it, and contained all that artwork. (Probably should've done some studying beforehand.) To me it seemed to be more than a religious landmark. Regardless of one's faith it inspired respect (if not awe). In spite of the foregoing accolades I must admit one of the main things I remember about the Vatican is Ardith—one of the ladies in another tour group with whom we were frequently crossing paths. It was difficult not to notice this proudly upright female person in a bare-backed, pink checked sun dress. As Jim and I hoofed it across the pavers of Piazza San Pietro she appeared to be gliding across its surface, with a long strong stride and her head held high. Apparently unaccompanied and to my eyes quite accustomed to that status. She wasn't a young girl, couldn't even call her a girl. Must've been at least thirty—maybe thirty-five. Although it was none of my business I felt a concern for her. She appeared to be alone and not mixing with the other members of the tour group. Don't know why I should have been worried about her welfare, but I was.

Waiting to get our souvenir envelopes franked at the Vatican Post Office she was in line right behind us. With the line not moving she opted to sit down at the base of one of those huge inside columns—directly alongside Jim and I. Sandals off she began examining her feet, most likely for developing blisters. (A ninety-degree-day tour of Rome is the perfect test for what you think are your most comfortable shoes.) I watched as she tilted her head back against the pillar and closed her eyes. The sun was now hitting her full-face. Thick auburn hair was pulled back from the temples, contrasting a fair-skinned, slightly freckled face. I suspected good up-bringing—private schools and that kind of life. When she finally stood up she was taller than I had anticipated (and taller than me, which was not so unusual). Rejoining us in line Jim's eyes met hers and he nodded a polite waiting in the heat hello. She did likewise, with a disarming smile. I suspected we had just met a proper and educated lady. Jim and I both felt an urge to appear polite and reasonably intelligent; do our best to uphold the American image. (For me of course that" reasonably intelligent" part presented a challenge in the company of her and other citizens of the Continent I would go on to meet.) We spoke first, introducing ourselves as pilots off a US carrier presently anchored in Naples. Just up here for a three-day tour.

The envelopes franked, Jim announced he was famished. I added "Me too." It occurred to us that now was as good a time as any, for the *three* of us to have lunch. We found a food vendor who had set up several small rickety tables (and *chairs,* which at this time—based on the condition of our feet, was as important as the food). Good thing lunch offered us that contribution, because our meal consisted of tasteless dry sandwiches (talk about thinly sliced ham) and a popular soft drink called *Orangina.* During this respite we had the opportunity to tell Ardith about ourselves and carrier life, and I think maybe even impressed her. On her part we learned she was originally from Scotland, but now lived in Knightsbridge (which I would later learn was an exclusive suburb just west of London). Jim asked her if she was working, and she said, yes, at Whitehall—a complex in Westminster where many rarely spoken about classified government agencies were located. Close up and with her no longer squinting in the bright sunlight, I could see she had beautiful green eyes.

I GUESS I JUST WASN'T THINKING

Up now and making our way along Via Della Conciliazone, still talking and taking in the sights, it was obvious Ardith was well schooled in the beaux arts. And once again I was deservedly embarrassed by my lack of knowledge in that area; feeling like a boy sent out to do a man's job. Fortunately Jim was doing considerably better than I was. (Now I really knew it had been a mistake to skip Music Appreciation in my sophomore year.) Made a silent vow to learn all I could as fast as I could, about the Renaissance artists and the eighteenth century composers that Ardith would frequently mention; at least familiarize myself with their most well known works. I would learn if you're going to make it in Europe this is a must. Our contacts with local vendors made it clear that she was fluent in Italian (and as I would later learn, French as well). Though I can't remember how the subject came up, I heard her tell Jim that she had never been married, which was difficult to believe. Jim told her about his family. I found myself remaining quiet.

Ardith was very courteous and agreeable in speaking with us, perhaps more so with Jim than with me—which was understandable. Jim was a John Wayne-looking kind of guy and could be very pleasant in these kinds of short social meetings. It was evident he wasn't harboring any ideas of wrapping his arms around her, so she was justifiably at ease with him. And I guess she felt equally comfortable with me, recognizing my innocent appreciation of the chance to have my first conversation with a real European (moreover, such a refined and educated one). Anyone would have been flattered to have been seen with her. I suspected now, right or wrong, the rest of our last day in Rome might coincide with Ardith's planned activities.

It was fortunate that we'd seen a good part of Rome already, because the rest of the day I would only observe it as it went past out of focus, while I concentrated on what Ardith was saying and her appealing English mannerisms. We learned she was an assistant to one of Britain's most renowned research scientists at a nuclear development laboratory in the respected environs of Whitehall. Jim surprised me by actually having heard of the institute she was associated with. (Told you he was smart.) Ardith said their mission there was to be the first agency in the Kingdom to find a safe and cost effective way to convert nuclear energy to a civil power use. But "Enough of that" she said, "Today is my third day of a short one-week holiday and I don't want to hear about Whitehall." In the months to come, I'd become more familiar with the term "holiday" (used by just about all the Europeans where we would say "vacation").

Part Two: The French Riviera, Leo, June, and Big Trouble

Our Chaplain's Tour would be over tomorrow and we would be heading back to Naples. I was now beginning to feel that might be too soon. Don't know where we got the courage, but after checking with Jim I surprised myself by stumbling over enough words that she understood we were suggesting the three of us have dinner together. Unfortunately it wasn't going to happen. She had a previous commitment: a dinner engagement with a Count. *With a Count?* She was quick to brush it off, telling us that it was nothing. Some friends of hers from England knew this gentleman and had arranged the introduction, so she had no choice. To my astonishment, she agreed—no, *volunteered* to meet us for a coffee or a *gelato* after her dinner engagement. I was surprised (and flattered) that she had even considered this. To give her an out, or *to back out myself* (as a married man on my very first trip ashore), I added, "But wouldn't that be a little late, with your earlier engagement and tour activities tomorrow morning?"

She thought for a moment, then looked up and said, "No, no, it's fine with me, I am accustomed to late hours. Dr. Whitehead calls me into the lab at all hours." (Yes, a Dr. Whitehead works at Whitehall.) Fortunately, thanks to the many kilometers around town Jim and I had made on the scooter, the cafe she suggested for a meeting place was one that we both remembered seeing (at least several times). It was set.

Jim and I caught the chartered bus back to our hotel and arrived—a couple of sweaty, foot-sore, weary travelers. Jim went down the hall to chew the fat with two of the Navy LSO's. (They sort of had their own fraternity—these guys who had been through Landing Signal Officers school.) Inside my room and "out on my feet" my freshly made bed looked mighty inviting. I for one was having second thoughts about the evening's planned activity. I could have easily crashed for the night right then. No, take a shower, lay down and think it over. I did, and dozed—easily. About seven-thirty I arose, got Jim and we low-balled it (and saved a lot of energy) by just going to a neighborhood pasta restaurant right next to the hotel. There we met two Italian Air Force pilots (who spoke good English) and we easily passed the time till we had to leave for our ice cream date with Ardith. We briefly considered not going, but since we had told her we'd be there, we were pretty much locked in. If she were to show up and we're not there, that wouldn't be very polite and would give American men (and commissioned officers) a bad name.

I GUESS I JUST WASN'T THINKING

At nine-thirty on the dot, Jim and I stepped up onto the terrace of the Caffe Della Parma. Neat atmosphere. Cellophane lanterns swaying in the breeze, lots of small metal tables with red paper table clothes (held down by large wooden clothes pins), and great music playing. Appeared to be a local spot. A neighborhood hangout. Lots of families with young kids—all enjoying themselves to the max. We'd gotten there early. Ordered Cinzano with soda. (We'd seen this drink combination on billboards all over town, and hoped it would make us look less like the rank tourists we were.) There was a lot to observe and the time went quickly. One of the most romantic songs I have ever heard was being played over and over again, a local favorite called "Al Di La." (It would end up being number one in Italy for most the year.) Was half hoping she'd show up and half hoping she wouldn't. *Man!*

Hmmm. Ten o'clock and still no Ardith. Not looking good (and Jim had already dozed off a couple times). But as late as they dine in Italy, even to me her estimate of nine-thirty had seemed too early. But now ten-fifteen and still not here. Maybe a hint. Maybe we should just leave now. Maybe something went wrong. But what? The meeting had been *her* idea. Wait a minute, I have the address of her pensione right here. She had given it to us. Maybe we should check there. She may have concluded it was too late and just went straight to her room. *Roger, what are you thinking.* That's ridiculous, for more than one reason. I was thinking of leaving, and Jim was doing it. He'd had it. I told him go ahead back. I'd give her another fifteen minutes and if she wasn't here, I'd be right behind him. Time's up and she's not here. Time to call it a night. I'm leaving tomorrow, maybe I should wait a hair longer—just in case, and be able to say good bye. Make sure she knew we didn't stand her up.

I may have been right. She may have been delayed, thought we would have left, and so went straight to her pensione. I took the day's already well-worn map out. Only one block off Republic Square. The Pensione Venezia, 334 Via Quirinale. Gotta be somewhere near here, know she said that. Dark, can't read the small print on the map. (Could have bought a good one for about three bucks, but opted for this free one from our hotel.) It'll work. Traced my finger tip across the maze. *Bingo!* Via Quirinale. There it is. Could just stop by on my way back to the hotel. Doesn't look too difficult. Halfway down Via Nazionale, turn right, one, two blocks, there it is. Turn left. If I remember right that will be downhill. Jim and I had been on that street yesterday afternoon.

Was late now and I should have been thinking of going straight back to my own hotel. But didn't. Jogged most the way, tie over my shoulder, perspiring more than I would have liked. Not waiting for lights, zig-zagging across the streets as necessary. 10:45—Via Quirinale! *Thanks map.* But finding the Pensione Venezia wasn't easy—even having the number. None of these buildings had names or numbers. Any one of them could have been her pensione, but no way to tell which. Asked an old man. Asked a kid. (I could easily see by the avoidance detours they were taking, the older Italian women were in no way ready for a conversation.) Finally, got directions from a guy in some kind of uniform. Back up the street about fifty yards. There it is. Just a tiny place.

Through the door, smack into a wall. Smallest vestibule I'd ever seen. A left turn, three steps. Another wall. A right turn and down an unlit, completely undecorated narrow hallway. At the far end of it—illuminated by one hanging bare light bulb, I could make out a years-ago framed, small boxy area. It appeared to be (and was) the concierge's station, and it would turn out—the manager's office and headquarters for the establishment. It was manned by an old guy with lop-sided spectacles, half-hidden on a rickety perch behind a narrow, four-foot wide, well-worn plywood counter. The crude handmade key box behind him indicated only six rooms in the whole place. I asked him for Ardith's room number. Much to my surprise—he gave it to me, and then went back to what he was doing. *Boy, some security in this hotel.*

Up two dark flights of tiny wood steps, into a musty, barely shoulder-wide hallway with jute carpeting. Spied Ardith's room at the end. Knocked. Knocked again. Nothing. Guess she's really running late. May not be going to come home at all. I was getting discouraged, and worrying, now that I had left the cafe—that she may have gone there, not found us and thought we had "no-showed." I was just smart enough to recognize that if so, it was probably for the best. And anyway, if she had really wanted to meet us, she could have. Decided to call it a night—head back to our hotel and just rest. *Rest and forget this kind of activity.*

Not too proud of what I did next. On the outside chance she was just late and was there waiting for us right now, and to try to save our reputation, I altered my route back to our hotel to take me past the Caffé Della Parma. Wow, that *is* a possibility. Maybe I left too soon. Now *she'll* be the one thinking *we* didn't show. I was out of the Pensione Venezia in a flash, my feet flying back up Via Nazionale—past ladies selling flowers, past overweight tourists raving about their lasagna, and Italian ragamuffins doing tricks with wooden matchboxes for 100 lire coins. Still a hundred yards away I could see there was no Ardith. My gait lessened to a trot, then a foot-grateful walk. *Give up Rog, this thing isn't going to come off, and it's probably a good thing it's not.* I'd lost to the Count. He'd be toasting her now, in his silk smoking jacket and ascot, his glass of sherry held high, her clear eyes fixed on him at the other end of the long table. I could picture his top floor balcony doors open, a soft breeze coming in from the terrace. Lace curtains wafting across a polished dark floor. *Who was I to be getting involved with this type thing anyway?* And what could I contribute to her Rome vacation in ten minutes? Certainly could add nothing to what she already knew about the city. Cultural comments? I don't think so. Not very smart there, that's for sure. And I was married. I'd be real temporary in her life (in fact momentary). The Count would be able to provide a lot more interesting conversation and lasting companionship than I could, and she deserved it. In fact, no doubt *he* deserved it more than I did.

I was investigating a possible shortcut back to our low-budget hotel when it hit me... *Caffe Della Parma?!* No wonder we had thought we had seen it several times on our trips. There were *two* of them! Or at least two of them with almost the same name. The other one was at the foot of Via Nazionale, even closer than her pensione. *No way.* Don't tell me. 11:00! Now *I'm* the one who will be late, if by some chance she's still there, which is not likely at this hour. If the trip to find her pensione was somewhat hurried, you should have seen this one. I was really moving. I kept telling myself it was a matter of two Americans having to keep their word. A matter of courtesy. The night scenery was flying by. Now past a gaggle of foreign language speaking kids wearing rucksacks covered with patches from Sweden and Norway. One more block. Via Del Corso. It's on this street, another half block. I saw it! The Caffé Della Firma. (Different last word.) Looked just like the other place. Same Cinzano umbrellas, striped awning, paper lanterns, and people drinking cappuccino or sipping liqueurs. Getting closer, seeing more, able to look past the hedge now. *There she is.* She's there. It's Ardith, sitting all alone.

I exploded into the cafe, all arms and legs, out of breath, bursting with apologies, and perspiration dripping off my nose. I'm sure I was a sight. Ignoring the waiters, other people and the world in general, I begged Ardith to accept my apologies, and Jim's—that he couldn't make it, and recounted the story (except the part about going to her pensione). Ardith thank God, didn't seem irritated that I was late. In fact seemed real happy I had finally shown up. *Am I lucky or what.* Out of such overwhelming relief to have avoided being a "no show" and finally find her, I reached out spontaneously and took her hand with mine. As soon as I caught my breath and realized I was holding her hand, I quickly let it go and nodded an apology.

We finished our coffee and sherbet and left for the walk back to her pensione. She had an early tour kickoff in the morning, and I sorely needed some sleep. We meandered like the real tourists we were, and by a circuitous route. Asked her how she ended up with such a prestigious life's work. She said she graduated from Queen Mary University with a degree in physics. (*Particle* physics!) And me with 60 semester hours. We strolled—even skipped for a while (which had seemed like a good idea at first). Up and down tiny streets, through deserted parks and along high wrought iron fences surrounding official looking buildings. We ended up at Piazza di Spagna and the famous Spanish steps (*scalinatas* Ardith called them). We decided to make the climb—first past John Keat's apartment in the building on the right, then eleven more levels. Tried counting the steps but lost track near the top—at about 130 of them. *Whew.* We took a much needed rest at the top, on the terrace in front of the Trinita dei Monti church. From there it was quite a sight; the sparkling night majesty of Rome beneath us, spreading to the horizon in all directions.

Ardith was standing close, smiling and appearing to be very comfortable with me—for what reason I can't imagine. It was a strangely easy and natural time, almost tender, which was not appropriate, and unusual considering we had just met twelve hours ago. I sensed I was with a valuable undiscovered person who happened to be female, and I was lucky to be able to spend a few hours of my tour in this person's company. I realized I could never do this type of thing back in the states. It just wouldn't be right, what being married and all. (In fact it would be unthinkable.) Yet here I viewed it as disconnected—*almost imaginary*, a momentary event that would not affect my marriage, or anything, when I returned to the states. Or at least that's how I was explaining it to myself.

Finally we both realized the way-too-late hour and knew it was time to conclude the evening. I offered to walk her back to her pensione (which was now *not* in the direction of my hotel). I continued to be taken aback at how naïve and trusting she was. It was as if she would have let me do with her as I wanted. I wondered what might have transpired if we would have been another couple, in another private place, instead of here leaning on this cold metal railing. We didn't kiss goodnight—of course, not even a peck on each cheek, and that was proper (especially for me). But it was a long and warm parting handshake. A few more of the stumbling, unsure, separating niceties you might expect, and I was (shakenly) on my way.

A long run and I was back in the hotel. Exhausted as I was, I lay there—mind churning for a long time before a much needed sleep overtook me. Just a couple weeks ago I was in my home, in bed with my wife. My children just steps away. *And look at me now.* Was this just an anomaly, a pleasant coincidence, or did I seek it out? Why had I found so much satisfaction in a foolish mini adventure like this evening. What good could possibly come of such a thing? The whole scenario, starting with the innocent few words at the Vatican was a weakly based, no—baseless endeavor. Stupid.

The bus ride back to Naples (to the carrier and my real life) was like the one up—no better, no worse, except my head was full of "what ifs" and "maybes." The other members of the tour group, hashing over their Rome adventures, seemed to sense I had a lot on my mind and didn't ask me to relate my tales. (Thankfully.) We were back in Naples and being dropped off at the pier a little after 1600 (4 p.m.). Unfortunately we'd just missed one of the liberty boats and had another thirty minute wait. Back out to the carrier by 1700. Finished up the niceties of recounting (most of) the details of our Rome visit with my squadron mates, went to the wardroom for a great (as always) evening meal, and hit the rack like a loose bundle of dirty clothes going into a hamper.

Back to My Real Life

Awake at 0600 and not feeling too bad. Had multiple dreams or a series of deranged thoughts, of which I could make no sense of and didn't try to. And yeah, though I don't remember a face having appeared, Ardith or something about her was somehow in them. But enough of that. That was then and this is now. Almost 7—time to get to the task at hand. Jim had already gone down to the wardroom for breakfast, and I was in the stateroom alone, and used the time wisely: I wrote a long letter to Sara. Three good pages bringing her up to date on the things we were doing and what I had learned about carrier-based aviation operations. Included how I missed her and the kids, and included a couple of questions. Would have been easier without the guilt I was feeling as a result of the actual events on the Chaplain's Tour. Luckily, with my first launch and recovery under my belt I did have a lot to say about that. Sealed it and dropped it at the ship's post office on the way down to the wardroom.

Great breakfast. Creamed beef on toast (known unceremoniously in the service as "shit on a shingle"). With it I had my usual accompanying drink—a tall glass of tomato juice sprinkled with pepper, and with a lemon in it. Had to answer a few more questions from one of the guys about Rome, and that was it. Outa there and on my way— ready now to concentrate on the tasks at hand. Had a big day ahead of me—in fact, two. Having been on the three-day Chaplain's Tour, I had not adhered to the "one day on, one day off" duty section work schedule for our in-port stay, and was now scheduled for two consecutive days of duty on board.

The non-flying duties assigned to the younger officers were more or less in title only, but not mine. Although I had not attended the USMC Maintenance Officers School (that all Maintenance Officer-In-Charges are supposed to have attended), I could still be a big help to Major Burnham. My daily schedule here in port was just about the same as while at sea: visit each of the five shops in the department (the Engine Shop, Electric Shop, Metal Shop, Hydraulic Shop, and Flight Equipment) each day. There, I'd go over the pending repair work, read all the aircraft discrepancies to make sure that what the pilot had written, was really what he meant to convey. (Some of the write-ups were ambiguous or barely decipherable.) I'd then edit his write-up and individually discuss it with the men from the shop tasked to repair it. In so doing, priorities were more easily assigned, efficiency was improved, and the outcomes noticeably better.

Besides the above, an important part of my job was to take the time to listen to the men. Show them that you *cared about them*. And there were always a myriad of small personal problems. Some days I would spend more time in one shop than the others, depending on the level and complexities of their current workload. Today turned out to be not unlike the ones I had before we pulled into port, and would resemble many I would have at sea. After finishing the real work in the various shops I made the decision to stay on in the Metal shop and just shoot the bull with the guys there. Meant I would miss the evening meal in the wardroom, but there were great late night snacks available. Plus, these unrequired and unrushed informal sessions with the men—recognized by them as being done on my own time, were much appreciated. And I was glad to do it. This evening I learned that one of the corporals had a discrepancy in his paychecks not arriving on time at his wife's bank. It took me two days, but I was able to get this fixed, and earned his gratitude (confidence and increased loyalty).

In each department, and working hand in hand with the *commissioned* Officer-in-Charge (Major Burnham or me) there is always a *non-*commissioned Officer-in-Charge. Ours was Gunnery Sergeant Baldwin—the senior enlisted man in the department and just below me in the chain of command. He was my main "go-to" guy for getting the "word" to the men. He was quite a bit older than me. Old enough to have been in during the last year of the big war, and to have been a Maintenance Chief at a Marine Base during the Korean thing. Out of courtesy (and a respect for his many years of service—albeit at a rank structure junior to mine), I tried to keep him in the loop. This meant not issuing any directives to his men without first bouncing it off him. Make it appear as a procedure we came up with together. Hate to say it, but it appeared Major Burnham's primary job (or only job), was asking me what was going on and forwarding all the status reports it was my job to create. The number one and not easy objective of the department was to have an Operational Readiness of one hundred percent at 0600 each day. This meant all twelve of our aircraft were in an "Up" status—everyone of them ready for flight (without a single "grounding" discrepancy). Most squadrons deployed aboard a carrier would only achieve this about one out of three days, and some days would only have nine or ten out of twelve ready for flight.

The following day touring the shops was similar, maybe even better in terms of accomplishing something big. I found out from Gunny Baldwin that one huge time-consuming problem was they couldn't do any electrical soldering on the flight deck. He said the colder temperatures and wind across the deck would cause what is called a "cold joint"—a weak connection that would leak voltage and ultimately fail. To avoid this they were spending hours attaching tugs to the aircraft, towing them from wherever they were parked on the flight deck, through the maze of thirty other aircraft, to the elevators, lowering them to the hangar deck, re-positioning them to the work areas on that deck, and then accomplish the necessary soldering work. And then the reverse of the whole procedure to get them back up on the flight deck. This meant for every fifteen minute soldering job they had over two hours of aircraft positioning.

"Well Gunny—tell me, how many cold joints have we had so far?

He responded (as I expected), "Well I haven't even risked doing it up there. No sense wasting the time. We're just biting the bullet, accepting the hassle of bringing them down here."

"Have you even tried one topside?"

"No need to Captain. Everyone knows the joints won't hold up."

I was successful (though pressing my luck and being as tactful as possible) in getting him to promise me that the next connection that required a solder job, they'd try it topside—without bringing the aircraft below. He said he would, but there was little doubt he was merely indulging me and already certain of the outcome. Surprisingly to him (and thankfully to me) the first one held up fine, and so did the second, and all the rest we commenced doing on the flight deck. Probably saved a hundred man hours a month. Back up in my stateroom by 2300 (eleven p.m.), after my late night peanut butter and jam sandwich, orange, and glass of chocolate milk. (Yup, still trying to gain a little weight.)

A Rome Replay

Woke up early the third day, which was an off-duty day for me. My section—the port section, had liberty. Everyone in the starboard section would have to stay onboard. Thought about hitting the beach and decided I would. No Jim this time. (He was on the starboard section, so I'd go it alone.) Put on what I thought were my most European looking civvies, and caught the 0830 liberty boat. Beating our way to the dock, while trying to stay out of the cold spray and making sure my teeth didn't chip I wondered what sights I might visit here in Naples. None of the guys who stayed had much good to say about Naples. Thought about the allure of Rome, and then thought about it a few minutes more. *I guess I could.* Didn't owe any debt to Naples. Maybe that would be fun—hop a train up to Rome. Just spending an hour on the Via Veneto again might be worth the whole trip (or at least better than watching the garbage scows and fuming trucks of Naples).

One thing about these European cities, the train stations aren't hard to find. Lots of signs. Every road, every alley, seems to lead right to them. Was able to jog to it in ten minutes, although I must admit, once three blocks from the wharves, Naples was beginning to show some promise. Inside the station it was easy to find the schedule board (*il Partenze Informazione*). Planted myself in front of it scanning the constantly flipping black metal cards with white letters, searching for the trains to Rome. (No LED readouts yet.) Evidently here—like in the states, they had "local" trains and "express" trains. Not sure how much time I would save, but time was again a factor. According to the schedule board there was a 0928 *Rapido* (I'm guessing—the "express") to Rome, leaving from *pista nove*, and my plan was to find track nine and be on that train.

Although the train system in Europe is a magnificent operation, the *Rapido* proved to be the mystery train of the Italian rail system. I would search for it many times in my travels, only to come up empty-handed. Today, was sure I had gone to the right track, but hard to believe it was a *Rapido*. I was seeing bicycles pass us. We jerked to a stop a hundred times and it seemed like I looked down at least one street in every town between Naples and Rome. It was taking more time than I had thought. Finally we arrived at the now familiar Statzione Termini. I was the first one off the platform and into the street.

Somehow it just didn't seem the same. Sure, a million tourists and the same great buildings, but the fulfillment of my previous visit was absent. Wandered about for almost an hour. Sat in Piazza Republica and enjoyed the same great sights, but had an empty feeling. It was then that it hit me: *Ardith*, that's what's missing. *Could I?* Should I try to find her? I would! A quick scan and *Bingo!* A pay phone. To it. Great—got a dial tone and had the right tokens. Dialed the number on Ardith's note. Ringing. Ringing. Still ringing. Nobody answering at Pensione Venezia. Well-meaning people from the tour agencies overhearing my efforts kept approaching me with hotel brochures and good deals. "No, no, I'm not looking for a place to stay. Thank you. No, I don't need a pensione." Double checked the number. It was right. I guess I shouldn't be surprised. What did I expect? Why would she be there in the middle of the day?

No time to lose. 12:50. Not too bad. Another marathon. This time even warmer. It's the end of July—middle of the day, and I'm tear-assing down Via Nazionale again. Shirt wet straight through. Into the Pensione Venezia and up to the desk. Can see why no one answered the phone. No one at the desk. Up the stairs to Ardith's room. I knocked and announced myself. "Ardith, it's Roger. I was able to get back to Rome. Are you in?" There was no answer, which certainly didn't surprise me. But, two seconds later the door swung open and out she came. Miracle of miracles. (Never did ask her what she was doing back in her room in the middle of the day.) Her eyes were sparkling and she had a great big smile for me. She was carrying a shoulder bag and wearing sandals. She did a complete spin and as her ruffled dress swished around her legs, I observed her long muscular calves.

An even bigger surprise, she gave me that standard European greeting, a quick kiss on each cheek.

We spoke—right there in the hallway for a few minutes, and then I broached an idea. I guess a ridiculous idea, that had just popped into the space normally occupied by a brain. I suggested a picnic, which by her expression was not something she had been considering. But there was no discouraging me, and I knew if it was to be I'd have to get things going right away. Why the rush? Well, once again, I had to make it back on the dock in Naples by midnight, and had a two-hour train ride before that. Even we officers had "Cinderella Liberty." The last liberty boat out to the ship left the dock at midnight—2400 hours sharp!

Two blocks from her pensione we were able to rent a scooter. The transaction took a lot longer than it should have (and I got a beat-up looking one to boot). I was hoping, to get the bread, cheese and wine, a single stop would do it. Not so. And just getting out of downtown Rome was a real challenge. I wanted to get to the outskirts where there'd be less confusion, be more rural, and I could start searching for some grassy hill. *Senso Unico* (one way) streets kept tossing me back into the thick of things. Went through the same clogged intersection a couple times before I got an escape route figured out. I'm sure Ardith was a little apprehensive on the back of our wobbly Lambretta. (If she would have seen my performance with Jim a few days earlier, she would have been even more worried.)

Finally we were out of the city, which was good and bad. Less traffic but less stores too. It was half an hour before I could find a place that sold everything I needed, except a checkered table cloth. I was really picturing a checkered cloth. Already going without a wicker basket. Surprisingly, found a checkered cloth. On the way again, but not in a nice area. Seemed like nothing but weeded lots with trash, abandoned commercial buildings, stalled construction projects, low rent apartments, and people fixing cars in the streets. *Please God, give me some scenery.* Where's my grassy hill? I could feel Ardith's hands on my sides for balance. They were there. They felt good. I cursed the extra pounds I had gained that settled right there under her hands. Would have liked my body to feel hard and lean to her. Don't think it did.

Shit. Cutlery? At least a knife. No way to cut the bread and cheese. I'd bought yogurt too, and needed a spoon. Another stop. *Damn!* (Don't ever try to buy plastic tableware in Rome. It's not available.) By now it's two-thirty, the sun is way past the halfway point. My afternoon is disappearing in front of my eyes. All Ardith can have by now is a sore rear. Find another store. No luck. Desperate now. On a new street with no ambiance, but I spy a restaurant with some tables on the sidewalk. Hated to do it, but had no choice. I leave Ardith by the scooter. I'm onto the patio, and off it—with two table settings. Over my shoulder, "I'll have them back in two hours—only borrowing them." Back on the scooter. Now, I have everything. On our way to the grassy hill.

Three o'clock. This'll have to do. Can't spend the whole day bumping around on the scooter. It wasn't really a grassy hill. In fact it wasn't even a hill. (A city built on hills and I can't find one.) I guess I was just in the wrong part of town. It was a grassy field, more or less. I would have liked more grass and less weeds. The saving grace was that on it stood the last remains of an old monastery-type structure. Hopefully somewhere on the premises we would find a picturesque spot. Maybe, but not likely the way my luck was running. Off the bike and into the ruins. Found a wing of the building with two walls gone (the floor half grass, half dirt) and a view out one side. Not too much trash. I spread the cloth. Things were almost falling into place. Not as I had visualized them, but it could have been worse. We ate. I drank my share of the Chianti. (Out of a paper cup.) The cheese was okay, but the bread didn't have a good crust.

We finished. I wiped the utensils and put them in my pocket. (I *did* plan to return them.) I could feel the wine, which I needed by now I can tell you. I'd like to talk about the warmth of the sun, but the afternoon had turned surprisingly cool. It was actually chilly. I don't know how much Chianti Ardith had. (For this project to fly she would have needed a lot.) Ready now to leave, maybe out of respect for all the effort I had put into this afternoon picnic, she got up, wiped off her dress, walked over to me, and gave me a nice big hug. The firmness of her body against me, scared me, but was exciting. She surprised me by holding the hug a few seconds longer than necessary. Two seconds like this and I thought I felt a slight jolt—her tensing. I didn't think I had caused this, but I could sense her discomfort. I pulled back to see a dismayed expression on her face. She was observing something behind me, then looked quickly down at her feet. I spun around. Ten yards behind me, some vagabond was noisily relieving himself against a wall.

We were out of there. And the late lunch would seriously delay or negate any dinner plans. The motor scooter ride back was no great time either. (I did swing by that restaurant and give back the tableware I borrowed.)

Ardith hung in there. I tried to return the scooter, but the damned place was already closed—at quarter to six! Knew I couldn't keep it. Had to leave it outside against their fence. I was glad I didn't have to bounce another foot on that damn thing. (Pretty sure Ardith felt the same.) Not having another plan at the moment, we commenced the walk back to her pensione.

You've felt this way before: You'd give anything to lay down and close your eyes. I was beat. Suspected Ardith was as well. We sat on the steps of her pensione. It was now seven (and neither of us hungry). Another two hours and I'd have to be on my way to the Stazione Termini. A two hour train ride back to Naples, a mad dash to the dock, and hopefully catch the midnight (last) boat to the carrier. Now I was even more tired, just thinking about what was left in my day before I would be back on the ship in my rack. What I really would have liked to do, was escape (with or without Ardith) to a dark, quiet, air conditioned room, and just fall asleep. Just sleep—until noon tomorrow.

In my condition and the late hour, I knew what I should have done. What I *did* was different. Out of my mouth: "C'mon with me, I know a fun place. We can walk there from here!" She was off the step and up on her strong legs and we were on our way. The other day in my travels back and forth between her pensione and the two Caffes Dellas, I had passed by a little restaurant with a terrace full of laughing, singing, story telling, leg slapping locals. Old and young, fat and thin. Lots of families. The smell of garlic and hot bread had been heavy in the air. It looked like a roaring good time was being had by all. And through a stairwell leading down from the sidewalk I'd seen a lantern-lit, brick-walled, underground room. Happy, romantic-sounding music and the sounds of off-key patrons joining in were flowing up the steps. Stooping down I had been able to see the feet and legs of people dancing up a storm. At least it looked great last night. *Here's hoping for tonight.*

Good fortune was with me. As far as I was concerned we had hit the neatest place in Rome. It was rocking! But not with the harshness of a chromed, strobe-lit disco. This place was warm and friendly. At first Ardith was a little apprehensive, but she soon gained her confidence, and in thirty minutes she appeared to be having the time of her life. There were lots of kids. In fact after our second dance a little boy in shorts ran out to dance with Ardith. She was thrilled. The two of them reeled around the floor to the cheers and clapping of his older brothers and sisters. I was happy for Ardith. Her eyes were shining. You'd think—so attractive and intelligent, she would have received lots of attention and had lots of happy times. But it didn't seem like she had. It was like all this was a first time for her, and she was so happy to finally be part of something. We were both drinking the Chianti like it was Kool-Aid. And it wasn't just any bottle. Not only had the owner boasted at length about this bottle, he had *given* it to us "*complimenti della casa*" (which was certainly appreciated by me, my cash having run real thin about now). The owner (who I had thought was one of the more rowdy patrons when we came in) was definitely enjoying his own establishment.

Finally, the Chianti was gone, my feet were aching, and my legs were being crushed under Ardith's weight. (Fifteen minutes ago someone had sat in her chair, and I had signaled she could sit on my lap.) I knew it had to be late. I was afraid to check my watch. When I did: *Whew.* 2200 hours! *No way now Jose.* I'm in big trouble. Too late to get to Naples in time to catch the last boat out to the carrier. *Shit!* But I had known what was happening and I let it happen. I just hadn't been able to leave. But now what? If I could be on board a train in the next hour, I could be in Naples by one. Then all I'd have to do is smooth-talk the Shore Patrol guys into letting me get on their next shift-change boat. That'd give me five hours sleep before my 0730 hours meeting with Major Burnham. I really bit off more than I could chew. Don't know what I was thinking. Or if I was thinking. I have to examine my priorities, but I don't want to think about that now. Not now, too tired.

Fortunately Ardith was as tired as I was, and more than ready to go back to her pensione. It had been a great night. The owner and half his family walked us out. Lots of handshakes and promises for another time. Maybe for Ardith. I was pretty sure I wasn't going to see Rome again, and was just as sure I'd never see her again. I knew I had done a foolish thing (lots of foolish things) in the last few days, and felt a little sad (more than a little). We walked silently to her pensione (as if she knew my thoughts), and of course it wasn't going to be just a simple good night, it was going to be a goodbye. Another guy might have tried that "Can I come in for a cup of coffee?" thing, in hopes of you know what. As fascinated as I had become with Ardith, I was married and that just wasn't an option. In fact, I knew I shouldn't even be standing here in this hallway. I was pleased knowing Ardith had apparently had the time of her life and appeared wholly satisfied. Even with another guy, the concerns involved and arising from a sexual encounter might have added complexities to this otherwise fun time..

Our time together had been so innocent, almost playful. She was like a little girl, all aglow. Maybe she would have liked me to spend the night. I don't know. I don't think so. I couldn't tell. She was still all bubbly. *She* thought we had lots of time: the fall, the winter, next summer, visits to London, who knows—perhaps a whole future. *Me?* Play-acting again. My heart hurt. The goodnight this time graduated from a handshake to a hug. Though I had not been computing the days passing, she blurted out that she would be leaving tomorrow. *Tomorrow?* Don't know why that should be an issue to me, but it was. Then she froze me with her next words, *could I escort her to the airport.* She had no idea the hoops I was jumping through just to get to Rome. And worse yet—even if I wanted to, tomorrow my section had the duty. I would be stuck onboard. "What time Ardith? When's your flight?

"I'm leaving from Fumicino at 8 p.m." Her head was down and she didn't look happy about this. I dared not to believe it was because we would be parting company. I knew that although my section had the duty tomorrow, there was one other pilot on the off-duty section who rarely went ashore. It was not out of the question that he would swap duty days with me. I might be able to arrange that. Get tomorrow off and work for him the next day instead. My mind was racing. Certainly not sure I should come back up at all, yet finding it almost impossible to exclude the possibility of a sweet goodbye, I surprised myself again: "Yes Ardith, I think I can. I might be able to." This seemed to very much please her. Her head snapped up and the look of anticipation I got was one that meant if I missed everything else in my life I should not miss this trip to the airport.

Of course I knew any number of things could come up aboard ship to squelch those plans, and I had no idea what motivation or second thoughts I might be having then, so I added: "I'll try. I'll surely try. But if I'm not here by five o'clock, just figure I couldn't make it and plan on taking a cab without me." Said it, gave her hand a squeeze, turned, and exited the pensione. Outside I broke into a run. My intention was to sprint all the way to the railway station, which was an ambitious goal at this hour and in my state. But I knew five minutes could be critical. I wasn't sure when the next train would leave. Tried to keep the feet flying, but couldn't do it. The legs weren't going to cooperate. Nothing left—slowed to fast trot. Midnight. Almost on my revised schedule. Exhausted. My short cut took me over an old wooden bridge, under a marble arch, past giant iron gates, in front of a long row of darkened store fronts, and finally, round the stone fountain in Piazza Republica.

I GUESS I JUST WASN'T THINKING

At last—Stazione Termini, and I couldn't believe it. It was deserted! Hard to imagine that any place having had such crowds, having been such a mass of humanity all day long, could be absolutely soulless now. And it wasn't that late. It was creepy. I felt safe, but alone. Like in the old movie *On the Beach*—when a radio-active shower had left nothing living, just a city full of empty buildings. Motionless. Not a moving thing in sight. All the newspaper and magazine stands were shuttered up. The cafeterias too. Hard to believe. Okay, at least there's two people here. Down at the far end of the hall was a guy and a girl (or a thin straggly haired guy) walking out the far doors to the street where the buses stop. *Oh no, what's this?* Don't tell me the ticket windows are closed too. If I have to get my ticket from one of those automatic vending machines I'll be screwed. (I'd tried unsuccessfully to translate the instructions and figure out those procedures back in Naples.)

The large *Partenze Informazione* that previously was lit up with all the departures was dark. Definitely not a good sign. Now I'm starting to get worried. Quick—through the doors to the platform, check the boards out there. Did. Not lit either! And it's only quarter to one. There were a million tourists here six hours ago. Somebody must still have to get somewhere. I can't believe it—a prisoner in Rome. Completely cut off from the outside world. I ran to a stanchion with a framed time-table. *Whoa.* A cold sweat. Big trouble. The last train to Naples was at 1205! The next one wasn't until 0443 with an arrival in Naples of 0622. And I had that 0730 meeting with Major Burnham. That was going to be close. What can I do? Go back to Ardith's pensione? Not now for God's sake. And no way I'm paying for a hotel (especially with half the night already gone). *I'm looking at three horrible hours in this place.*

After some canvassing, I found an empty baggage cart and pulled it over behind some stacked pallets for a little privacy. Located a few relatively clean cardboard boxes, flattened them, and layered them on the metal bed of the cart. It was tolerable. Boy was I tired. Don't feel too suave. Glad Ardith can't see me now, curled up on a baggage cart, my clothes all wrinkled and needing a shave. Ugh. Still hard to believe there's no one in this whole terminal. Even the baggage check place was locked up tight. It's crazy. Like the place was quarantined and somehow I got in. Gotta sleep, but I better not sleep through my train; assuming I could even fall asleep. If so, I was pretty sure the noise of the early shift coming in would wake me up in time. Flat on my back I found myself shaking my head in dismay. We had been talking about meeting each other on another vacation. *About me visiting her in London!* I had listened to the words coming out of my mouth in disbelief. There had been little I could say that was true. Little I could have proposed that could ever be brought about. I did not feel good about my conduct and the falsehoods I had uttered (or truths I had kept to myself). I knew my life and my future. Who I was and who and what I could never be, no matter what my fantasies or what temptations I exposed myself to—and that's what this was.

Well I was right about one thing, unfortunately more than right. While still positioning and repositioning, trying to get comfortable, trying to get my bones away from sharp corners and hinges—at about three o'clock the early shift workers came in. All manner of inconsiderate crashing, banging, and shouting commenced (along with the prompt loss of my bed). The train station was reborn like a dry fossil erupting into a live creature. It was the end of any chance of sleeping, that was for sure.

I wandered about, checking my watch, waiting and wasting time. Stumbling through the doors to the street I observed a black sky turning gray and even slightly whitish just over the tops of the buildings. A bundle of newspapers came flying out of a passing truck, just missed my legs and continued tumbling across the sidewalk. My mouth had a terrible taste. Guys with trays and boxes of bread and rolls were running in and out. The metal shutters of the newsstands and coffee bars were clattering open. Things were happening. Cabs and buses out of nowhere were suddenly everywhere. A new day was beginning in Rome, but I wasn't going to be part of it. And I shouldn't be. I didn't belong. I didn't deserve it. I had been on borrowed time. I was leaving as I should. I wasn't part of this world anyway. (Winced at the thought of my wife being able to observe me right now, or worse—last night!) My stomach was upset, but the cafes still weren't serving. Another thirty minutes to waste. Feeling real ill. Hard to believe that I'll be on the carrier at 0700, but I better be.

It was by accident—I hadn't hoped for as much, but luck was with me. At 0440 I again (mercifully) climbed aboard the much sought after *Rapido*. (Thank God for small favors.) An hour and twenty later I was in Naples. Good thing it was a short ride, I was ill the whole trip. Caught a cab to the dock. (What a ride. Didn't help my stomach any.) 0625: So far so good. Got the first liberty boat returning to the ship. I'm gonna make it. I'm going to make it this time, *but how many next times?* I thought of not even attempting the trip back up to Rome tomorrow. Let Ardith get to the

43

airport on her own. What was I doing to my mind and with my life? Even if it were just for now, just while I was gone and never going to have any effect my life or my marriage afterward. Even if it were only a new foreign experiment, only a temporary event, I was allowing myself to do things and begin considering things that are out of the question. I just wanted to sleep, to get away from these mental interrogations and behavioral reflections. It was possible I could become more involved in my temporary "play-life"—an impossible fabricated one, than in my real life.

I struggled up the least used aft ladder to the flight deck, praying I wouldn't run into any of my men, or any of the other pilots (let alone the Colonel). Jim—my roommate would know I had not come home, but he should be the only one. Now, if I can just make it across the hangar deck undetected. I did. So far still good. Now through the forward hatch and towards my stateroom. Walking through the narrow (and fortunately—dimly lit) passageways, I could feel my socks rolled up in uncomfortable wrinkles under my arches. My shoes had trod a million steps and my feet in them were aching. My collar was wet around my neck, and I'm sure, badly soiled. I probably shouldn't even wash these clothes, just throw them away (or burn them in an effort to destroy any lingering memories).

Made it into my stateroom. Home free. Weak, embarrassed, confused and tired, but safe in my stateroom. Fortunately Jim was already gone. That's good. I'd rather not face him right now. A quick shower and shave. Dressed again. Might look okay. I had to be careful, the ship and its whole operation was beginning to seem menial and foreign to me. As if I were only a visitor, popping through from time to time, grudgingly co-existing with it as it interfered with a possibly new and exciting life.

Arrivederci Ardith

0720 hours: No time for breakfast and too ill besides. Down to the maintenance office to meet with Major Burnham. Got to give him credit. He gave me all the time I needed to explain a potentially new maintenance procedure; a way of tagging suspect aircraft parts that had been removed, but that may not have been bad. This way they could be identified for further checking, and possibly even reinstalled. The Major who was usually slow to get excited about a junior officer's recommendations, was impressed with this innovation. I was flattered. Only one problem. He was so excited he wanted me to hold meetings with all the shop heads right away. Explain to them exactly how we would incorporate the procedure.

Whoa, who knows how long that will take? It'll cancel out a badly needed nap, and maybe even cause me to not get up to Rome in time to take Ardith to the airport (assuming I'm successful in convincing myself to do it at all). Started on it right away. First to the Engine Shop. The "troops" (that's what we call the enlisted men) there, and in all the subsequent shops were really excited about the new procedure. They agreed wholeheartedly with the presence of the addressed problem. And most importantly, Gunnery Sgt Baldwin seemed impressed and optimistic. (As I think I told you before, if he wasn't with it, no matter its merit—it wasn't going to work.)

Checked my watch as I exited the last shop—1130 hours. Good. Better than I expected. Could still make it if Tripp had not yet left on liberty and was willing to swap days with me (and I didn't pass out from lack of sleep). You can bet I was tired—real tired, and confused. But somehow unable to resist putting forth some level of effort to bring about this final visit with Ardith. Went to Tripp's stateroom and he wasn't there. Down to the Ready Room where the guys often hung out. Three guys but not him. The good news was Brad said he saw him about a half hour ago in the wardroom. Maybe. Miracle of miracles: There he was, spooning in some of our Filipino cook's famous peanut butter soup (and still in his uniform)! Promise him the moon if necessary. Didn't have to. Pulled the chair out next to him and made my plea. "No sweat," he'd be glad to stay on board today—take my duty. (Though I would never understand it, there were a few guys like Tripp who seemed to have no desire to go ashore.)

Back in my stateroom about noon, organizing my mind and body, and figuring out what outfit to wear, when Jim walks in. *Good news.* He had already heard about my new maintenance procedure and was obviously pleased at my contribution. In fact, he made a neat compliment about me *sure earning my pay*—which I most certainly didn't deserve, but was real glad to hear. (Made some points there which I'd undoubtedly need later.) Ten past noon and I was waiting at the top of the ship's forward ladder, and great, spied a liberty boat about halfway to us from the dock. Twenty after and making one of those teeth jarring, butt bruising, wet trips again (that I would do much too often in the months to come). Half past and at the dock, hailing a cab this time. (Had to save every minute possible.) At the train station in just a matter of minutes. Couldn't complain, things were going as good as I could expect. Was on board a train a few minutes after one and what's more, it was a *Rapido*. (Three times in a row now—a record for sure.)

I GUESS I JUST WASN'T THINKING

In the Stazione Termini at two-forty-five. Not bad. But once again my phone calls to Ardith's pensione just rang and rang. No answer. Already knew that half the time the old geezer wasn't there, and so there'd be no one to transfer the call to her room. No sense wasting time here. The same marathon again. Was real familiar with the route now—got there in record time. Evidently the guy at the desk was getting used to me too. He barely glanced up. I was past him and bounding up the poorly lit worn wood steps. But there was no Ardith this time. My heart sank. I leaned against the wall, thinking. But no time to lose. Back to the concierge. Talk about a jerk. This guy not only had no information about Ardith, he gave it to me with great disdain. I could have yanked him out of his little plywood cubby-hole.

Out into the street, looking left and right, mind was racing. Where? Where could I even begin looking? What had we talked about? I didn't even know which hotel her friends Martin and Mia were staying in. Nowhere to look that made any sense. Rent a scooter? That's it—rent a scooter. I'll be able to cover more territory that way. Flew the four blocks to the Vespa Rent-a-Scooter place. Got one for two hours, not a great rate, but saved six bucks. *Please God, let it be that I don't need it longer than that.* I'll swing by the pensione every half hour just in case. She may only have gone out for an errand, or for a sandwich, since it is near lunch time. Damn, I'm missing that chance too, we never did have a leisurely meal together.

I could have gotten killed a half dozen times, actually touched fenders on several occasions. There'd be that sudden *bonk*, a yank of the handle bars, and jamming my foot down to the pavement just in time. *Wow that was close.* The traffic was horrendous and I wasn't looking at it. I was scanning the crowds with fiery intent—desperately probing for a familiar walk, a familiar profile. No tall auburn haired woman escaped my scrutiny. She had to be out there, somewhere in that sweltering sea of humanity. Several times I was sure I had seen her; thought it had to be her—the same hair, the same shoulders, the same walk. *It's her.* In two seconds I'd be off the bike, leaving it—wheels spinning, half up on the curb, on my way after her, weaving through the crowds behind her, heart pounding and breathless, only to be crushed when some strange face turned to me. It was all I could do not to shout at them that they had the *wrong face.* I was becoming frantic. I was all over Rome, from the catacombs to the Vatican. And she never returned to her pensione either.

May as well admit it. I've lost. It's over. This is stupid. May as well turn the scooter back in. An hour and a half on it in this traffic, under the July sun, cutting through the diesel fumes and just staying ahead of the horns, was as much as I could take. I have to think. That's what I have to do. Just think! If—*just if* she was planning to meet me, besides her pensione where would she be? But what makes me think she even knows I'm in town? What makes me think she wants to see me? She could have even had another date with the Count.

The Caffe Della Firma? Could be, it *is* lunch. (No, it *was* lunch.) Maybe a late lunch. One last check at the pensione. The guy had no idea where she would be, and still not friendly either. I'm off for the foot of Via Nazionale and the Caffe Della Firma. Maybe—just maybe. *Please God one last favor.* Again, Rome for me was just a blur. I was spending all my time running full tilt—either late or searching. I was one tourist in a serious hurry. I didn't look like I was on a summer vacation. I didn't *feel* like I was on a summer vacation. I was on another mission, albeit a very questionable one. I skidded to a walk 100 yards from the cafe. There they were, the striped umbrellas and white metal tables. A light breeze gently moving the young cypress trees on each side of the patio. Everything like it was. But no Ardith. My energy was being sapped by an overwhelming feeling of frustration and discouragement (and an awareness that this was probably a fitting outcome). There was no earthly reason to suspect I'd ever find her. I plopped down at one of the tables, physically and mentally exhausted. There was no way. It was now quarter to five. I should have made a contingency plan. I should have anticipated a screw-up and designated a special meeting place. Just in case something like this happened. *Ardith, where are you?*

I was completely preoccupied with my own thoughts and wishes. I didn't notice anything or anyone in the restaurant. With an eight o'clock flight, she'll have to leave the city by six thirty at the latest. *God, give me a break.* I did nothing because I had no ideas. When my feet and legs felt like they would support me, I decided to make another check of her pensione, though I'd made three trips already, without success. Still, she has to come back there sometime. Why didn't she leave a message for me? That really had me puzzled. I didn't run this time. I couldn't. But no one passed me on the sidewalk, that was for sure. In the door. To the office. Same deal. Same old guy with no news or idea about anything. I was getting to hate this guy. I had yet to see him smile, and I had been polite from the first time we met.

I GUESS I JUST WASN'T THINKING

Five-thirty. Why didn't I think of this before—*the underground restaurant!* Do you think? Maybe, what have I got to lose. On my feet again, running again. Remembering, while my feet flew down the street, how much fun Ardith and I had had at this spot just twenty-four hours ago, with the music and dancing, and the Chianti. I'd give anything for one more night like that. It was not far and in five minutes I was closing on it. At this time of the day, they wouldn't be serving any meals, but the place should be unlocked. You can usually see them sweeping and dusting and setting up tables between meals. I rounded the corner. No one was on the terrace. It was empty. The tables were piled one on top of the other. Not ready to be used. Put on hold, like my afternoon. Things can sure seem dead when you're not part of anything. Completely out of ideas, I was standing with my head drooped, my jacket hanging from one hand and my bag in the other, like a real loser, when I heard a voice from the downstairs. *It is! I know it, it's Ardith!* She was there. If we hadn't seen each other for ten years, it couldn't have been a more joyous occasion. I think she was really glad to see me. She hugged me with all her strength (which was a lot). I was ecstatic. I could have leaped over the building. I didn't deserve such luck, but here it was. We were together! I didn't know for how long, or if ever again. But for now, all was right with the world. The owner and his wife were beside themselves observing our reunion. I knew we didn't have any time to waste but the guy made us sit for one quick glass of his *Riserva Speciale* Chianti (which we did, and did enjoy, but while checking our watches). And guess what? Ardith *had* left a message for me at the pensione: A detailed itinerary with this exact rendezvous point. She had written it all down, and told the old guy there to be sure I got it if I showed up. *That son of a bitch!*

In view of the critical time issue here—which she must have known, Ardith was acting so lackadaisical, it almost appeared as if she didn't care if she missed her flight. Based on my calculations we had to be on our way to the airport in thirty minutes. And I had a plan. One I'd worked out in advance and just had to put in action: The place that rented the Lambrettas, also rented used sedans, and it was only about three blocks from Ardith's pensione. I would rent one while Ardith checked out of her pensione. I knew it would take at least thirty minutes to get to the old Fumicino airport on the coast, and that meant we had to get back to her pensione right now. She would have to be checked out and us on the way by six-thirty at the latest.

We said good-bye to the owner and his wife (again) and walked briskly to her pensione. She begged me not to make a scene with the old guy. I didn't. I wanted to, but it wasn't as important as our imminent separation, and the few minutes we had before then. Ardith was concerned about the necessity of renting a car, and didn't want me to go to that expense. Kept saying she could take a cab and I could go with her. That would be fine. (It probably would have been fine.) But I wanted the privacy, some time alone. Taking a drive together would be the first normal activity we'd tried. She finally agreed. While she finished packing I ran the three blocks to the place I rented the Lambretta and used my credit card (again) to rent a beat up black Fiat.

Murphy's law. As much of a hurry as I'm in, the transaction is in slow motion. And the only car they have is low on gas. I ask them if I can get to the airport on however much is in the tank. They say something in Italian that's the equivalent of "No sweat." Just as I'm about to drive out (onto a one-way street that's going to take me about four blocks out of the way), the guy I rented the picnic Lambretta from, comes running over shouting I owe him an overnight payment. I explain how I left it right there against the fence, couldn't get inside. Not now I tell him! I'm in a big hurry, but that I'll be back by eight o'clock. Don't worry. (He looked worried.) I was out of there and back to the pensione at six-twenty. Ardith was ready and we were on our way. (You can bet the old guy dodged me the whole time.)

In spite of the fact the wheels were out of line, it leaked fumes inside, the AC didn't work, and my window wouldn't open, the trip was what I had been anticipating. We drove past contrasting green and yellow fields, and neat wooded areas—due west towards Fumicino. I wasn't wild about the gas gauge. It read one needle width above empty. There had been lots of gas stations before we got out of the city, but I knew we were late, and I wanted to get some miles under us before we stopped. Bad idea. Now there were no gas stations. I hadn't passed one in ten minutes. Pretty soon we'd be to the airport. If I can just make it there. *Please God, don't let me run out before I get to the airport.* Ardith didn't seem sad to be leaving. I can't say that. But she was happy we were still together. We talked about visiting. My mind was stalled, in sludge—bogged down. I didn't know what I could say and mean it, or have any chance of bringing it about. I felt like I was slipping and sliding on a stage. Experimenting with two lives. Becoming two persons—not much liking either one.

We made it to the airport (the gas gauge needle a hair below empty).

I GUESS I JUST WASN'T THINKING

Into the parking lot. Out of the car. Into the terminal. Checked in. Having some coffee together. She was so strong, so tall, yet so quiet and passive. I watched as she clutched her purse on the table, fingered the clasp, and hung on to each word I said. Based on this show of respect and other actions on her part, I guessed she would be a respectful and devoted life's partner to someone, someday, somewhere. We passed the last forty minutes almost in silence. I don't remember the flight announcements. I don't remember the good-bye. The next thing I knew I was walking away from her gate and she was gone. I was alone and I needed to be alone. I was tired. I wasn't sure of anything. I ran out of gas before I got to a service station. I had to walk a couple miles with a two-liter plastic bottle. I didn't care. I did it quietly. I turned in the car. I paid the extra for the Lambretta. I caught the eight-twenty train to Naples.

Chapter Five
SEARCHING FOR AN EXPLANATION

Back on the ship at 2300 hours and in the rack at midnight, but not sleeping—not yet (and deservedly so). Just lying there staring up at the metal frame under Jim's mattress. *What in the hell am I doing?* Our first time in port and just look at me. If my time in Rome is any indication of my future activities, I'm in big trouble. I spent the whole damn time engaging in a foolhardy mini adventure—something I should never have been doing. Why this need to search for new and different life's circumstances? (Wasn't seeing it in any of the other guys.) But I did know this much: As far back as I could remember I had a diabolical curse. *While I may not have known for certain where I wanted to be, I did know one thing for sure: It usually was somewhere other than where I was!* And where had I been? Where did I spend my youth—just about all of it? I can tell you and in a few words: "Far from the action." I was not where it was happening, ever. And usually because I was working. Dad never actually told me I had to earn all my own spending money (whether for a movie, that new Schwinn, or even a pair brown corduroys for school), but there was no question that he expected it, and I unquestionably responded.

But I have to admit, I had a wonderful home life. A great mom and dad, never a cross word with my sister or brother, we ate all our meals together, and I had my own bedroom! But as far as what I was doing when I wasn't seated in a classroom, I was nowhere (at some kind of job). It started with paper routes, and early on—having my first one when I was twelve. And guess what, even worse, it was a *morning* route. At 5:30 a.m. while all the other kids were still asleep I was pumping my bicycle up and down the still-dark streets. Having done this three straight years, I promoted myself to an afternoon route for 9th and 10th grade. In my junior year I quit delivering papers and graduated to stocking shelves in a local grocery store for the next two years. *You want to find me after school?* Just go to the Godwin Avenue Co-op, look down enough aisles and you'd find me, on my knees ripping open cartons and writing prices on cans of peaches with one of those old grease pencils (while all the other guys were at baseball practice or doing nothing). The minute the last school bell rang you could color me gone—on my way to work. Forget about any afterschool activities like trying out for a sports team, float-building projects, forensic clubs, pep rallies (or just being slouched in a booth at the soda fountain having a cherry coke *with those rich kids from the Heights).* That would've been something! Oh how neat it would have been to be able to be hanging out with that always-ogled group. The Heights was a super exclusive residence on the west side of town, where the rich people lived. I heard it was high enough that from their giant front porches they could look over the Hudson and see the buildings in Manhattan—twenty miles away. (To me and my friends it was a place we knew we lacked the credentials to even consider taking a quick drive through.)

And the weekends? Saturday mornings (every Saturday morning) I belonged to Dad. I was at his disposal for any one (or two or three) of a seemingly never ending list of property maintenance projects: replacing shingles, creosoting wood posts, shoveling furnace ashes, putting insulation in the attic, cleaning the garage, filling the ruts in the driveway, straightening bent nails on the cellar floor—whatever. When he was a kid that's what his "Pop" had him doing. It worked for him and I was going to have advantage of it as well. Sunday's agenda was no better. We kids left the house at 8:30 to walk the half mile to church, where we attended Sunday School first, then waited for mom and dad—to accompany them to the 11:00 adult service. When it was over we went home, took off our "go to meeting" clothes, jammed ourselves in the 38 Olds (that we'd gotten in the Will when Mom's dad died) and made the twenty minute car trip up Route 17 to Saddle River for the weekly chicken dinner at Grandpa's house. This outing usually had us home about four. *My free time each week was Saturday afternoons and from four till dark on Sundays.*

And the summers, for most kids the last day of school would mean neat vacations with their parents, or one fun day after the other at Graydon pool. Or best of all (my dream) playing baseball in a summer league—on a real team, with uniforms, on manicured diamonds, and having your parents there watching you. But not for me, I'd be working. And I guess even if I wasn't I wouldn't be having all that much fun. I'd probably have spent half my time sitting on the curb with Wes or in the backyard doing nothing with Rolly. What I could only fantasize about (and did just about every day): not have to work and be popular enough to spend the lazy summer days cavorting with those cool rich kids from the Heights. The guys were always laughing and having such good times, wearing Bermuda shorts and mahogany-colored penny loafers, *without socks.* (No matter what stores I checked, I never saw the clothes those guys wore.) And the girls from the Heights—wow. They were all pretty. You couldn't miss them in school, sashaying through the halls dressed in their white blouses and pleated Scotch plaid skirts, crossed arms in front enfolding their books (and hiding their emerging bust lines). And now at Graydon pool—in bathing suits! Well I couldn't even imagine spending a day (even a half day) like that, being there that close to them and just wasting time.

Don't know why, but never felt that I was eligible to give some girl a call for a movie date. I was so envious of all those Heights guys kicking back, fritting away their time and talking to the girls from their forbidden neighborhoods. They never had to give a thought to having a part time job. Their dads carried briefcases, caught the eight-fifteen train to Manhattan, bought a new car every year, and took the whole family to Florida during winter vacation. They had it made. I was a phantom student gliding through the halls unnoticed. I would have given anything to be part of that "in-crowd." Share in some of their activities, even just waste time with them! But I never tried, never even gave it a shot. So while I'm sitting here complaining, in truth I guess I really have no one to blame but myself. I probably could have made the time, I probably could have gotten up the nerve. I just didn't. Might have to say it's my own fault I missed all those precious teen years.

Chapter Six
OUR MISSION IN THE MED

We steamed out of the port of Naples—myself and many others I suspect, more than ready for the structure and normality we'd find within the confines of the ship; things familiar and things of order. Unfortunately, even if I chose to I knew I would find little solace in relating my escapades or confiding my concern to any of my squadron mates. My time ashore was for the most part—dishonorable. No critical occurrences perhaps but not defensible in intent. Obviously I was doing a lot of second-thought thinking and should have. The other guys were laughing and reminiscing about stupid (but blameless) activities. Somebody having a few too many beers, races in cabs, great meals, night club shows. What stories could I share without deserved embarrassment? Of course Dale Hornsby (the Navy Cajun guy from LSU) was always willing to listen, hanging on every word and wanting more details. As you might imagine, I was more than ready for this at-sea period. Turn-to on my job. Clean up my act. Get with the program. Write to Sara.

With no flight operations scheduled the first day, I set out on my standard "visit-all-the-shops" tour. One hour each. I hit the Metal Shop, the Hydraulics Shop and the Electric Shop—all before lunch. Learned that too many inflight discrepancies were taking multiple sessions to be fixed. Many being worked on three times—each time for several hours, without resolution. It's not uncommon for a discrepancy not to be fixed the first time, since many problems only occur in flight, and therefore the maintenance guy can't be sure he's fixed it, until another flight is flown. One malfunction in particular, an intermittent low hydraulic pressure warning light, had been worked on three times. Interviewing the three technicians who worked on it, I discovered the second and third guys were to a large extent repeating the same trouble-shooting procedures the first

54

guy had already done. They were checking, adjusting, and changing the same components (without success).

To avoid this problem, I designed a new worksheet for aircraft discrepancies. As another form to fill out (more paperwork) you can imagine it didn't get a very warm reception from the troops. However I was convinced it would help eliminate duplicated efforts. On the form— each aircraft having its own, the first technician assigned to trouble-shoot the malfunction, would enter the discrepancy number, briefly list his conclusions as to the reason for the malfunction, and then a rundown on the systems or parts he had checked, adjusted, removed or replaced. If the same problem cropped up again (not fixed the first time) the next guy to tackle it, had somewhere to start. He'd know exactly what avenues had been explored the first time. It went on to become a form used fleet-wide (and Major Burnham got a lot of credit).

Second day mail call I got a serious letter from Sara. As usual she was doing a first class job running the house and taking care of the kids. No wife could have been more wholesomely occupied with what was truly important. Things were not complicated for Sara, she knew all about her world, her husband, her children (and her Eastern European relatives in Toronto and Ypsilanti). Everything she did was designed to make things safer and better within that circle. Turns out some guy had seen our oldest daughter Donna swimming, and been so impressed that he had a swim coach from Atlanta check her style. Sara was confused because it turned into a real production. After having Donna swim, they did muscle mass checks, tendon tensile checks, and rotator cuff range checks. She must have passed because they said they would be willing to enter into a contractual agreement. Donna would go to some place in Texas first. Then if things worked out, maybe to a place outside San Diego—a camp that trains Olympic and professional athletes. There'd be special tutoring and everything. It would cost some money at first, but if she progressed like they anticipated, and won or even placed in some of their "step meets," there would be decreasing expenses, and it would end up being "more than worth it." They had Sara call some parents in Jacksonville whose son was already in the program.

I could see she was confused and more than a little upset by the whole thing. I knew this was something I should respond to. As shaky as I was beginning to realize I was otherwise, I valued being a father, and at least some things you could do as a husband. I would never stand for Sara to be hurt or taken advantage of. Fortunately (according to her) Donna didn't seem to want to do it. At first, I was excited for what it might mean to her. Then after more thought, got less excited about what it might mean to the family, and even Donna in the long run. Now she was a great little swimmer, and even at her young age was popular because of this. Her talent brought her happiness and there was no pressure to knock two-tenths of a second off her time. She swam because she liked to and it was only one part—a small part, of her young life. I wasn't sure I wanted two-tenths of a second, and grinding out another victory, and winning another medal, to be the big things in her life—especially at six. I wrote a long letter as I should have. Sara deserved it, and I certainly wasn't writing her enough. I knew some guys who wrote every day. (There wasn't another way. This was decades before texting, email, Skype and webcams.)

I used this at-sea period to hit the weights. Spent a lot of time in my hideaway up on the forecastle, much of it trying to keep my benches from sliding and losing my balance on overhead lifts. It was a neat and private place. No one ever came up there. Dale had brought a couple of dumbbells up there from his little gym, and he and I had some good workouts there. Got some great "pumps." I had been making two between-meals trips to the wardroom each day. Once in the morning and once in the afternoon— for a thick peanut butter sandwich, a glass of chocolate milk, and an orange. I think I was starting to gain weight. Dale said I looked like I was bulking up (but then your workout partner is supposed to motivate you). Don't know why—my whole life, at least since I was eleven, I would have been so preoccupied with being bigger. If I had spent as much time on anything as I spent lifting weights and worrying about my darned pecs, I would have earned a Ph.D. in it.

The scuttlebutt on the way over, had it that we were being followed by some Soviet ships. We knew that, but now—today, the word was passed down that they had been spotted entering the Med. A whole new attitude began to permeate the ship. There were classified briefings, 24-hour watches, and lots of telex's. Even had a couple "General Quarters" (Emergency Station drills), and two "Pilot Alerts". And then yesterday it reached a peak when the word from the SONAR section was that we might be being followed by a Russian sub. They had started picking up a strange kind of "ping" that they had never heard before. I found myself— even with everything else on my mind, getting caught up in the fever. But nothing was as exciting as when the "ping" was identified. *That* caused a lot of excitement around the ship. Up in the forecastle, one of Dale's dumbbells had been rocking back and forth, tapping an adjacent steel gunnel. That was the strange sound the SONAR guys were hearing. The Soviet Sub turned out to be a thirty pound dumbbell. Colonel Cunningham was *not* amused.

You might imagine (now—at the peak of the cold war) that the US had a massive and well-coordinated retaliatory plan in the event the "Evil Empire" initiated hostilities. (Translated that means should Russia launch even one missile westward, or should someone at a console somewhere *think* they did!) Well you're right, we did have a plan. And although we weren't going for Russia, you can still sleep well, because about a thousand Air Force planes and aimed missiles were waiting—24 hours a day, to do just that. Our mission was to knock out a bunch of strategic targets within the Eastern Bloc, and milling around here in the Mediterranean we were well within striking distance of them. But who's gonna get what? A lot of coordination was required. (I guess that's one of the things the Joint Chiefs of Staff get paid for.) In any case, the Navy had its targets, the *Forrestal* had its targets, VMA-331 had its targets, and *Roger Yahnke had his!* Wednesday in the most classified briefing I'd attended to date, we were assigned our individual targets. I got mine. The one I would keep for the whole cruise—my very own thing to personally demolish—a supposed Russian military installation on the outskirts of a small village in an unsuspecting Eastern Bloc country.

I don't know if I told you, but VMA 331 was not just an attack (bomber) squadron, we were ready to attack with *nuclear* weapons. Yup, we're talking mushroom shaped clouds in 1964. And obviously, on board was where the nuclear weapons were stored—twelve of them, four for each attack squadron. (Great thing to think about in the middle of a storm.) In any case, as far as the Marine Corps was concerned, I was no longer called an "Attack Pilot," but rather a "Nuclear Weapons Delivery Pilot." And the procedure for dropping an atomic bomb was a lot different than a regular bomb, because survival of the pilot was not guaranteed. The shock wave and radiation spread so quickly, it required a special release maneuver by the pilot—actually "tossing" the bomb, to get out of there fast enough to avoid being himself killed in the blast.

In order to facilitate the required hasty retreat, the profile for dropping a nuclear weapon was referred to as a "Loft Maneuver." (A far cry from the old dive-bombing.) You sped in at exactly (and I mean *exactly*) 500 knots True Airspeed, as low to the ground as you could get, and that was supposed to be just 50 feet over the ground (to stay under the enemy radar) until you passed a point, exactly 24,000 feet (four nautical miles) short of your target. This point was known as the "Pull-up Point," and everything was math and physics from there on in. That's why you had to be exactly 500 knots.

As soon as you got overhead this pre-briefed landmark (a building, a bridge, a factory or whatever), you hauled back on the stick—mightily, until you pulled four "G's". This would have your lips drooling, your belly over your belt, and all the blood trying to pool in your legs and feet. As you continued upwards and went through a nose-up angle of exactly 45 degrees, there was a small "click" (the parameters were met) and the automatic release circuitry cut loose the weapon. It wasn't a matter of *seeing* the target, because you never did. Inertia, centrifugal force and gravity, guided it to its target, in a high arcing trajectory. Meanwhile you didn't stop the backward pull, the aircraft continuing right past straight up, and you didn't stop there. You kept pulling back until the nose of the aircraft came back down to the horizon behind you—pointing back in the direction from which you had come (albeit, now you're upside down). This method of reversing course was supposed to keep you out of the injurious effects of the blast; get you turned around in the least amount of time.

The fourth and fifth day our flight ops were dedicated to practicing this maneuver. We used small, twenty-five pound projectiles, which theoretically had the same aerodynamics and flight trajectory as the actual nuclear weapon. The ship would act as our Pull-up Point, towing our target (a beat-up wooden sled) exactly 24,000 feet behind it. We would start about twenty miles away, and speed right at the bow at five-hundred knots. Passing over the ship, we'd yank back, and loft our dummy nuclear weapon towards the sled. Radar following gave us a "read" on where our shot had gone—where it impacted and how close.

In addition to the necessity of maintaining exactly five-hundred knots, you had to hold a consistent pull-up force of exactly four "G's" throughout. These two elements were vital parts of the physics that determined the trajectory of the arcing projectile. Furthermore, the weapon had to be released as the plane passed exactly forty-five degrees nose-up. If it released too soon, or too late, the impact area would be too short or too long. To me, the most difficult part was keeping the damn wings level during the pull up. That was real important. If one wing or the other was down even a little, you'd be in a slight turn and you'd loft your weapon off to the left or right. Even if it went the correct distance, it could end up way off to the side.

Finding these targets, getting from the Mediterranean Sea (actually for our targets, from the Aegean Sea) to a town—say, in the middle of Romania, was another thing. A three-hundred mile journey over a route you would be taking for the first time. There was a meeting at 2000 hours (8PM) in S2 (Intelligence) and they supplied us with a whole bunch of very detailed, large-scale maps of the Balkan states. The next day each of us spent almost the whole day gluing a series of them together, to construct a mosaic stretching from our "entry point" on the nearest coast, to our assigned target. On these maps (using a swell selection of colored felt-tipped pens) we would trace our specific route, making navigational notes, and "tic" marks each three minutes, to assist in ascertaining our specific geographical position. (Could be real easy to get off your necessary track.)

The finish line on these maps was your individual Pull-up Point. Hell with the target, first you had to find the Pull-up Point! Every pilot took great pride in how accurate and detailed his strike map was (and what hot info he might have included on it that the other guys hadn't thought of). It was the most important part of our target folders. We were told that to maintain the necessary familiarity with our routes and the terrain features, we were going to be required to log at least five hours each week—studying these maps. But let's say you knew where your Pull-up Point was on the map, and maybe following your carefully drawn yellow high-lighted line, you could even arrive there. *But would you be able to recognize it*—approaching it at such a low altitude and going five-hundred knots. It would be real easy to be *past it*, before you'd identified it. If so, the whole Loft Maneuver is wrecked. You couldn't complete your delivery. You're screwed. Can't even start over. At tree-top level and scenery-blurring speed it would be real difficult to see and identify a ground level Pull-up Point, so they were usually tall, man-made structures, with enough vertical height that they would be outlined above the horizon for some distance before you got to them. And even then it would be difficult. To make us more able to recognize our Pull-up Point, it was announced with great fan fare, that soon, we would each receive a U-2 photo of our individual Pull-up Point.

I GUESS I JUST WASN'T THINKING

Friday was the day when we were scheduled to receive this much ballyhooed photo. Everyone was real excited about receiving the final (virtual) part of their (almost sacred) target folder. It would be a special computer-enhanced 8 X 10 glossy. The photo interp guys told us that the resolution of these prints was incredible: *You could read a license plate!* It was going to be just like being there. The photos were being passed out and signed for. Each pilot scurried off to his own corner to study his radio tower, or crane yard, or suspension bridge. I snuck away to an unoccupied table to view mine—the photo of the Pull-up Point from which I would launch my morsel of death and destruction (which would vaporize about 10,000 people immediately, and cause another 60,000 deaths in the next 24 hours). I could see every detail, like I was up in a hot air balloon looking down. It *was* like being there. Except, my Pull-up Point was a church steeple! It was a friggin Catholic church. And the damned photo must have been taken on a Sunday, because worshippers were filing out. The steps were full of families. Old ladies and little kids. *Geez! There's a guy and his wife walking down the steps holding the hands of their two little girls.*

Chapter Seven
THE FRENCH RIVIERA

Wow!

Spent most of the last chapter describing our potential mission here in the Mediterranean. This at-sea period was a twelve day crash course in the discipline and exactitude necessary to live through flight operations at sea: formation flights, loft maneuver training, exercises with live ammo, being slung off the bow praying like hell, and then (scrounge up your last bit of nerve) for one more wide-eyed, tight-jawed, shipboard landing (called a "trap"). Seemed all we were doing was passing each other on the way up to or down from the flight deck. Day after day of clamorous, fast-moving, chaotic precision. (You just kept hoping someone was in charge, that they'd done this before, and knew what they were doing.) Resolve and sinew were put to the test. We were learning as we went. Thankfully each launch seemed a little less hectic. Perhaps because of the lack of any alternative or not enough time to consider and falter (or the butterflies in our stomach had been shaken senseless), things were becoming tolerable. Almost matter of fact. Sometimes the returning flights would meet overhead the ship and a hellacious unscheduled and unapproved dogfight would ensue (where my main goal was to avoid a midair collision)!

One good thing: the above described flight operations having been so furious, this at-sea period was over before we knew it and we were headed for our first real port of call: Cannes, the center of the glamorous French Riviera. No spot, no place in the world would leave a more indelible mark on my life than the Cote d'Azur and Cannes. Seeing it, feeling it, smelling it, I would never be the same. Who could forget the fresh early mornings full of the satisfying redolence of freshly baked croissants and café au lait, seeing the men raking the beaches and washing the streets, and the old ladies setting out their flowers on the sidewalks. I know I for one wasn't ready for it. On the outside it was crisp and clean, light blue, golden, and white. Inside, it was crimson with sequins and eye shadow. I had been to stateside seaside vacation locales such as Atlantic City and Miami, but I had never ever been to a place like this. Never would I see so many beautiful people committed to pandering themselves. To this day when I think back to it, a provocative array of intense and sensual images whir past my eyes. Cannes was a lady, an exquisite and expensive lady, leaning back on her elbows against the cliffs of the south of France, exposing her body to the baking Mediterranean sun, knees drawn up, feet apart, offering herself to those willing to pay the price.

There was a great deal of excitement as we secured flight operations Friday afternoon and steamed due north toward Cannes. Those of the ship's company who had been here before were more than willing to educate and prepare the first-timers. And boy did they. While the ship's PA system played old songs by Edith Piaf and Charles Aznavor, the seasoned voyagers described their previous adventures and romantic encounters. Hearing all this we were lucky some of the young sailors didn't just jump overboard and swim for it. We knew that Cannes was the site of the renowned World Film Festival, and a hangout for international cinema celebs. We'd heard about the French movie stars (Brigitte Bardot and Alain Delon), the topless beaches (St. Tropez and Antibes), and the gambling (roulette at the Palm Beach Casino). The air was electrified. We were going to be there—smack dab on the Riviera, and who knew what adventures were in store for us.

Unfortunately we didn't arrive in the harbor until almost midnight— too late for any liberty. When the anchor chain made its usual bone-jarring plunge, half the ship was on the flight deck ogling the twinkling lights ringing the shoreline, and making hopeful plans for the morrow. As usual we were mooring a mile out—directly off the hotel beaches. You could almost hear the music and laughter. A real paradox we were—this bunch of crew-cut regimented worker bees inside their huge gray hive, about to come face to face with a complete lack of discipline. Talk about "off the turnip truck." Good thing we didn't realize our naiveté. If we would have known how outclassed we were going to be, we might not have been so hip on venturing ashore. I hit the rack at midnight, anxious for the morning.

Saturday 0900 hours: This was going to be a good group: Bob Harmon, the "Goffer" (Don Goft), Nick Cassopolis, Mike Ballard, and yours truly.

If there was a liberty party to be in this was it. (Seriously doubted there would be any museum trips for us.) Bob and Don could hold their own anywhere. They were tall and good-looking, with winning ways. Always an asset. Nick was recently married, but with his dashing good looks and flashing smile he kept the ladies wondering till late in the evening. Mike was married as well, but the chase was in his blood and he would find himself in the thick of it frequently. Major Burnham (my boss) never recognized the extent to which he didn't fit in and unilaterally attached himself to our party. I think the guys were figuring on playing along for a respectable time, and then losing him as the sun went down.

And we couldn't have asked for a better day. It was a brilliant postcard morning with clear skies and sparkling colors. The liberty boat was light, and at full RPM it was quickly eating up the distance to the dock. Unable to take my eyes off the magnificent view of the shoreline, I reached out like a blind man—groping for the gunnel to steady myself against the boat's jolting. Those aboard not straining to take in every detail raised their faces to the early warmth of the sun. The closer we got, the whiter and more luxurious appeared our destination—the beautiful and prestigious *Marina de Cannes!* And of course, it didn't let us down, picturesque and replete with multi-decked yachts and large sailing vessels.

The engines were cut back and our boat swung nicely against the seawall at the far side of the marina. I felt a little apprehensive clambering up onto the dock, already sensing that we could be uninvited guests who would not fit in. On foot we began to negotiate the pier, past a panorama of dazzling white hulls, lacquered teak decks, colorful pennants, shining stainless and gleaming brass. As we tentatively made our way single-file down the narrow walkway we passed only a few yards from the privileged people and their valuable possessions (much closer than I would have imagined ordinary citizenry would be allowed). I could have reached out and touched the stern decks, where the proud owners and their guests (in navy blazers and coral ascots) were casually seated or draped just right on pastel deck cushions. Twirling their glasses, and throwing their heads back, they seemed to me to be laughing and joking artificially (almost for our benefit). Amazingly to me—on almost every boat, at their feet lay one or two strange looking dogs that appeared equally aware of their station in life. If this place wasn't going to be prohibitively expensive, I would be surprised.

I GUESS I JUST WASN'T THINKING

Within earshot now, I had my first exposure to the melodious and manipulative *langue Francaise*. An obviously much superior method of communicating (if the demeanor of those wielding it were any measure). I was beginning to be ashamed of what my voice would sound like. Bountiful as it was I would discover Cannes was *not* user friendly to Americans, particularly to those who did not speak French. The mile long, immaculate and arcing grand avenue in front of the big hotels was called La Croisette. This beautifully manicured, divided boulevard bordered a long and carefully gussied beach. It boasted three separate lines of hundred-foot tall Royal Palms. One along the sidewalk in front of the hotels, one on the center island, between the two-way traffic, and one along the raised walkway that ran the length of the beach. The traffic crawled by to see and be seen. Black Porsches, silver Jags, and open red Mercedes. All were occupied by well-tanned handsome men and alluring women behind dark glasses, who seemed dedicated to taking little notice of the foot-bound population. We walked the half-mile long La Croisette from end to end—several times, never quite being able to become part of the revelry. Rather, continuing to appear to be just what we were—overwhelmed gawking aliens.

From the elevated esplanade alongside La Croisette we ogled the beach below. The women-watching was of dizzying proportions. There appeared to be little doubt that these jeweled and lotioned female specimens had come to be watched. They coyly performed in every manner to arouse and devastate any males who would pause to take notice. Nothing they did was functional. Everything was a charade of vanity. They strutted, sat, bent over, turned, and crossed and uncrossed their legs artfully. Each apparently innocent movement designed for effect—to produce the best possible exposure of the parts of their anatomy of which they were the most proud. But this was the south of France and this was what they did best. One of the guys said, "All of Europe can't be like this. Who would ever live in the States?"

From eighteen to eighty (most in their 30's, but many in their 40's or 50's—*even 60's*) the vainest of all women came here to flaunt. They caught your eye and stared you down. Never had I seen so many apparently educated and refined women, wearing such outlandishly undersized shorts and bikinis (along with all manner of raffish bangles—to include seductively draped gold waist chains and beaded ankle bracelets). And even in the hotel lobbies when these bodies were more appropriately clothed, breasts, buttocks and crotches of all shapes and sizes strained for release, pressing outwards at every opportunity. And I must admit the European men hanging around this beach were no slouches either, though they all looked the same. Imposing heads of wavy black or salonized silver hair, bright silk shirts open to the navel, white slacks, and red suede moccasins. (Not a single guy was wearing socks. Guess that's the fashion.) On the beaches, they strutted their stuff, their muscular abdomens well exposed and their thin nylon bathing suits leaving little to the imagination. You could see right off that these men were not at all embarrassed about advertising their bodies either. (And I'm sure they didn't have to be home at midnight like we did.)

There were three big hotels: The Carlton, where I guessed the rich-rich with a name to go with it bedded down. Stately and sovereign, it was obviously the ranking lodging. It towered well above adjacent structures and there for mere mortals to ogle from a safe distance. A half block down—the Miramar, looked like I *might* be able to afford a night there. (I would go on to learn that just about every seaside town in the world has a Miramar hotel.) Another two blocks, and the wonderful, famous (and always faithful to me) Martinez Hotel. All three had large hedge-screened terraces in front, for evening dining and special affairs. Throughout the afternoon an endless parade of beautiful couples strolled past us, perfecting conspicuousness. We had no idea which way to turn.

On the water side of La Croisette, every hotel had its own private beach with showers and change-rooms underneath the elevated esplanade. On the beach there was barely any sand visible, just wall-to-wall chaises and parasols. Bow-tied attendants squirted between the bright cushions and towels, ready to bring an iced Cinzano or a steaming cappuccino. For more than an hour (and what a crude foreign sight we must have been) we plodded up and down the bricked esplanade above and bordering the beach, taking in the brilliant aquamarine and gold, and spellbound by the endless glistening copper carpet of shameless female sunbathers below. We were like rabbits in a lettuce patch. Never had any of us seen on display so many well tanned and well oiled bulges and crevices. It was truly public eroticism.

Finally, feeling like the absolute voyeurs we were (and likely becoming somewhat of a spectacle ourselves) we decided to take a break—lay low for a while. Some of us went to check out the beach shops, others to explore up the hill behind the hotels (into the real world of dry cleaners and grocery stores). I chose up the hill, returning thirty minutes later with a strange cache: a pair of hardwood shoe trees, a neat tortoiseshell hood emblem for a Ferrari, and a pair of soft gray suede Italian loafers. (The last representing the best part of my future Continental disguise.) We rendezvoused back on La Croisette at one o'clock and decided it was time to tackle lunch. As boldly as we could (now well aware of our status and limitations) we set out to find a friendly place to do this.

Ten steps below La Croisette, right on the beach each hotel had its own restaurant, where dedicated sun worshippers could take the noon meal and get their rays at the same time. Under an array of umbrellas, small tables with pastel colored linens were set to accommodate the most discriminating patrons. This arrangement spanned almost the entire stretch of the Cannes beach. Since there were at least ten hotels there were ten of these restaurants, side by side (separated only by colored ribbons). We had our choice, but it wasn't that easy. Leaning over the railing on the esplanade we peered down at the sea of flamboyant diners. Large-mouthed and sun-glassed, they too were tossing their heads about and sending out throaty laughter. It was not immediately apparent where we would fit in best (if anywhere). We wandered back and forth, stoking up our courage. Finally picked the lemon and turquoise restaurant belonging to the Miramar. (Having had a tough time deciding between it and the peach and aqua one run by the Martinez.)

It was a delightful lunch. We all had the plat du jour: Avocado stuffed with shrimp as an aperitif, a huge croissant sandwich of shaved country ham and melted cheese (and authentic Dijon mustard) as the entrée, and then for a postre, the world-famous *Fraises a la creme*—strawberries and fresh cream. All of which was abundantly washed down with ice cold Amstels. The food and the surroundings were great, but this was my first experience with service in a French restaurant. I have sampled it many times since and my opinion remains the same: The waiters are there at their own convenience, preset to their own speed, at serious odds with both the management and the customers, dedicated to the art of showing complete disregard if not disdain. All of which (according to the unwritten rules) the diner feigns not to notice, and then upon leaving, professes to have enjoyed immensely.

During this great lunch (with all the nearby female diners practically naked) I couldn't help noticing a fully clothed lady at the next table, observing us. She was wearing an ankle length black dress, which along with her accessories appeared to be of the highest fashion. She had long dark hair and fair skin, and was reserved and gracious in her actions. Her apparel was more appropriate for an evening embassy function than this beach café. One time I think I caught her looking straight at me (probably in disbelief), but hard to tell since she too wore those super sized dark glasses. After lunch we all got the downer that follows a great meal and some alcohol. (Would have given anything for a hammock in the shade.) Someone suggested we ought to get a room somewhere convenient to the beach, where we could take a rest or change clothes without having to go back to the carrier. (And do away with two liberty boat rides.) Jim asked what my plans were for the rest of the afternoon. I answered. "I don't know, what are you going to do? You want to go back to the ship for a nap?"

"Hell no!"

"Okay, just a suggestion."

A familiar mid afternoon sinking spell was starting. I knew I for one could use a nap. Especially if I were planning to be part of any late night action. But the guys decided they were going to stick with it, stay active— play it for all it was worth. Down on the beach owned by the Martinez hotel we heard some great music coming from a circular, thatched roof bar. It was presently surrounded by fifteen or twenty of the previously mentioned beautiful people, who all seemed to be reveling in brazen social indulgence. Didn't know about the other guys, but I was feeling a little inadequate. Our outfits (JC Penney sport shirts and polyester trousers) had looked reasonable enough when we got into the liberty boat, but here on the beach, we looked like a delegation from the Country of the Nerds. I was afraid that if we went down there and tried to mix, we could well be the brunt of a few jokes, or at least some deliberate dismissive glances.

Still—down we went, and we weren't the brunt of any jokes that I could notice. But in a way it was even worse. Sitting only two yards from them we couldn't have been less acknowledged if we were transparent. Engaged in thespian-like orations and then exaggerated laughter, they acted completely unaware of their recently arrived nearby audience. I've since learned, on the continent this behavior is called "theater" (and it's pandemic in France). To occupy our time, we set about rating the bikinis. And there was some assortment: white silk, gold lame, knitted with pearls and sequins. All of ridiculously inadequate coverage, and many being worn by women who—based on their age and body type, you would have thought would not have been caught dead in something like that.

Bob and Don and the rest of the guys ordered up. Cold beers again. I was too full to take one more swallow of beer (or even imagine it going down). Decided on a Bloody Mary. Got it and tried to look as if I were not completely outclassed on all sides on my first visit to the Cote d'Azur. My preparation for all this was limited to two years in the Boy Scouts and three paper routes. I looked exactly like what I was: "Just off the ship." We spent the waning hours of the afternoon here, disappointedly watching as the crowd began to thin out. (Many I'm sure, to hotel rooms for ardent "afternoon delights" while we told old jokes.) We saw our share of topless bathers, but all agreed the farce and taunts of the preposterously dressed (under-dressed) older women, strolling the esplanade and staring you down, were the best. I was toying with the idea of maybe doing some exploring on my own, but it was clear I would have a hard time getting away from the group. Major Burnham was already organizing a dinner party at a special restaurant he was touting. What the hell—these are the guys I live and work with. I'll stick with the group. Secretly I wondered if I had the courage to split and test the waters on my own. If so, it would have to be after a rest. I was ready to collapse now and it was only five. We wouldn't meet at Le Bistro until seven-thirty. That's enough time.

I slipped away, jogged all the way to the dock and caught the first launch back to the ship. Unfortunately, didn't get any real sleep. Took a much needed shower and at least got horizontal for about an hour. Even got fifteen minutes in front of my sun lamp (which before we shipped out, some guy told me would be a good thing to have if you're going to spend ten months below deck, completely out of the sun). Changed shirts, put on the coolest-looking sport jacket I owned, and my brand new (half size too small) Italian moccasins. Picked up another credit card and was in line for the next liberty boat to the beach.

Cannes At Night

The dinner at Le Bistro was great. Although the restaurant had too many tables for its size, and was crowded and noisy. Major Burnham became almost a spectacle, insisting that everybody—not just some of us, try the onion soup. *What a jerk.* (Although the soup *was* delicious.) Had my first Chateau Briande and first taste of Béarnaise sauce, and a bottle of old Bordeaux. If I wasn't hooked on Europe at 3 this afternoon, I was a goner now. If this meal was any indication, everything they say about French cuisine is true. (And it felt good to be on liberty and doing something normal with the guys. I was proud of myself.)

About ten-thirty, the day's accumulated fatigue must have overtaken us and the party broke up. I was alone, for whatever that was worth (at least no more making conversation or laughing on cue). I started back down La Croisette, past the Carlton which seemed to caution passerbys, "Think it over very carefully before you start up my steps." And I'll admit, I for one wasn't ready to challenge it. In its upward sloping circular drive was a line of expensive cars, spilling out and receiving the creme de la creme. Past it. Past the Miramar. *Hey, what's that?* What kind of music is that? Great sounds were wafting up the street from the Martinez. Happy music with a great beat!

I began to jog towards the Martinez. It was such a glad sound I didn't want to miss another minute of it. The front patio at the Martinez was about 50 ft. square, surrounded and protected by a tall hedge. Peeking through it I was surprised to see there were only about twenty or thirty people still on the patio. All in formal attire. A live group on a small stage (set up under the awning where dinner had been served) were singing their brains out. (And in English!) A funny looking set of kids with weird hairdos. I nearly leaped over the hedge. I definitely wanted to be part of this. I didn't see a way to get onto the terrace (without first going into the hotel and then coming back out through glass doors on each side of the stage area), so I squeezed through a cut in the hedge. No one anywhere to collect any money. Could this thing be free? I glanced around for a ticket booth. None that I could see. Must be the last throes of a private function. With all attention directed forward it was easy to emerge unnoticed and work my way up to just behind the outer circle of spectators. Short of them were a half dozen tables, all vacant. Invigorated by the music, but weary from the day's activities, I availed myself of a chair at one about ten feet behind the last row of observers.

Although they only did one more song, the music was infatuating, with delightful lyrics. I was humming what I had never heard before, joining in on the simple chorus and clapping my hands, as was everyone else. I didn't want the music to stop. However, much to everyone's disappointment, after a valiant but unsuccessful effort by the crowd for a curtain call, it did come to an end. It had been positively enchanting, but the group was gone. If I was any judge *this* group was going places. I'd never heard of them, they were a new group from England. I was willing to bet that in visiting Cannes, we had seen our best port of call first. There would be no way to top this place, no matter where we would put in.

I GUESS I JUST WASN'T THINKING

Most if not all of the crowd disappeared in a matter of minutes and the terrace was all but deserted. I remained seated, remembering the music, heavy in the chair and my tired legs outstretched. The day's activities were taking their toll. Suddenly I realized, at a nearby table—the only other one occupied, was the same dark haired, well-dressed woman with big sun glasses who had been next to us at lunch. I was not good at this, like some guys are (Bob for instance), but when our eyes met, I surprised (in fact, shocked) myself by nodding a respectful "Hello." She responded verbally with a disarming smile, and motioned me to join her. *Whoaa, what's happening?* Somehow girded with an only seconds-old bravado, I amazed myself by managing to do just that (almost as if I was accustomed to being asked to join a lady). A waiter arrived at the same time I did and we ordered drinks. Fortunately, earlier in the day I had done some careful observing, and now felt reasonably chic ordering a Ricard liqueur in a cute little ceramic pitcher. She asked what I was doing in Cannes. Before I had a chance to think of some adventuresome tale to obscure my origin or embellish my station in life, it was out—the plain truth. And a good thing too. We hadn't fooled anyone earlier in the day. She had known we were off the carrier, and politely (in perfect English) asked me some questions. Wary me, I'm remembering the security briefings about enemy agents, and keeping our mouths shut. Enough of that caution. I answered her questions. She was definitely not one of the kind we had ogled all afternoon.

Surprisingly she seemed pleased that I was an American. We did small talk though I could see it did not fit her. She was French by birth, had married an American, and was now divorced or widowed (never got that clear). Her last name was Kennedy. What's more, by coincidence her first name was Jacqueline! Not *the* one of course, but worth a few laughs. She said she had met the real Jacqueline Kennedy two times—at New York Art Association benefits. And she herself owned an art gallery on Fifth Avenue, with an apartment above it, where she resided most of the year. *Wow!* Again she was dressed conservatively, in a high neck frock with its taffeta collar turned up nearly to her cheek bones. And she was still wearing the same tinted glasses, so it was difficult to tell her age (but I guessed about ten years senior to me). We talked and she made me feel very comfortable. We got onto the subject of the JFK assassination and the controversial Warren Commission report. At last, I thought I was engaged in an honorable activity, and it was good not to feel guilty or manipulative. Throughout, our repartee was respectable, and absolutely without any overtones of impending activities.

Feeling worse for the wear, I didn't have any problem declining a second drink. Glanced at my watch and realized the last liberty boat had departed fifteen minutes ago. Slumped there, head down, I heard her speaking and tried to collect my thoughts. "Well, young man, shall we make our exit. Are you ready to go?" A shock went through me, ending in an actual, physical thump in my chest. I was pretty sure I knew what she meant, but I had not expected it and I was not at all ready for it. Up till now everything today had been a game, just speculating. And here, up to this point it had been harmless banter. My neck was pulsing. *This type thing happens to other guys, but not me.* I hadn't been working up to this. I truly hadn't considered this outcome at all, particularly with someone like Jacqueline. I was incredulous and not prepared to answer, but I did—not believing the sound of my own voice, or the words. It was almost as if there was no option. I had the split second to consider that responding negatively would have been poor etiquette (maybe even an effrontery). To her question I weakly smiled and stammered the affirmative, in spite of a frightful awareness of what she would suppose I was agreeing to. My confusion must have been evident, but she appeared to take no notice of it, or to my lukewarm acceptance of what was likely an opportunity to be relished.

She rose and turned towards the large arching entrance to the foyer, reaching back for my hand. I took it. What was I doing? *Rog, what's happening here!?* We were inside, through the lobby, into and out of an elevator, on her floor, in the hallway and in front of her room before I knew it. During the journey Jacqueline was quiet, smiling gently at me from time to time. My stomach was churning, and deservedly my dogging thoughts were back in the States. I waited at the doorway as she entered her room, puttered around a moment or two and then flicked the switch on a low-watted, small, fringed-shade table lamp. My feet took me into the room. Judging from what I could see now, as externally grandiose as the hotels were, the rooms (at least this one) were not large or modern. I stood uncertainly (awkwardly) scanning the dimly lit room, and almost got the feeling we were in her own tiny summer cottage. And I was right. "Yes Cheri, it's mine. Stays locked up all year. I only use it for my summer holidays." Not only was the room of small dimensions, it was crowded with an array of large personal furnishings, including a ceiling-height dark teak armoire, an old roll-top desk, a brass-strapped antique trunk, and low black marble table. There was a small bathroom (with an only slightly opaque glass door)!

I GUESS I JUST WASN'T THINKING

She sat down in the only chair in the room. I was still trying to convince myself I would be able to shortly and politely work out a way to leave. I searched the room for some alcohol or glasses, with a goal of turning this visit into no more than a parting drink. But nothing resembling a small bar. I had no idea of what to say, or do. I guessed if I were to play the part I'd allowed myself to audition for (and got), now was the time she would be expecting me to walk over, raise her up and take her in my arms. No way I could do that. If I did there'd be no chance of keeping this just a nightcap; the result of my presence would be assured. My thinking was disjointed and without conclusions.

While I was still in paralysis she got up and started straight for me, arrived and pressed herself firmly against me—head to toes. In solely a reflex action I allowed my hands to grasp her sides, which I immediately knew was a big mistake. She was now kissing me full mouth! A long kiss. Done, she stepped back , never taking her eyes off me, *and began undressing!* I reflected on the oft portrayed scene of the two lovers standing—facing each other, slowly undressing. I had no intention of carrying that out, but did pretend to fumble with a shirt button. In the limited light I observed her nude body. She wasn't as tall as I had thought, and perhaps a little fuller than I had noticed. Her thickening waist and not-so-round buttocks gave away her years. She was considerably older than I was, that was evident. Her skin was truly alabaster, pure white; an apparently finely cared-for lady. She did not seem to take note that I was still dressed.

Completely naked, she turned, climbed on the bed, pulled down the quilt, leaned up against the pillows and beckoned me with an extended arm. Talk about one confused male. I was frozen. She smiled, allowed her knees to spread, and again motioned me to join her (with increased urgency). No alternative response seemed available and I reluctantly (frightfully) lowered myself to the edge (the very edge) of the bed. I didn't remain upright long. With both hands she pulled me down alongside her. Never mind I'm fully dressed (still wearing my shoes). It may have been the softest bed I'd ever been in, sinking terribly in the middle. I was becoming mired in a cloth sex pit. *I would have given anything to be back on the ship.*

The room seemed warmer by the minute and my skin was becoming damp. I had almost no choice now. *And it was all my fault.* On the terrace I could have said no—feigning sorrow, claiming some excuses (which I certainly had). My present plight was pretty much destined the minute I reflexively nodded and took her hand out on the terrace. Her head was now on my chest, with her face nestled into my neck. She began kissing me, hard, wet and repeatedly—with serious intent. To avoid the certain outcome of this; to extricate myself now, would border on the impossible. Whoaa, she rolled over full on top of me, holding my head in both her hands. Hardly believing what I was doing, and despising myself for it, I let my arms go up and around her. I persisted in delaying, maintaining a status quo for longer than she would have expected. In these circumstances though I felt obligated to do something, I did the least I could as far as returning any affection. She started sighing and thanking me in French; multiple cheri's (and urgent sounding words I would try to remember to look up in my French dictionary).

I was sure she was wondering why I hadn't leaped out of bed pulled off my shoes, shed my trousers, and climbed back in on top of her. She had to be wondering what the hell I was waiting for. The insides of her thighs were wet and shining. She let her knees fall wide apart, pulled her heels up to her buttocks and began tossing her head from side to side on the pillow. But I was not physically responding to her heated female efforts; not in the slightest. I'd like to say, strictly because of my guilt as a married man, but no, Oh no, not again! *Shades of my failure with Connie on the hard wood floor and with my wife on my wedding night and thereafter.* I felt no desire, no heat in my loins, not even the start of an erection. I became more and more sweaty, and more and more concerned. In spite of my brain being riddled with remorse, any healthy male should have 'risen' to the task. But not me. There was no question she was ready, but I was not. (Perhaps a blessing in disguise.) Even were I desirous of doing so, (which I wasn't) once again *I was not in possession of what would be required.* I didn't know if I was more disheartened or relieved by the condition.

Finally; can't disappoint her. Confused and embarrassed I pressed my fully clothed pelvis against her mound and began a series of rhythmic upward motions. While doing so I flattened my hands against her back and kissed her shoulders, hoping that would distract her from what was actually not going on below. Of course—without reaching it myself, I felt her reach hers. Her legs locked straight out, she strained and puffed up her white belly, let out a long crying moan and then curled up in a ball. I was smothered in her arms, the recipient of words and tears. Certainly I hadn't done my part to deserve such a response—that was for sure. And I was already wishing till it hurt that none of this had occurred. While catching her breath she began coughing. It got worse—seriously worse. I began to really worry. Her lungs sounded terrible. Fortunately, after several minutes and about the time I was considering calling the hotel doctor, the coughing began to subside. Once in control of it, she confronted me with the fact that she knew I had not "taken my pleasure." She said she couldn't sleep, could not go on, until—in her words—she had "killed me" (evidently not realizing I was already mentally and physically dead).

With great urgency she set about this task. I was kissed and touched in every conceivable place. She made short work of my belt buckle and zipper. Avoiding the tendency to recoil, yet in a defensive mode, I heard her exhorting me to respond. For my part, I was so taken back by her procedures, and so much aware of the mechanics of her techniques, mother nature now had even less a mind to take over, and I continued magnificently limp. In spite of her not discovering anything similar to what she must have been expecting, she manipulated what she held, while trembling and uttering frantic incitements. In the midst of my discomfort I suspect her fitness caused her to falter and give up—without succeeding, collapsing on my chest, sobbing.

I was flat on my back, stunned, completely drained; replete with deserved regret, and also, unfortunately—once again, the familiar crushing chagrin of my inability. Jacqueline positioned herself into a half sitting position against the headboard. Once settled she pulled on me, urging me upwards to join her there. Difficult as it was, I did. Once there she took my head in her hands and guided it over onto her large and soft white breast. Holding it there, she stroked my head and whispered to me in French. I was more than tired. I was a wreck. My mental clutch was slipping. If I didn't sleep soon I'd be hallucinating, but needed to get completely horizontal to do so. I was able to pull out one of the way too-thick pillows and inch her down until we were almost lying flat. In that position and after an extended time of deserved torment, I finally lapsed into a state of semi consciousness; dreams awash with undecipherable, disjointed scenarios (other than a constant theme of distress). I didn't feel good about anything. I could not shake that I knew I was where I shouldn't be. Finally—mercifully, I slipped off into a deeper and less fitful slumber.

I woke up with a start, a headache and moderate nausea. Nightstand clock showed slightly after four. Raised myself upright. Jacqueline was breathing heavily and didn't stir. Though I felt very ungentlemanly about it, I had no choice. Carefully slid from the bed, collected my clothes, partially dressed and stole out the door. Wanted to get as far from the scene as fast as I could. As if distance itself could erase my shameful activities. All I could think of was a long, hot shower (try to get clean), and a couple hours of real sleep. I went quietly down the deserted hallway, down two flights of steps. Circumvented the lobby. A quick trot to the furthest set of doors. Escaped. Onto the abandoned patio, but still not feeling any better. Not by a long shot. Outside, I found the "exquisite lady" was now deserted. La Croisette was bathed in silence under the soft sodium light of the frond-muted street lamps. Not a single thing moving. I guessed all those laughing people had gotten what they wanted and were mercifully dead to the world. No one here now. As for me, a quick half mile to the dock and try to talk my way onto one of the special Shore Patrol launches back to the ship. (These would become the saving graces for late revelers dragging themselves to the dock after midnight.) Thank God for one petty officer. He let me onboard the next boat bound for the ship, no questions asked.

Into my stateroom without waking Jim. Left my soiled clothes in a damp pile on the floor. Back out and down the passageway to the "head" (Navy for shower and toilets). May have been the only thing moving on the ship. Scrubbed myself thoroughly. Twice, for whatever good it would do. Back to the room. Quiet. Didn't want to wake up Jim. No teeth-brushing, but one good, long mouthful of Lavoris. Into the rack. Tired and weary but unable to sleep, I lay there wondering what had I let happen. Could I say it wouldn't count? That it was an anomaly? Something happening in a parallel universe? Not be part of my real life? Not be a blemish on me as a married man? An experiment? An exception? No, while I truly felt that was true, there'd be no acceptable rationale to explain this away. While I wanted to swear that it would never happen again, I wasn't so sure. Could this one tryst be the type of thing I would continue to blunder into? I would hope not, but I wasn't so sure. Here—alone and far away, if I could bear my own reproaches, I might finally experiment. Explore heretofore unknown territories, without it ever affecting my wife and children.

A Squadron Mascot

0730 hours. Jim was already up and gone. A new day was starting. I could hear increasing clattering in the passageway outside our stateroom. Gotta get up. Have to pop out of the rack and look ready. (If I was going to soar with the eagles at night, I couldn't hide in the shed with turkeys during the day.) God, I would have liked to have stayed in bed. Needed to. Still had a headache. No wonder, best I can recollect: two Amstels, a Bloody Mary, three wines, and two liqueurs. All in one day, after not drinking at all. (Why wasn't I thinking about that then?) But for now—this morning, Jim's in a hurry to go on liberty, and wants to discuss some Safety-of-Flight maintenance item before he leaves. Whatever it is I've got to be sure it's taken care of. I've got to perform. I've got to pay the piper. I've got to be worth my salt, especially in Jim's eyes. I can crash afterwards. Jim left. Maybe I can last an hour. I did, plus some. I got twelve CAUTION placards engraved for the cockpit, announcing the possible non-functioning of an overspeed protection circuit. Got em all installed and had been seen round and about. Accomplished that. So okay for a dash to the stateroom and into the rack. Awoke again at 1400 hours. Think I felt a little better. In any case, on your feet again. Get out there, make a contribution. Have to hold up my end of the bargain. I'll visit the shops, review a bunch of worksheets, and find out if any of the men have any problems I can help them with. (How about me, who's helping me?)

Forget last night. Cannes. *Geez.* Everything there is to see and do in a city like that, and I ended up in a tiny dark hotel room with a not-well, older woman. All that sun and all that fun, and all those girls, and all those other activities (whatever they are), and I ended up like that. Do I even know how to just plain recreate? Or if I have to end up one on one with a female, why can't it be an average one and have an innocent afternoon. Can't I just do something normal when I'm ashore? Maybe not. Between my nonsensical campaign in Rome and now this first night in Cannes, I was worried—*real* worried. Right now, I don't feel like ever going ashore again. Guess it'll pass, even though it doesn't feel like it will. I don't feel proud. I'm glad my sons can't see me. *Let alone their mother.*

Two days passed before I could look at myself in the mirror. Then another day of just squinting at the distant Cannes beach shimmering in the morning sun. It was beckoning me for all it was worth. Remembering the sidewalk cafes with their tiny tables and colorful umbrellas, the lotioned and bangled hard bodies, and listening to the stories coming back, after three days I was ready to give it another try. (And as a result of my prolonged self-imposed stay onboard, I had *saved* a day of liberty, which could come in handy at some later date.)

Part Two: The French Riviera, Leo, June, and Big Trouble

Almost the same liberty party as the first day: Bob, Don, Nick, Mike, and I. (No Major Burnham this time.) Braced ourselves during the ride to the dock and clambered ashore. First thing on the schedule, visit the local shops and purchase some souvenirs to mail home. Finished with that we strolled to the Miramar, and having brought our swimwear with us this time, actually went into the water (which it appeared the local sun worshippers thought was a completely unnecessary beach activity). We played water polo and volley ball—were so darned All-American and clean cut, it was pitiful. Tried to act like we weren't all but overcome by the salacious vistas in every direction. Paid way too much for an hour on water skis at the famous Martinez Beach *Ski Nautique*, but it was worth the price—we met Erica!

Erica was one big, noticeably healthy (chesty) German girl. A dynamite-looking, flaming redhead, about 25 years old, with what I guess some people would have called, too-big hips and thighs. Freckles everywhere and a smile that made you melt. (And maybe too tall for me—at least 5ft 9.) Out of nowhere she had just shown up at the ski boat ramp and started a cute teasing banter with the five of us. No timid soul this one I could see. She wore a modest bikini, but had a body whose most eye appealing parts, refused to be hidden. They were coming out of that bathing suit everywhere. She rode in the back of the tow boat while we skied behind it, and laughed heartily as one by one we undertook stunts of increasing difficulty and repeatedly wiped-out royally. It was looking like we just might have found a great female companion for this in-port stay. At one time, two older European guys did come by, spoke to her a couple minutes, then left. Couldn't tell if one of them might have been a boyfriend. Didn't seem so. Surprisingly to all of us she quickly accepted our invitation to join us for lunch.

Another great lunch. Most of us did a repeat on the menu from the yellow and turquoise restaurant that first day ashore. One of the guys posed the idea of us all going to the Palm Beach Casino that night and win big. And the surprising good news was that Erica wanted in. And I was afraid, from her enthusiastic response that she might really have the gambling bug. Oops, too bad for Bob. Major Burnham spied us, came over and asked him if he would go back to the ship and check on travel arrangements for the major's skiing trip to Garmisch, in December. *"Now? This afternoon, you want me to do this right now?"* Bob certainly wasn't wild about a trip back to the ship, but the Major didn't give him any choice. The Major (who used to live next door to Mike back in the states) then asked Mike about his wife and kids, and Mike shortly excused himself. Twenty minutes later, after the strawberries and fresh cream (again), Don Goft (almost never seen without Bob) also left. Nick had separated earlier, having been personally invited onto the private launch of some rich Greek over here. By chance, I was the lucky recipient of these developments. By default I had ended up alone with Erica.

Sitting there in her company, at least to all outward appearances I was as qualified as the local studs, and was beginning to consider that I could actually become a bona fide part of the scene. She continued to talk about trying the roulette wheel that night. In fact, I was beginning to think she meant *we* should try it, together. Thinking ahead to this eventuality, before they left I had managed to borrow thirty bucks from Bob, and twenty from Mike, besides what they left as their share of the tab for lunch. (And based on the tab it's a good thing we enjoyed it as much as we did.) Don had said he thought he had some extra cash in our recently acquired squadron hotel room.

Erica's sexy green eyes, wide mouth and big body had all my attention (and every guy's for six tables in every direction). I'm thinking she's got to be teasing—just wasting some time with me. Certainly she has better things to do (which turned out to be half true). I didn't think she would stay with me too much longer. We got looking through old photos in her wallet. She told me about an American baseball player she had met here last spring, at Antibbes. She told me they had had a real nice time. She showed me that photo. It was Roberto Clemente! It was two-thirty. We'd had a lot of sun. I felt good, but didn't need any more beach and had no idea for the next activity. Fortunately, two minutes later Erica asks me if I would like to leave, to go meet her friend. "Sure, why not." We went for the walk. Would you believe, I'm strolling La Croisette with my own huge-titted European female.

Turns out her friend was the guy who had stopped by at the beach, and was staying in a high rise a little further down La Croisette. When we entered, he was playing cards with another guy on the balcony. He may have been a permanent resident, or here on an extended vacation. I think it was his place alone. Erica gave no indication of having a room there or any belongings on the premises. His name was Fritz and he was German that was for sure. His companion was French. While neither one looked real successful, they weren't acting like money was a problem either. I couldn't tell if Erica knew Fritz from Germany or met him here. I think from Germany. Both guys were in their forties and were of small stature. *Good, for once I'm not the smallest guy in the room.* They were both balding, wearing open-necked sport shirts, smoking (a lot), and nursing drinks. Erica introduced me. Fritz didn't appear at all jealous. (I had been worried about that aspect of things.) While at first he didn't look thrilled to see me, he shortly relaxed and was quite sociable. Told me to have Erica fix me a drink. Though I didn't feel like drinking, the process would at least give us something to do. Erica fixed me a red-colored drink in a tall glass. It had a strange taste—bitter, but a good kind of bitter. Hard to describe. It was my first Campari-soda.

Erica started reading a slick French fashion magazine. I did my imitation of a guy standing awkwardly in the middle of a room. She looked up and motioned to me to go talk to Fritz. *Great! I can see Fritz is waiting for that.* Both guys were leaning on the balcony railing, pointing across La Croisette, and talking seriously in low tones. I felt like I had stumbled in on some kind of plot, like they should have been wearing shoulder holsters and poring over the floor plan of a bank. I knew I couldn't talk to the French guy, I'd have to speak to Fritz (who had spoken to Erica in English). I realized I was so far out of my element, to have any credibility at all I would just have to admit my status and talk about the things I knew. *Whew—a* good decision. They had already guessed I was an American and off the ship. Good I had planned to tell the truth. Fritz wasn't a big fan of the US military, and I had to downplay our role over here. I got the impression the two guys were expecting another person to arrive any minute. I suggested to Erica that we step out for a breath of air, stroll La Croisette again. Thank god for small favors. She agreed.

I somehow made the mistake in describing our upcoming jaunt, of indicating we could "do a little shopping." It was thirty minutes and 300 Francs later that I got her out of the most extravagant accessories shop I'd ever seen. *Damn.* Had a feeling I was going to need that cash later. Why didn't I use my American Express card? Bad thinking. But the good news: Evidently it's true, buying stuff for women *works.* There was a marked increase in our closeness, and her rubbing against me after the belts and earrings were in the bag. We were now strolling hand in hand. And I had a *lot* in my hand I can tell you, with Erica. She was being extremely agreeable. We passed several guys I knew from the ship, and they gave me some "Holy Shit" looks. (It was hard not to gloat.) I was already wondering how this would wind up by late tonight. A dinner date never got arranged. I think she intended that it wouldn't. But, are you ready for this: She made me promise to meet her at the Palm Beach Casino at nine! I told her she could count on it. I jogged back to our squadron hotel room, met the "Goffer." Got almost thirty bucks worth of Francs from him. Jogged back to the boat dock and caught the first launch back to the ship. I had time to lie down for an hour, get a great (free) supper, log another fifteen minutes in front of my sun lamp, and prepare myself for who knows what. (Though I was determined it would not replicate my recent unanticipated late night tryst with Jacqueline.)

The Palm Beach Casino

It may not have been Monte Carlo, but for me it was more than enough. Just like in the James Bond movies. Lots of tuxedos and floor length dresses. Me? I was wearing a cream colored, hieroglyphic print Egyptian linen blazer that I had bought when I was stationed in Japan. (The guy who ordered it didn't have the nerve to pick up.) It was either a powerful fashion statement or tacky as hell. Fortunately, most people never could determine which. I climbed the fifty foot wide, brass-edged marble steps, through the columns, past the guards, and to Reception to show my passport. Yeah, I did have my passport. Lucky for me, just as I was leaving the ship one of the guys told me that you needed your passport to get into the place.

One of the tuxedoed casino staff at the far side of the entrance gave me a wave of approval, which made me feel even better (knowing how little I deserved it). In fact it was almost a "Hi," like we were old friends. Things *were* looking up. All the money I had managed to collect was wadded in my pocket. I touched it to reassure myself, though I had the feeling it would not be there long. I had my pass and was in the door! *So far so good folks.* Wow. Large carved oak archways, high ceilings, huge frescos and tapestries on the walls. Lots of highly polished, lustrous woodwork and paneling. Wall to wall Oriental carpeting throughout. I was in what was just the first of several gambling areas. Looked like at least two large main rooms and some sort of recessed private gaming alcove, protected from prying eyes by rows of intricate mahogany latticework. (It kind of said the same thing to me as the Carlton had: *"Think carefully before venturing in.")* Considering that people were winning and losing thousands by the minute, it was pretty quiet. No moans, no cheers, no cussing, only nodding heads and hushed conversations.

Bingo! There's Erica at the *Cachet d'Argent,* surrounded by at least six guys. (Talk about being the center of attention.) How was I gonna get in there? I'd be surprised if they were speaking English, probably French or German. (Erica spoke perfect French.) What luck, she saw me, and what's more—right in front of my wondrous eyes she was excusing herself and coming my way! This was too good to be true. To contrast her rust colored hair she was wearing a Kelly green ankle length gown. She was a knock-out! Once again it was as if I had been assigned a part in a script. In no way was I capable of achieving this in reality. I was going to need a lot of luck this evening. I was in over my head, again.

Everything went great, though I wouldn't have been able to carry it off, had she not been on my arm almost constantly, and, surprisingly—giving me lots of attention. (A doorman once told me: "The best credentials in the world, is a beautiful woman on your arm. You'll get in anywhere.") Erica was my credentials in the Casino. Seeing her on my arm, no one screwed with me. Believe it or not, even the usually rude croupiers were passably respectful. I got bolder and bolder, which in turn caused her to fawn and coo all the more. I felt like saying, *"Wow Ma, look at me now."*

The downside of all this upbeat ambiance was that we were in a gambling house, and Erica was bound to want to try her luck, and likely with my money (more accurately—the whole squadron's money). I've done this several times since, so now have something to compare it with. She was *not* inconsiderate. She was actually concerned about our losses. Acted as if she knew I was there on a shoestring (but never voiced it). In fact she cashed a check of her own. Get that? *Checks!* I did have one with me, but was already thinking how a cancelled check from a casino would look back home. Mostly she made small bets, which helped. But she made a lot of them. One time we had a minor streak going on the wheel. We were playing the 20's, the even and odd 20's—all *ten* of them, on *every* spin. We won about six times in a row! Had a big pile of chips in front of us. In fact, more than I thought we had won. Good, I saw her pocket a couple of the largest denomination rectangular chips, probably for safe-keeping (for the comeback we would likely have to stage after blowing our present winnings).

I had a drink in my hand the whole evening. Don't know how many I had. Never felt tipsy. Actually in this place I might have looked too young to drink. Erica smoked, which was hard to believe with her gleaming white teeth. Maybe she just smoked on these occasions. We slipped away from the activity, over to an eighteenth century brocade loveseat. It was right next to that private alcove I had seen earlier. She waved at two men who were in there playing some weird game. One of them was Fritz. Erica explained the Baccarat game to me. Not for the meek. High stakes in there.

It was then that the 500-Franc chips came out of her purse. Four of them! She giggled. I had only seen her take two. We were in better shape than I thought. What's more, she gave me two of them—as a gift! A helluva gift, considering they were worth about $100 apiece. Boy, would I like to hide one of these babies somewhere, and sneak it out at the end of the evening. If I can just hang on to even one of these—nothing more, I'll at least be semi-solvent in the morning. *Please God.* We tried other tables and other games. She was always by my side, and kissed me often. I have *no* idea why. And she didn't care in front of who. *Keerist, what a night!* We were in and out of chips so much I never knew where we stood. Most the chips were in her bag most the time. Somehow, we got way ahead several times, and believe it or not (I was impressed) she went to the cashier and cashed out, twice! Usually gamblers don't do that. She stuffed a bunch of money in her purse both times. I'll bet she'll remember *this* evening. Maybe just maybe, I'm bringing her good luck.

The gambling gods were with us is all I can say. And I *did* manage to stash away one of the big chips. I hadn't let Erica see me hide it. I would come back tomorrow and cash it in. Didn't want her to know I couldn't afford to lose. Erica was good to me. Real affectionate. Going where I wanted to go. Doing what I wanted to do, standing when I felt like standing, sitting when I felt like sitting. More than just accommodating, in fact—inexplicably wonderfully submissive. I had never in my life been the recipient of such respectful (let alone beautiful) female company. We were a good couple and you couldn't miss us in there. But a little while later, after checking her watch, with a simple nod Erica indicated the evening's over and *Bingo* we're on our way out. What's next? Where are we going? I don't have a hotel room. Don't know if she has one, or is staying with Fritz. (I tried to coax it out of her several times during the evening, but never got an answer.) She knows I'm on the ship, and if I'm planning on spending the night on it, this might be the time to split. No way of knowing what's going to happen yet (but I can suppose). The lingering guilt of my recent late night incident here in Cannes was appropriately haunting me. *Again—so soon?* Might as well start worrying right now.

Part Two: The French Riviera, Leo, June, and Big Trouble

Couldn't believe how easily we got out of there and away from her two friends. They saw us leaving—came out of the Baccarat room all smiles, shook hands and asked how we did. Fritz was real friendly. Erica gave him two of the big chips she still had, a quick hug, and then they said good night. (He got the best of that deal!) Out the main entrance. Saw that Casino manager again, the one who waved to me going in. Now I recognized him—it was the French guy from this afternoon, in the apartment. Erica didn't seem to notice him. Even away from the group she kept giving me kisses and squeezes. We were out, down the steps and into a limo in two shakes. But we hadn't yet established *where* we were going. We'd gone about 100 yards when the driver slides open the privacy glass, looks over his shoulder and asks me for directions. Unable not to reflect on my recent episode with Jacqueline and remembering what took place (or didn't take place) and how I felt afterwards, I was more than a little confused. I had serious mixed emotions and faltered, uttering nothing in response. Fortunately, in the midst of my confusion Erica shouted something in French and we were off. At least she had a plan, and I was ill-prepared to object to anything.

Five minutes later we were being dropped off in front of a small, ultra-modern (smoked glass and stainless steel fronted) private club, right across La Croisette from the *Palais des Festivals* (where each summer they hold that famous Cannes Film Festival). A bunch of SL's, Jags, unknown Italian sports cars and stretch limos were double-parked in front of the club. You might imagine I was getting worried. I'd pulled off the casino bit, but I was sure—here, I had a good chance of being exposed for what I was. Found a small, unlit and unmarked door. Opened it and entered. Once through it I had even more reason to feel out of place. Two steps inside the door and *Bam!* fifty sets of eyeballs were on us. We'd walked in onto an empty, two-foot-high platform that spanned the entire width of the front of the room—an apparently makeshift stage probably still set up from an earlier presentation. The door we'd come in—the only one I'd seen, was right in the middle of it *and we were now the center of attention*. It was evident, to come through those doors you were supposed to *be* somebody. The dimensions of the club were unusual. Quite deep front to back, but only about twenty feet wide. Just a few yards in front of the stage was the first row of a sea of at least thirty or forty small round tables, wedged tightly together—with no aisle. There was no way to proceed further. *We were stuck*. Floor to ceiling mirrors ran the length of both side walls and the rear wall, doubling the impact of all the formal jackets, shiny lapels, black ties, sequined dresses, high coiffures and sparkling jewelry facing us. There were all kinds of international cinema memorabilia hanging about, but *not a seat in the house!* The place was jam packed. We were stranded on the only free floor space there was, still under unanimous scrutiny.

But fortunately I had those best credentials: Erica on my arm. One glance at her and the waiters immediately began yanking tables around (practically pulling chairs out from under people), brushing crumbs, dumping ashtrays, and smoothing new table clothes. *Bingo!* We were seated. I knew that this kind of treatment required the maximum tip. The first thing my hand hit in my pocket, was the 500 Franc chip I had saved. I don't know if I thought it would be cute, or if I didn't think at all. I'm not sure. It happened too quickly. I pressed the rectangular slab of plastic in his hand. We're talking a big tip—around one hundred U.S. dollars! We're talking stupidity! As soon as I did it I felt sick. Erica saw the gesture and a strange expression crossed her face. She caught herself, but quickly grabbed it back and pressed a couple fifty Franc notes in his hand. The waiter didn't seem to care either way. Everything was okay except I was a little embarrassed. Erica brushed it off. She smiled, lit a cigarette, reached across the table and took my arm. She was leaning way over and smiling, very invitingly. I'm thinking, this can't last, *what does she have in mind?* We had our laughs, coffee, a great dessert called Crème Brulée, a couple liqueurs, and at last (finally) after what seemed like twenty-four hours together, it was time to call it a night. We were at the cutting edge. I knew *I* was the one who should make a move, but I didn't. I just tarried, worried, and waiting to see what she might say.

No, I don't believe it—we *were* going to spend the night together. In fact, from the way it was brought up and handled, she may have never considered otherwise. *Will I never learn?* Butterflies. Reasonable panic. I ended up with an outcome that just about anyone else would have predicted (and mightily appreciated)! And having gotten it, I'm *not* feeling good about myself—on two counts. While the eyes and body of this super-sexy Deutsch moll should leave no male with any doubt about a more than satisfactory response, if I pulled a repeat performance of my late night tryst with Jacqueline, and I'm forced to pull off another pseudo-screwing thing like I did then, Erica would certainly know the difference, and why. And it'd be way more than humbling. She told me her hotel room number (and had me repeat it twice). My instructions were to wait 30 minutes—

give her about a half an hour, and then come on up. But, are you ready for this, *she's staying in the Carlton Hotel!*

Penetrating the Carlton

I nervously circled the area for thirty minutes, in fact forty to be sure (while in the throes of the great debate, alternately deciding to make a break for the dock, and then shamefully finding myself turning towards the hotel again). One o'clock. Still a block west of the Carlton I could feel it peering down on me disapprovingly. Later, as I closed in on it, I think it was either grinning or shaking its head. *The joust was about to begin.* No way without being registered that a person could just walk in and past the staff. Fortunately at this late hour there was very little activity, so it was not quite as intimidating (but no chance to slip in with the crowd either). I'd attract anyone's attention in that huge deserted foyer. From a safe distance, I observed three sour-looking hotel clerks behind the desk, like vultures on a limb. *Whew.* This was not going to be easy, or at least it would not be comfortable. I was shaking more than a little. However, now—at this point (without remembering making the final decision), my plan was to somehow do it. *No matter what, get to Erica's room.*

I checked the rear and both sides of the hotel, hoping I'd find an unmanned entrance. No such luck. Possibly another way: On the front of the hotel, to the right of the main entrance, was a long line of sliding glass doors, opening onto the now damp and deserted marble terrace. The far right ones were almost a hundred feet from the main entrance. *Maybe one of them's not locked.* Peering (best I could in the dark) through the furthest right ones, they appeared to open into a large and unlit—apparently no longer active, formal dining area. If one of those doors were open I could slip in through it, sneak across the darkened dining room, and get to the base of a wide stairway at the end of the room, without being seen. *Please God, let one of those doors be open.* Considered it one last time, but knew there was no way I could just stroll past the concierge desk in the main entrance.

I made my way up onto the patio. Not a soul in sight. Bent low like a stalking commando I snaked my way through the white metal tables, now topped with upside down chairs. Arrived at the front wall. Crouched there under the awning, breathing heavily. I could see the well lit reception area through the other glass doors, but they'd have a hard time seeing me. Tried the furthest set of doors. Not open. Tried the next set. Locked too. *Shit!*

Didn't really want to get any closer to the main entrance. But great! The next one was open. Slowly, get it just a little further. *I'm through.* Good. Here—for the moment, I was in good shape, out of the line of sight (thanks to a series of columns inside the foyer). I could rest a second and think. But once inside, in order to reach the marble staircase on the far wall, I would have to cross a 50 ft.-wide area, completely open except for a couple statue pedestals and an empty acrylic display case. During the midpoint of my crossing I would be in full sight of anyone at the reception desk.

The three guys in front of the concierge desk were still talking among themselves. Probably weren't expecting any new guests, and appearing to be disinterested in anything beyond their circle of light. *Here goes,* about to make my break for West Berlin, crossing the mine field before the wall. Checked my watch. I wasn't going to be early, that was for sure. Damn near an hour. *Shit.* I mustered all the courage I could. Ready? Deep breath. Now or never. *Go for it!* I'm on my way! Moving quickly but not running (yet). Halfway across I feel eyes and can't resist looking towards the lobby. *I'm nailed!* The guy who had been behind the desk had chosen now to come out into the lobby. He was in plain view. *I was in plain view!* He was looking right at me. We were eye-to-eye! I picked up my gait. He started walking towards me. I quickened my step. He was pointing his finger in my direction and yelling something to me. Now he's *running* towards me. *Shit!* No way to justify my presence. No chance of talking my way past him.

I burst ahead. My legs under me. I was moving! Preservation now outweighed morality. Raced up the steps two at a time. The guy was at full speed now himself. I could hear the clatter of his heels on the polished stone floor. He was shouting now, calling to the other guys as well. I heard more footsteps. The Carlton had been violated and it wasn't sitting still for it. *Shit, what now!?* What floor!? 304, 304! Should be the third floor! I already passed the first floor, and the second—I think. *Here* then, get off now! Grabbed the banister, swung around. Almost tore my arm off. I was full speed down the wide carpeted hallway. Flying! I could barely make out the room numbers. Running so fast, when I turned my head around to catch a glimpse of my pursuers I lost my balance and barely avoided going sprawling to the floor.

Oh no! *How could that be?* The numbers going by were in the 200's! *I'm one floor too early.* The hotel guys rounded the top of the stairs. I could hear them behind me a hundred feet. I could feel their eyes burning holes in my back. They had me in full view. End of the hall, round the corner, up the staircase again. *I'm out of their sight for the moment!* On the right floor now—the 300's! This is it! If I can make it inside her room, before they clear the corner at the top of the staircase, they won't know which room I went in. *Wrong end!* Room 320, 318, 316. *Shit!* Too far. I'll never make it inside her room before they round the corner at the top of the staircase. They weren't out of the stairwell yet. Any second though. I slowed to a short stop in front of 304. I could hear she was on the phone! "Erica. Erica" I voiced in a loud whisper. "Unlock the door, but don't open it! I'll be back in a minute!"

I was off again, out of the blocks and away from her door before they had me in sight. I gave it all I had. I accelerated. They couldn't possibly be gaining on me. One more lap, one more time around. I'd be far enough ahead, I'd be able to get inside her room before they got out of the stairwell. *Stride! Pull!* Up the steps, now three at a time. I'm getting stronger. Down the hall, down the steps. Only hit them once. In the third floor hallway again, at her door, on the knob. She was right there and I was in! What a girl. Finger to my lips. *Shhhh.* A half minute passed before the footsteps went thudding by. They were out of luck. I'd lost them. I was home free. I plopped down in a chair. My lungs were on fire. My legs were trembling. I was completely drenched. But I was there. Erica went into hysterics, and then me too. You couldn't help but feel good when you saw this girl laugh.

I was surprised (in fact astonished), to calmly—with an understanding of the consequences, find myself mentally prepared to go through with whatever sexual encounter I may hopefully be capable of. I had convinced myself that it would be occurring in that "parallel universe. *Just an experiment I had to carry out.* She made us both a drink and we talked about our time together. Unlikely as it should have been, I was able to laugh and demonstrate a carefree, even cavalier attitude (somehow having dismissed the fact that I would forever after have to answer for the remainder of the evening).

Erica excused herself and went to the bathroom. I heard the shower. A minute later she peeked around the curtain and motioned for me to join her. *No good way to turn down that invitation.* I joined her, though next to her I felt short, thin, and generally inadequate (but maybe soon). Reasonably embarrassed too, but it was steamy and soapy, and she never seemed to be sizing me up. *Thank you God.* Out of the shower and dried off, she made straight for the bed, flung the cover to the floor, slapped the sheets and invited me to join her. I did. I should have been more nervous, but the love-making this time, however it would play out, would fortunately not be the main event of the day. I think Erica could have done it or not done it, and it wouldn't have made any difference to her. So much exciting had already happened, it seemed (I ventured to hope) the act would not be the measure of our time together. While we were joking and kissing I noticed the phone dangling by the cord off the night table. I pointed to it. Erica leaned over the edge of the bed and picked it up. Would you believe, after our talk, the shower, and ten minutes more in bed, *a guy named Peter was still on the line!* She talked to him about five minutes, and ended up saying: "But Peter, truth is love, love is truth. Good Night."

It seemed like Erica really liked and trusted me. For what reason, I don't know. We could have been high school buddies. Maybe I felt less guilty and more confident this time because it wasn't a seduction with expectations to fulfill. It would just be how the evening ended. Other much more important things had happened today. Although true enough I was shutting some things out of my mind, and praying that I wouldn't disappoint her. Suddenly she jumped out of bed, went to her purse and came back with one of the big 500 Franc chips, that she called a *plaque*. She must be growing those friggin things. I was secretly hoping it was going to be a gift. (She still had my other one from the afterhours club.) She was excited. She was giggling and squeezing my arm. "Look at this, isn't it beautiful?" I didn't know what she meant. She rolled over and got up on her hands and knees, held the chip out, and looked me straight in the eyes with the damnedest expression on her face. I focused on the chip in spite of the fact that just behind it two pendulous breasts hung almost to the mattress. The chip was like a hundred I'd already seen tonight, a quarter inch thick plastic—about two inches by four inches.

"Yeah it's neat."

She was out of bed again and over to her closet, some ruffling around and back to me with another 500 Franc chip. "See this," she said, shoving this second rectangular slab under my nose. "This one is a real one! Put them together. Go ahead. Compare them, I want you to." Amidst gleeful laughter and almost breathlessness at times, the details of an incredible story unfolded. Fritz was her brother. He was a composite materials engineer with the Krups company in Germany, who had his own lab and R&D fabrication unit. He developed prototype molded plastic appliances. It all began a year ago when she met a cashier from the Casino. (He's a manager now.) He convinced Fritz it could be done, although it turned out to be no easy task. Even with access to all the Krups facilities it was a frustrating, long and expensive process developing the mold for just one chip—the 500 Franc chip of course!

"I don't believe it" I said, *"Counterfeit chips?"*

Erica was giggling and squeezing my hand as she rattled on in great detail. A lot of trial and error before they got it right. It hadn't been so hard to get an exact mold for the precise size and weight. Finding the right combination of dyes took a while. The real complicated part was the conductors: thin ribbons of copper foil that went into each chip, from end to end. They had to be layered in during the molding. Every night the chips are counted and placed in slots—like cassette holders. ("Bins," they're called.) These bins slide, like metal drawers, into a steel cabinet. One turn of a key and a voltage is applied to all the drawers, and each one has to pass an amperage continuity check. One bogus (or even cracked) chip, and the drawer won't pass inspection. What's more, but this wasn't as complicated, the engraved Casino logo was inlaid with a light-frequency sensitive material. Every time the chip went across the cashier's counter, with special glasses he was able to verify its authenticity.

"How in the hell did you learn all this? From that cashier guy?"

"Some of it yes, but mostly Fritz did it. We kept five chips after last summer's holiday. Didn't cash them in. Took them to Fritz' laboratory in Solingen and he went to work on them." They had needed the cashier for something else. Another thing had to be avoided: an *overage* in the nightly count. There couldn't be a surplus. They could only cash in as many as had been walked-out with. Fritz had almost given up on the project several times, since at first it was costing them so much, and one of the other workers got wise to it. Without access to the high tech equipment it would have cost more to make them than they were worth.

I told Erica there was no way they were going to be able to continue getting away with this. I hated to think about her getting caught. How many chips did they start with? How many did they have now? What if someone saw a difference? She just laughed and slapped the bed. "We're not worried." We lay there holding hands and looking at the ceiling. I had to laugh at myself, and the evening, and my inexperience. It all came clear to me now—how it always seemed we had chips we didn't win. Why she cashed out twice, and finally, why she grabbed back the 500 Franc chip I had tipped the club waiter with. (And me, thinking she'd remember this night because of the luck I had brought her.) *Geez!*

I GUESS I JUST WASN'T THINKING

I was successful in not letting my mind wander. How could I while watching Erica, kneeling above me, grinding her pelvis just above my abdomen. *Please God, even if just this one time.* And blessedly I did feel something not familiar—something new; not a rigidity, but hopefully a slight fullness. She lowered herself carefully, took hold of me and guided me with her hand, to where *I think at least a small part of me was inside her.* Blessedly—with her making the major (if not sole) contribution, it must have been sufficient. She made no comments or gave any indication that it was unsatisfactory. I was greatly relieved. It was a fitting end to our time together. I lay there comparing the extent of my regrets of infidelity, to the joy of having been able to consider myself having been (at least partially) inside a woman, and now begin to imagine to some small extent, *the pleasure every other man can know and takes for granted.* Could there be a chance for me? On this cruise?

Chapter Eight
GETTING A RADAR STEER

Woke at 0700 hours sharp, surprisingly (and undeservedly) rested. Had just finished in the head (showered and shaved) and put on my newly shined shoes when Jim popped back in. Asked me if I'd like to go with him up to the flight deck before breakfast, to watch Cannes slip over the horizon. Well that was the plan anyway. Once topside we were shocked to discover we were already out of sight of land. The schedule had changed, we'd up-anchored a couple hours earlier than scheduled. No trace of the Cote d'Azur. Knew we couldn't be more than sixty miles out, but by the razor-sharp line of the horizon we could have been in the middle of the Atlantic. I couldn't stop thinking about what kind of exciting and sensuous activities might be starting up along La Croisette right about now—without me. Would they miss me? (Who's *they* for God sakes. Get back to reality Roger.)

It was slightly reassuring to discover that I wasn't the only casualty from the South of France. I saw a quite a few mindless faces with glazed expressions; bodies without souls, moving mechanically. Many I'll bet with haunting memories, a few regrets, and wallets empty. By the third day, I didn't know anybody that hadn't checked the in-port schedule, to see when we would be back in Cannes. And I learned later, that the various ship's captains on these Med Cruises, had their own running bets, on how many "hands" they would lose to the Riviera. Not just return to the ship late, *actually never see them again.* (And you can be sure I now understood why).

My activities in Cannes (on the heels of my escapades in Rome) had me a little worried about having lost a keel beam. I was just smart enough to realize I could begin spending more time thinking about potentially exciting scenarios ashore than I was about my squadron and its mission.

And aware of this I was determined to mount a concentrated effort to restore myself during this forthcoming at-sea period. I'd be the hard charging Marine Corps Officer that everyone (mistakenly) thought I was. *Shake it off and get with the program!* And unfortunately, the de-prioritizing of my shipboard duties was only one of my problems. I was finding it harder to transmit meaningful things and ideas in my letters to Sara.

How in the hell could I be thinking about my kids as much as I was, picturing their sweet smiling faces looking up at me, and still be carrying on like I was? The kids—they were the valuable things in my life, in my *real* life. The one I would be going back to. I was playing with fire and I knew it. My quest—the need to keep on searching, was either in my genes or spawned quite some time ago and present ever since. Thing is, this cruise could just end up providing a solution, and if so, likely be my ruination. It was a little frightening and I certainly didn't feel good about myself. And based on the two in-ports so far, I had good reason to doubt that I would be capable of regaining control. But I was going to try.

Departing Cannes we steamed south for six hours before Air Ops surprised us all by announcing an immediate launch of sixteen birds. Somehow (thank God) I wasn't part of it. However the following day I would be, and also for seven out of the next ten days! It was during this at-sea period we commenced our first *night flying* operations, something justifiably dreaded and which would surely test one's skill, nerve and mettle. As you might imagine, as hard as it is to land aboard a carrier in the daytime, it is woefully more challenging at night. A real chance to experience what we pilots affectionately call a "leemer"—*a cold shot of urine right through your heart.* And it was on one of these flights that I'd have my first real carrier-based scare, but it wasn't the landing.

Every now and then the navigation equipment in the aircraft goes on the blink. When this happens you have no electronic guidance back to the ship. Even if it's daylight, all the water looks the same. No identifying features, no railroad tracks, no Super Domes, no interstate highways to follow. No landmarks at all. Trying to find the ship with no nav aids is worse than trying to find a needle in a haystack. It's more like trying to find a needle in Iowa. You can't help worrying about this. If this equipment failure happens to occur during a night flight, you're really in trouble. It's pure total black out there. (As one guy said: "Like being inside an ink bottle, in a coat pocket, in a closet, at night.") And I was scheduled for my first night hop tonight.

So if you do lose your navigation equipment, how *do* you hope to get back to the ship? You radio them and ask for a "Radar Steer." We have a small electronic device in our aircraft called a "transponder" that can respond to a signal (interrogation) sent from the carrier. The guys in the radar room "paint" this "return" (see it) on their radar scopes, and can then give us headings to fly to return to the ship. The alternative to not finding the ship, is finally (before you've run out of gas) pulling the aircraft up and "punching-out" (ejecting). Out you go, with a loud searing roar, feet and elbows flailing—into the night sky. With metal buckles bruising your chest, hard straps ripping at your crotch, nylon cords cutting your hands, and the wind buffeting your face, you plunge down towards a cold sea just waiting to swallow you up. All the way down you're praying you don't get knocked unconscious on impact and drown immediately, which to avoid you're instructed to inflate one half of your life vest on the way down. (If you inflated the whole vest, upon plunging into the water its buoyance might cause it to be forced up over your head, and off.) If you make it through that, start praying all over again that you don't die of exposure before dawn (when the first chance for your unlikely rescue occurs).

A night-time bailout over the open sea is the one terrifying and statistically fatal event no pilot wants to contemplate. Unfortunately, the guys up in the radar room—all nice and comfy, sitting in armchairs and eating their late night snacks, don't really appreciate your situation. They don't know what it's like out there. They can't truly appreciate the frightening and all too real possibilities facing us when they hear our call in. (They know where *they* are.) They watch their scopes in a safe, warm and friendly environment, munching a tuna sandwich and listening to the *Top-Forty* on the Armed Forces Radio.

Checked my watch—almost midnight, was sitting in the Ready Room with my wingman, Tom Keller (an easy going guy and no problem to fly with). Wondered if he felt as queasy as I did. I had briefed for a rendezvous after take off—on the ship's 010 degree radial, 50 miles out, at 25,000 feet. We'd join up there, practice night formation flight, and then get back to our holding point an hour and twenty minutes later for recovery. "Recovery" looks like an easy word—not hard to say. In reality it means controlling every axis of your aircraft down through the night sky, into an increasingly narrow chute, at hurricane wind speeds—without varying more than three or four feet in altitude or five to ten feet left to right! All this culminating with a teeth jarring slam into a completely darkened, lurching, listing, wet and windy deck, blessedly catching a wire, and walking away. No small task. To preserve our night vision, when night air ops are scheduled there are no white lights allowed on the ship, just low watt incandescent red lights (which don't affect night vision). In the resultant muted scarlet glow, now only four feet away Tom's facial features were barely recognizable. We looked more like a couple of sallow ghouls than hard charging Marines.

There it was, the PA boomed with the now familiar announcement: "Attention 2nd launch pilots. Man your aircraft. Attention 2nd launch pilots. Man your aircraft." I nodded to Tom and he fabricated a weak smile. We rose with our flight paraphernalia and started the always adventuresome trek up to the flight deck. Once there, in the pummeling cold wind we stumbled and searched, finally locating our aircraft. Not as easy as daytime, but got strapped in. Two back for the number three catapult. Engine running, going through my checks, not able to see a damn thing outside. *Oh no, may have a problem here.* The friggin directional gyro was not showing the proper heading. I'd heard the maintenance guys saying that there was so much metal in the ship's nearby superstructure, it could affect the remote compass in the wing, giving a false north indication. If your aircraft was parked near it, you could *expect* to see erroneous readings. Only trouble is, after about fifty take-offs, I had not yet seen this error. My conclusion was that I might actually have a defective compass system—a really bad thing for a night launch. *Should I shutdown and ground the aircraft?* Maybe. But canceling out of a night flight was not good for your reputation. (One pilot ended up with the nickname "Strep," since he came up with a sore throat every time his name appeared on the night flying schedule.) And now in my case, this compass discrepancy had recently been described as possibly a normal indication. Don't have too much time to mull this over, my launch turn is coming up fast. If I cancelled out and there was no discrepancy, I'd never live it down. Had to come to a decision quick.

Whew—that's better, looks correct now. Maybe it's okay. Yeah, I think so. I'm on my way onto the cat. *Uh-oh, what's this?* I don't think my DF (direction finding) needle is pointing where it should either. *Geez!* Don't tell me it's malfunctioning too. It's not pointing to the location of the ship's transmitter. Wait a minute. Yeah, okay, that could be correct. Oh well it better be, cause I'm getting hooked up right now. There's the launch signal. W*hoa!* I'm going! Head pinned back. Halter's away. Off the deck. On my own! Sinking just a bit, holding my own, nose up ten degrees. On the gauges. No horizon. Hold it, hold it. Got flying speed! I'm accelerating. Cheated death again.

I turned to the northeast to intercept the 010 degree outbound radial. Climbing 4000 feet per minute. Tom should be off in about a minute. Ten miles out, twenty, thirty miles out. The DME (distance measuring equipment) was working okay. There, established now on the 010 degree radial (according to my instruments). But my CDI (course deviation indicator) was not acting properly. It stayed full left too long then didn't center like it should have. And now it's wandering way around to the right. Can't be a proper indication. Level 25,000 feet. Shit, there's fifty miles already. Set up my left orbit. Nav lights on dim for Tom. (Leave them on full bright and they're too bright for the eyes of the joining pilot.) *Don't have a good feeling.* Five minutes. Seven minutes. Ten minutes. No Tom. Where the hell is Tom? *Frig!* Damn DME unlocking. Now I have no distance measuring equipment either. Gotta call Tom.

"Fast Fleet 505, this is Lead, where you at Tom?"

"I'm where I should be Rog, dead on the 010 radial. Where are you?"

"I may have a problem. Standby." Goddarn compass. Wait a minute, lemme try something. *Shit,* that's what I was afraid of. This is not making sense. I've got the crab angle in and I'm not seeing the needle swing. I know, only this far from the ship and at this speed, I should be seeing more progress with the needle swing. *If you left Kansas, going to Georgia, you know that Ohio should go by on your left side. If it went by on your right side, you couldn't be heading east!* According to my navigation instruments, that type of thing was occurring. All my high tech gadgetry wasn't meeting a simple test of logic. I double checked the primitive, not too accurate but reliable, non-electric "wet" compass (a 360 degree disc floating in a kerosene filled housing, mounted on the windscreen). It's an original *Spirit of St. Louis* instrument still being installed in every new 757, and it was not agreeing with the electrical or gyro driven compass. This is the worst kind of situation, two kinds of trouble at the same time: A *directional* error—my compass system, and combined with that, a *positional* error—my navigation receivers not working properly. I take that back! I got *three* kinds of trouble! My DME isn't working either, so now I have no way of knowing how many miles I am from the ship! In a nutshell, I was in *big* trouble. My instruments (*three* of them) were lying to me. My CDI showed me on the 010 degree radial, but I wasn't. My Directional Gyro showed me heading to the northwest, but I wasn't. My DME showed twenty-one miles from the ship, but I was a lot further than that. *No telling where I was.*

"FastFleet 505, lead here. Lost all my Nav, you may as well go back to the ship."

Tom answered: "Roger 504, You sure there's nothing I can do?"

"Naw, you'll never find me. I'll get a radar steer back."

Bad thought: Not only was I not going to be able to rendezvous with Tom (since I had no way locate the real 010 degree radial or the fifty mile fix we briefed on), but *worse*, I was going to have one helluva job finding my way back to the ship! Aware of this more serious problem I did a "one-eighty" (a 180 degree turn, reversal of course), and started back towards where I had come from—where the ship ought to be. *Wait a minute. Bad idea.* If I were to continue back for it, I could easily pass over it without seeing it, and then not know for sure whether I was still north of the ship, or south of it. Better stay right here. Start orbiting right here. If I stay here, at least I'll know for sure I'm still north of the ship, and I can tell the radar guys to just scan the top half (northern area) of their scopes. Found the switch and put my exterior lights full bright. One of the other guys *might* see me (Hah). If I would be so lucky, they could join on me and lead me back. The one thing I *did* have, was my radios. Thank God they were working. I had no way of determining my position, but at least I could communicate. I could talk to the ship and explain my predicament. I could ask for a Radar Steer. *Remember?* From those guys back on the ship, eating midnight snacks and drinking coffee. Let them locate me by using their radar scopes to pick up the signal from my transponder. It makes a large and unique symbol on a radar scope. Once they had that, they could give me vectors to fly back to the ship. Hopefully!

First things first: Fuel! That's the precious thing. No gas stations in the sky. And too far to make it to dry land. Pull back the power. Conserve, stay at a high altitude where fuel consumption will be less. Only when the muscles in my jaws started cramping, did I realize how tightly I had my teeth clenched. *Relax Rog, relax.* My whole body was tense (and soaked). All alone in the middle of nowhere. Made me think of the Helen Reddy song "You and Me Against the World." All alone in this small and fragile capsule zipping through an ethereal huge cavernous black ball, somewhere in the space of the world. I knew from the ship's heading during the launch, and my continuing heading thereafter (with one small orbit here), I had to be to the north or northeast of the ship. Had to be. Perhaps 75 miles out, and maybe only 20 to 30 miles off the 010 degree radial (if I was lucky). *Time to call the ship for help.*

"Pancake, Pancake, Pancake (the ship's call sign). This is Fast Fleet 504. How do you read. How do you read?" Silence. Nothing. More silence. *Shit.* "Pancake, Pancake. This is Fast Fleet 504 how do you read, over?"

"Aircraft 404, this is Pancake, go ahead."

"Pancake, this is Fast Fleet 504, repeat, *five*-oh-four, I'm about 50, maybe 75 north. Lost all my nav, need a steer back to the ship."

"Say again 504, sorry, busy. What do you need?"

"I need a steer. Lost all my NAV. I need a steer back to the ship!"

"Roger 504, Squawk Emergency for fifteen seconds, and then back to common." (This meant switch that "transponder" thing to a mode that caused the already unique mark on their scopes, to flash even brighter.)

"Okay. Doing it!" One minute of silence, nothing, still nothing. *Come on you guys!*

"504, say again your approximate position"

"Yeah, Pancake, I'm north of the ship. Gotta be. Somewhere near the 010 degree radial, about fifty, maybe sixty miles out."

"Standby, we're changing operators here. We'll be back with you. *Jesus Christ!*

"504 (mumble) this is Pancake, we're not painting your squawk. (mumble) try emergency again."

"Wilco, you got it." *(Godammit!)* " And Pancake, you sounded garbled on that last transmission. I had trouble understanding you."

"Yeah 504. Sorry, my mouth was full. Still nothing, are you sure you're east? What's your fuel state?"

"No Pancake, *not East*. North! I was on the 010 degree radial just fifteen minutes ago ...don't know how much I'm drifting, or what course the ship's been on. Fuel state, ..ah...my fuel state is 2,500 pounds...only forty, maybe forty-five minutes more." Whew! This thing was getting serious! *Where did they get East from?* I told them north! They shoulda had me by now. Really black outside. No visible line where the sky met the water. No horizon at all. Even on nights when there is no moon, you still have starlight. (Believe it or not, the stars *do* make a difference.) But tonight, nothing! No moon, no stars, no up, no down. Tom called twice. No way he would be able to locate me, so he went back to orbit over the ship for recovery.

I could almost *see* the fuel gauges going down. It was October, the water would be cold. Pilots who don't drown in it, freeze in it! I was circling in a steep bank trying to stay in the place I thought I was. But not too much bank. (Takes more power to maintain altitude in a bank—got to save fuel! Shallow it out a bit.) Fuel, that's the thing. Power's already set at max endurance.

"504, I think I got you, turn due west and hold it."

West? *That didn't compute*, but: "You got it. I'm coming right to (I think) a heading of west. Only using my wet compass so the heading may be off just a little."

"We're looking for you. We got a target. Got ya! You're south of us 504. Got you forty miles southeast."

Forty miles *south?* Even southeast. *Doesn't compute.* I couldn't have drifted *that* far in twenty minutes? No way! I'd taken off to the north, turned northeast, flew ten minutes, then orbited. I *couldn't* have drifted that far south, I don't think. *Could I?* Or could the ship's speed have factored in. Maybe. Jesus Christ, now I *was* getting worried.

"504, turn to the northwest. Fly 330 degrees and we'll bring you in."

"Rog, Roger, I'm doing it, but I don't think so Pancake. Double check. Double check that target on your scope."

"Rog 504, are you steady up on 330 degrees now?"

"Yeah, I'm dead-on as best I can tell, but I only got my wet compass, and it's bouncing around in the glass. And, oh shit! There goes the light in it. The little bulb in it went dark. No light. Can't see it. Got a short in the light. Using my penlight. But close as I can see, yeah, yeah, I'm on 330 degrees."

"504, this is Pancake."

"Yeah, 504 here. Go ahead."

"Uhm, ...um, you still maintaining that northwesterly heading?"

"Affirm, Affirm! Just like you said, 330 degrees, but I don't like it!"

"Ah, 504, reverse course, turn south now, turn left to 180 degrees right now, start letting down to five thousand feet."

"*South!?* 180 degrees? Now you say South? You mean now you got me north of the ship like I thought?"

"Yeah, yeah. North. We got you now."

"What happened, how did you paint me southeast, and give me that northwest heading?"

"I thought I had you on the bottom of my scope sir, but it was a speck of mayonnaise."

Part Two: The French Riviera, Leo, June, and Big Trouble

Once safe back from this white-knuckled flight, having survived it, I think I considered myself "bullet-proof," destined to survive the cruise. The rest of this at sea period went pretty good. Was feeling confident and part of a worthy effort, but not so enthralled that I wasn't looking forward to a break from flight ops and our next in port stay. We' be in Genoa in twelve hours.

Chapter Nine
A VERY PERSONAL ADMISSION

The First of Two Painful Recollections

The continuing humbling lack of success during my last two in-ports caused unwanted reflections, to wit I mentioned the name "Connie." In college she and I were the campus's most seen-together twosomes. Although at Central Christian a hot relationship consisted of strolling hand in hand between classes, or at night—walking your girl back to her dorm and giving her a good night peck on the cheek. Sadly, our romance was put on hold at the end of my sophomore year. In spite of a great time at college, I left Central. *And why?* Well now with our "All-Volunteer Army" you wouldn't think of it, but back then we had a draft—a hell of a draft! I could very well be called up in my junior or senior year. This being so I decided to put college on hold and get my military obligation out of the way. In volunteering as a Naval Aviation Cadet, I could earn my wings and become an officer and a gentleman (instead of wielding a rifle in a muddy trench). I'd just have to manage short visits with Connie for the next couple years.

While in flight training at Pensacola (the "Annapolis of the Air") a mandatory Christmas leave was announced, and on the way home I was going to visit Connie! It had been six months since we parted and I was anxious for this reunion. On the final leg to Minnesota (at two in the morning and in an old propeller-driven aircraft—with no heaters) I contemplated what might be awaiting me. Her town of Grand Meadow had a population of only 1,700 and her farm was about five miles outside of it. Tried to imagine what her mom and dad would be like, and what life on a real farm (wind swept and snow crusted, a ten minute walk from the nearest crossroads) would be like. I'd only have three days there, but wow, could hardly wait.

Even with the separation it caused, I was content with my decision to have left college early. I was proud making my way in the world; especially being on my way to become a Navy jet pilot. I was no longer just a student wandering a small Midwest campus, I was doing something patriotic. To make sure this fact would not go unnoticed by Connie's parents, I was wearing my uniform—or selected parts of it that I liked best (and had combined in a completely unauthorized fashion).

I would like to say the visit was great, but it was not. It could have been. Lord knows I wanted it to be. We took short walks, watched some late night TV, and visited a couple of her high school friends. All that went okay. Her mom was nice—real nice. Her dad seemed to be frequently overly cynical, particularly when it came to my military status. A couple times I think he went out of his way to say something "to get my goat"— unnecessary belittling things. Hopefully it was just because he wasn't ready for his daughter to be getting serious about some guy. I don't know. I hadn't given him any reason to dislike me or disapprove of me. He was a big man and one time (perhaps I shouldn't have been wearing my uniform) he took my small-sized hat and plunked it on top of his large, wavy gray-haired head. The hat looked absolutely ridiculous, like a piece of doll's clothing. It made me think, if my head was that small, how small must the rest of my body look?

The evening of my second day, he asked if I would like to join him for chores the next morning. Ever since my morning paper routes I've hated early get-ups, but you can bet I said "Sure!" I was up and ready to go at first light. And I was a real trooper—up to my ankles in manure, wet to my armpits milking, having my teeth rattled on the back of his feed cart. I was wholly and vigorously involved, lifting barrels, shoveling grain, and tossing hay. I went at it like it was my own farm. Someone arriving on the scene would have been hard pressed to tell which one of us owned the place. It was a matter of me establishing credibility. (He already knew I was from New Jersey and that wasn't in my favor.) I was surprised and saddened when later at breakfast, he jokingly—but only half-jokingly, described my contributions as *what you would expect from a city kid.* That comment hurt, but it was far from the worst thing to happen on my last full day in Minnesota.

I GUESS I JUST WASN'T THINKING

Talk about surprised! Talk about shocked! On the last day of my visit I was caught completely off guard and reduced to bewilderment. At a quarter to eleven, lying on a throw rug on the cold board floor in her living room, next to an old gas heater (*and only fifteen feet from her parent's bedroom door*) this wonderful young woman—the light of her mother's eye, *wanted to have sex!* I was numbed, struggling to believe what was about to take place. Sure, this is how these things end up—I think. (I know.) But I never thought about when or where it would be. I'd heard it many times: *A girl saves herself until she's married.* And Connie? God sakes, other girls maybe; other girls but not Constance Luedeke, with her thick glasses and long-sleeved, high necked blouses.

But there were no two ways about it. She had decided she was going to give up her body tonight! And from the way she was frantically undressing, she wanted me to take it in the next two minutes. She had thrown all caution to the wind and was going to do it right here and now. I couldn't help feeling as if I was about to take the "final exam." What I do know is—*I wasn't ready for it.* Not by a long shot. I might have been out on my own planning vacations and buying airline tickets, but I guess there were a few things I wasn't doing: I hadn't been hanging around any working girls or lonely women. I was twenty years (and two months) old, but had not yet lost my virginity. Sure, I'd thought a lot about the act of losing it. (In fact I fantasized a great deal more than I felt was normal.) This would be my first time, but oddly enough I wasn't preoccupied with that fact. I was concerned about everything else. At the bottom of the list (if it was even on the list) was any possible physical pleasure that might be in store for me. But there was no altering the course of events. I was going to have to perform, and quick.

What followed was probably the most awkward and unsuccessful effort ever devoted to satisfying a woman. I think I started out okay, nuzzling her and stroking her now exposed female body, nibbling and kissing her. I did all those things which I had understood to be expected of me and pleasurable to her (even though to me they seemed to be artificial—contrived mechanical motions). Finding myself in this situation, with its definite requirements and larger-than-life expectations, I was not feeling confident. After a goodly time conducting the aforementioned activities, irrespective of what Connie might be feeling, I was aware of a frightening 'nothingness' precisely where I should have felt some growing activity. And I had no reason to believe that five more minutes was going to make a difference. A dominating fear began to overtake me, knowing I had to consummate this act. I had to. I was striving and straining, pleading to the gods of love making, and talking under my breath, beseeching myself with desperate urgency. *C'mon. C'mon. Please! C'mon.* But no luck.

This complete lack of arousal was in stark contrast to my hormonally charged youth; to the daily if not hourly (and often untimely) erections that had plagued me from the time I was twelve. God knows I had spent more time than I should have thinking about being in this exact situation. In bed at night I'd made up exciting scenarios (such as myself and some voluptuous woman handcuffed and bound together on the floor, the length of our bodies unavoidably pressed against each other) and every time—in a matter of minutes (if not seconds), I'd find myself in possession of a hardened device that demanded satisfaction.

Due to my lack of readiness, I had to delay "going for it." I continued to position and reposition, avoiding and postponing. All the while my pretty Connie lay there, twisting and anticipating. I looked down at her—head back, eyes closed, mouth raised, hips raised, and cursed myself. Embarrassed and ashamed and becoming more so with every minute, I prayed she was not aware of my difficulties and that some miracle would occur. Some minutes later we were a mass of tangled clothes, elbows, perspiration, and floor burns—*with me in no better condition.* I could have cried. I was ready to scream. I could have wrung it off and stomped on it. With jaws clenched tight, lest I fill the air with profanity, I was wildly distraught. I tugged her this way and that, transmitting stupid instructions (when I was the one who needed help). I got her to allow me to slide a pillow under her hips—which some guy had told me, "positions the woman's pelvis just right." (As if the previous angle was part of the problem.) But she did it. She was going to try anything to get this thing on the road. She tugged it under her full white buttocks, wiggled a bit, and indicated she was ready. *God, if I just was!*

Hard to imagine I was not overcome by her warm, damp body, and round, heavy thighs. I wasn't in the slightest overcome with the lust or desire that I knew should be consuming me. I was just a man on a mission—totally dedicated to overcoming his plight, wholly concerned with it. A goal that left no room to savor the moment and let nature take its course. I lessened the touching and kissing I had been doing. How could I continue without being able to consummate it? And for sure Connie needed no more foreplay. Her movements and moaning indicated she was ready for ignition. If she would have had further physical arousal (in addition to her gritty determination to cross this bridge tonight) my lack of performance would have been even more devastating (if that's possible). I was exhausted, discouraged, and never before fraught with such embarrassment.

The mental anguish, futile contortions and flailing about was abruptly interrupted by a resounding loud metallic clang! My heavy Navy brass belt buckle had struck the base of a metal floor lamp. With the sharp noise reverberating in my ears I could visualize her father (*in the next room*) bolting upright in bed. Like a boxer in the throes of a hopeless loss, I would be "saved by the bell." This would be my reprieve. I scurried for distance in mortal fear that any second the bedroom door would be yanked open and I'd be looking up at her father. Connie must've had the same thoughts, as out of the corner of my eye I saw several articles of her clothing all in the air at the same time. Any pending activity was over!

I was quite sure in the days to come she would spend a fair amount of time reflecting on this non-event. (I sure knew I would.) I was afraid that after this—to her, my male attraction would never be the same, and I guess I was right. The big fade began soon afterwards. From down in Florida (no email or skype or texting back then), but with letters, flowers, telegrams and hours in phone booths, I tried desperately to win her back. She had begun dating another guy at college. I knew him. An older guy there on the GI Bill. He'd been in the army, been overseas, smoked, drank, and almost immediately seemed to have some kind of mysterious hold on her.

The Second of Two Painful Recollections

And are you ready for this? My wedding night with Sara was an exact and equally confounding repeat of my experience with Connie! I again completely failed to become armed. I was totally demoralized. No matter what I tried it was to no avail. Thank God Sara must have been forewarned and to comfort me had said "Don't worry, this is not at all unusual." Maybe not, but for me, I was real worried. *I now had a track record of 0 and 2!*

Now, on this cruise, I was haunted more than ever: my track record worsening to 0 and 4. *"Am I ever going to find that one woman with the right chemistry; the one that would unlock my manhood?"* If ever I am, right now—on this cruise, here, free to explore and meet exciting Continental women, would be my best (and only chance).

You Might Wonder How It Was That I Got Married

After graduating from flight training (only three years after graduating from high school), my first duty station was El Toro, California; the choice duty station, located just a few miles inland from Laguna Beach (and just thirty minutes from Hollywood). And I got it! It was ground zero for new and daring activities. There were movie stars, health nuts, sports cars, cool surfing dudes, and throngs of tanned, hard-bodied, golden haired females wherever you looked. It was everything and more recanted in the familiar lyrics of the Beach Boys' songs. It was just about all any young bachelor could dream of. I can see now, this would have been it! However I never gave it a chance. After only a few months at El Toro; still at the fringe of understanding steady employment; early on in the experiment of living an independent single life; not yet having been responsible for a residence; having never lived with a girl, and in no position to be qualified to even consider moving on to any next phase, I let events shape my life.

At just twenty-two years of age, in spite of well-founded fears and before I knew anything about myself, before I ever gave a thought about what words or actions of a life's partner would complement my yet undetermined temperament, *I found myself married!* And more important, I never gave a thought to what would be required of me! I never stopped to consider the permanency and commitment I was making; how I would no longer have the freedom to explore other interests (including a chance romantic interest, should one occur). Gave no thought to that. Had no idea of the word "perpetuity." Surprisingly not a single friend or family member hinted I might want to give this marriage thing a little more thought. After hearing the coming account of how my marriage came about, you will be even more sure I am doomed to live in the present; incapable of futuristic thinking, unable to think more than a month ahead.

Upon my arrival at El Toro I had chosen to live on the base in the Bachelor Officers Quarters, while most of my hip friends opted to live off-base. One of them, Mark Yatsko (Remember in Part One—my PreFlight roommate, fervent Texas Aggie, and I guess—best friend) and his lovely wife had really lucked out. They found an A-frame perched on stilts, on a cliff overlooking one of Laguna Beach's most beautiful hidden coves. They were living the life they deserved and could only be envied. One beautiful, stress-free day after another. She the beaming, happy, stay-at-home wife, and he the swaggering "top gun" of what used to be Pappy Boyington's *Black Sheep* squadron (about which they made that popular

TV series). This night they'd invited me over for one of their famous spaghetti dinners.

Along with me they had invited Tom Blake, a fellow Marine we had both known in flight training. Prior to entering the Naval Cadet program, Tom had been the starting quarterback for the University of Missouri. He was a sturdy, frequent bar-fighter, fire-plug guy, with freckles and close cropped red hair. As usual Tom would be there with his fiancée—an absolutely gorgeous local girl. Up till tonight I had never seen Valerie not in a bikini. And a bikini that was never quite up to the task of confining so many luscious areas anxious to escape. Tonight she was dressed in a lavender tank top (also failing to restrain) and stretch white cotton shorts which seemed to be lifting her off the ground (making me feel as if I should give a tug down on the hem of my own boxer shorts).

A good time was had by all (helped along by one innards-warming, world-softening glass of wine after another). Caroline would leap to her feet at any request from Mark, accomplish the mission and return to the table with a big and loving smile. And Tom and Valerie while finalizing the plans for their October wedding were obviously getting along just fine. She was sitting on his lap with her tan arms around his neck and ample breasts pressed against him, never letting more than thirty seconds pass without planting another long kiss. By the end of the meal the room was delightfully aglow and full of contented smiles (and the sink full of empty Chianti bottles). The world was a wonderful place to be. I was favorably impressed by this married and about-to-be-married lifestyle. It was my first close observance of a young husband-wife relationship, and would have convinced anyone that it was a union to be highly sought.

In the midst of this warm conjecture I realized Caroline was speaking to me. "And Roger, how about you. You must have a girlfriend somewhere." I had to think. No one came to mind (which made sense, because there *was* no one). But then I commenced to tell her about Sara, who I had met at a church summer camp in high school and taken on a couple movie dates. They all chimed in with "tell us more" and "so what's happening now." I obliged—still for some unknown reasons exaggerating all aspects of the relationship. Between sips of an after-dinner Mexican liqueur (that Mark had bought in Reynosa and insisted we try), I continued to embellish all my new girlfriend's admirable traits. The other four were all ears. I heard the relationship between Sara and I getting more real; better and better. I can't remember who suggested it or why in the hell I went along with it, but after fifteen minutes of this escalating dialogue, the next thing I knew I had been directed to the phone and was dialing information for Sara's number. I don't recollect any details of the conversation, but when it was over I was being roundly toasted and slapped on the back. I had somehow said (no—no I didn't say it) but I must have allowed Sara to conclude that I was not just calling to rekindle a relationship, but was using verbiage *that permitted her to speculate on a possible engagement!*

After a couple months and several more phone calls, though I cannot remember what mood or conversation could have possibly prompted it, a diamond ring was in the mail. The next few months, I did my impression of a stray leaf. While I can't say I wasn't aware of things progressing, I was in a semi-conscious state, failing to take any action, neither guiding nor resisting the course of events. Four months later on a brisk December afternoon two complete strangers were pronounced man and wife; no earthly idea about each other or themselves. At least I had no earthly idea. Sara probably thought she knew what she was doing. All her girlfriends were doing the same thing. Our parents were real happy. *It was about thirty minutes after saying "I do," that what I had just done took my legs out from under me.*

Chapter Ten
GENOA AND THE DA VINCI

I was on the flight deck when the anchor hit the water. The skies were gray and the winds were gusting. *Not* my kind of weather. I watched the liberty parties clamber down the ladders and drop into the boats below, and was relieved to note that I could observe all this with little or no urge to join in. *Thank you God.* Perhaps my lack of interest was due to the cooperation of the elements, which were doing their best to make the Genoa shoreline even less appealing. A wet smog hung heavily across the horizon, obscuring the upper reaches of most smoke stacks and any building over three stories. Sooty emissions drifted upward and then merged with the low gray clouds. It might even be easy to stay on board. But for most of the ship's company it was shore leave and there could be new things to do and new people to meet. I was pleased that I still felt no beckoning. So far, so good. The scuttlebutt was that Genoa was definitely not a hang out for the jet set. I was pretty sure I wouldn't be swapping duty days here. If this turned out to be true, I would only use my assigned liberty days, and no more. Better to save them up. (We'd be back on the Riviera in six weeks.)

The second day in my section was the scheduled duty section. In view of Genoa's dreary appearance and reputation, I didn't mind waiting another day to "hit the beach." I decided it would be smart to again spend this day with my nose to the grind stone, "scoring points" if you will. (In case I need them later.) I'd make my rounds first. Make sure I was seen all over the ship doing everything an Assistant Maintenance Officer could do (without usurping the authority of the Maintenance Officer). Gotta be careful of that. I spent most of the day visiting the Engine Shop, jawing with the men there, and assuring myself that there were no parts or labor problems. The level of readiness we had maintained so far had been impressive. With twelve aircraft on board, there was only one or two mornings that all twelve weren't ready to go! (A couple times we *just* made it.) I could see that if this kept up, it would look good for Major Burnham and myself.

During my rounds I encouraged the men to bring up whatever they might have on their mind, even if it wasn't a work issue. When they did I tried to show a real interest. I'm still trying to master the art of listening. In any case, the men appreciated an audience other than their workmates. From time to time they did have a legitimate bitch, and with my rank I frequently was able to do something to help them, and I felt good about that. Most of these men were darn good citizens, husbands and fathers, but based on their lower military rank did not receive the respect and consideration they deserved for other worthy accomplishments in their life. I looked forward to any opportunity to support them.

Day number three was scheduled liberty for my section, although I didn't yet have any special plans. There hadn't been any exciting feedback from the first couple days' foragers. However I decided I may as well see what was out there, and began to assemble my best casual outfit for another Italian holiday. This would be my khaki suit (albeit from JC Penney), a cool cashmere pullover I'd bought in Rome, and my new suede loafers from Cannes. I'd just carry the jacket in case it was needed. (I'd borrowed Nick's paisley ascot, which would be part of that outfit.) Hopefully that would be a sufficiently Continental outfit for Genoa. (Though not likely I'd be mistaken for Pierce Brosnan or Sean Connery, even if one of them were five feet eight). Who would I go with? Once again—*no one*. Although this time I had no itch, no expectations, I just felt more adventuresome going it alone. Had this idea it enhanced my anonymity and increased my chances for more interesting introductions. True enough this solo status pretty much excluded a fun afternoon with the standard pair of giggling American college girls on vacation, but I'd be willing to forego this for a possibly more worldly and stimulating "one-on-one" meeting.

Off the Liberty boat and ashore I found myself in a city jam-packed with overloaded buses and dilapidated trucks, inhaling my share of smoke and fumes. The rumors had been right. Not likely there was going to be any movie stars mingling about in this place. However, as always, I was fascinated by the hubbub of a strange big city—observing the bustling downtown activity (even if it meant breathing in a lot of diesel exhaust). A good thing too, because there was very little girl-watching to be had in Genoa. Say what you want about Sophia Loren and Gina Lolabrigida, eligible Italian girls do *not* make a habit of wandering the streets in search of escorts. The city of Genoa, for a guy of my perhaps latent inclinations, turned out to be no better than it had been described.

During the day (try as I might to maintain my conjured lone wolf image) it seemed every time I turned a corner I was bumping into a boisterous group of my squadron mates. It soon became apparent that the social and professional thing to do, would be to just join up with them and be a sport. Forget any mysterious activities for the rest of the day. One among them, Captain Nielsen (who had been enlisted previously) and had been in port here many years ago as a young sailor, decreed he would show us the greatest little restaurant in Italy. He then proceeded to lead us on a wearying quest to locate it. After much too long of an excursion (several of the more hungry guys dropping out), we did find it. I was introduced to Cannelloni, and I have to admit, it was the best I would ever eat, and would become my favored Italian dish—to this day.

Somehow, perhaps just because of the law of averages, or destiny intervening to help me keep my promise, nothing great was happening for me in Genoa. In fact I was about to conclude that my first two ports of call were just flukes. Two times I returned to the ship *early*. On a later liberty, Bob Harmon and I did run into two young and kooky American girls on a shoestring-budget travel odyssey. They were a kick in the ass I can tell you that, broke but "good" girls. We provided them with some great pasta, and let them use our squadron hotel room for a much needed and appreciated hot shower. (And I think Bob almost scored after that show of kindness.)

My workout partner Dale, told me he had found fantastic twin resorts about twenty minutes south of Genoa. Availing ourselves of the charming (but sooty and packed) Italian rail system, we jerked our way there one afternoon. Dale was right. They were postcard paradises: Santa Margherita and Porto Fino. These villages, nestled in picturesque coves and surrounded by charcoal cliffs, ended up as the subjects of many a jigsaw puzzle. The curving shoreline was a series of unmanicured pebble beaches and partially hidden rocky inlets. Lapping against the stone overhangs, the deepening water was an appealing dark blue. The beaches were strewn with a colorful mélange of overturned wooden rowboats, many of which had a couple old fishermen perched on the keel beam, laughing and smoking their pipes while busying themselves mending nets. The hotels ringing the tiny bays were not giant chrome and acrylic monstrosities. They were all small—

many wooden, mostly cream or pale yellow with brightly contrasting red, blue, or green shutters. They appeared to be family-run, comfortable and unpretentious establishments with grandmas and grandkids peeking out of their doors and windows. It was the Italian "working man's" version of the Cote d'Azur. But nothing like Cannes. This place was humble and honest—full of ordinary citizens.

Notwithstanding the above exception, Genoa continued to remain conveniently unspectacular. So much so that again this day (our last day in-port) I had returned early from liberty. I was just finishing a late evening snack when Mike Ballard came bursting through the wardroom hatch with potentially exciting news.

"Rog! There's an American cruise ship two piers up the wharf, loaded with tourists."

"So?"

"Might not hurt to stroll down there. See what's cooking. Meet some stateside people. Have some harmless fun."

"Okay, why not? I've never set foot on one before." To convince myself of my honorable intentions (and perhaps bolster my chances of not getting involved) I didn't even spruce up. Maybe we'll have just good enough of a time that Genoa won't slip away with nothing at all to report.

From the bow of the liberty boat, banging in the heavy chop, trying to avoid the salt spray and dirty wet canvas, we eyed the city lights, just visible through a fine drizzle coming out of the dark sky. The trip took about ten minutes, during which time we joked about the colorful and exciting onboard activities that might be awaiting us. Unfortunately—as usual, our adventures, whatever they would be, would have to be carried out and culminated in time for us to be back at the dock by 2400 hours (midnight), to catch the last launch back to the ship. One exception, the Navy officers whose wives were paralleling our cruise by inland ground transportation, and visiting their husbands during the in-port times, were allowed all-night liberty. There was a special liberty launch for these guys, which left the dock at 0600 hours each morning. This married officer's privilege really pissed-off the bachelors.

On the darkened dock now, we were trodding on wet concrete, navigating around coils of old rope and stepping over assorted piles of trash. Making my way through the refuse I didn't feel as sophisticated as I would have liked. We waited only a couple minutes before concluding a cab ride wasn't going to happen. On foot then. No time to lose. This evening would be Genoa's last chance to get in the record books. Mike was excited. (Good to know there was at least one other guy with some adventuresome spirit.) We could see the cruise ship now with its strings of colored Christmas lights strung up and down from the superstructure. Maybe gaudy, but it set a festive mood. As we closed on the ship I could make out its name. Huge, black painted metal letters, leaking rust stains down the white hull, spelled out: *Leonardo Da Vinci.*

"Doesn't look like an American ship to me Mike."

"It's gotta be. The guy told me it came from New York."

"Funny name for an American ship, but maybe there will be some American passengers."

As we walked out the pier towards the spot where the *Da Vinci* plank rested on the gouged concrete seawall, we saw some of the ship's company—what looked like security guys, checking some sort of ID cards. *ID cards?* That could be a game breaker. As is, I didn't think we looked much like the other passengers. Mike had more confidence and went straight towards the gangplank. *Voila,* he was past the agents and quickly but not too gracefully making his way up the burlap covered boards. Steadying himself with one hand on the white vinyl-wrapped hand rail and beaming a look of self-satisfaction, he was waving me to join him. I did. (The guy at the foot of the gangplank didn't even look at me.) Even though we knew nothing about a tour ship, we had this false sense of security in that we had just come off a giant sea going vessel. Our legs were with us. All we lacked was a plan, some idea of where we were going. It was about nine. We hit several dining halls full of jabbering people, but so far no abundance of Americans, especially no young single American women. Let me go further; no abundance of *women,* young, single, *or* American. Some older women, in groups, not speaking English. The anticipated scenario was not falling into place right off.

We discretely probed one passageway after another, keeping in mind that we belonged nowhere and could be accosted at any time. Things were not going as well as in our earlier speculation. We found several groups and did make some small talk with a group of proper "Brits." You can always count on them for agreeable conversation. (I would learn that better in future travels.) About ten minutes later we got a good steer from a person of unknown origin: Second deck on the bow, he thought, there was some sort of festivity—a buffet or dance, or something like that. With live music! Could be it.

Part Two: The French Riviera, Leo, June, and Big Trouble

As a Marine, once you have a mission, the effort and accomplishment are historic. We plowed forward reacting to each momentary setback with a bounce to the left or right as necessary, and then renewed progress. *Ah ha.* At last, we could hear the sounds of music and laughter straight ahead. The best kept secret was compromised. We were within striking distance. Bursting through the last hatch we found ourselves on a small open deck. *Bingo!* This was it. Once again into the cool night air, replete with twinkling lights and banners. A band was banging away on a portable stage. A long buffet table draped with bands of pastel colored paper stretched half the length of the exposed deck. On it were giant punch bowls, pitchers, baskets of fruit, and flowers. Around it, about fifty well-dressed multi-national passengers were having quite a time, laughing and singing with glasses raised on high. We were on target. Now, what to do or how to do it.

For a better look we strolled confidently (like properly invited guests) to the farthest deck gunnel. There we leaned back (as casually as we could), our elbows atop the cold wood railing, supporting us in a passably casual pose, while we screened the animated crowd. The musicians appeared to be either Latin or South American. (My very little Spanish might come into play.) Mike said that should we be so inclined and get up our nerve, asking a lady to dance could be internationally acceptable, and a good way to effect a meeting. Unfortunately just as I was nodding a half-hearted agreement to his suggestion, the band went on their break, which would put this option on hold for at least twenty minutes. (And twenty minutes could be critical inasmuch as it was almost ten.)

We unsuredly ventured into the arena—up to the buffet table. As we moved around it (helping ourselves to some of the more appealing looking offerings), by chance and heretofore unseen, I found myself next to a very eligible appearing woman—about my age. By the sharp lines of her face, her hair arrangement, and her thin lips, I was pretty sure she was European, and thus not optimistic about any chat in English likely. (Couldn't imagine that mouth forming sloppy American slang.) I was beginning to discover (as you no doubt have noticed) that for whatever reason I had a strong attraction for the striking features and differing mannerisms of these European females. There was both strength and sensitivity about this one. Maybe even a sadness—at least to my eyes.

When I finally got up the nerve to speak, the result wasn't very impressive, just an awkward smile and a weak "Good Evening." It didn't sound very confident. And although she was now looking at me, she wasn't answering. *Wait now. Give her a chance to respond. Maybe she's translating.* There's a smile—a beautiful smile. Another pause, and exactly what had I feared. While those lips did form English words, they certainly had spent more time with another language. Went on to learn she was French. Her name was Paulette Bonfils (which I later learned means "good son"). She had been in the States for six months, working as a nanny to a rich French family on Long Island. She was now returning to her home. She was happy and sad at the same time. She was glad to be talking to me. This basic information took about fifteen minutes to compile. I don't care what you look like, or how you try to dress, I was discovering that if you don't speak French, you are *not* going to be a superstar in Europe. I now had renewed intent to correct my deficiency in this area (which I did, providing much good fortune later).

When the music resumed Paulette gestured that she wanted to dance. *Uh-oh, don't tell me it's happening again,* we molded together as one, breathing in unison. Years later I realized, some women just fit against men. To the man—at the moment, he is sure it is his manliness that creates the union, not realizing it is her natural gift. (And her burden as well, since she fits well against *all* men.) Her accent was delightful, but strange it should be so strong after her extended stay in the States. She said when she left New York she was speaking English well, but that in speaking French on the voyage, in just ten days she'd lost most of her English capability. At the time this sounded unlikely to me. In later years, with my own second language work, I would find this happening repeatedly. We weren't communicating all that well, so we continued to dance. When our eyes met she smiled and looked back. Gotta be careful here, *I'm out for a little fun and falling into the same scenario as the last in-port.* We snacked and talked to the band, which was Argentinian. I spewed out all the Spanish I could remember. They thought it was great. I'll tell you what it was: *It was late! Shit.* Almost eleven o'clock.

About this time, Mike—who had danced twice—with two different women, shot me a thumbs-up, signaled he was calling it a night, and was gone. I was as I would often be: on my own in an unwarranted location. Obviously I was dissatisfied with myself, my position and talents, but maybe beginning to figure out why.

Paulette and I took the same stroll Mike and I had taken earlier— to the stern of the ship, separating ourselves from the thinning crowd.

Once again leaning against the now wet railing. But it was different now. I was with this thin honey-haired French woman with the shining eyes. Together there, we could look up past the awning to the black Italian sky, which now (maybe just for us) had more than its share of stars. Without expecting it, next thing I knew she had given me a quick kiss. It certainly wasn't a very sexy kiss (which was fortunate since I never was good at that anyway). I guessed it was okay—the right kind of kiss for Paulette at this time and with me. She didn't say anything, but didn't move away either. I felt her arm slide around my waist. Not too many minutes later we were walking across the stern deck, past the crowd, and towards the interior of the ship. *How long was I going to let this play out.* I was not giving her any signals that she could interpret—either way. I was fully aware of what could happen. Gotta go one way or the other, not just hang around in case she wants to do it. I knew these things often fell in place, especially on nights like this. I was at the same time fearing that it would, and yet it titillated me that it might (as well as frightened me, aware of another possibly crushing experience).

Based on the distance we had wandered into the bowels of the ship, I was pretty sure we had left the stern deck for good, and were likely on the way to her stateroom. What else did I expect. None of my actions to this point would have indicated I was adverse to culminating the evening in such a manner, when in fact I had very mixed emotions about such a conclusion. On the one hand I knew I might not be able to resist the chance to lie next to this fine woman and touch her bare skin, and attempt to share her secrets. On the other hand, in so doing I would be promptly abandoning my on-again, off-again resolve and confirming my weakness. And almost worse, if I did end up in her bed, I would have bet (just because I would have so wanted to please her and make her especially happy) I would have jinxed myself. And we *were* headed towards her stateroom. As usual, at this time in these situations, apprehension and a deadening weariness suddenly overcame me. I was thinking about a lot of things. Some of them things I should be thinking about. In addition to what you might imagine, one of the things I was thinking about, was having already missed the midnight boat! Hate to admit it, I was also thinking about if this were to go good—the likelihood of a future meeting with Paulette. *I don't know what the hell I was thinking!* Unbelievable to me that so many people have given me credit for being smart, when time and time again I've proved that isn't true.

I GUESS I JUST WASN'T THINKING

It was a tiny stateroom. You could barely turn around in it. No windows. All stainless steel and laminated plastic. Not much for aesthetics. Good for ease of cleaning. Anybody could live there for a week. Right about now things were a little awkward. She rummaged through a drawer and brought out some photo albums. She pulled a small cassette player out of a locker, then searched through a plastic bag of tapes. And we soon had some lovely French music. As tired as I was, I knew there was something I had to do. I located a small alarm clock on the metal dresser, and set it for five. She watched and was surprised to see the early hour. I wasn't going to tell her I had to catch an 0600 boat back to the carrier. I'd absolutely positively have to get on that morning one for the married Navy Officers. None of those officers would know who I was, or whether or not my wife was accompanying me. I'd just join them on the dock at 0545, and hop on their boat with them. No one in the squadron would need me between now and 0600. I'm sure Paulette had all along assumed I was another passenger, from another class or deck. I don't know, we didn't talk about that or much of anything for that matter.

There was just one chair in the stateroom and I collapsed into it. She plopped down on my lap, kissed me sweetly on the mouth, and opened one of the albums. I wasn't sure if I was relieved or aggravated at this harmless photo checking activity on her part, knowing it had arrested any possible sensual progression of the evening. But then I hadn't done my part to make this easy for her. She went through the whole album. Mostly pictures of her stateside employer's home and their kids. She looked very happy in all the shots. I realized I was fast succumbing to the day's and evening's activities. I tried as best I could to listen to her narration (one English word then two French words) as she described the photos. But I couldn't help it, I dozed off, and was brought back when she leaned over me and snapped off the light behind my head. I was being led over to her narrow bed. She pulled off only her outer garments. We were in bed, but on top of the covers. Each still wearing our underclothing. She had made the decision. We were going to call it an evening without making it complicated. Still in her half-slip and bra, she put a leg and an arm over me and snuggled her head into my neck. As best I could tell in my stupor, her body felt warm and good next to me, and she seemed to be very content that I was alongside her. The next thing I knew she was breathing heavily. Nothing, absolutely nothing happened. A night with a woman without the pressure and worry of warranted anguish.

Part Two: The French Riviera, Leo, June, and Big Trouble

When the alarm went off at five I had to claw my way out of a deep sleep. I felt drugged, but good about myself—even though it hadn't been a result of appropriate decisions or actions on my part, there had been no transgressions. I had a slight headache and felt a little queasy, although I didn't think I'd had too much to drink. (Though it had been one of those mysterious fruit punches, about which you never know until morning.) It was going to be a rough day at work, I was sure of that. But as always I would get through it. Knew we were scheduled to up-anchor at noon. Regroup. Rest later. Dressing wasn't easy either. The room was dark and I had trouble standing on one leg. Trousers, then shoes. (Put my socks in my pockets.) Paulette made sure I had her address in Lyons (which I *did* want). Maybe only my interpretation, but she seemed sad. She reached out and held on to one of my hands, which didn't make my dressing any easier. Kept at it. Boy did I feel bad. I kissed her good-bye, as she did me. It was difficult leaving, especially since I had never explained my origin, or where I had to go at this ungodly early hour. She didn't know I was going to leap off the ship and run like a thief, a half mile down the waterfront to catch a greasy boat, and start another life. Out of her stateroom.

We often say "My heart jumped out of my throat" or "I was scared to death." I now believe either could actually happen. When I emerged from the interior passageways onto an open area along the exterior decks, for the first time I was able to see outside the ship. What I could see was water—water everywhere, only water; left, right, front and behind. Only then did I feel the hum in the soles of my feet, and realize *the friggin ship was underway!* It must have pulled out some time in the early morning. *We were at sea!* I was a prisoner, or worse—a stowaway! Suffice it to say I was in big—very big trouble.

Decided to fess up, explained my predicament to the *Da Vinci*'s radio operator. Could he make a call? Well he'd never tried to contact a US Navy Shore Patrol station before. Couldn't this time either. But wait, he had an idea. He could get ahold of the Genoa Yacht Club. They in turn could send a driver to the US Shore Patrol office, carrying a message for them to relay to the Commander of VMA 331, aboard the USS *Forrestal*. *Whew. Sounds complicated, but could work.* The radio operator on this ship was a good guy, his suggestion might save my career.

Coincidentally (in fact miraculously) for the only time during the entire cruise, the carrier had only a one-day at-sea period this time. Just a short repositioning—from Genoa to Marseilles. With no flight operations scheduled! And the gods were really with me, because the *Leonardo da Vinci* was also on a one-day trip—to Nice, not too far up the coast from Marseilles. With a one-hour cab ride, I'd be able to hook up with the ship tonight! I'm sure I didn't deserve this good fortune. The *Da Vinci* could have just as well been going to Tunisia.

It was going to be a long seven hours. I hated to do it, but, yes— you guessed it, I returned to Paulette's stateroom. When I finally got it all explained—which wasn't easy, she laughed, really laughed, like it was the first time she had in a long time. When we hit Nice, I was down the gangplank as soon as the lines were tied. Caught a cab and was pulling onto the Marseilles dock an hour and a half later (paying the French driver with Italian Lire). Waiting for the liberty boat out to the carrier I was a nervous wreck. Everyone else looked like nothing was wrong. No one was showing any concern. Funny about how the extent of a disaster depends on perspective. I was the first one in the boat and scrambled forward (as if my position in it and the three seconds it would save could make a difference).

In fifteen minutes I was on my way up the aft ladder to the flight deck. The Colonel met me at the top step, along with all the captains and most the lieutenants (all grinning knowingly). Among them was Bob Harmon, perhaps my only squadron confidant (who had been an avid listener when I narrated my Ardith and Erica stories). He would be anxious to know the reason for my late arrival and was holding up a cardboard sign that said *"Benvenuto Signore Fortunato."* (A reference in Italian to the adventuresome main character of the currently popular TV series named *Mr. Lucky*.)

As you might imagine it was a humbling evening—attempting to explain away my activities. I smiled a little, but not much. I was talked to. I lost one day's leave. I deserved to. The Colonel was if not understanding, very tolerant. Finally in the rack I felt relieved, half safe (born again). Let sleep take over, refresh and renew me. I knew that tomorrow by the time I awoke, we would be fifty miles to sea—starting another at-sea period, with who knows what shipboard adventures awaiting us.

A Change in Our At-Sea Routine

Surprisingly (and gratefully) awoke refreshed. Ventured up to the flight deck to breath the clean salt air and squint through the bright white haze at one more Mediterranean horizon. This at-sea period was going to be a two-weeker with the emphasis on conventional ordnance delivery. Old fashioned rockets and bombs—just sighting your target visually, and rolling into a steep dive, (what feels like) almost straight down at it. Once again the target was a sled (wood raft) towed behind the ship. But this would only be part of the at-sea period. The other training maneuver slated to occur on this at sea period was going to be something new and much preferred. A certain number of pilots from each squadron would fly to a US Air Force land base near Licata, Sicily, and stay there for three full days—using their "live ammo" range. (A chance for some liberty *during* an at-sea period.) Luck was with us, VMA 331 got assigned one of these boondoggles, and I was going to be the Division Leader for it.

Thursday afternoon the four of us made the now well travelled trek up to the flight deck. Before strapping in we stuffed our liberty togs, toiletries, and an extra flight suit in a small, usually empty avionics compartment accessed by a hinged door on the outside of the nose section of the aircraft. The launch went like all the others and we were on our way. Landed late in the afternoon, checked into the Visiting Officers Quarters, and later had a great steak and a couple of Heinekens at the Officers Club. The following morning we received our briefing, marked our maps and took a short written test on their "Range Rules." At 0900 I was airborne with a flight of four to the range, where we subsequently deposited our ordnance in a superlative manner, if you don't care about "duds." (Instead of a ball of fire, it seemed every third or fourth bomb just made a puff of dust.)

Being so close we couldn't resist the temptation. After we'd expended our ammo we flew up the coast and did some low-level flyovers around the blistered lip of Mount Etna. Peering down inside that gaping, charred aperture gave you some idea of the inferno that's at the center of our planet. Brad got too close and took a bump that damn near de-winged him. That night at the "O" club we hoisted our share, gave our Air Force brothers a friendly razing, and closed the place with the Marine Corps Hymn. Had to pour Brad into the rack again. (He was having a fine time away from the scrutiny of Colonel Cunningham.)

Little Things Mean a Lot

The afternoon before we were scheduled to return to the boat (Yup, we called the carrier, the "boat"), I decided to take a cab into the city of Licata. There was something I needed to buy. The weather had turned cold and gray and reminded me of the fact that since my sunlamp had burned out I was losing my color. Maybe I could pick up a sun lamp on my afternoon off here in Sicily. Once inside the city I had the driver leave me off at what appeared to be a major shopping area. Spied a big store—looked like a stateside department store. Only one floor, but about a half-mile across. I entered (shivering), coming in out of the cold damp air. (The store wasn't all that warm either.) But it was well stocked. Certainly I would be able to find a sun lamp here. I navigated my way through aisle after aisle of tools, linens, shoes, lingerie, etc., straining to pick out what would most closely approximate an appliance area. Thought I saw it—an aisle with toasters, blenders, fans, and other electrical devices. Made my way over to it.

As hard as it is to believe, the following story is true. Absolutely true to the last detail. After circling the shelving a half dozen times, I had not yet spied any cartons showing a picture of a sun lamp on it. I found an infrared lamp—for muscle soreness, etc., but no sun lamp. Time to seek help. The sales lady was eager to help, in fact almost desperate to assist me. I asked her (in English) did she have a sun lamp? Her expression registered only panic. I was sure she was not expecting such gibberish. She had not understood a single word. She stood there wide-eyed, waiting in silence (as if time alone would solve this). I repeated myself slowly and with exaggerated articulation: "I would like to buy a sun lamp." Her countenance did not change one iota. This was a complete bust. She did not blink, sigh, or move even an eyelash.

Part Two: The French Riviera, Leo, June, and Big Trouble

About this time she was joined by a male salesperson from the adjacent section. His face radiated the same "ready-to-serve" expression that hers had, moments earlier. I enunciated slowly and carefully, "Sun lamp. Sun lamp." *Talk about a repeat.* Maybe not so much panic as the girl, but let me say, nary a glimmer. His face a perfect blank. By now, in my new European travels, I had picked up some Italian and French words (mostly from romantic songs I had heard in Rome and along the Cote d'Azur). I was gaining a tiny vocabulary. I knew the Spanish word for sun was *sol* (and maybe in Italian too). I tried again—with this small language innovation. *"Sol Lamp, Sol Lamp."* With this I think I noticed a slight look of anticipation on their faces. This might have struck a chord. I might be on the right track. However, while waiting for the response that never came, I watched helplessly as the initial favorable light flickered, faded and died, and both countenances returned to their previous total blank. Each was looking to the other for help. Two people drowning.

Within a few minutes I had drawn another half dozen sales persons. They were all getting involved, asking each other questions, and trying with great energy to discover *what in the hell this foreigner was after in their store.* In case it might help I grabbed one of the infrared lamp packages and pointed to the picture on the box, and made motions to indicate that this was *almost* what I wanted (looking upward, as if at the sun, closing my eyes, and tapping my cheeks and forehead with my index finger). It was like a game of *Charades,* or *Twenty Questions.* All eyes were fixed on me as they waited with bated breath for the next clue. A competition was emerging. Some shoving ensued to get the best position to see and hear my next clue.

An idea. I remembered that in most European languages, the adjective *follows* the noun! So it wouldn't be *Sol Lamp* (as I had just said). Rather, it would be *Lamp Sol!* Hard to believe this little "switcheroo" would make any difference, but you never know. At the rate I was going I was going to run out of time. Had to try something. So here goes: *"Lamp Sol, Lamp Sol."* I pursed my lips and flicked my upper teeth with my tongue, as if I were giving speech lessons. And I think it might've paid off. A few *oohs* and *ahs.* Some hushed conversations. *Had I made some progress?* They were almost there. They were pleading. Couldn't I help them? They just needed another word, one more clue. I had none. Once again the flames flickered and died, not even an ember. I couldn't believe it. Another sea of blank faces in front of me. I was nowhere.

121

Still, *another* idea (I was no dummy): Not "sun lamp," or even "lamp sun," but *"lamp of sun."* Maybe I needed the word "of." Lamp *of* Sun. I had seen this word lots of ways, in French and in Spanish. It was usually de or du, or I think, in Italian—da. I could try that: Lamp of Sun—*Lamp de Sol!* That should do it. My audience was still on the edge of their seats, waiting for the next clue. Who would be the one to break the code? When I was sure I had their attention. I fired away: *"Lamp de Sol, Lamp de Sol,"* and waited. Boy, this might be it. A breakthrough! Several faces in the group (which now numbered half the ground floor sales force) began to light up. But once again, only for a moment. They were whispering to one another, each hoping to be the first to solve this great mystery. They were hollering all sorts of answers at me, and more questions (none of which I could understand). But so far no one had left to get a sun lamp. They were all back to just watching and waiting. I could tell we were still at square one. They didn't have the slightest friggin idea what I wanted.

After a few moments, I tried again. This time just a little different: I'd try "New York" Italian. I would add a one vowel suffix to the first word: *"Lamp-a," "Lampa de Sol."* As soon as the words were out of my mouth, they were gone in a cloud of dust, scrambling over one another to bring me my sun lamp! By adding *one* letter—just one vowel to one word, forty people, instantaneously—for the first time, understood exactly what I had meant.

Sometimes Things Happen

The following day—on the morning of our departure we heard some disquieting news: The Navy attack squadron launching their flight of four to Licata—to relieve us, had a very expensive screw-up. Not five minutes after they were airborne the number four man in the formation came up on the radio hollering about a fire in the nose compartment of the section leader's aircraft. *"Pelican Three you're on fire! Pelican Three, you got flames coming out of your nose section!"* And I can tell you, anybody that thinks a fire at sea is the worst thing that can happen, has never had a fire in flight! When you're on fire the airplane may only stay together a matter of seconds, so an immediate ejection is the only recourse. It's standard policy throughout the military.

The wingman kept yelling and the Division Leader ordered his number three man to "Get outta there!" The canopy flew off, the ejection seat hurtled up, and an unmanned plane sliced down into the sea and was gone with a gulp. Only one problem: just after the pilot ejected, one of the other pilots got close enough to ascertain that the flames coming out of the nose section, was really one pants leg of a day-glow-orange flight suit that the pilot had packed in that nose baggage compartment. It had gotten sucked out through the hinge, and was flailing and shredding in the windstream (looking like flames). The pilot was rescued okay, but more than a little embarrassed. The Navy was out about three and a half million dollars.

A Scary Ride and More

Back on board the ship, the second week—a real tragedy. I was scheduled for the 0900 launch. At 0840 my assigned aircraft was not yet "topside" (on the flight deck). It was still being worked on, on the hangar deck. Looked like it might not be ready in time for the flight. At 0850 it finally got the "thumbs up" from Maintenance. Sgt Baldwin said I could climb in the cockpit right there on the hangar deck and ride it up on the elevator. *Whoaa. Not* a fun job! The elevator is just a bare flat 50 ft. by 50 ft. platform protruding outward from the hangar deck, skimming along just twenty feet above the turbulent water racing below. It has no walls, just a one half inch cable stretched between some spindly stanchions (to sort of make you think they'll keep you from being jarred off). Battery on I made radio contact with my wingman, Earl "the Fox" Freeman, who was already in his aircraft on the flight deck. I told him I'd be topside in a minute. In case he was launched first, I rebriefed the initial rendezvous procedures.

They shoved me out onto the elevator—backwards, finally halting me—with a hard jolt, my main gear not a foot from the edge of the elevator. (One wing and fifteen feet of fuselage completely out over the water!) With the ship rolling and pitching, I could just imagine the tread on my A4 Skyhawk tires breaking loose and starting to slide. *What a dangerous operation!* It was going to be at least a fifty foot vertical journey up to the flight deck. I waited nervously for it to begin. When the gears suddenly engaged to start the elevator on its upward travel, the whole platform dropped a good foot! I could feel the airplane fall and then bounce. Christ, I hope I'm still chocked. Okay, we're on the way up. I watched the gray, smudged and salt-streaked steel hull slide downwards past me. Half way up I realized one hand was vice-griped on the eye-level glareshield, and the other one with a similar grip, on the stick, as if I could fly myself out of any trouble that might occur on this ride up.

I GUESS I JUST WASN'T THINKING

Topside! *Made it.* The white-bright haze of the overcast morning sky, silhouetted the activity on the flight deck. But I wasn't safe yet. I spied a pig-faced tug with its grease-stained grill racing towards me. It would snatch the tow bar (already dangling from my nose gear axle), yank me off the elevator and pull me over behind my designated catapult. Once again, up here—unprotected, the wind was fearsome. The whole plane buffeted and leaned. The cats were firing test runs. The radio was blaring the launch sequence. Steam and oil vapor everywhere. *"Clunk."* The pin was in the tow bar. I was moving. I never thought I'd consider the flight deck a safe place to be, but as I moved onto it, off that damn elevator, I felt mightily relieved. Safe on the flight deck I saw the elevator shudder twice and start its slow descent back down to the hangar deck level. *Hope I don't have to ride that thing again.*

The first planes were already being strapped onto the cats. I was late—rushing, trying to catch up, trying to keep my nerves in check, trying to accomplish my interior setup, trying to spot my other guys, when I suddenly had that feeling something somewhere was wrong. One of those conclusions that starts as a vague impression and slowly gathers credibility. Whether it was aural signals, a change in the tempo, many people apparently distracted at the same time (lots of heads turned to one direction), I don't know—not sure. Then I heard the Flight Ops emergency siren howling and lots of shouting over the radio. "Hold! Hold! Launch Hold!" The launch was cancelled. Never went.

Evidently the parking brake had not been set on one of the auxiliary power units (those four-wheeled, thousand-pound electric starter units) up here on the flight deck. The carrier listed and it had rolled over the edge, plummeted forty feet straight down onto the elevator—right where I was three minutes ago, and right on top of one of the mechanics for the Navy Crusader squadron. Out of the blue, unexpected and certainly unnecessary, some mother's son, an eighteen year-old Seaman Deuce from Lancaster, Pennsylvania was our first fatality of the cruise.

Four more days of flight ops, touring my shops, and lifting weights with Dale in his workout area—since I'd relocated my weights from the forecastle down to his low engine deck. We had some good workouts. Got some good "pumps." I was eating often and beginning to gain some weight. Finally bulking up—which I told you, I'd been trying to do (unsuccessfully) since the sixth grade. Also and much more importantly, I finally got around to something that *was* worthwhile: I caught up on my delinquent letter writing to Sara (and my dear folks)! That important activity (and the browsing through old photos that it inspired) made me feel much closer to the family. During these sessions, I could almost imagine terminating my inexcusable activities ashore and just enjoy some normal times "with the guys." *Recreate in a normal fashion.* And it might be easier to stay in line in our next port—Rhodes, a small island off the coast of Turkey. Supposedly—although not now, but during the "holiday" season (July and August), was a low budget vacation spot for Brits and Germans. Inasmuch as it was now November we figured it would be pretty much abandoned. I hoped the limited expectations of Rhodes would assist me in living up to my intentions of beginning to cool it.

Chapter Twelve
THE ISLAND OF RHODES

Reflections and a Reconnoiter

I'm anxious to tell you what happened during our stay in Rhodes (which the rest of the world correctly refers to as *Rodos)*. I vaguely remembered reading about it in high school, the island of the Cyclops in Ulysses' travels. Now another traveller was about to set foot on it. Only 25 miles off the Turkish coast, but owned by Greece. Not even half the size of Puerto Rico. In fact, small enough that when we were just thirty minutes out I could still see both ends of it.

Unlike Cannes with its luxurious white marinas and golden beaches, but not as bad as Genoa and Naples with their battered trucks and rusted tankers, our first impression of Rhodes was still a little bleak. Maybe because of the weather. It was one of my unfavorite gray and windy days. Before steaming into the harbor we had been disappointedly observing the shoreline; an assortment of small villages at the base of brown dirt buttes strewn with big gray rocks. Only rare clumps of greenery. When anchored just a half mile out, we still couldn't see any encouraging activity onshore. Nothing bright or festive. Astonishingly, not a soul was visible in the dock area. It was deserted. I could just imagine a hand-drawn *Out of Business* sign hanging on the city gates. It was doubtful that much exciting would be awaiting us here. Still, there was always that chance—even this late in the year. I'd heard that no Mediterranean vacation spot could get too cold for northern European tourists. Supposedly a lot of them came here for a late summer, lower cost holiday.

I wasn't very proud of my behavior during our stay in Genoa. It had started out okay, but then I weakened and made that late night jaunt to the *Leonardo Da Vinci*. While I had escaped without the most serious transgression, it sure as hell wasn't because of any firm resolve on my part. You might think I was optimistic about extending my one port, blemish-free record, doing even better here in Rhodes. And maybe I would have, except surprisingly, I got a letter from Ardith! She was still remembering our time together in Rome, and had suggestions about future times together. We could visit the Scottish highlands in the summer, attend some plays in London, go skiing in Switzerland. I was immensely flattered knowing this refined and educated woman up there in the UK was still thinking about me. With my lack of stature, minimal accomplishments and common American ways, I had not dared to think my mediocrity would go unnoticed by one of these European women.

With the recollections of my escapades with Erica, the short but exciting meeting with Paulette, and now this letter from Ardith, my head was beginning to fill with reckless speculation. I was ready to believe that maybe—just maybe, my life was *not* already a closed book. Something else, whatever it was, may be awaiting me. It was possible that the one special woman who would finally excite me and ignite my passion, might still be out there. And if so—if this were true, from what I had seen thus far on the cruise, it was going to have its best chance of happening now—here in Europe. As indefensible and dishonorable as my behavior had been, as ashamed of it as I was (and I certainly was), I say again, I felt I had no choice but to allow myself to see strange new places, do different things, and meet new people. Knowing what blessings and good fortune I already had (a wonderful wife, four beautiful children, good friends and a fine reputation), you can be sure I spent many a worrisome late night hour questioning myself, delving into my anima—trying to nail down exactly which personal deficiency it was that held me on this course of apparently reckless experimentation.

We'd docked early. Great for the guys with liberty the first day. Once again my section wouldn't draw liberty until the second day in, and I could easily wait. (Especially the way Rhodes was looking from here.) On the other hand, as a result of everything discussed previously, as bad as it sounds, I halfway talked myself into just giving up resisting the urges. Confess a major default and go ashore—not denying the deceitful nature of my conduct. Just give fate a chance to lead me where it might. Prove me right or wrong. I knew I was deserving of all the recriminations that could be heaped upon me, but feared I was now committed to staying the course. As I surveyed the washed out, stagnant appearing harbor facilities and adjacent areas, it looked as if a lackluster in-port stay was indeed very likely. Rhodes sure didn't look like it was going to be able to provide the adventures of Rome or the French Riviera. Summer was over and a chill in the wind across the deck was remindful of this. I doubted there could many tourists here this late in the season. Sadly for me (now that I was considering perhaps drinking to my fill) I was afraid the ambiance and frivolity of the summer holidays were over. Maybe for the rest of the cruise. Maybe for the better.

I strolled across the hangar deck with Bob Harmon and Don Goft, who did have liberty today. I'd get the lowdown from them when they returned tonight, and that report would determine my itinerary for tomorrow. Even though the shoreline had looked so drab, now having given myself permission I was eager to see what Rhodes might hold for me. Bob and I joked together at the top of the ladder for a couple minutes waiting for the boat to get properly positioned below. Finally the chief looked up and waved the eager sailors and my two squadron mates to come on down the ladder. The day was young and the liberty crowd was anxious to sample the wares of this legendary island. In less than two minutes the boat was full to capacity. After a couple waves from Bob and Don, a high pitched whine from the engine, and a wide sweeping white curve, the liberty boat distanced itself from the carrier. All right, so much for that. Now it's time to set about earning my pay.

They say "It's okay to play hard if you work hard." I didn't know about the adage, but knew since I'd been really pressing my luck when I was off the ship, I was damned sure going to be super industrious while on board. More than just appear industrious, I had to get things done—meaningful things. I knew I was spending too much time either reminiscing about past in-ports or planning the next in-ports. I had better buckle down here today. The Skipper directed me to make sure all the men received a real fired-up safety presentation. Get everybody involved! And in what: That accident I told you about—the tug falling on the kid on the elevator. A freak accident on the one hand. On the other (and no question about it), *somebody's fault.* The brakes probably were not set on the power unit, or the wheels weren't chocked, or it had not been parked parallel to the edge. Three "fail-safes" that hadn't been in place. The carrier leaned, and there it went.

It was 1930 hours by the time I wrapped up the last presentation. Procedures, procedures, procedures. Boring and most of the time not critical, but skip them just once, and someone can die. Unfortunately that's the rule in aviation. Having missed chow, I made up my "Special:" a thick peanut butter sandwich, a large glass of chocolate milk, and an orange. I was still on my (stupid) weight gain program. Besides the normal meals, I now had this snack at least twice daily. I had gained six pounds so far. Don't know how it looked on my small frame, but Dale and I were hitting the weights regularly, and I think I felt stronger. (Dale *said* I looked good.)

Bob and Don popped back on board about 22:30 (10:30 p.m.). I met them in the wardroom for some coconut-cream pie, eager to hear a critique of their day's activities. And here it was: According to them, there was just one tourist beach—about a half-mile long, no sand, just gray round pebbles; not even a quarter mile from where the liberty boats tied up. It was not crowded and those that were there were mostly overweight, gray haired European senior citizens on a cheaper, off-season vacation. The beach was directly across the street from four "so-so" hotels. They said there was a small downtown area (with Cyclops statues for sale everywhere) that could use some modernizing, and its empty streets gave further testimony to the lacking midsummer crowds. However, some good news: They had seen two large tour groups in town—a British group led by an effeminate guy in brown suede shoes, and a German party led by a giant woman with wild hair.

"Yeah, so did anything special happen; any good places to go?"

Don shot a look at Bob, and Bob responded that he met one German girl—Ingrid. Pretty nice too. Her group had been on the closest beach to our dock, right in front of one of the older hotels. They suspected she'd be there tomorrow and recommended I forget town and just hang out around the beach. According to the guys Ingrid didn't speak English very well, but they thought she should be checked out further. That was the extent of my briefing. They obviously had not had a rousing time (and those two bachelors always found where things were happening).

Got a good night's sleep and had a great breakfast. A new day—*my* day. My section is off-duty. Made the second liberty boat and at 0940 hours was plowing towards shore, ready to seek my fortune. I was carrying a small bag containing some necessary toiletries and a couple changes. (Just in case.) To my delight, the sky was clearing. It was going to be a better day. Same old ten-minute, rough, always wet trip to shore. Tried to balance myself in the middle of the boat to stay away from the crusted salt and grease on the gunnels. I was wearing that same neat black cashmere sweater I'd purchased two doors down from the Spanish Steps. Had my own gray ascot this time, but even to me it looked phony. (Back in the bag.)

From the dock (for once) it would only be a short walk—about 200 yards along a narrow curving road, to the small beach area where Bob and Don had come upon Ingrid. The sidewalk I was using was actually the paved-over top of the harbor's sea wall. Clumps of dried kelp hung off the edge attracting their share of flies. A worn smooth, skin-oil-glazed pipe rail—originally there for safety, now supported a half dozen ragamuffin kids with fishing lines (no poles). Don't know about fish, but the water lapping just below them contained its share of trash. Just like the guys had said: ahead of me to the left I saw four small (only two to three stories high) wooden hotels. They were set back quite a distance from the road, each with an expansive, table-flat, barely grassed front lawn. Not a single shrub or flower bed (and appeared to be in desperate need of watering). They were unpretentious but respectable appearing establishments, each with its own inviting terrace. Easy to imagine they catered to the same people each year. The street—which continued past the hotels, separated them from the pebbled beach now commencing to my right. There was very little traffic, just a few small weird-looking cars crawling by. I couldn't see a single restaurant. Maybe the type of vacationers this place attracted availed themselves of the most economical "holiday" packages, which I later learned, offered breakfast and required them to take their evening meal in the hotel dining room.

I was disappointed at how many middle-aged (in fact downright *elderly*) people were on the beach. They may have been from England or Germany, but they looked like they were off farms in the Ukraine; pale skin, bowed and bent, most overweight, varicose veins, gray hair. *Whew!* This was no Cote d'Azur I could see that. Adults—men and women alike, were doing full-clothing changes right on the beach. They took turns holding up large towels around their spouses during the critical steps. Compared to other Mediterranean beaches, this one was not at all picturesque. Then again, I might not be in the best area. That's happened before and will again. In keeping with the plan, I strolled the beaches in front of the hotels. Tried to look just like any other relaxing vacationer, enjoying the warm sun (thank you) and the fresh air. Glancing out to sea I could understand how the beach goers might wonder what that strange gray shape was on the horizon. If I was lucky, I would be being mistook as some eligible European guy. (But not likely)

Found Her

1330: *Bingo!* I stumbled on Ingrid. No question about it. That's German I'm hearing, she's blond, and with a black bikini. After three not-necessary trips to an ill-stocked concession stand, which took me right past her and her girlfriend's blanket, I stopped and told them I was a shipmate of Bob and Don that they met yesterday. The guys were right. Ingrid (who was the prettiest) did not speak much English, but hopefully enough (considering I spoke no German). She certainly did not seem to be "on the make." Our chat was forced and her girlfriend didn't speak *any* English, which made it even more awkward. I hoped to improve the conversation by feigning an interest in learning something about the German language. Ingrid smiled and nodded that she would be more than willing to help.

Having been introduced to Latin in high school, and remembering the strange grammar (*agricola, agricolae, agricolaram?*) I decided to find out if in German, a noun had a different suffix depending on whether it was the subject or object of a sentence. To discover this, I would ask Ingrid to give me two sentences in German: *The man kicks the dog*, and then *The dog bites the man*. With these two examples I would be able to listen carefully to the word *man* when used as the subject of the sentence, and then see if it was altered when used as the object of the sentence. When I asked her the first sentence I received an understandably non-complimentary, quizzical expression. I then realized, without her knowing my grammar objective, this sentence must have sounded real dumb. With not much enthusiasm, and waning interest in me as a student of much potential, she responded, *"Der Mann tritt den Hund."*

I guess this was getting boring enough for her girlfriend who excused herself right there and then. Seeing this reaction to the first sentence, and worried about my chances of clearing it up, I couldn't believe I still went ahead with the second sentence. Ingrid—now sure she was in the throes of being picked up by a complete jerk, snapped back, *"Die Hund bisse der Mann."* I could see she had lost all interest in giving me any further German lessons. The subject was changed. I rallied somewhat in the next hour, being as polite and friendly as possible. About four, she decided she had best join her travel companion. We bid a warmer than expected farewell, and I was able to arrange a dinner date for that evening. Her bus would be dropping her off right in front of this beach at seven-thirty. *Great, we'd meet right here.* I guess I kind've took a break from my search for that special woman. Could tell Ingrid wasn't going to be her. But it'll be a chance to practice my jargon and technique (in case in one of these Mediterranean seaports I do spy one)!

Uh-oh, one oversight. With hampered communications and being preoccupied with just winning points, I had failed to find out which hotel she was staying in. You see (for you present day Lotharios) at one point in time (right now for me) in most places in Europe, and I was sure—here, an unregistered man didn't just come waltzing into a hotel and march over to the elevator (or in this case start up the steps). We're talking serious verification—passport checks and showing room keys. This could be a problem. What to do? I wasn't sure which hotel Ingrid had gone into. She started out towards the one on the left, but may have veered to the middle one after I quit watching her. Could be staying in either one. Geez— should've watched her all the way. Could be an expensive mistake.

I was feeling a little tired and didn't know how long the evening was going to be. I had a few hours to kill, and knew I could use a rest. Should I go back to the ship? I'd be able to get some good rest in my stateroom, but what a hassle getting there and back. To get my rest this afternoon and make sure there were no unnecessary obstacles tonight (in case things worked out) I decided to get a room here in town. Just picked the one in the middle, and it wasn't too expensive, but two credit card crunches later I wasn't feeling all that smart. Tried to sleep—knew it would be for the best. Mostly just laid there and hypothesized.

Eight o'clock and not looking too good. No bus and no Ingrid. Wait a minute, I think that's it coming now. It was and she was on it, but with some bad news for me. Without a translator, the best I could decipher was that there was another activity scheduled for her group this evening, that hadn't been on their printed schedule. And no way she could get out of it. I was proud of myself though—kept my cool. Managed to appear only mildly disappointed. Ingrid surprised me by suggesting we just delay our dinner date till tomorrow.

Decided to spend the waning hours of daylight exploring the far end of the island. The road in front of the hotels continued (with even diminishing attractions) for several hundred yards, became unlit, and made a surprise U turn down the other side of the island. In view of its lack of promise, not sure why, I continued walking. Dark now, but give it a chance. Surprise of all surprises—about a half mile down the completely deserted road I came upon a really first class resort area. *How in the hell did Bob and Don miss this side of the island?* It had bigger, flashier, and more modern-looking hotels. Surely this was the place for the more affluent vacationers and someone of my curiosities. I stopped in front of one large, gleaming white, jet set hotel. It must've had 200 rooms. Unfortunately, as I scanned the front of the building, I noticed only one out of ten rooms were lit up. *Not a good sign.* But then again, probably normal. It was October and the season was over.

Decided to check it out. Entered as casually as I could (having already had some practice today). After gaining some confidence and feeling up to the task I sauntered up to the reception desk. Started with a "Good Evening" and followed up with some small talk—weather and soccer, and the nice points of the island (insofar as I could think of any). Remembering my discouraging view from out front (no lights in the rooms), I asked what their occupancy rate was, suggesting that in this gray, off season, it might be way down. "Oh no sir, we're almost full." (*Full? He's saying "full," after what I had observed.*)

"Well where was everybody" I asked. "The lobby and restaurant look deserted."

"They're all up in their rooms sir," was the reply.

Remembering all the darkened rooms, without trying to be humorous, my response was: "Oh yeah, well if so, they're all up there developing film." (This was way before digital cameras.)

I didn't spend the night in the hotel. I retreated to the ship. Would have to be back on board at 0800 in the morning anyway. And I needed time to find somebody to switch liberty with me for tomorrow evening. I was hoping *that* dinner date would materialize. On board, I owned up to the fact that I had found Ingrid. Bob kidded me about *stealing his girl.* I was a little worried about him stealing her back during the day tomorrow while I was stuck on the ship. Checked with Tripp. *What a Guy!* He'd cancel his evening's liberty tomorrow so I could go ashore. (He was in a conversation with the "Strep" I mentioned earlier, regarding pilot's coming down with sore throats when scheduled for a night launch.)

A Dinner I Won't Forget

Accomplished a lot during the day. Took a late afternoon rest and caught the 1900 liberty boat to shore. Good thing too, because Ingrid was right on time! She looked happy to see me and took my hand almost immediately. *Could be a good sign.* We decided to eat in town, so perused the beach hotels, finally choosing the center (and most upscale) one. The right side of its ground floor was completely open, displaying a spacious and well appointed banquet hall. Diners could look out at the sea over a low, carved stone wall holding a ring of colorful potted plants. White-jacketed waiters were scurrying about, covering the round tables with peach colored linens, setting the silver and putting out crystal. Classical music was coming from somewhere. (Glad I was wearing a coat and tie.)

It looked as if it was going to be (for once) one of those nights when things just go right. As soon as we entered the maître d' rushed over, greeted me with more respect than I deserved and escorted us to a choice table. The ordering went smoothly. Asparagus soup and then the always acceptable avocados stuffed with baby shrimp. A chilled beer for me and a bottle of Tavel on order. More folks filing in. (Good thing we got here when we did.) We both decided to go with the plat du jour—veal marsala. The whole meal went great. The food was just fine and Ingrid seemed to be enjoying herself, and the waiters were refreshingly pleasant. Gratefully but undeservedly, it was an elegant dining experience.

Halfway through the meal an incident occurred which could not have done more to bail me out after my previous afternoon's (apparently stupid) German language lesson. A scruffy dog had somehow gotten up onto the terrace. When the Maitre d' spied it his first reaction was panic, but quickly regained his composure and attempted to conceal his distress from the diners. He began some urgent signaling to the closest waiters, but it was as if the mutt was intercepting these signals; trotting this way then that way, just managing to outmaneuver his pursuers. The staff appeared to believe their concern and frantic efforts were going unnoticed by the diners. They tried to carry out their other duties as if there were not a ridiculous farce unfolding. They came and went with their silver trays held aloft. The ones who passed close enough to the mutt to have some influence, either hissed or shook a foot in his direction.

Ingrid and I (and by now most all the other diners) were doing our best to avoid breaking out laughing. Finally one waiter realized firmer action was required. He started straight for the mutt—who upon seeing this, backed up under a table, pushing the low hanging cloth further under with his backside. A second waiter anticipating the dog's exit on the other side of the table, ran around to position himself there. When the dog's backside began to protrude out the hanging linen on the other side of the table, he hauled back a leg and booted him! I looked at Ingrid. She looked at me. I said, "Der Mann tritt den Hund!" The look on her face—it was worth a million! But more: As a result of the kick the dog shot forward, back out the front side of the table, smack into the other waiter. Alarmed and confused the dog took a quick chomp out of his pants leg. I looked again to Ingrid. She knew what was coming: "Die Hund bisse der Mann!" It was great, to this day I don't know that I've ever laughed as hard.

The meal was a success, thanks in part to the dog incident. I felt relaxed and was not concerned about the evening's eventualities. This was fortunate, since while we were having a Cointreau in the hotel lounge, in comes her travel companion—beat after a group dinner at a monastery somewhere. The two of them had a short conversation, and Ingrid said they were going to call it a day. In a sweet "Good-Night," I thought I heard, *Don't worry, there will be another time for us.* Trying not to seem like I was rushing things, I harmlessly suggested a dinner date for the following evening. No way I could come in during the early part of the day, I'd be paying back Tripp for tonight.

Another Dinner and the Crash

Back on board and after a good night's sleep, I was ready to "turn-to," and would have no excuses not to get some things done. The tension that abounds during our at-sea periods (with life and death flight operations going on) is mercifully absent, in port, the tempo is reduced, and at any given time half the people are off the ship. All this being true I was able to feel relaxed (in spite of all else I had going on). Made my usual tour of the shops, spending about an hour in each one. Found a minimum of "snafu's" and the troops had only a few personal problems that needed looking into. (Each of which I made detailed notes of, to use later when I met with the Admin department OIC.) Did spend an extended period of time in the Electric Shop, where they had a mysterious problem with the AC (alternating current) system in one of our aircraft. There was sufficient voltage, but it would unexpectedly vary way out of limits. I made several suggestions, of which (thank you God) one led to the cause.

The above finished, I still had time to have a short workout with Dale—who was obsessed with developing his calves. He had this stupid theory that if someone watched the muscles while he worked them and kept up an out loud running commentary on them, there would be better results. He kept asking, "Can you see them working? Can you see them pumping?" About 1500 hours I discovered that the guy I was going to swap duty days with had come back early and I would have been able to go ashore at noon! No problem. Better to have stayed on board. Felt good about having made the contribution. Was beginning to feel tired, snuck away to the stateroom and was able to take an hour nap. Awoke a little before 5 p.m., dressed, and made another of my now too-frequent trips to the liberty boat ladder.

Met Ingrid in her hotel lobby, and she looked great wearing an open-necked sequined black sweater, but I noticed for the first time, that she did not have good teeth. (Me either for that matter.) Found out also, that this was going to be her last night on Rhodes. So where to go tonight? She had an idea, and a good one as far as she was concerned. Seems there was a neat little Turkish restaurant about thirty kilometers out of town—up in the hills somewhere. I hadn't yet had a reason to check into the taxi situation. However, I could see that Ingrid was intent on going to this restaurant, and I was going to do my best to get us there. I checked with the concierge, and in a few minutes we had our own chauffeured (not new) Mercedes limousine. Five minutes outside the city an initially reasonable route had deteriorated into a rutted, barely two-lane road, winding and difficult to navigate at dusk. It would not be a fun drive if you had to do it yourself. I wasn't sold on our chauffeur, but forced myself to ignore his lack of application, in order to concentrate on what Ingrid was trying to say. With the language barrier, even a simple conversation bogged down quickly. It took us about a half hour to make the trip.

The restaurant was indeed quaint, but evidently word-of-mouth travels quickly, as half the tourists on the island were availing themselves of this "unknown" authentic taberna. I made the best of the meal (fish) and my share of the wine. We were there to have a good time and we did. We finished eating and it was still early, only nine-forty-five. Outside I was at first unable to locate our chauffeur. Finally spied him about a hundred yards up the road with a gaggle of the other drivers. He was engaged in some animated story telling. I waved and yelled until I got his attention. Not too enthusiastically he signaled with a beau geste wave that indicated he'd recognized me, and *don't worry he'd make this his last story*. It was a good ten minutes before he finished, and trotted over to where our limo was parked. We were in the car and on our way back to town, and maybe an extended evening.

Our chauffeur had not been studying any driving courses while we ate, that's for sure. Although I was bent over Ingrid, listening and whispering, and working like hell, I could not avoid sensing the road noise and became concerned regarding our speed. I craned my neck to see the speedometer. Only 100 kilometers an hour, but too fast for the blind curved road we were on (and us with no seat belts). I tapped the driver on the shoulder and pointed at the speedometer. He nodded *Yup, that was a speedometer.* Back to Ingrid. Three minutes couldn't have passed before there was the sudden stab of brakes and the awful screech you fear. In the split second before the impact I yanked my head up, to see emblazoned in the headlight glare—about six feet in front of the hood ornament, a gigantic silky brown, *horse's ass!*

Thud! We hit it head on (ass-on)! The car snapped in a half-turn towards the center of the road. The amount of turn stayed to the left, but the car just skidded sideways ahead in our lane, snagging and almost tipping, threatening to go over on its side in the next half second. I could feel it was going to happen. This meaningless deduction in a quarter second. And no seat belts! I already had one arm around Ingrid. No time to speak. In this same half second I thought of a plan. If we could move our feet and legs towards the downward tipping right side of the car, we could try to walk/quickly crawl up the side, and then the roof, during the roll. If it were only one roll maybe, and not too fast of a roll. I actually—stupidly, had time to contemplate this—which possibly could have been executed by a carefully trained stunt man. But as you may well imagine, I was not up to the task. When that Mercedes started rolling, I never did figure out which way was up or down, or have a moment's clue about which way to move to avoid injury, or do a single thing to save my life, except close my eyes and holler. Then all was quiet and dark, and smelled bad, like gas fumes, burnt rubber, and hot metal.

We were upside down! I could tell that. The wheels were spinning. The engine was running. (That wasn't good.) Half the windows were out. I didn't hurt anywhere. (I think.) There was glass everywhere. Ingrid and I were wrapped up in a ball on the felt-lined ceiling. She was moving and talking a blue streak, although I had no idea what she was saying. I tried to move. My left foot was stuck. It didn't hurt, but I couldn't retrieve it. My left shoe was clamped tightly between the driver's side doorpost and the edge of his seat. There was almost no pressure on my foot. The stiff leather sole was protecting it. If I could just twist it I would be able to pull it out. *Fire, what about fire?* With a yank, my foot was out of the shoe. So much for a neat pair of cream-colored crocodile shoes (that—like my hieroglyphic linen blazer, I had bought when I was stationed in Japan). I couldn't get either of the back doors open. We exited through where the rear window should have been. The driver was inside yelling, and *his* door

137

was wide open. Suddenly he realized he was free and crawled out on his hands and knees. He had a broken finger for sure (since it was pointing back at his elbow). He kept yelling. The engine was still running. It turned off with the key.

More confusion popped up on this previously deserted country road. A third hysterically screaming guy appears out of nowhere to join us, near the dead horse, and our Mercedes on its roof. Don't know why, but he's really frantic. Ingrid, now looking at me very seriously, says, "I think we are very happy." *Happy, my ass, my evening could be over!* (Later I found out that with her limited English she had meant to say "lucky," not "happy.") The deranged newcomer is at my side, has ahold of my sleeve, and is tugging me to come with him. I can't understand a word he is saying. There's no alternative, so without a clue I let him begin dragging me into the darkness. It's then I spy *another* car a ways back the road—also upside down. I didn't know there was another car involved. I had only seen the horse. What the hell had happened here?

Shit, there's a kid in that car! I could see a young boy in the back seat. A puddle of gas was burning on the ground right in front of the car. The crazy guy runs up and stomps on it, which does nothing. He runs back to me frantically gesturing at the side of the car, and of course I know the problem. He can't get the friggin door open. But neither can I. It was a big car, but I tried rocking it. *Surprise!* It rocked easily, being almost perfectly balanced on the center of its roof. I holler at him to pull on the door while I do my luckily not difficult impression of Superman, easily tilting and then holding the side of the car up. While apparently amazed at my strength, he yanks the door open, and the kid clambers out—amazingly calm considering the accident. The crazy guy, who I guessed was the driver, grabs the kid and runs about a hundred feet from the car. Keerist! I didn't need this. *How about my evening?* By now several cars had stopped. As the participants pieced the story together, the guy with the kid had been traveling some distance in front of us. He tried to avoid the horse and lost control of his car. The horse stayed in the road until it got rammed by us. *Whew!*

Having gained enough composure to begin considering *what now?* I gave a hopeful "everything's okay" glance over to Ingrid. Fortunately, she was now looking reasonably calm and (please God) just might be up to concluding the evening in the anticipated fashion. Tiny pieces of broken glass in her hair were reflecting the moonlight, as if she was wearing some kind of squashed tiara. You can be sure, in spite of this mishap I was still ready to make the best out of what remained of the night. This meant— first, I had to secure us a ride back to town. While retrieving my left shoe from the limousine and answering questions from new arrivals, I was able to get one of them to let us ride back to town. Being so preoccupied with getting a ride back to town, I barely paid any attention to the crazy guy with the kid. He was jabbering to me a-mile-a-minute. With the help of an English speaking local I was made to understood that the boy's father, who evidently was someone special here on the island, would want to thank me. I had to visit tomorrow—tomorrow for lunch. At the same time, he was shoving a card at me with a raised gold inscription that read *Konstantinos II*, and listed an address. I nodded okay, mostly to get rid of him. Can't get bogged down with that now. Plus I wasn't even sure I could get off the ship tomorrow. Let's take one day (or night) at a time here.

The ride into town was devoid of any romantic conversation or foreplay. (Easy since I was in the front seat and Ingrid was in the back.) I was wondering how this all would pan out. Now my left foot did hurt, and I had a bad cut on my right wrist. But I was still hoping. We strode into our hotel like celebrities—survivors, fresh from the front. We were above menialities at this point. She retrieved her key, took my hand, and we were on our way *straight to her room.* No invitations, no explanations, no charades. I don't know if she had decided the excitement of the evening just called for finishing it up this way, or if she felt like she owed me something after my three day investment, or if she had it planned from the beginning, or if it was just the end of her vacation. I don't know.

The room was small, certainly a package deal, and wasn't air conditioned. The window just above the sidewalk was propped open. The one yellowed ceiling light was not mood setting, and the walls were pale green. Looked like a room in a Tijuana medical clinic. Not in there thirty seconds and *Bingo,* her skirt is sliding down her legs to the floor and her sweater is coming off over her head. Saw her wince as she pulled it over her shoulders. There were still shards of glass in it. Looking at her there I could better admire her cute (but somewhat odd) figure. She was short-waisted—in fact almost *no* waist. And she would not have needed a bra for support; her breasts were not full or bulbous. Instead they were just small pointy cones, unusually wide apart and facing even further to the sides. (Amazing I hadn't noticed this on the beach.) They were delightful and I could imagine fondling and kissing them. The gray nylon panties she was wearing were ordinary, but they were sumptuously packed—front and back. Even in the dim light, just below them I could see the soft, fine blond hair on her thighs.

Studying the silk undies, staring at that well tanned little belly and the puffy mound of her most private part, I was thrilled to think I felt myself becoming aroused. (It may be that there's something with these German girls.) We spent about ten minutes in the bathroom, Ingrid now naked and me in my hopefully (praying) beginning to fill undershorts. I tried to lightly swipe off the tiny glass particles stuck all over her. They wouldn't wipe off. I had to pick them out one by one. Got most of them out. Enough of that. She was into the bedroom and the ugly light was snapped out.

I could see it was going to be up to me. She certainly wasn't the aggressive type. (No Erica here.) So I started my contribution; the things I thought would be the most arousing to her (and me). After a few minutes I was greatly relieved to feel some fullness right where I would need it. Must be working, she began moving rhythmically in apparent greater anticipation. I threw one leg over her and propped myself up on my hands and knees above her. Before attempting an insertion, I reached down and snuck a feel of myself; *maybe*—just maybe! I gave her one long kiss on the mouth. That done, with one hand I reached down to assist an insertion, *and realized it was gone!* During the two-second kiss it had disappeared. I was completely de-armed, stalled—sick. Again!

Certainly what transpired, as intimate as it was would not qualify for the legal definition of "penetration." Whether or not she was fully aware of my deficiency seemed not to matter. She was evidently on a mission and put everything into it. She was going to take her pleasure come hell or high water, irrespective of me. When she finally reached it (talk about no waist) her hips went right up under her armpits. For me, as you might imagine that while I was grateful as hell for that, I was way more than a little discouraged by the same non-performance I had lived through many dozens of times since my wedding night. Here on the cruise, after the slight breakthrough with Erica, I thought there was a chance some European sexual miracle might be in the offing. I dared to think that maybe, just maybe I was about to have a life. After tonight, perhaps not.

Again (and as usual) I laid there after the act, feeling as if I was in the wrong place. Like I should be somewhere else and the sooner I was there the better. Should I just go back to the ship, now? Couldn't shake it. Finally—I guess about two, I got up, dressed, tip-toed out, and caught a liberty boat reserved for the shore patrol guys (who I was getting to know real well by now). Was real tired by the time I got to my stateroom. Slept till nine the next morning, and then couldn't remember if it was a duty day or liberty. Let's see: First day in port I worked. Second day had liberty, met Ingrid, dinner date got screwed up. Third day, shoulda worked but switched with Tripp to go to dinner with Ingrid. Fourth day, my liberty day, Turkish restaurant and the car accident. Yeah, I should stay on board today. (And God knows I feel like I should. Need to!)

Lunch With the King

About 1100—by accident, straightening my clothes and going through my trousers, I found the card from last night. The one the crazy guy had given me—with the kid's father's address on it. Wasn't really sure I was sufficiently interested to go to the trouble of getting someone to stand by for me while I did lunch with his dad. But you never know, it might add more color to what has turned out to be a reasonably unanticipated colorful in-port stay. In spite of a good start on a couple maintenance projects, after mulling it over and reflecting on the driver's plea that I meet the boy's father—*Hell, I'm gonna go.* Just need to find someone to standby for me for a couple hours. Got ahold of Tripp (again), before he'd left. In fact, he wasn't planning on going ashore until 1800. Great! He'd standby for me till then (without a "pay-back")!

Ashore, it was only about 100 yards to the taxi station. I had the father's address, but evidently it was not a trip any of them wanted. Either they weren't familiar with the area, or there was another deterrent. In any case they were flustered. It took several tries before I was halfway sure I had a driver who wanted to take me to this address. A long ride, but finally, upon arriving—*wow.* This address is bound to be someplace special. Even though I could not see over a high white stucco wall, covered with ivy and fuchsia flowers, I could imagine a large well-kept estate behind it. And I was right. An amply built, stern-faced guard grilled my driver then swung open a huge wooden gate, exposing a spacious, manicured lawn, sloping uphill—at least 100 feet, to a stone cottage (a *large* stone cottage). There appeared to be nothing behind the cottage, as if it were perched on a cliff. The driver pulled in about ten feet and stopped. I was out and he wasted no time in making his exit.

A little scary. Standing alone inside the gate, scanning the expansive lawn in front of the house I noticed a half dozen men lounging at various locations. They appeared to have little to do, almost as if they were just stationed there. Took a breath and started up the drive towards the house. None of the men approached me (although they all were watching my every step). There was a wide shaded wood porch with several pieces of summer furniture spanning its length. With some apprehension I mounted the steps to the front door—which was wide open. In fact every door and window in the house appeared to be open, attesting to the wonderfully balmy day it was. The sun was brilliant and the air was skin temperature. My kind of day.

The guy who met me after a short wait in the foyer, that contained an upright shelf filled with old stone and metal artifacts, was not the father. While he wasn't dressed like a butler, he acted like one. Fortunately he appeared to be expecting me, because I could see he wasn't a guy to be fooled with. I was invited in and guided past a step-down, to a long terra-cotta-paved hallway that led to the rear of the house. To my right was a spacious room furnished with large and comfy looking wicker chairs and loveseats, each with big cotton cushions. The room was full of light from the wall of windows that opened onto that front porch. Beyond it, and now a little further down the hallway, I was able to see the rear wall of the house, which was all glass—about four sets of French double-doors, side by side. Through them I could see a stone veranda (which also appeared to span the whole width of the back of the cottage). Beyond it's railing lay a breath-taking view of the Mediterranean. Somehow (though not through my calculations) I had arrived at a much higher elevation than the city. The cottage was high on a cliff overlooking a private lagoon that tourists would have killed for. (I could now see our first impression of Rhodes had been the result of a too limited sampling.)

A family was on the terrace. Upon seeing me they stopped what they were doing, came quickly inside, and spent five minutes showering me with praise and thanks. Talk about nobility, aristocracy, earned status. They say when you see it you recognize it, and there was no question about it. From their attire, mannerisms, and surroundings, I could see these were privileged people. Suddenly it dawned on me, remembering the name on the card: *Konstantinos II*! I was about to have lunch with the recently exiled King Constantine of Greece! I was on guard immediately, *way out of my league here*. But from them—for the next two hours, came no statement or question (or even a mild reprimand of the help) without a kind expression. They had no doubts or fears, you could see that. The father was about 35 years of age, handsome with straight black hair. His wife was similarly attractive, also with straight (and long) black hair. Both spoke perfect English. We went over the previous night several times, then dropped it for good. I was in for a wonderful, leisurely Mediterranean midday meal on their elevated veranda. The wrought iron railing next to the table was fifty feet above the first rock ledge below, and the water far beneath it. Looking down, around, and at the host and hostess, for sure I had never been in such special surroundings. I felt the corner of our turquoise table cloth flicking against my ankle in the soft breeze. The meal started with (of course) a Greek salad, then a plate of sliced meats and a wide assortment of breads. Dessert was a fruit plate containing at least two fruits I didn't recognize. Throughout the meal they kept my glass full of a light Rosé Greek wine. *I was living that other life I had up till now only fantasized about.*

Finally it came time to go, as I knew it must. I hated to see the afternoon end. I was in a different, uniquely polished world. I could feel it in the air wafting past my skin. I had been whisked high and away from the world I knew. My host and hostess had been so gracious, so well educated. They had spoken with such awareness about current world affairs (and *the arts*, again). I only hoped I'd held up my end of the conversations. While bidding farewell in the foyer I saw a uniquely hammered silver bracelet on that shelf with other artifacts. I couldn't help admiring it. The father, noticing my attraction, reached down, picked it off, *and gave it to me!* A gift I would always treasure—found in a cave on the island over a hundred years ago (and being worn as I type this).

On the way down the hill my heart was pounding, my mind was racing, and my feet were flying. I was hardly touching the ground. Didn't ask for a cab to be called, or even think about the distance. I was still euphoric from my experience. I'll jog now and then think about a cab when I get to the bottom. Any future in-port adventures would have even more to measure up to now. After *this* day, I doubted I would have the strength to refrain from searching for more of whatever like this might still be out there.

Chapter Thirteen
FACING UP TO IT

Stating the Obvious

I started out rationalizing my indiscretions ashore as periods of exploration whose time had come. Unavoidable excursions to avenge my missed youth. *But that excuse just isn't holding up.* There is a distressing pattern to every one of them (which I'm sure you've noticed). They end up not just being limited to exciting new escapades on foreign soil. Rather, each has had an added twist: *a real or fabricated interest in and pursuit of yet another woman.* I'm ready to admit that most of the energy being spent is not as I originally claimed: because of an understandable effort to make up for the fun times I missed during my high school days, or even a refusal to give in to the fact that my life is a closed book. No, I'm at last (better late than never) ready to confess it is because of a third calamity; something much more worrisome. Something that radically skewed my perception of the world, every social situation, and every other man.

And what would that be (not that you haven't already noticed)? You remember the narration of my late night disaster with Connie? Well as I mentioned earlier, *I encountered the same crushing inability on my wedding night with Sara.* (Thank God for some unknown friend who had previously told her this occurrence is not uncommon on one's wedding night.) I concluded that as fate would have it, I'd matched myself up twice—two times in a row, with a woman with whom there was *no chemistry.* (And critically I'd made the last one permanent!) If an evening with my wife was leading up to an intimate union, early on, rather than being filled with anticipation, I would feel a justifiable concern and approach the hour filled with fears of failure. Fortunately as the years passed I was able to improve to a just-tolerable performance (about two hits in five "at bats"), that my wife mercifully seemed satisfied with. But certainly not me. I was all but mortally wounded. I couldn't do other than cling to the desperate hope that somewhere out there was the one woman with the *right* chemistry, who would unlock my manhood and save my life. She was my Holy Grail. I just had to *find* her!

My Excuses, No Matter How Truly I Felt Them

With alarm I now recognize that *because* of this devastating deficiency, no matter what the circumstances or situation, I was viewing almost every female creature (and I mean the woman in the car next to me at a red light) as a potential sexual partner, who would perhaps be the one I would finally be able to satisfy. And I'm just about sure the enslavement to this *is specifically because of my inability to do so.* I realize now my apparent womanizing springs from an inordinate lust, the strength of which— enflamed and heightened by my impotence (there I said it) eclipses that of a normally potent male. That man has no reason to give a thought to my kind of pain, fitful longing, and embarrassment. He'd never feel the fury of my hunger to one day triumph and emerge from this bitter blight. He would have no reason to be constantly searching as you see me doing. And remember, this was 1965—decades before "E.D." was the subject of nonchalant conversation and the all too familiar Viagra ads. Now—at this time, it was untitled and not discussed. Something without understanding or treatment. Each sorely affected man left to suffer his own fears, frightful encounters and recriminations—alone, *holding the knowledge that he is incapable of consummating any romantic endeavor.*

Could There Be Hope

Shamefully, throughout my marriage I could not banish the thought that someday—somehow, I'd come face to face with that one woman; the bones of whose face, the penetrating gaze of whose eyes, whose words and moves, the silkiness of whose skin, would provide the stimulant that had thus far been lacking. Sighting of such a female person had already occurred twice. (I'm sure there's more, but unfortunately only two such temptresses come to mind at the moment.) Once, all flights cancelled and snowbound in an unheated Wichita airport, it was a hazel-eyed, braided, honey-haired, too-thin, rock band singer, who I could not take my eyes off. The other, on a dock in the Bahamas—a glowingly innocent, fair skinned and freckled, red-headed newlywed, oozing succulence and appearing so ready to be taken, sitting with her bashful (and lucky) husband. Both times, even though passing yards away it was close enough to have entered their field of entrancement, causing me to lose track of my gait and whatever thoughts had previously been in my head. I reveled in the sensation of their demanding aura tugging on me, and when our eyes met I felt a strange, wonderfully powerful warm force and fullness arising in my loins; the extent of which left no doubt as to its mission and what I would be more than capable of.

Irrespective of the overpowering need to—even if only once, experience what every other man has, trying to portray my activities as somehow justified, something that would not now or later affect my marriage, would make no sense to any of my friends, or probably anybody (especially my wife)! However, if I'm ever going to have my manhood awakened, for sure my best chance is now—on this cruise; traipsing the Continent, just an arm's length from these foreign appearing, foreign speaking, foreign thinking, mysterious European women. (Though true enough, so far on this cruise it hadn't happened; not with Erica, not with Paulette, and not with Ingrid.) And while I'm facing up to it, irrespective of the validity of my analyses and my inability to curtail my quest, I'm appearing (even to myself) as a person with no conscience. I know my behavior would be worthy of unanimous condemnation. How come I don't see it that way? Even if it were completely out of my control—wholly unable to refrain from (which I believe it is), why is my remorse insufficient to deter further experimentation? If not for what this infidelity represents to my good wife—who certainly deserves no such treatment, how about my children? Did they deserve a father like this. A case could be made I am not mentally sound.

Chapter Fourteen
ISTANBUL

Tea Time at the Hilton

As usual we would be moored about a mile out, and also as usual—when the anchor hit the water and the ship heeled, most of us were topside checking out a another new shoreline. Squinting through a bright haze we saw a strange landscape; an expansive horizon of rose tile roofs, glinting gold domes, and a hundred minarets poking skyward. A large city that seemed to stretch from horizon to horizon. Built on high rolling terrain it was split and divided by two large rivers and a bunch of smaller tributaries. Looked like it could be real easy to get lost in Istanbul. First-timers like me had some doubts about what restrictions we would have put upon us in this strange city. Turkey is a predominately Muslim country and although it tolerates an Orthodox church, it still had some strange civil laws on the books—drawn directly from the Quran. I know that now and am surprised the Navy didn't schedule some "appropriate behavior" briefings for us before letting us go ashore. (Lucky we didn't have a lot of guys get in trouble.)

First day in my section had the duty and I was glad, since it would give me a chance right off to earn my keep and impress Major Burnham. I'd get to work verifying the waiting and completed work orders and fire up the men (while watching most my buddies trot to the liberty boat ladder). The second day was my day off and although I had planned to stay on board and work (and in so doing pay back Tripp for the day he lent me in Naples), I weakened and ventured ashore. Downtown (I think it was downtown) it didn't look that different, at least where I was hanging out. Most women on the street weren't wearing veils or in that long black garb. It wasn't difficult getting a drink and the sidewalks advertised lots of "shows upstairs." I say it didn't look different, well maybe it did a little. And Bob said that last night he saw a guy with an ugly looking automatic weapon on just about every corner, and several on the sidewalk in front of the El Al (Israeli Airlines) office.

In addition to (and in contrast with) the many mosques and orthodox churches, Istanbul had some ultra modern hotels, chock full of exciting people. In my wanderings I came upon the Hilton and decided to investigate. Evidently every Sunday afternoon was "Tea Time" and I had picked a good time to be there. Lots of I guess Turkish, but western looking, frosted haired, large earringed, middle aged socialites with darkly painted lips. They appeared to be there catching up on the latest gossip and doing some men-watching. Or in any case that's how I saw it. The area was not well lit (they could have started the film anytime). The carpeting was a deep maroon color and the tables were black. A strange night-clubish atmosphere at two in the afternoon. As usual I was alone. By now you can see I must prefer that. It has its good points and its drawbacks.

While seated at one of those small, round black tables and imagining the possibilities that this occasion might afford me, I was jolted back to reality by a loud, "Hey, how ya doing." A Navy officer from the ship, that I'd only seen once or twice; a supply officer from the ship's staff. I was sure he must have ulterior motives. We were not only not friends, we weren't even acquaintances. Our sole commonality was being US servicemen. Why would he be coming over to join me—without an invitation? I couldn't deflect his advances—a real "glad-hander." He approached, reeling off a purported list of mutual friends. What's worse, in contrast to my efforts to appear continental, he was in a bright plaid blazer. It shouted "I'm an American." Smoking a big cigar too. Not my kinda guy. This was going to be ugly. (I was already constructing my excuses to leave.) He pulled back a chair, occupied more space than two people and began talking loud as a platoon sergeant. I tried to make small talk while he went through address books, waved down waiters, clicked his ballpoint pen, and spread his tobacco paraphernalia in front of him. Looked like he was opening an office at my table.

It wasn't long before his true colors and real motivation for joining me became apparent: a platinum blonde two tables away. I was occupying a strategic location. That was it all right. Only one problem for my friend, she was already sitting with a very successful looking gentleman (who could have been an American as well). But this wasn't going to stop my new friend. He boisterously got the attention of her companion, who it turned out was a Senior VP with Ford Motors in Turkey. Discovering this he then promptly set about establishing that they knew so many of the same people in Detroit, they were practically old friends. Personally, he was making me sick.

But let me tell you who he was really pissing off—the blonde at the table with him. Her male friend had succumbed to my tablemate's flattery and was commencing to ignore her. He was now twisted around in his chair, conversing over his shoulder with my obnoxious companion. She and I were left out of the loop. It was obvious to me that my new friend was working up to another table hop—to join Mr. Ford Motors and his attractive blonde companion. I'm not sure I should have started off calling her blonde. She was an older woman. At least in her late forties if not fifties. (In fact I hadn't been too proud of myself homing in on her.) Her hair was more silver than blonde, could well have been bleached gray. But this was not a detraction, it only enhanced her respectable beauty. She was wearing a sequined black sweater and large chandelier earrings, and was strikingly made up with a *Roaring Twenties* black beauty mark on her cheek.

She was obviously not accustomed to the kind of inattention her companion was presently offering. After five minutes of the back of his head she'd had enough. She maneuvered her purse so that one end of it was against the base of his tall tropical drink. While gazing nonchalantly across the room, using the end of her purse she slid his drink to a spot alongside his forearm and right at the edge of the table. Once having placed it in this precarious location, she suddenly called out his name. He spun around, lofting half his drink two tables away.

As he jumped up, shaking and dusting off the cigarette ashes and wet napkins down his front, without a word she picked up her things and left the table. I watched her make her way to the far side of the room and settle into an over-stuffed loveseat. My tablemate was a little surprised at all the activity, and having seen his plans dashed, withdrew to the main bar, where he would undoubtedly locate someone else to annoy. Finding myself once again alone and observing the blond to be momentarily alone, I mustered the courage to approach her and compliment her on her effective retaliation. A nod of the head and a nice smile, and we were talking. She spoke perfect English, and being so blonde (if it were) I was surprised to find out she was 100 percent Turk. Belkis Soylemengoza, the daughter of the Minister of War. But not enamored with politics. She'd been married to a politician once—the Mayor of Istanbul. She told me with considerable emphasis, that she'd never get involved with a man in any type of government again! Things evidently weren't much different than in the States. (I learned later from one of her friends, that her husband had not been voted out, he had been shot out!)

For once I had not picked a 5'9" female. Belkis was petite. Now, from close quarters I could confirm her years, and considered easing out of this in view of the age difference (not to mention the likely *experience* difference). But it can't hurt to just spend a little time with her here in the lounge. I was just smart enough to realize I might be in the company of a very interesting person. She looked like a thin Mae West and acted and sounded like Zsa Zsa Gabor. Every other word was "Dahling," and it was perfectly natural for her—she could get away with it. It seemed like everyone that came in the hotel knew her or knew of her. Our conversations were frequently interrupted by demonstrative waves, kisses, and hellos. She could flash a smile in a heart beat, and instantly come back to her story as if the greeting had never occurred.

It wasn't too difficult to carry on a conversation with Belkis—mostly you listened. She was a raconteuse of the first order and I a captive audience. If you feel a little inadequate in conversing, don't worry—just pay attention and act real interested, you'll get invited everywhere. (I've found that most people would rather engage a good listener than a good speaker.) And in this case, my limited world experiences definitely put me in the inadequate category. We spent quite a while this way—me on the "ear-end" of her wild tales. After two British ladies stopped to say hello, she began yet another scarcely credible tale. "Have you been to England darling?"

Embarrassedly I admitted, "Only at Heathrow, and then just a couple hours."

"I went to school in England—after secondary school here in Istanbul. I guess I was seventeen. No, eighteen. That's important. I remember now. Eighteen. Pass me that ashtray. Thank you darling. In any case Roger, as you might imagine, my family wanted the best for me. Here in Istanbul all the well-positioned families spoil their daughters. And of course I was no exception. Certainly not. I was sent off to a proper school in London. That's very nice, a gentleman always offers a light. I'll teach you. You're going to be a good student, I can tell. We're not Muslim you know—

generational Christians, but darling, no way they would send me alone. My Aunt Eda, bless her soul, came along to chaperone me.

"We resided just outside the city, on the second floor of a charming old inn. We had a big bedroom and a sitting room with a lovely balcony. It was quite nice. On the ground floor was a pub with a restaurant, which served very satisfactory food. One night while we were eating I noticed a dashing Englishman sitting across the room. Even as a young girl I recognized the meaning of his glances, and I felt myself blush. I couldn't avoid responding to his quick smile and our little game was initiated. I knew it could have no culmination of course, but darling, I must tell you, my young heart was beating ever so fast. I barely ate a morsel." With this Belkis reached across the table and grasped my arm, and added with a smirk, "My aunt Eda thought I was catching a fever. Later, upstairs in our room, while brushing my hair—which she did every night for twenty minutes, she asked me 'Belkis my dear, you didn't by chance see that man in the restaurant tonight did you?' As you might imagine darling, not being daft and thinking already to tomorrow evening, I responded as innocently as I could, What man aunt Eda?"

"Then you didn't see him. Good! Because he is the biggest playboy in all of England!"

Belkis went on relaying the story as if it happened a week ago, and it wasn't difficult to keep paying attention as she continued. "I laid awake half the night, unable to stop thinking about this bold man with his black hair combed straight back. I could hardly wait to see what tomorrow's evening meal would turn up. And it was the same Roger, he was there when we arrived. I spied him immediately and he lowered his head, but he had acknowledged my presence. Like this Roger, sneaking a glance, you know, one eyebrow up. These are important things. Signals. You should know that. You could be charming too Roger. I will help you." She tilted her head back and laughed. "No No, I'm serious. Back to the story now, don't interrupt me. Where was I? I chose a seating which would exclude Aunt Eda from a good vantage point, and our stolen glances could continue without notice. I felt special and warmed inside by the attention I was getting. Of course I knew no direct conversation or actual meeting could ever occur. Evidently we had been sufficiently discrete in our little dialogue, because that night in our room, my dear Aunt Eda never brought up the subject of the gentleman at dinner.

"But Roger, listen to this darling." I guessed this would be something special since before continuing she leaned over and grasped my wrist in both her hands. "When I awoke the next morning, my bedspread—from the foot of the bed to the ruffles at my small white neck, was completely covered with roses! It had to have been him! He had somehow gotten someone to enter our room and delivered these, without either myself or Aunt Eda waking. You can imagine my state at this point. Aunt Eda also, but with far different concerns. That day—after the roses incident, I was surprised, and excited that she chose to again take our evening meal in the pub. My knees were shaking as we descended the steps into the dining room. And Roger, he was there!"

According to Belkis, she and the charming Englishman played their game. The delightful exchanges continuing throughout the meal. Increasingly titillated by the arousals she was experiencing, she toyed with her meal to prolong the encounter, playing with her creme caramel until Aunt Eda reproached her for her manners. Well the time to leave arrived. The meal was finished and Aunt Eda was getting impatient. It was then that Belkis looked up with a start, to see the young Englishman approaching their table with long quick strides.

"And Roger, he was at the table before Aunt Eda could speak or react. In the next second he scooped me out of my chair, and I was off my feet and in his arms like a small child. He turned on a heel and carried me straight to the door, and through it. We were outside—in the chilled night air, and before I knew it I was being lowered into the front seat of an open Mercedes." She said she was stung into a paralysis by his sudden and unexpected actions, "...or of course darling, I would have leaped out and ran." And then—still before she could move, Belkis said he was at the wheel and the side of the pub echoed the sound of the engine as the dew soaked open Mercedes roared away.

She continued, and the story became even more interesting. The small coupe knifed through the dark village roads, the headlamps stroking the undersides of the low-hanging branches. They reached the M-5 ramp and accelerated up and onto the motorway, beginning their secret journey. The speedometer was frozen at over 100 kilometers an hour, as Belkis sat their rigid, considering her actions and listening to the whine of the wheels on the wet roadway. They drove without speaking. Neither offering a word. She was sure she was being foolish. She wondered about her family and Aunt Eda. "....and I knew this was wrong Roger, but I was more excited than fearful. In fact, and I'm a little ashamed darling. I wasn't fearful at all. I knew I should have been afraid but I wasn't. I knew I was being a bad girl." For an hour or more they raced the moon through broken clouds. The night wind buffeted her ears and whipped her hair forward onto her face, bringing tears to her eyes. She said she knew one thing for sure, her boredom at school was over. Exactly for how long and with what consequences, only time would tell.

There had been nothing but the drumming of the wheels on the rough macadam since they left the motorway, but now they were slowing, and suddenly the gravel was flying as the Mercedes took a sharp turn between two massive stone gates. While the grand stone house wasn't completely dark, only a few windows gave evidence of lit rooms. A house of this size must have a staff, but no one appeared. Belkis said that only at this moment did some apprehension blot out the tingling and exhilaration she had been feeling. The engine and night were suddenly quiet, his door had opened and closed and he was at her side of the car. He took her hand, helped her out, and led her up the slate steps to the entrance. She followed without resisting. Her young body alive.

"We entered a foyer, poorly lit by one high and dimmed chandelier. Its ceiling, obscured by the darkness above the hanging fixture, was three floors up. You might imagine now darling, I was a little scared. The foyer opened onto a large room—a library, with a huge fireplace. Both side walls were floor to ceiling book shelves. Thousands of hardbound books. If it was this man's house, he was a man of letters. I could see two large writing desks and several pieces of grand leather furniture, but we did not enter the room. Instead, with one hand in the small of my back he guided me a few steps to the right—to the foyer staircase, and up it to a long banistered balcony. Oh thank you. Yes. I'd love a gateau. No, that one— the cheesecake, with the pineapple. That was lovely of you Roger. There's hope for you young man. Now where was I? Yes, at the top of the stairs.

"The balcony—on the second floor, stretched the length of both side walls and the rear wall of the library. He smiled and motioned me to start down our side. Almost to the end, just before turning across the rear wall, he stopped me in front of a door to what I guessed—was going to be my room. For the first time, he spoke: 'Belkis, I'm sure you're tired. Please get a good night's sleep. You will find everything you need inside. No need to rise early, breakfast won't be until nine. See you then my darling woman.' It was the first time that anyone had called me a woman, and I suspected that quite soon I would have every opportunity to become just that."

I GUESS I JUST WASN'T THINKING

The following day was the first of many that Belkis would spend at this remote fortress. Of course she made the necessary calls to Aunt Eda (who understood all, and who would relay a properly edited version to her parents), assuring them of her good health and virtue. She described the first few weeks as a slow and tender courtship; from the parlor to the porch swings, from candle-lit dinners to boat rides on the lake, from the flowers on the terrace to the far reaches of the estate. She said he was very kind, and ever so patient. Sweet smiles. Small gifts. He would touch her softly on the shoulders and arms. After about three weeks, there was something new, "....when he would brush against me I was aware of a strange empty feeling inside, that was crying out to be filled. And somehow," and once again she reached across the table, but this time laced her fingers in mine, "....somehow he knew darling, because finally, one night, he came into my room." (Though she added that this night she had left her door ajar ever so little.) She said it was wonderful, he was wonderful. They were very happy. She would remain for over three months as the young and willing apprentice to the affections of Master Adrian Conan Doyle, the son of Sir Arthur Conan Doyle.

"You've heard of him of course, haven't you Roger—the author of the Sherlock Holmes series." I allowed that I had (and for once I didn't have to fib).

Adrian did not cease showering her with affection, lovely gifts and exciting weekend excursions. She wanted for nothing and had the run of the estate. And although he never spoke of it, she knew from talking with the staff that there was a "lady of the house"—a frail woman from Scandinavia who was not in good health and was currently convalescing in a kurhaus in Germany. Sooner or later she would return, and Belkis knew her stay would become most inconvenient.

And that day arrived. One evening at the end of an especially quiet meal, Adrian excused himself and went straight to the garage. A moment later—ears tuned to the exterior of the house she heard the Mercedes engine. She heard it backing out, and then nothing. She had a premonition about Adrian's journey that evening. He left often, but this time it was different. He was gone more than two hours. She was at a third floor window behind a half-drawn curtain when the Mercedes appeared through the gates and came up the drive. A thin woman stepped unsteadily from the car. Two women of a now plentiful and enthusiastic staff hurried to assist her. They stayed at her side, half-supporting her up the steps and into the house. What would happen now? Did this woman know about Belkis?

She did. That night while Belkis lay awake considering her future, she thought she heard a faint knock upon her door. She opened it, certain of who would be there. And she was correct. There she was—Adrian's wife, in her robe, standing unsuredly in the hall. Belkis was justifiably embarrassed, but invited her in. She did not accept this offer. "She just looked at me Roger, for a minute or two—with no facial expression, and then said, 'Belkis, you are young and beautiful, you can have any man you want. Please, leave my house. Give me that peace. I beg you.'" Belkis said it wasn't a difficult decision. There is a time and a place for everything. A beginning and an end. She put together only a small bag of necessities and slipped out of the house. And it was not a pleasant night; through a cold drizzle she walked the mile to the village, bought a ticket, and within the hour was on a train for London's Waterloo Station.

She was understandably worried about what kind of reception awaited her in Istanbul, and chose to stay with her cousins in London for another month, till things cooled off. Her Aunt Eda was no old fuddy-duddy, and came through to save her hide in this one. I asked her if she ever saw Adrian again. She said—but not convincingly, that she never spoke to him again. When the story was over, it was almost five, the crowd was thinning, and it just felt like it was time to call it an afternoon. As much as I had enjoyed this and a half dozen other stories, by five I was feeling a little weary from sipping tea and listening. We parted, but not before there was no doubt she expected to see me when I next came ashore.

Seeing Istanbul with Belkis

Whenever I could get ashore, I was with Belkis. It was always different and to say—amusing, would be an understatement. We spent a lot of hours together (most of them in cabs). She was a celeb in this city, that was for sure. Everyone seemed to know her. And from the stories she narrated, she had me convinced—she was a historied Istanbul femme fatale. I knew I was not the first to catch her fancy, nor would I be the last. But once again, for me it was new and exhilarating. She was constantly flattering me and I felt important. One day she took me to lunch on the terrace of the notorious Political Club. It was a light and airy, sophisticated early afternoon dejeuner (with its share of eccentric souls). She afforded me a lot more respect and attention than I deserved. In conversations with her friends, she consistently took great pride in wildly exaggerating my attributes and accomplishments. Had I earned or deserved any of this, I would have been greatly complimented, as it was I was greatly embarrassed. I could see a lack of actuality made absolutely no difference to Belkis.

No circumstances occurred and no day ended where it seemed like a whole night together was likely to occur. For me I was satisfied just to be in her company. As far as I could see, I never came close to being asked to spend the night. But in her eyes and in her touch, I knew it was not out of the question. But it would only happen at such time as she chose, and after I had earned it, and she felt the setting was just right. There was always that tantalizing suspense of the when and where.

One night we had plans to attend a concert. When I arrived at her apartment (she didn't live in a house, she lived in a polished, dark and sterile, sparsely furnished, and I think, government-provided apartment) she informed me that we were invited to a pre-concert party. It would be held at the home of Turkey's Laureate Tenor, Khlavik Zawregh, who would be the soloist later in the evening. According to Belkis, she and Khlavik were very old friends, and she was excited about introducing me. (I was already wondering what I was going to learn about myself in that introduction.) We took a cab. I don't think Belkis owned a car, or even drove. It was an exercise I could not imagine Belkis putting up with. A thirty minute drive out of the thick of the city and finally into a fashionable area of manicured lawns, pruned shrubs, high, brass-plaqued walls, and massive iron gates. We'd arrived. Must've been fifty cars parked outside. Navigated our way to a huge main entrance. Once inside my discomfort was measurably increased. I didn't know anyone except Belkis of course, and only a few people were speaking English. I didn't recognize any of the items of food set out on the buffet. There were no beers or brand name whiskeys, although they were serving some type of alcohol beverage in the form of a brown punch.

Belkis was eager to introduce me to Khlavik, but while it was his house, he was nowhere in sight. Well "Soon" she giggled, pointing a finger upwards. Belkis took some joy in sharing with me, one of Istanbul's inside stories: Khlavik's affection for young boys. Turns out he was about to appear. Word was he and his young companion had just finished their bath together. And true enough, a few moments later—amidst cheers mixed with some tittering and quickly subdued guffaws, the duo appeared on the second floor balcony, side by side (in fact, arm in arm), wrapped in a single, large striped bath towel. Their emergence garnered applause from the group, especially from what would be the guest of honor, the bearded

Emir, *who would accompany Belkis and I to the concert.* I'm not sure how we got paired up with Sheik Abdullah-Whatever. He spoke no English and had not been a friend of Belkis. But he was visiting royalty, that was for sure, and I think—the concert may even have been scheduled for him. I found out that Belkis—as the official welcoming committee for Istanbul, was to oversee his well-being for the evening's performance.

Our caravan of black, seriously-appointed vehicles (with fender pennants and police control) sped through the city and to the hall. Once again I was definitely in over my head and was beginning to feel the inadequacy of my dress. Belkis had said "wear a coat and tie." She had not said: black coat, and black tie. I was "out of uniform" again. Fortunately, I don't think the bulk of the attendees recognized what was or was not, appropriate dress for an *Ameriqui.* The Emir was in what appeared to be a loose fitting, white dressing gown, and wearing a checkered cloth on his head. (Belkis called it a *thobe and gutra,* I think.) But unlike mine, his outfit (with ample bands of embroidered gold and members of his entourage frequently adjusting it) was not being questioned by anyone.

We were led to seats in the second row. (And it appeared the first row was not going to be used at all.) Before the concert started, the musicians went through the drill of tuning their instruments, which to me sounded like the screeching of a gaggle of starved alley cats. *Whew.* Once that was finished, there was some sort of long presentation (part in French), a couple speeches, and a flowery introduction of the Emir (our charge) by the maestro. The concert itself, at least most of it, was beautiful and moving. I was beginning to understand—just beginning, to have an appreciation for the power and beauty of classical music. (Once again I was ill-prepared to recognize or comment on any individual composers or their works.) The concert took almost two hours, intermission included. At its conclusion and after the encores, the beaming, penguin-appearing conductor announced they would play a selection for the guest of honor (seated next to Belkis). He could choose the piece he had enjoyed most, and thought to be the most beautiful, and they would do it again—especially for him. A great deal of confusion arose, as the Emir with little Turkish dialect or English language capability, was unable to describe the exact movement he had enjoyed the most. A translator was summoned, the program was examined, fingers were pointing. Finally—*That's it!* They had discovered which piece the Emir had most enjoyed, and the orchestra would do it again. They would spend five minutes tuning their instruments!

157

I GUESS I JUST WASN'T THINKING

It killed me to spend the next two days aboard the ship, but I was five liberty days in debt. My time had come. I had to start decreasing the number of days I owed guys before the damn cruise was over. But it still hurt, wondering what was going on in town without me. Nick Cassopolis came on board Friday with a message from Belkis. He had seen her in the Hilton lounge. (By now—and I should have been worried, Belkis and I were becoming a familiar sight to the other guys in the squadron.) According to her note, I was to be sure—absolutely sure, to be at her apartment at six Saturday evening. Great, she was sending me messages. But what about Saturday morning and afternoon? Guess she's got something else scheduled. Okay, Saturday night it will be.

Probably a good thing. I could get some good work done during the day. At least I'd be seen scurrying here and there like a conscientious junior officer (and on a day I was scheduled to be off duty)! Got in several good morale visits, and they're important. The guys in the shops don't get a lot of recognition, and nothing would work without them. Frequently the enlisted man is often considered to be less well educated and to have only limited potential, and statistically this might be true. For the most part they were only high school graduates (or drop-outs). Few if any college men in the enlisted ranks. I would see many of these same men, after a stint in the military, return to college, graduate and become very successful contributors to our society. Often times ultimately surpassing their commissioned officer supervisors.

I was excited about what lay in store for me as the cab rounded the last corner to Belkis' apartment. (Do you think it would be tonight? Has she decided?) No, it would not be tonight, however what did transpire, eclipsed anything so far. We were going to go to dinner and it was going to be a "double date." Although somehow Belkis could make it seem like I was her commanding masculine escort, I had about as much control as a flea on the back of a dog. Where she went, I went (followed). I thought we were going to meet the other two people at a hotel, but no, we picked them up at what looked like a large private residence—and it was: the residence of the German Ambassador! Our cab driver was given the third degree at the gate, in fact I was afraid if he didn't calm down, we were going to be run off. Cooler heads and Belkis' smile prevailed. We were permitted to drive through the gates. At the large and pillared villa entrance, we were met by four noticeably sturdy men, who I'm sure were more than domestic staff. We were politely ushered into a spacious white marble foyer, walking across a spectacularly inlaid black and yellow coat of arms, and under a massive crystal chandelier, into an adjoining sitting room furnished with not-so-comfy looking furniture. *Whew.* You might imagine I was impressed.

A bit unsure does not adequately describe my condition at the moment. However Belkis was in her element, carrying on an animated conversation with a well dressed gentleman who could have been the executive secretary, the Vice Consulate, or the Ambassador himself. Fortunately this interlude would be short. (Because so far I wasn't having a good time.) I heard voices, footsteps, and some commotion in the foyer. Belkis aborted her conversation with whoever and motioned to me to follow her—which I did once again. Basked in the brilliance of the huge foyer light, we were about to meet our companions for the evening. Belkis was hugged and kissed, and all sorts of niceties were exchanged (this time in English and French. No Turkish). The gentleman and his lady—both, were indeed elegant. Seeing him I was secretly vowing to buy some sharper looking clothes. (While sport jackets and slacks might be great in the states, they weren't hacking it here.) He was about forty, and she I think—a little younger. He was well groomed and dressed in a tailored gray business suit. She was stunning—in fact, regal, in a long white knit gown, hair piled high, with a tiara. Wow, what friends Belkis had!

I knew that I had seen these faces before—somewhere; not necessarily together, but they both appeared familiar—famously familiar. But where? In the newspapers? In the movies? Where? In another minute I would know: He was Maxmillan Schell, the German movie star. And the lady? *Whoa...* Princess Soraya! The wife (or ex-wife) of the Shah of Iran. *Holy Shit*, would I be in over my head or what. Belkis introduced me with her usual editorial flourish. My ancestry, nationality, and life's work, while somewhat vague, left one with the idea of good blood, notably fine accomplishments, and even greater successes lying yet ahead. The next couple hours were a whirlwind before my eyes. There was never a moment that I wasn't afraid of making some giant faux pas. I'm sure we went to the best restaurant in Istanbul. As usual Belkis had everything under control and we were shown to a prominently located balcony table (being greeted about six times getting to it). Once seated I was on my guard to avoid making any foolish comments or other conversational blunders. (Observing the room's décor and clientele, I was real worried about what would happen when the check arrived.)

I GUESS I JUST WASN'T THINKING

It could have gone a lot worse. As I gained confidence, I managed to get into the causerie, relaying a couple of what I hoped were interesting anecdotes. Once alone with us our guests became more natural, and the chosen topics were not what I would have expected. He was concerned about the problem of unwanted pets in Germany—dogs and cats without homes. She asked lots of questions about suburban life in the USA—particularly about women (wives) working. But the real surprise of the evening was yet to come. Upon leaving the restaurant we hailed a cab, whose driver was a real crank. Belkis had some trouble giving him the address. I was in the front seat. Belkis, Maxmillan, and Princess Soraya were in the back seat. Although Maximillian was the perfect gentleman, for some reason the driver appeared to take an instant dislike to him. Halfway to the German Embassy, while joking around, Maxmillan kissed Princess Soraya—a light peck on the cheek. The driver saw this and went ape-shit. I later learned, the first problem was that Maxmillan—a Christian (which translates to "infidel" to a member of the Islamic faith) was with a possibly Muslim woman. Unthinkable in the first instance. And worse, he kissed her, and in public! A giant "No No."

The driver, while spending some time watching the road, managed a harsh and prolonged turn-around every 30 seconds, to let go a string of derogatory-sounding berations of Maximillian. Belkis got involved and started reading him the riot act, but this would be one time Belkis would not win. In a few minutes we were stopped in front of a concrete building with white and green globes out front. Looked like a police station. The driver was out, up the steps, and inside. Not two minutes later he emerged with a uniformed officer and began shaking his finger at Maximillian in the backseat. I could guess what the beef was. At first I thought Belkis was mad, then suddenly she was laughing. Whew, everything's going to be okay. Or is it? The three of us followed her and the Turkish police officer up the steps and into the station (which may not have been a good idea). Maxmillan tried to straighten things out, and he was impressive; stayed calm and never raised his voice. Belkis seemed amused at his efforts and plopped down to watch, on what I guess was the chief's desk. The cab driver was acting real satisfied, like he'd won and was just waiting for something—I don't know what, to happen.

Well here's what happened: The four of us were marched into a holding cell! I could hardly believe it. From how Belkis and the fat chief were talking, I got the idea it was a temporary thing, just done to appease the driver, until he left. He did (and I paid a bunch of Lira for the ride, plus the time on his meter). What was supposed to be—I think, a momentary appeasement of a local Muslim citizen, turned out to be an overnight stay in the Istanbul "hoosegow." I'm pretty sure Belkis could have made one phone call and had us out of there in a minute, but to her it was a grand opportunity for "theater," and she was playing it for all it was worth. About three in the morning (I guess Belkis was responsible) our meal came: a large flat piece of bread, several types of cheese, and a bowl of a light green, creamy herb dip. And to top it off, a delicious cake made out of dates and brown sugar. (We even got some homemade wine from the jailer.) We played cards—a strange game, like "Go Fish," with cards having only symbols (no numbers).

Maybe because I was so tired, I don't know, but I loosened up and told a few of my favorite jokes; actually had Maxmillan laughing. I couldn't believe where I was and what I was doing. An ordinary (not even ordinary) A4 pilot, here—with *these* people! Belkis and the princess hardly stopped talking the whole night. (I think they might have somehow crossed paths in their youth.) It was a helluva night, I couldn't believe it. Me in jail in Istanbul, with Maxmillan Schell and Princess Soraya! Who's gonna believe it? Talk about an in-port visit! We were out in the morning. I was back on the ship. Our stay in Istanbul was over. I knew we were scheduled to put in to Istanbul again in a month, and I was sure I'd see Belkis.

Chapter Fifteen
A SERIOUS MEDICAL DISCOVERY

Another at-sea period. The bad news: Even aboard I couldn't stop thinking about my adventures with Belkis. The good news: Each at-sea was becoming less fearsome; in fact almost methodical. The routine was fast and easy. The time was flying by. Daytime flight operations were even becoming tedious; usually just "boring holes" in the sky. Very little live ammo firing. Evidently the ship's company didn't like the hassle of lowering and recovering the target sled—and were now down to setting it out only twice a week. This then had us mostly just practicing formation and navigation. Since we were attack pilots, seems we should have been doing more "attacking" (and less of this "straight and level" flying).

Guess we were starting to get a little frisky. On just about every flight—on our return to the ship, and while waiting for our recovery times, we engaged in even more realistic four, (or worse) eight-plane, unscheduled and unbriefed "dog-fights." (Incredibly disorganized, simulated air-to-air combat sessions.) I didn't see a real point in these gaggles, especially since we weren't fighter aircraft, and the chances for a mid-air collision were plenteous. You'd be pointed straight up, just off a four "G" pullout, real narrow field of vision, head pinned against the cushion, and *Bingo*, the sky would go dark in the shadow of another A-4 tumbling out of the sky, right past you, fifty feet off your wing tip! (Neither of you in real control of your aircraft.) As you might imagine, my roomie Jim Stremlow loved these exercises. And this at-sea period—in addition to these airborne adrenal pumping events, a personal shipboard situation caused me some real concern.

I was in the ship's dispensary (medical clinic) for over an hour and a half, waiting for the Flight Surgeon. (Though he's certainly not going to be operating on anybody. "Flight Surgeon" is the approved title for an MD who accepts a military commission and is assigned to a tactical Squadron.) He wasn't here, but for sure he wasn't off the ship making house calls. Ours was a dead ringer for Tim Conway from the old Carol Burnett Show. Three years in the Navy and he still wore argyle socks with his uniform. His two claims to fame: really being serious about keeping us healthy, and not giving up when stumbling through an unfunny joke. We used to say he joined the Navy to save up money, so that when he got out he could afford to go to medical school.

Geez—1500 hours. Half the afternoon gone and still no doctor. Fortunately nothing much scheduled today. Cold in here. Temperature just at the goose pimple level. Checked out the standard sterile environment of vinyl and stainless steel. Same tile floors as always. Trying to pass time now—counting them crosswise and lengthwise; trying to figure out which side of the room they began to lay them from, and which side did they end up at—slightly out of line, and have to trim them. Glass cabinets with short legs, containing the standard array of scary looking, variously shaped instruments inside. This was not a soft and friendly place. If he's not here in another five minutes I'm outa here. But not to worry, I wasn't sick. I felt great. It was the dentist who told me I had to come over here and get a "blood coagulation time" test before my impending wisdom tooth extraction. The dentist had said it could require substantial surgery and a lot of bleeding could be expected. (Some bedside manner huh?) He wanted to be sure my coagulation rate was proper and that he wouldn't have any problems with post-operative bleeding. (These are *his* problems?)

Hooray, the doc—at last. A quick greeting. He checked my record and the request from the dental section. No Sweat. This would be easy—just do the standard check. (I was to find out in the sessions to follow, "standard" can mean different things to different people.) Was hard to believe he was that busy, but the doc briefed a corpsman (a Navy physician's assistant) on how to do the required procedure, apologized to me profusely, and promptly left the area. With the manual on the table at his side, pages held open by a heavy stapler, carefully reading while tracing the lines with his index finger, the young corpsman set about administering my "coagulation time" test. Better I should have said "tests."

Things did not go as anticipated. More than one—I think, four test tubes (*large* tubes) were filled with my blood; each the result of a separate penetration, and I am not brave about needles. (Especially those wielded by a 19 year old apprentice.) A nice kid though, carrying out each step (attempt) with due diligence. The most recently filled tube was set upright in the wooden rack. The clock was ticking and the blood thickening, I hoped. "What, you say seven minutes? Only *seven* minutes and it is supposed to be hardened enough on the surface to turn this tube completely upside-down, without the clot breaking?"

"Yes sir."

"No way! Where does it say that?"

"In the beginning. The page before."

"Well how about the diameter of the tube? Read that again. And how deep is the level of blood supposed to be? How high you fill the tube has got to be real important. If you have it too full, the weight of the blood will be more, and yeah, it'll break the clot. I think you're putting in too much blood."

Within the hour and as a result of the ensuing discussions, we ended up with three more corpsmen—each with varying opinions on how to interpret a navy medical manual. But the test results were always the same: Wait seven minutes, tilt the tube, and Oops, watch Roger's blood run like water. The doc was notified. I was told that for now things were finished. I should wait in my stateroom. (With my aching arm.)

No word and dinner time. Back in the room, still no word. Well I'm not worried. A little pissed. Write a couple letters and hit the rack. Tomorrow's another day.

Next day, 0900: A call from the doc, and I responded, "Yeah sure Marv, I can be down there in ten minutes."

"Well what do *you* think Doc?"

"Not good Roger. I've got a couple other tests I need to run."

"What are they, and what for?"

"The first one I'd like to do is a capillary integrity check. You didn't pass any of the "coagulation times" tests. Your times were way out of limits." Here we go again—my arm still aching from yesterday, but surely there's an explanation. This test was going to be carried out by the Flight Surgeon himself. (A fact that at first I thought was good news.) The tools: A yellow plastic metric ruler, a US Government black ballpoint pen, and a small stainless steel ball peen hammer. Interesting. Not overwhelming. Worthy of my continued attention.

A twenty—precisely twenty millimeter circle was measured and drawn on the inside of my left forearm. (I might add, the same arm which had undergone severe abuse eighteen hours ago.) I suggested the right arm, since I could barely straighten my left arm. The left was what they said in the book. So it's gotta be the left. I can handle it. (I think.) Two attempted erasures later I wasn't sure. We had now finished with two of the required tools: the ruler and the pen. I was a little concerned about the third—with good reason.

Marv commenced with the frenzy of a mad shoemaker, wielding his ball-peen hammer, to beat (as best as he could) the center of the circle on my arm. That is to say, after I had initially yanked my arm away to get an explanation. We were going to do this as specified: 25 strikes, within the circle—within 30 seconds. I can tell you—for Marv, 25 hits inside the circle required about 100 total tries, and we didn't make the time limit either. The criteria: Count the number of tiny red spots that would emerge within the circle 30 seconds later! I failed this test too (or rather I should have gotten a grade of "Incomplete"). You weren't allowed to have more than 15 red spots. I had *no* red spots, just one huge, pulsating pink blotch. But no spots!

"Rog, you've *got* to have the dots. We'll have to do it again on the other arm. I have to put down the number of spots."

"Marv, be serious. No spots at all has to be a passing grade."

"Nope. The other arm." This time it got botched early.

"Wait in your stateroom. I'll give you a call."

I could see that the doc was definitely concerned. He told me he had done this test before (although I certainly was not convinced). I would have considered all this as just a damned inconvenient joke, if it weren't for the fact that the Doc looked genuinely worried. He kept reviewing the results of yesterday's coagulation tests. I told him I couldn't wait in the stateroom, but that he could get ahold of me if need be by calling the VMA 331 Maintenance Office. I think I was successful in convincing myself everything would turn out okay. Just another military medical "snafu." However I could feel a little tightness in the pit of my stomach. Lunch in the wardroom was great as always. My own silver napkin holder. My same seat. The same teak paneled wall to look at. Peanut Butter soup, and would you believe, good! Shortly after lunch, while drifting into a light doze, the phone buzzed, and it was the doc.

"Captain, can you come on down?" Of course I could, but this was no longer a fun thing (and he called me Captain instead of Roger).

Inside his office, he spoke: "Roger, let me tell you what we *do* know: You don't have leukemia."

(Pause)

"Leukemia? *Holy Shit!* What are you talking about?"

"Do you have a history of hemophilia in your family?"

"Christ No, what are you thinking?"

"Roger, your blood is not coagulating. Not at all."

"Who says? Based on these friggin tests?"

"We've gone over them ten times. I don't know about in the past, but right now your blood is taking more than twice as long to coagulate as it should. A bona fide hemophiliac sometimes does better than that."

"Well what do you think? There's gotta be an explanation. Hemophilia is hereditary, I couldn't be just getting it now!"

"I'm going to do another test in the morning. But for now, don't shave, don't do anything where you could get cut or scraped. I'm serious. Matter of fact—you actually should probably stay in your room, and be careful even in there!"

Back in my room again, not knowing if I was crazy or the world was crazy. Surely this was a ridiculous mistake. But how could the doc be so wrong? He said he had messaged the US Naval Hospital in Bethesda with the test results and questions. I laid there thinking, and worrying—just a little bit. Hell I'd seen these screw ups before. The phone again. Christ I hope not the doc. It wasn't. I was soon to wish it was. Instead, it was Bob Harmon (the Crew Scheduler). Would you believe, *I was scheduled for the 2330 (11:30 p.m.) late night launch!*

"No sweat Bob. See ya later." Jesus Christ! Now what? Can you imagine me bopping down to Bob's office and telling him, "I'd love to fly tonight, except I'm a hemophiliac." No way! Even if it turned out I *was* a hemophiliac, I'd be drummed out of the Marine Corps by the time anyone knew. What the hell, maybe I'll just do it. What's the doc gonna say. He didn't specifically tell me not to fly. (Of course I think he thought that was pretty much understood.) Some deliberation, lots of mulling it over. No way, no matter how phony this whole thing is, I just can't come up with this story; my reputation would be down the drain. I'll fly. I have to. I'll just be careful as hell. Move slow. Wear my gloves.

1800 hours (6 p.m.)—in the wardroom for the evening meal. As you might imagine I didn't have much of an appetite. (In fact, may have been a little nauseous.) Wasn't much of a conversationalist. Back to the stateroom. Lie down for a little while. *Whew.* 2100 hours. Down to the Ready Room. Stumble through a one hour briefing for a night formation flight; an hour and fifteen minute sortie. My wingman would be Doug Shannon, a good guy, from a liberal New England state, and smart like Bob Harmon. Hope he didn't notice my hesitancy and weak briefing. Back up to the room for a quick thirty minute rest (prayer session).

2300 hours (11:00 p.m.). Thirty minutes to go. We were all draped around the Ready Room, where once again—to protect our night vision there were no white lights, only dim red ones. And those damn red lights; you can see them, but they don't give off any worthwhile illumination. For some reason, in the red glow, your beard shows up like a two day's growth, everybody has black hair, and your teeth look terrible. A regular Halloween party. Uh-oh, could feel the ship heeling as it turned into the wind for the upcoming launch and recovery. Not long now. It was going to be rough tonight, a fine rain was being blown across the deck.

Whoaa! Loud! In preparation for our launch, the damn catapult checks were underway—three, four, five shuddering, ship-shaking slams. And I may have told you before, although I wouldn't hear it, as soon as we four had cleared the deck, the catapults would start giving off another kind of hair-raising scream. The guys who took off at 2200 would be coming back, and every thirty seconds when a tailhook caught a wire, the turnstiles would shriek as the cables were yanked out. And then after that scare (as soon as the cable had dropped free of the tailhook) you'd hear the high-pitched whine as the rewind operation pulled the cables back in taut, for the next landing arrestment. Once again (unfortunately), tonight I wouldn't be here in the Ready Room listening to these sounds. I would be out there and up there, alone in the cold, black soup.

2310: There's the call. Time to start up to the flight deck. The same winding passageways, hatch after hatch. A labyrinth. Six months at sea, a hundred launches, and I was still searching for the best way to make this trip. Had already gotten lost about ten times (real easy at night with just the red lights). Finally, up and onto the flight deck. Wondered what the Doc would say if he could see me now—his newly diagnosed hemophiliac up here on the way to his aircraft. Careful. Careful! No sharp edges! Don't scratch yourself. Step easy, reach slowly. *Keep your hands off any metal corners.* Windy, black and wet. Made my way towards my assigned aircraft. Should be parked right behind cat number three. I'd be the third bird airborne. Doug would be fourth, right behind me. Almost got run over twice by swabbies "tear-assing" across the deck in their heavy tow tugs; zipping in and out between the moored aircraft. Tiedown cables everywhere. *Step high.* Straining to see. Can't afford to trip, especially tonight. Brrrr. Cold. Where the frig are my gloves? Shoulda had them on, would've helped protect my fingers. Good, in my helmet. I'll get em on as soon as I climb in.

The cockpit looked high as a steeple, just barely silhouetted against the black sky. Sgt. Parker already had the pilot's ladder installed in the mounting holes on the side of the aircraft. Big step to the first rung. Hanging on. Be careful with the hands—sharp edges here. What a deal. Okay. First things first. Still on the ladder, before climbing in, remove the first ejection seat "safety" pin in the rear of the headrest. It was a large straight pin, thicker than a hanger wire, always installed from the ladder-side towards the far side. (Once again, the plane captain would remove the second—*final* seat safety pin, after the pilot was strapped in and ready to go.) While buffeting in the wind on the spindly ladder, blinking and straining to see, I reached for the first pin.

Yeow! Sharp pain! What the hell? *The safety pin had been installed backwards!* The sharp beveled point was sticking back towards the ladder. I had rammed the end of it right into the fleshy pad of my thumb! *Keerist!* Wetness—a lot of wetness. In the red light, blood would not be visible. Everything looks red. But no question about what it was. *Geez!* I had meant to put on my gloves *before* I came up here. But that wouldn't have stopped that pin. Wait a minute, get em on now! Get the right one on, tight over the thumb. Squeeze it! Wait—an idea. I had a rubber band on my kneeboard. Quick. Got it. Stretch it and wrap it around my thumb—real tight, down by the base. Get it around one more time. Can feel "pins and needles" in the end of my thumb, but at least the blood flow should be shut off. Might be okay.

I was in the seat. Things happening fast. Sgt Parker handing me the last of my equipment. Dark, noisy, windy. I don't think he was aware of what I had just done that was causing all my yelling and twisting about. The canopy's down. The ladder's away. There's the startup clearance. Eyes outside now—reacting to the taximan's wands ahead. On the cat. "Thumbs up," there's the circling wand—now full forward. I'm away! (I hope not forever.) The thought entered my mind that if I did pass out from blood loss, no one would ever know why I crashed; just conclude I'd done something stupid. But I did make it back, and made a good landing too. Now, safe and laying in my rack and still alive, I was willing to bet that no matter what the damned tests said, I wasn't a hemophiliac. The wound was not just a puncture, it was a tear as well, and it had bled profusely, but stopped by itself. Time to go to sleep. I deserve it.

The next day, back in the dispensary—one last test. After the previous night's experience, I was not interested in continuing this medical misadventure, but decided not to fight city hall (especially since the Doc was so excited about some specific instructions they had received from the Charleston Naval Hospital). But this test was going to be the one to end all tests. I stood like a shackled Transylvania monster, between two hefty chief petty officers, each holding an arm. Directly in front of me—Doc Marv, with a book and a stopwatch. To my left front, a corpsman with a full needle, ready to make a deposit. To my right front, a corpsman with an empty needle ready to make a withdrawal. The timekeeper was ready. (*"Ready on the Right. Ready on the Left. All ready on the firing line."*) I was standing vulnerable, like a wino in front of the judge, just hauled in off the street, head down awaiting his fate.

First, my left arm was yanked out. The corpsman with the injection came to life. Pop, in went the needle, and into my body went so many cc's of what looked like beer. Out came the needle. *"Start!"* hollered the timekeeper. An out loud countdown ensued. Finally, "..fifty-eight, fifty-nine, *sixty seconds!"* The corpsman with the empty syringe came to life. My right arm was yanked out front. Bam, in went the other needle. Out of my body came the same amount of something—I think mostly blood (and my supply was getting low). This was it—the end. Far as I was concerned, I was finished with this program. I was allowed to straggle back up to my room to await the results. I'm not sure what results, or for what malady, or anything. Since I'd flown late last night, I was justified in resting during the day today. Thank God. The phone never rang with results. The Doc never gave me any results. I never had any more tests. I never had any more problems. My wisdom tooth came out easy.

Chapter Sixteen
VALENCIA

A Great Chance Meeting

The anchor had made its now familiar plunge. Another in-port, and I wondered what adventures might await me. Some time ago I mentioned considering my activities ashore as being almost carried out by someone other than my real self —that "parallel universe" thing, although certainly this analysis could not hold up. How and why was I was letting myself get into these terribly wrong relationships? The thought of my wife or my mother (or even one of our Marine married-couple friends) being aware of my conduct caused me to grimace ashamedly. But I was hooked. There was no way I could not continue on this path, abort this journey, though I truly did—did believe (or at least hope) that all of it would be external to my marriage; an unavoidable individual project that would be left on European soil when I returned to the States. It had to be. It *would* be! While it was real time now, it was a series of detached events; almost dream-like occurrences that would not affect my future committed situation. *At least that's what I thought up until Valencia.* It would be the switch that turned on a new regard for a second life; sabotage my theory of being able to later just forget it all.

I can't remember much about the city itself—a Spanish seaside town in the dead of winter, gray and deserted. Must have always been ashore at night, since my only recollections of it are during the hours of darkness. Valencia in November was a lot like Philadelphia in November—windy and cold. So far it had not been reaching out to me. Dale and I had forty-five minutes before we had to be on the dock (to catch that midnight liberty boat back to the ship). Enough time to grab a late snack. A week here already with nothing much to report. And this night had been more of the same. Four times ashore and nothing special. No recordable adventures. (And it's true what they say about Spanish girls: *you meet em at church or not at all.*) Up to this point Valencia was not going to be part of my memoirs.

But I can tell you, that was before we walked into *this* restaurant. Things were about to change. It was a tiny—about five-table, neighborhood "hole in the wall." Much too well lit and harsh looking, with light green walls and a white tile floor that needed a good scrubbing. Meant to be functional. No ambiance at all. Still, a few steps inside we got a real jolt. There at the back of the restaurant—at two tables pulled together, were about ten heavily made-up, wild-looking girls, laughing, clowning, chowing down like mad, and *speaking the King's English!* Talk about talking with your mouth full—all of them at the same time, arms waving, fingers pointing. Salt shakers, pitchers, food samples, magazines and 45 RPM records were crisscrossing the table at a quick pace.

We were stopped in our tracks by this promising sight and plopped down at the closest table. As striking as they were in their striped bell-bottom slacks and high heels (and raincoats hiding bare midriffs), as much of an audience as they must know they would attract, they appeared oblivious to the other patrons; totally engrossed in their own conversations—not trying to put on a show. They seemed much too comfortable in this strange eatery. Their animated cockney dialogue and spontaneous gesturing were a joy to hear and observe. Dale and I looked at each other: Were these Brit girls having fun or what? Talk about carefree. Talk about being on top of the world. Talk about not being bored! Long legs were sticking out everywhere. Vermilion red hair. False eyelashes. We must be in the theater district. There must be a theater somewhere near. These girls gotta be some kind of show girls. And as I said, lucky for us—speaking English!

I encouraged Dale (who between the two of us was far and away the best candidate) to go over and try to strike up a conversation. He did, and I was shortly being waved at to join him. I was not very confident, having some real doubts about how much of an impression a couple of square Americans would make on these girls. For sure they had been chased and courted by the best and the worst. While I'll admit they didn't fall all over themselves when we walked up, it appeared they were at least going to give us a chance. Most of them stopped talking, looked up politely, and listened patiently as Dale went about introducing us. Which he did it in his most gentlemanly and charming Cajun fashion.

I GUESS I JUST WASN'T THINKING

"American chaps are you? Off the ship I'll wager." We owned up to that. Couldn't deny it I guess, though I would have rather been an international arms dealer who had just flown in from Zurich. *We'll start with the truth and exaggerate when we get the chance.* I think they spent the first few minutes deciding whether we were a couple of jerks or worth talking to. I can't imagine why, but we must have passed the test, because the next thing I knew (with no apparent signals between them) they were making room for us to join them at their table. So far, so good.

They were dancers! Not "show girls." Big difference I would learn. *Don't ever call a dancer a show girl.* They were part of a twelve-girl troupe from the London-based Stafford Ballet. (Not really *ballet* ballet; they did complex, leaping, balancing choreography routines between the acts of popular vaudeville-type shows.) They were five months into a one-year contract, traveling the country with *The Tony Le Blanc Show,* which was presently doing a stint here in Valencia. (Tony Le Blanc was the Milton Berle of the Spanish stage.) In Spain, nighttime entertainment and particularly burlesque type theater, was very well received. Sellout crowds every night, and long runs.

These girls were a breath of fresh air. (A *gust* of fresh air.) I don't know exactly what I was expecting out of "these type" girls, but now, eavesdropping on their little tête-a-têtes, I was taken aback at the honesty and caring I was hearing and observing. They would "ooh" and "aah" at each other's stories, then lean forward with lowered head and finger extended, to offer motherly advice in hushed tones. To me, their sincere and down-to-earth behavior did not at all go with their bawdry appearance. They loved Spain and said Valencia was okay, but not as *sympatico* as Madrid or Barcelona. They'd already done a stint in both these cities and evidently they were great. The girls couldn't wait to return there. In Spain, under Generalissimo Franco the streets were clean and safe, the people were honest, and living was cheap. And evidently the audiences were loyal and appreciative—returning to see the same show over and over again. They did two performances a night. They had just finished their first one. The second act was on right now, and they had to be back in a few minutes for their next routine. What a buoyant ride it was to be in the midst of them. They sure were making the most of their short break.

Unfortunately, I knew we had to be back on the dock in just ten minutes (or miss our Cinderella liberty boat). But I knew another thing too. In the couple more liberty days I had, I was going to make every effort to get to know these girls better. In fact there was one in particular I had been watching since we first sat down. Her name was June and she was the ballet captain for the troupe (which translates to a cross between a mother hen and a drill instructor). Heavily-dyed long dark red hair contrasted a knowing face with an honest smile. Her eyes shone with optimism and innocence, yet at the same time I suspected she was someone not to be fooled with. I had a feeling this girl could size up anyone, any situation— come to a fair conclusion, and mete out firm justice. I was anxious to know more about her, her family, her home, how did she get into dancing, and what countries had she already been to.

We were running out of time and I decided to go for broke, try to schedule an official date for tomorrow night. Dale and I proposed to attend the performance and then invite them all to dinner. *They went for it!* This accomplished and reeling from our success, we excused ourselves for a speed run to the dock. I was excited on the way back to the ship, and still excited as I lay in the rack, trying to get my mind off the Stafford Ballet and June Rice. Excited about what might still be awaiting me here in Valencia.

At breakfast Bob and Don were enthusiastically describing a deal they had uncovered to order an XKE while on the cruise. There was a military purchase option to buy European-made cars, and have them delivered in the states at a major savings. In this case a Jaguar. Made me reflect on the life of a bachelor; no heavy considerations, no wife, no kids, no baby-sitters, no domestic schedules. What freedom. I told them about the English girls Dale and I had met, and invited them to go ashore with us. We'd all go to the show and have a great party afterwards. Bob and Don did their share of chasing girls, but they weren't as excited about the offer as I suspected they'd be. (Of course they hadn't seen these girls either.) Anyway, I was too busy arranging my own activities to worry about setting up dates for other guys. I excused myself to take care of some of my shipboard duties (and to be alone while I speculated about how our late night plans would pan out). Good ol' Tripp. Now I owe him *another* day. (At the rate I was going, when the cruise was over, I'd still owe him a bunch of days!)

The Stafford Ballet in Action

Dale and I were in town by six o'clock—a couple hours early. The same restaurant as last night. Berated myself for not having told the girls we'd buy them a drink *before* the show—wasted a valuable opportunity. We found a different crowd in the restaurant at this time of the evening. Last night, what few people came in were second-shift workers wolfing down a plate of beans before reporting to their nighttime job. At this hour it was mostly families. Seated at some tables were what appeared to be three generations. Easy to identify the gray-haired grandparents, their son the mustachioed hard-working husband with a dutiful wife and mother, and the dark-eyed kids in suits with short pants.

After nursing a Dry Sac sherry for about an hour, I decided to go get the tickets. Who knows, the damn thing might sell out early. And that'd do it if we missed the show. Better take care of the tickets now. Jogged the two blocks to the theater and managed to buy a pair of tickets. Think I got reasonable seats. I never have understood those damn seat sections: *Stalls, Lodges, Orchestra, Dress Circle?* Had to try to interpret a seating diagram (viewed upside down through a small glass window). I purchased seats in the mid to upper price range. (Two kinds were cheaper. One, more expensive.)

As great as the restaurant had been to us, by eight o'clock we'd had our fill of it and chose to wait on the sidewalk in front of the theater. At eight-fifteen the doors were unlocked and we were in the first group through. Inside the theater we were both duly impressed. It was immense and lavish. Huge chandeliers hung from a high domed ceiling, which was ornately carved with gilded cherubs. Large tapestries and twenty foot high murals adorned both side walls. A live orchestra was tuning in the pit. I had never been in a theater like this (of course I had only been to one other stage play in my life). The stage must have been seventy-five feet across, maybe more. What a place.

The real theater goers began filing in about quarter to nine, but not so many. A bunch of seats were still empty. I was beginning to feel sorry for June and the girls, and Tony Le Blanc. After being so elated at the quality of the facilities, I now had a sickening feeling about a too empty theater; about a show going broke and dancers returning to England. But, wow— five minutes before showtime they must have opened the flood gates. In they poured, and all well-dressed—every man wearing a coat and tie. Lots of older people, in their fifties and sixties. I was impressed. And would you believe, as best I could see there wasn't a vacant seat in the house.

Even without understanding a word, the show was great. Bawdy and burlesque, but not X-rated. I guess Tony Le Blanc was the country's favorite standup comic, this show being a three act comedy with lots of

174

mimic and slap-stick. Tony's Spanish leading lady was a six-foot bleach blonde, with huge bazooms (and this attribute had not been overlooked in the writing of the script). The crowd loved the repartee and harmless sexual innuendos. They were glued to the stage, bright-eyed and totally engrossed, laughing heartily and unembarrassedly on cue. For me, I watched it in nervous anticipation. I knew the girls danced between acts, so I was anxious for the first act to finish. When the curtain finally swept closed—to the swell of applause from the crowd, I was anxious and tense, and happy for the girls when almost no one left for the foyer. After about five minutes a rhythmic prelude rose from the orchestra pit. It increased, the lights dimmed, a pause, and then a primitive drum beat.

When the curtains parted, I laid eyes on a set that I don't know how anyone could have gotten onto that stage in just five minutes. A foliated jungle panorama with a real waterfall, and rock cliffs going up into the catwalks. The set was adorned by twelve, luscious, gold-dust covered Amazon women—*who would be our dates for the evening!* The bright klieg lights shone off their glistening bodies and sparkling costumes. Three stood tall and proud right at the front edge of the stage, towering above us with their spears held overhead. Three or four were high atop the rock ledge, a couple hanging from vines, and one on a huge throne. What a set! I searched and examined, but surprisingly could not be sure which one was June. They all looked the same, with their shining hair pulled back and sequined, heavy makeup, huge lashes and glitter on their eyelids. All of them with the same large red mouth and white teeth. It could have been one girl on a stage full of mirrors. No way to find June. *Wow, talk about legs!*

When the show began I was at first shocked at the intricacies of the routine, and second, mightily impressed by the timing and athletic ability of these food-munching girls of last night. The amount of energy they were expending was amazing. I was also embarrassed at how I had undervalued their skills and commitment. There was determination in their eyes and intense concentration as they carried out each movement. They would explode into each new challenging feat, suddenly demanding their strong legs and backs to arch and spring, and thrust them across the stage. Sitting this close I could see the clenched teeth, and hear the gasps and restrained grunts as they put forth maximum efforts. It was obvious they were as dedicated to their profession as I was to mine. (Can't believe I said that. *More* dedicated, I'm sure.)

I GUESS I JUST WASN'T THINKING

The crowd loved it and I was filled with pride and excitement that I knew these girls, and that I would get to know them better. I was having a hard time believing that these leaping, tempting sorceresses were the same sprawling, famished young girls I'd met the night before. Boy, could they be proud of what they were doing. I knew Bob and Don would have liked to have been in on this. Maybe if I could find them now, I could get them here in time to catch the girls' next act. (If I could find two seats.) For two cents I'd run out and try to find them. Most the guys hung out in the hotel where we had our squadron room. I'd probably find them there. Naw, the hell with it. The final two acts of the play were as funny as the first act, and the girls' second performance was as fabulous as the first.

If you thought I was nervous in the theater, you should have seen me waiting in the restaurant at one-thirty in the morning. From the minute this evening was planned I knew the midnight boat was out of the question. I had already decided I would most likely be on that 0600 boat for the married guys. (Matter of fact I had Tripp standing by for me until noon tomorrow.) Not too many people in the restaurant. Almost the same crowd as last night. Same too-well lit interior. No romantic mood going to be set here I could see. But I learned, to these girls no mood-setting stuff was needed after their mood-setting job. I would learn that what they were interested in were simple things, real people, recipes, their cats, their "mums." Who would have ever guessed?

I don't want to say it was a disappointment; certainly it was not, but it was a little bit of a shock. Three of the girls were almost to the table before I recognized them as the previously spectacularly beautiful creatures we had seen gliding and leaping across the slanted boards of the Teatro Principal. In place of tall, glistening, statuesque figures, with classic features, a frolicking gaggle of almost adolescent girls in old sweaters, faded jeans and army surplus jackets bounded through the door. Instead of cascading platinum and burgundy locks, there was straight, thin, straw-colored hair. At our table, scrubbed faces with absolutely no makeup (and no eyebrows). Up close, some bad teeth, a few bruises, a skin rash. Entirely human.

Their liveliness, their joy, their shining eyes, and truths as they saw them, captured us again. Snatching chairs, joking, poking, laughing and consoling, it was them again: June, Laurie, Wendy, Claire, the rich girl from Manchester, the real redhead from Ireland, the twins originally from Argentina, and more. I wanted to go some place special. I didn't know where, but someplace that would dazzle them. June kept saying that this place would be just fine. I guessed it was, but I wanted the girls to remember this night. I wanted to impress them for June. Oops, a couple of them were already ordering Cokes. Gotta get this thing organized quick.

Dale and Wendy were sitting together at the next table, heads close. He was getting with it. Before June could decide on which special place we should hit, a couple of the girls gave Dale and I unusually big "thank yous" for the invitation and bowed out for one reason or another. I was a little sorry; would have liked to have brought the "whole catch" along. Maybe just maybe we would have bumped into some of the other guys (and boy would they have been jealous)! But nope, the verdict was in. That's it—we're eating here. Later I decided maybe these girls were no dummies. They weren't about to jump in a cab and go away with a couple guys they really knew nothing about—clean-cut Americans or not. No problem. We'll eat here and enjoy it. *Por Favor, traiganos las cartas!*

Boy, did these girls enjoy eating or what!? It was one activity they made the most of—especially June. She gave me a big—a wonderfully big and mischievous smile, and then snatched up the menu. She studied it only a minute or two, and then with a look of complete self-satisfaction slapped it down on the table convincingly, leaving no doubt that this phase was over and done. With an impish grin, she clowned for me, hunching up her shoulders, smacking her lips and rubbing her stomach, signaling her anticipation of the treat in store. Checking out the rest of the girls, most of them were acting just like June—joyously animated and obviously unafraid to show their emotions. I could see they were in the habit of making the most of the moment at hand. *Enjoy it, whatever it was, wherever it was.* Boy, would I like to be able to think and live like them. Surprisingly and gratifyingly (*thanks God*) June appeared to be perfectly content to be here with me. No signs of restlessness. Nothing to indicate she had any regrets or second thoughts. Even in this dinky little restaurant with a new American friend, she was going to enjoy herself, no questions about it. And though I don't know how or why, from the beginning she seemed absolutely at ease with me. "Old shoe" after fifteen minutes. I wondered if she was like this with every guy, or if maybe I was going to be something special.

Suddenly she cocked her head to one side, closed one eye and squinted at me through the other. She was daring me to guess what she had selected. Whatever it was, I was sure it was going to be great. Or if not she was going to devour it anyway. If it was a total bust, there'd always be another day. You could tell that was what she was thinking; that was her philosophy. I suspected no one ever had more fun or enjoyed herself like this Brit lass. I told her about life on the carrier. Not much else I could say. (Don't know if she noticed how many areas I *wasn't* getting into.) From my end it was not fun and required some quick thinking. I wanted to paint an attractive picture—perhaps even one of eligibility, but I didn't want to lie to June. Already that didn't seem right, although as you might imagine I failed to tell her I was married. Embarrassedly I'll admit of recent I wasn't starting any conversations by telling people I had a wife and kids. And certainly it wasn't because I didn't have a family I could be well proud of (or that anyone would not be proud of). It was just that the opportunities I was now experiencing precluded me dwelling on the fact that my life's story had already been written, with no more chances, no more relationships, no more mystique.

I tried to let June do the talking, although unless she was encouraged to do so, she was very content to listen. And what a listener. From the way her eyes stayed on me I couldn't believe that she wasn't seeing right through me. When she did speak, for a change I listened.

"You bet. Born in England—Birmingham. A couple hours northwest of London by motorcar. We're called 'Brommies.' Everyone from Birmingham is called a 'Brommy.' Birmingham is what you yanks would call a blue collar city, with lots of factories. You know, mostly just trucks and smoke stacks, and labor demonstrations. In the early 1900's Birmingham was the chosen area for all the Irish immigrants. Now—for the last ten years, the Pakistanis and Indians have been joining them. In fact Roger—and it's cute, because of this crazy ethnic cross section, a UK-wide expression has arisen: *A typical Brommie with a shamrock in his turban.*"

June was one of three sisters; the daughter of a Scottish shoemaker, who from her description was a cross between Jimmy Durante and George Burns. She had wanted to be a dancer since she was a little girl doing soft-shoe routines at his side. She opted out of school in the eleventh grade and enrolled in the only dance school she could afford. It was located on the unheated third floor of an unoccupied building right next to the Birmingham railroad station. She did her moves to the clanging of the cars hitching and unhitching; did her pirouettes to the circling of the locomotives in the roundhouse below. With the sniffles, cold ankles and chapped hands, she spun and leaped, and peered through soot-stained windows, picturing new and strange places, and imagining audiences in Europe and all over the world cheering her on.

Concerning this troupe, June had been hired first and then recruited the other girls. All of them were seasoned troopers with at least one tour under their belt, except for Claire—she was only 17 years old and it was her very first tour. Looking past two tables at her bright young face and wide eyes, I wondered how in the hell her parents ever let her leave England. June had been concerned also, and said she'd told the owner that Claire was too young—give her another year or two. He agreed, but just before they left one girl cancelled out and they had to call up Claire. The girls had danced in many countries but liked Spain the best. The theater company here lived up to its agreements, the girls were able to rent comfortable flats within their budgets, and the food in the markets (or the restaurants) was good and not too expensive, and it was safe.

June got an omelet and some kind of pork sausage. I ordered a steak. June made me get a plate of *Espinaca a la Crema* to go along with it. Couldn't tell what Dale and Wendy got at the next table. A few girls had split to different tables (some with their boyfriends—which I guess I should have suspected). I was concerned that having invited them to dinner, I would not be able to track down the checks, and that the girls would just buy their own dinners, making me look like I had reneged. Some did buy their own and still thanked me profusely. (I think June was involved in that decision.) The girls—all of them, were great. They didn't want to be impressed. They asked us lots of questions about the USA. Dale told them all about New Orleans and the Mardi Gras celebration. I was dumbfounded, as with no special effort on our part, the girls seemed to be having a perfectly good time, right here in this small dingy restaurant. I had spent so much time of recent, envying the European men for their appearance and worldliness, and now all of a sudden I find that these girls are not only interested in America, but in average American guys.

The girls adored June. At least a half dozen times during the meal, one or two of them came bounding up to our table, gave June a big hug or a kiss, and excitedly related this or that about herself, or her boyfriend, or her family in Blackpool. It was obvious that as their leader, she was someone the girls looked to for advice. And I was sure of one thing; it wasn't because she had just been *handed* the title of Ballet Captain. It was because they knew her credentials and she had earned their respect many times over. At twenty-four, June was a veteran on the dance tour. She had been here before. She'd been everywhere before! I felt (and maybe for the first time in my life) that June was a person I could easily respect and admire, and be faithful to. Already I found myself hoping for good things in her life; that she would get what she deserved, that things would turn out all right for her, that there wouldn't be tough times for her, or even mediocre times. I should have hoped harder, or just stayed out of her life.

Wrapping up dinner and paying the checks—*at three-thirty*. Whew, was I going to be exhausted tomorrow or what. And what next? As much as I wanted to spend more time with June (and she showed no signs of wilting) I felt myself slipping. Dozing off in the middle of my own sentences. Pins and needles in my legs. Need to rest, need to charge up. But I also knew tomorrow was the last night the carrier would be in port. If not tonight, it would have to be tomorrow night. So, unable not to, and in spite of what shipboard problems it would incur, Dale and I made sure we had another date laid on for tomorrow. We could go dancing—just the four of us. (No more need to impress the rest of the girls.) And the good news, they went for it!

We were able to talk our way back to the ship on the first Shore Patrol boat (which wasn't until five o'clock). I was really dead by then. And we wouldn't have gotten on that boat if it weren't for Dale knowing the chief. In the stateroom at 0600. Jim was just getting up and gave me some mildly disapproving looks. Not a good deal, but he doesn't know. He's never gotten involved in something like this. But the cat might be outa the bag. People might be giving up on me. I'll fix it later, gotta sleep now—at least a couple hours, then I'll get up and tear the place apart. Fell asleep like a dead man.

The alarm went off. Pushed the button down. Fell back asleep. *Shit—11:00!* Showered, shaved, dressed, and to the shops. In fact, the shops and half the ship. Good, it appeared most people hadn't noticed the decline and fall of Roger Yahnke. I was surprised (and gratified) at how much the other guys and the men in the shops *didn't* know about me. *Thanks again God.* And guess what? Today is my own liberty day. Don't have to swap with Tripp.

A Scary First Date with June

Same restaurant—one-thirty in the morning. Girls should be in here any minute. I was nervous. Don't think Dale was ever nervous. (And he shouldn't be. He looked like Dean Martin and could bench press 300 pounds.) There they were! I saw June. She was first. A good sign. Followed by Wendy, and Laurie? *Oops an extra lady.* We jumped up and got the three of them seated. I could see right off that Laurie was not comfortable. Maybe concerned that her tagging along might be a monkey wrench in Dale and my plans. But the dating gods were with us: "No June, you and Wendy go dancing. I'm out on my feet anyway. Plus I have some letters to write."

Funny how you size things up. I was almost sure that June was going to plan the evening so that we would have more time together. But for now she was going to share a few moments and some good times with her true friend Laurie, who ended up staying about thirty minutes and I have to admit—even for me, it was time well spent. A pleasant experience. Seeing them together I could sense the bond and see that Laurie was the only one who approached June's level, and who June would confide in. I suppose with June's job she needed at least one sounding board. As they talked it was apparent that they went back a long way. And guess what, Laurie wasn't really a dancer. June had just hired her to help her out. Laurie was a singer. (And June said she was "smashing!") She had brought down the house last year at the Summer Festival in Liverpool and had been on tour with Shirley Bassey! And then her agent had really screwed her. Not literally. Financially. Contract stuff. I think the rights to a recorded song.

Laurie was just here for a six-month stint, earning money to return to the UK to cut another record. She had a deal being financed by Granada TV (the only purely entertainment independent TV channel in England). I quickly began to feel a respect for Laurie. She was okay. She wasn't dating here (as hard as it was for me to believe). She had a steady boyfriend back in England and was true blue. The five of us had a good time together, and I think—a longer time together than any of us had anticipated. When Laurie looked at her watch and saw it was almost two, she jumped up, grabbing her coat and scarf, and apologized profusely for delaying the start of our evening. Of course based on the hugs from everybody at the table, she knew no one was holding a grudge. She wished us all the best "night on the town" (or whatever was now left of it). As late as it was, Dale and I weren't sure what our options were. We were still hoping that this last night in Valencia would make it memorable. We asked the girls if they had a favorite spot, or knew some after-hours club where there might be live music at two-thirty in the morning. Wendy responded. "Junie, how about the place out on the beach, by the bus parking lot?"

181

"Don't know Wendy, haven't heard much about it. Can't imagine it's a late one though."

"Yeah June, t'is. Claire's been there; she said it had a good band."

"Claire's been out there? I could see that June was not at all happy that Claire had been there.

While she was still shaking her head and before Wendy could answer, Dale and I decided to jump on the idea.

"Let's go!" We hailed a cab and were on our way—a long way, to our beachside destination. Miles of nothing. Long unlit stretches. Empty crossroads. Deserted neighborhoods in a winter ghost town. And still windy. Finally, must be getting close, small sand dunes on both sides. Ten minutes later (still in Spain I think), a forlorn cluster of buildings—some signs of civilization. Next thing I knew we were pulling into what must have been the bus parking lot Wendy was talking about. A helluva trip, but maybe it'll be worth it. And sure enough, in the middle of this large but completely empty macadam parking lot was a completely unlit, one-story concrete block building; from all outward appearances—abandoned. No outside lights. No signs. The few windows there were, were shuttered. We made our way across the lot, past a couple parked buses, over two curbs, and up to an unmarked small door that we decided, had to be the only entrance. And it was.

I was about to enter one of the least explicable public places I'd ever ventured into. Once through the unpainted front door we stumbled into a black abyss—had to stop and allow our eyes to become accustomed to the darkness that enveloped us. When we could finally make out a few rudimentary outlines, we were able to deduce that the interior of the building was just one, large, bare, unfurnished, cement-floored room. From front to back, halfway across the emptiness there was a floor-to-ceiling lattice work divider, separating the space into two rooms. In our space—the area we had entered, there was a reception counter with no one behind it, but not another piece of furniture—nothing. Could it be this building is the bus terminal during the day, and they just move all the benches and counters somewhere at night? There was a dim glow in each of the far corners, where a recessed ceiling light did nothing more than mark its own location. We stood rooted to the spot. No one approached us. We were being totally ignored. No hosts or hostesses; in fact I couldn't make out a soul who appeared to be an employee. One or two patrons (I *guess* patrons; more accurately—shadows) milled by us, but no colors or features were visible.

It was apparent the area on the left side of the divider was where things should have been "happening." In the farthest corner a band was playing (also in the dark, minus what slight illumination the nearest recessed ceiling light afforded). Through the divider I surveyed the other side. The far side wall, the back wall, and the whole length of the lattice divider in front of us, were lined with straight back chairs—from corner to corner to corner; all of them occupied by hunched over, motionless beings—guys and girls; about half and half, but not speaking to one another. Hands clasped in their laps, they were staring straight ahead. No laughter and not a smile that I could see. On that side there were no tables, no bar, no waiters or waitresses moving about; nor could I see anyplace that appeared to be selling drinks (one of which would have come in real handy at this point). In fact, as I scanned the people sitting along the walls, it did not appear that any of them were holding drinks. The dance floor was completely empty. Everyone in the place was seated, not a single person on the dance floor. A little flustered our eyes searched for something familiar. Something *normal!* Another small gaggle of silent alien figures glided past us. *What in the hell kind of place was this?* As far as I could see, no one was having a good time. Dale and the girls appeared to be as cool to this place as I was. A weird atmosphere to say the least. June looked at me and drew the corners of her mouth way back and rolled her eyes. Dale shrugged his shoulders and Wendy (thank God) said "Oh well, as long as we're out here, let's go for a walk on the beach." *Best idea I'd heard yet.*

Only five minutes from the club we found ourselves on an uneven sidewalk, making our way through a slightly rundown, almost abandoned, seaside area. No large or modern buildings. Only some small, derelict cottages on the beach. I didn't yet know what great beaches Spain had; on the Costa del Sol, at other locations on this—the Costa Brava, and on the islands of Majorca and Ibiza. What I did know, was that *this* area was not very enticing. Not a new structure anywhere and what was standing was in bad repair. Screen doors banging in the wind. Weed clumps blowing across the street. A dismantled car up on the curb. Other than the bare-bulbed street lamps above us, there didn't appear to be a single source of light anywhere. We were now stepping over foot-deep drifts of sand across the sidewalk, which fronted a row of old wooden hotels (that hopefully came to life during the summer). We passed a couple that I think might have been open for business. Dale and Wendy—about a hundred feet ahead of us, were stopped in front of one of them.

I GUESS I JUST WASN'T THINKING

Uh-oh, I was reading Dale's mind and suddenly felt a little uncomfortable. Didn't know if June was sensing a turn of events here, or how receptive she would be to it. We hadn't been talking too much—still just innocently holding hands. Decision time. Not likely that we're going to venture down to the beach for the aforementioned walk. This was it. A hushed conversation ensued between Dale and Wendy that would either end up with the four of us mounting the rickety stairs to this clapboard hotel, or an awkward outcome that would involve a "U" turn back to the parking lot to search for a cab. My suspicions were confirmed: Dale had done it. He'd sweet talked Wendy into agreeing that at this late hour, they'd best not try to make it back to the city. Just bed down here. (The way my legs felt and as tired as I was, from a physical standpoint, hitting the rack did sound pretty good.) But this hitting of the rack, of course, would result in some serious involvements. Of course I had to go along with it. I don't know how I mushed it by June, or how enthusiastic she was about it, or if she really even understood what the plan was. I just kind've blabbed that we would just hang around in another room, and let Dale and Wendy do what they wanted to, in their room. We would just waste some time, or doze, or watch TV, or something. *Yuk.*

Dale was up the steps and into the hotel. About three minutes of uncomfortable silence and he was back out, flashing a big smile and waving us up. (Shades of Mike Ballard waving me up the gangplank of the *Leonardo da Vinci*.) Inside—just one old guy. I took care of the formalities. The place smelled like mildew. Creaking floors. Worn carpeting. Dim hallways. Narrow wood stairs. Cracked glass in the pictures. Onto the second floor, and with some forced wisecracks, into our respective rooms. Me, with measurable discomfort. Once again, here I was on the threshold of a tryst, and feeling a lot more worried than lustful.

The one large window in our room fronted the street we had just come in from. It had no curtains and no shade, and was letting in altogether too much light (from one of those bare-bulbed street lamps). This harsh illumination did nothing to flatter the blank plaster walls and old furniture. There was a bathroom. One bed—a small single bed. (Almost a cot.) What next? *Gotta start sometime.* June was silently following me in—maybe too close. I stopped and turned and she walked right into me. The first things to touch me were the fronts of her huge well-muscled thighs. I was a little nervous as it was, and this sudden hard pressure from her big lower body served to intimidate me further.

I was halfway there, so I put my arms around her. Gave her a kiss. Our first kiss. Her hair smelled good and her firm waist was enticing. I think she may have been prepared to see it through—sort of in a "wait and see" mode at the moment. I think she sensed I had an honorable interest in her and was thus going to tolerate my advances, although she probably had envisioned it would occur in another way, another day. Maybe after a couple dates. Maybe in her apartment on a lazy afternoon. Maybe a nice hotel room, after a night of romantic dancing. Still in my arms, June reached around and gave me a good whack on my backside—a mock spanking, and shook her index finger at me while sporting a tension-relieving look that said, *You're a real bad boy Roger.* I think her levity at this time made me feel a little better. "No plan June. Just happened. Believe me."

"Don't worry, look here." She flipped on the TV. "BBC, we watch it almost every night when we get back from the theater; wind down with some news from home. And today they're supposed to have a special with Cilla Black. You should hear her." June eyed an overstuffed loveseat against the wall, strode over to it, hoisted one end like it weighed nothing, and commenced dragging it across the room; in fact, running backwards with it—to a spot right in front of the TV. The illumination from the TV did nothing to soften our hardened confines. We watched for a while. I'd never heard of Cilla Black before, but she was great. She sang her number one hit in the UK, "You're My World" ("…every breath I take, every move I make"). It was a serious love song, and June and I were very quiet during it. The show over, June was up! No hesitancy, no fudging.

She marched over to the bureau and matter-of-factly began undressing *in full view of me.* (I was feeling awkward enough for the both of us.) But it was quick and functional, as if she was in the dressing room with a bunch of girls. It definitely was not done in a manner to arouse me. It was the furthest thing from a seductive disrobing. She braced herself against the wall with one hand, reached down with the other and pulled off her scuffed shoes. One, then the other. After inspecting the soles, she shook her head disapprovingly and flipped them over her shoulder (as if into a trash bin). She whipped her sweater off over her head like a track athlete lightening up for an event, took aim and tossed it across the room where it draped over a straightback chair.

I watched in amazement at her nonchalant behavior. She undid the zipper on her hip-huggers and started tugging them down, only to find they would not make it past her knees. Thumbs hooked in the material just above her hobbled knees, she hopped like someone in a sack race, over to the bed. Arriving there she twisted around, flopped over on her back, swung her legs overhead and yanked the trousers off. She popped back up and stomped around to the foot of the bed. There (in her bra and panties) she assumed a not flattering pose. Legs planted wide apart, flat footed, and hands behind her back, she mimicked a Marine at the Parade Rest position, guarding some monument, and gave me a salute. She was clowning!

For some reason, June was making this thing the least erotic as possible, *perhaps for both of us.* I don't think she was ashamed of her body, but she was not proud of it either, and certainly not displaying it as any prize. I guessed as far as June was concerned, it was just there. No better, no worse—hers, the one she was stuck with. And thank God, it worked. It leaped and spun, and danced for her—well enough that she wasn't dependent on her parents or anybody else; paying her own way through life. Next thing I knew she had turned on a heel and was marching (now imitating a drum majorette) knees exaggeratingly high, arms swinging, straight towards the bathroom. Before going through the door she did some little stage maneuver, leaning backward and blowing me a kiss over her shoulder. *God what a girl!* Evidently she wasn't bashful, she didn't bother to close the door. And no matter there was no hot water, she took a cold bath, in a deep old fashioned tub, under an unshaded hanging bulb. I peeked. Her white skin was a great contrast to her dark red hair, which was now wetly stuck across her shoulders. Out of the tub and standing there, her legs appeared much too long and large for her torso. Her glistening buttocks were strong and beautifully rounded, and her muscular thighs were well-shaped (and hard, I already knew). But June was not big on top. Her arms and shoulders were thin, and her breasts were small. This was of no matter to me, my escalating interest in her (including both respect and affection) was not in the least effected by any physical shaping.

She strutted out of the bathroom, wrapped in a faded towel, and leaped—I mean *leaped* onto the bed. A giant yank and a flap and she was under the covers. I wasn't sure if her natural boldness was making me less nervous or more nervous. *Goddamit, this time it would be serious*, and as usual I wasn't feeling inclined. Not by a long shot. And worse, I had no reason to feel optimistic about any changes for the better. I made a quick trip to the bathroom. The cold water discouraged me from taking a bath. Just did a thorough wipedown. Came out shaking. Don't know if it was the cold water, the chill in the room, or my nerves. Into the rack. Our bodies smelled half of the cheap soap and half of perspiration. Thank God the sheets felt as if they might be clean. Didn't know where to start.

Petted. Petted some more. June was quiet and patient. She wasn't smothering me with hard wet kisses, or any kisses at all. I don't think it was a plan, but she just laid there passively, giving me time (which I sorely needed). She wasn't throwing her legs apart or grinding her hips, thank God. If she would have started out like that, I would have been spread-eagled against a far wall. She was quiet. I kissed and caressed her. I kissed her some more. This big physical girl—so demonstrative in every other way, was lying perfectly still. What movement she made was slow and without sound. Still not ready and delaying as usual, I moved my face lower, past her smooth stomach, to begin kissing the sweet hollow where her big legs joined her groin. My face there, I was surprised by a clean, sweet smell, like the fragrance of a recently bathed and powdered baby. It wasn't perfume and I hadn't seen her use any lotion. Maybe it was just that soap smell, but June's mons seemed to have an innocence, a purity, that I'd never had reason to consider before.

However in spite of all this (or because of all this), as I had feared from the beginning, nothing great happened. In fact nothing *at all* happened. Like I had no blood flow. As if my groin was anesthetized. I tried and waited, and tried. Mentally shaking my head at myself, my body, my hormones, my fate. To say I was woefully lacking would be accurate. If I had it to do over again, I would have opted to please her another way; just hide my ineptness. *Or better, have avoided entering this hotel in the first place.* I was disappointed and embarrassed, but worse—almost ready to resign myself to my condition. She never commented one way or the other. God what a let down I must have been (again). I slid my arm under her head. She kissed me on the forehead, gave me a big, 'little-girl' smile (just like at dinner the other night), rolled half over, made a project of slapping a hollow into her pillow, and flopped her head into it. She was calling it a night, no question about that. I can't remember when or if I fell asleep.

I do know that when Dale pounded on the door about seven o'clock, I was in no shape to rise and shine. Felt terrible. Mulled over the previous late night. No way I was going to brag about that. Hard to even imagine laughing or joking. The good news: June didn't act like there was anything wrong in the world. She held my hand, patted me on the back and kissed me on the cheek. The four of us straggled out of the hotel and made a brief attempt to stroll the beach. Have to admit, the area looked a little better in the daylight. Not great, but at least it appeared as if it could be salvaged during the summer season. Started searching for a cab around ten. Finally got one, and with the girl's good directions arrived downtown in just fifteen minutes. We stopped in front of our destination—the Cafe Andalusia, a little before noon. It was a neat place and the Stafford Ballet's favorite breakfast haunt. (They normally ate breakfast about noon.) Inside, we ordered up two liters of fresh orange juice and four huge omelets with everything. Thankfully the girls didn't appear to hold any grudges. We'd escaped. The girls made an event out of the meal, just like the night before (and as I would see—every time they ate, no matter where or when).

Unfortunately, the girls (all of them—the whole troupe) had an appointment with some Spanish TV station at two o'clock; so this was going to be our last few minutes together in Valencia. This was going to be it. Neither of us was anxious to part (of course after my lack of performance last night, I don't know why June would have had any regrets about seeing the last of me). We walked—dilly-dallied, the ten or so blocks to the *Edificio De Periodicos*. There, stalling outside the carved stone entrance, while Dale and Wendy did their talking, June and I did some serious future planning of our own.

They'd be leaving Valencia in three weeks for a stint in Barcelona, where we were scheduled to anchor the end of February. With earnest intent June gave me what information she had that would help me locate her in Barcelona. She pressed the piece of paper into my hand, folding my fingers around it; then pressed the tip of her index finger square against my nose and said, "Now Rogey, you be there, I'll be waiting for you!" I was justifiably surprised; couldn't imagine our time together would be very high on her list, but she *did* seem a little sad at our parting. Not that June could ever be described as looking sad; from what I'd seen so far, she was an upbeat, determined, resilient person, always ready for the obstacles and disappointments that she knew were out there. I was pretty sure that nothing could be devastating to June. It was no accident she was in charge; along with those beautiful green eyes and innocent face, I sensed she had a degree from the *school of hard knocks,* and could always put things in perspective. I bet when any of the girls were down in the mouth, it was June they counted on to cheer them up; get them back on their feet and through the tribulations that were part and parcel to their livelihood. Already, I felt for June, something I had never felt before: a deep respect and wholesome affection. Yet sadly—tragically, *she was not proving to be that one woman who would awaken me.*

Chapter Seventeen
CHRISTMAS IN CANNES

Paulette Again

This was going to be a first—twelve days in port. Almost two straight weeks of liberty. Before this we'd never spent more than five or six days in port. Now we were going to celebrate the whole Christmas season here in Cannes. (Although it sure didn't feel much like Christmas, I can tell you that.) The ship's company was doing as much as they could, hanging up artificial pine bows, tinsel, candy canes, and playing Christmas carols over the PA system. But we all felt something was missing. And was something missing from me? I'll say—the expected and heightened seasonal sentiments. Away from my family at this time of the year I should have been more "down in the dumps," busily spending my time writing Christmas cards and wrapping gifts for Sara and the kids. And I was! I was—at least to some extent, although perhaps in a much too perfunctory a fashion; not giving sufficient thought to the choice of the gifts I was choosing and buying. Instead of being in the heartfelt swing of things, I was ashamed to find myself preoccupied visualizing events that might evolve on the two days leave I'd be taking when we pulled into Cannes.

It's not that Sara and the kids weren't in my thoughts. They were. I could imagine them cheerful (hopefully) and full of the Christmas spirit (mercifully oblivious to my less than honorable activities), bustling around my low end of the market, car-ported house. *My* house? *Their* home. And much more appreciated by them than me, I'm sure. I was embarrassed at the thought of Sara's undeserved concern for me; out to sea, doing my duty, making the sacrifice. How could anyone who knew me—no matter how far away, not somehow sense my flagrant activity? Of course in the midst of my own dilemma, I wasn't considering my previous short involvements (and now my feelings for June) as "womanizing." But what else could it be called? Objectively, even I knew my behavior was such, and could not be explained another way.

But this was going to be my only chance to know. If I didn't discover it now on this cruise, I wouldn't—ever. Rome, the Riviera, and Istanbul. Wow! Don't see how I can rein myself in. Having sampled a whole new world, I would be unable not to keep on exploring it. I didn't see how I could do otherwise. I would continue experimenting and searching, in case somewhere out there, there might be that one situation, or much more importantly—that one woman who would validate my masculinity. I found myself unable not to be thinking about finding her. And then a real fright of what that find would mean. The unthinkable things I would have to do to, should I decide I wanted her with me from then on. Where was it all leading? *Talk about the moth and the flame.*

And even after all this soul-searching, here I was readying myself to go again, hyped-up and dreaming about this Cote d'Azur rendezvous with Paulette (from the famous *Leonardo Da Vinci* escapade). Through international mail (her written English was fairly easily deciphered) we were able to set up this short winter weekend meeting. The memories of the sun-soaked beaches and glistening bronze bodies of Cannes were still fresh to me. The mere mention of the place provoked visions of pleasures and adventures, that I could never considered being restricted to just July or August. Thinking ahead now to the next few days, I was (with difficulty) able to subdue the guilt feelings that were lurking just under the surface. But I did recognize them and knew I was being negligent in not being more preoccupied with the family's activities during this yuletide season. And what time I was not thinking ahead, I was thinking back—to Ardith, and Erica, and Belkis, and Ingrid, and now, more than the rest—June! *God help me.*

As soon as we rounded Antibes' point, I could see that the weather was not going to cooperate. For the past twenty-four hours I'd been praying for blue skies, but no such luck. There lay Cannes like the North Jersey coast, shrouded under a cold and wet, gray overcast. I could spot at least two or three small squalls between us and a disappointingly dismal-looking shoreline. It wasn't beckoning this time—with the glittering enticement of the past July visit. Not by a longshot. *Could this possibly be the Cannes I remember?* And worse, it was windy. (Told you what I think of the wind.) Standing on the flight deck I felt the ship shudder in the Captain's ordered

190

final turn before mooring. Thirty more seconds. There it was—first the rumbling of the chain rattling out and then sound of the anchor pounding the water. The splash sent a spray across the flight deck that felt like ice pellets. Regardless of the elements I was determined to have another memorable time in Cannes. An uncontrollable shiver went through me. Decided to get below. It was a wet forty degrees and I had been topside since we were twenty miles out.

For once there'd be no worry about swapping duty days here. It was all "leave," *official* leave. So no wheeling and dealing. My plan was to catch the first liberty boat and be at the train station when Paulette arrived. I was all packed and had clothes for any occasion, except as I mentally ran down the list—clothes for a cold, wet occasion such as the one likely to take place. But I'll tell you, no chills, not even pneumonia, is going to wreck this weekend. I'll have a nice visit with Paulette, and some time to get to know her; find out about her family, her living arrangements, her job, and what thoughts were running around in the back of that attractive European head.

Unfortunately, after recognizing the attraction I felt for these strange, lithe, intense and differently educated females; what limited intellect I had was saying: Rog, be realistic. *How can you even consider something worthwhile happening out of all this?* True enough, gotta face it. First and foremost I was married. Well-married! A husband and father, with kids, and in-laws and stateside neighbors. How could I even contemplate the event that would have to take place first? And once announced and carried out (incomprehensible in itself) what chances would I ever have of sustaining an existence in Europe? What work could I find that would provide the income to maintain the type of life I had been observing and sampling on my times ashore.

Or on the other hand, if I *was* able to convince myself to do it, and managed to snatch one of these European women off her natural turf, away from the organized fineries of her culture, and whisk her off to the good old USA. How would she adapt to the K-Mart, U-Haul and Denny's way of life? Especially now after what I had seen over here. Whew, not pleasant to think about. One of those "you can't get there from here" type situations. I had real doubts about what I was doing and how I was thinking. 1400 hours. My roomie Jim Stremlow, watching me pack, kidded me about bugging out again. Hard to tell when he's kidding, one of his fortes was a cutting sarcasm. Not really sure what he thinks of my activities.

I GUESS I JUST WASN'T THINKING

I was back down the same passageways I'd run up many a late night. No problem getting to the liberty ladder. Passed Ernie on the hangar deck. He kidded me about the pointy toe shoes I was wearing (that I had bought in Genoa). He said they were only good for *killing cockroaches in corners*. I could see that most the guys took my frequent absences as harmless cavorting (not realizing the obsession). I was becoming more and more a loner. Two other guys signaled me a thumbs up, and wished me a good time. Others had grown so accustomed to only seeing me briefly—leaving and arriving, they had given up trying to keep track of my activities. I gotta keep in touch; can't become an outsider in my own squadron (especially with Jim). I'm pressing my luck there already. Jumped down from the ladder two rungs high, and landed, suit bag and toilet kit swinging, struggling to keep my balance on the uneven boards in the bottom of the rocking liberty boat. As usual it was a bumpy fifteen minute ride, and wet too. The wind was off shore, about twenty knots and cold. Seemed to take much longer than usual to tie up at the west end of the Cannes Yacht Basin, where we were told we were privileged to be able to dock. (And we were. In Genoa we couldn't use the Yacht Club. Had to use some commercial concrete slab pier a mile north of town.)

Though I hadn't noticed it last time I was here, there was a lone hotel situated on a rocky point that jutted out from the far west side of the marina. True, staying there would mean ten minutes more to walk to the town center, but it seemed to be beckoning me. It was a white, wood-sided building that actually looked friendly (and that I was sure would be less expensive than those big ones across from the beach). Maybe I should just register there right now. Naw, better wait on that decision until joined by Paulette, in case she had a preference. Although I could've at least got that step out of the way. Think I finally discovered one of those things women don't admit, but actually prefer: it's when the guy just takes care of things without always asking, *What would you like to do? C'mon now, what would please you?* (And had I got this hotel, I would not have had to carry my suit bag and toilet kit all over town while waiting for Paulette.)

By the time I got to the end of the cement walkway the cold damp air had me shivering, and the skies had turned dark and threatening. Not surprisingly, just as I turned right onto the famous La Croisette—with a good ten minute walk ahead of me, it began drizzling. While it was still the wide, palm lined and curving esplanade I had cruised in July, it was certainly not boasting any vacation splendor now; not being baked in the summer sun, nor graced with exciting people in daring outfits. And to make matters worse they had obviously chosen this time of year to tear up the roads. Ahead of me was a maze of yellow and black tape stretching between white and orange stanchions. Making my way along the sidewalk wasn't easy. About every fifty feet, next to a gaping hole there was a huge mound of dirt and broken pieces of pavement. Had to pop off the walkway and out into the middle of the street. Even there, I had to juke left and right to avoid fluorescent-vested, turtle-necked, chain-smoking laborers, who were doing their share of grumbling while hoisting rubber-coated electric cables from muddy excavations. My shoes and trouser cuffs were wet and splattered. I broke to a fast walk to facilitate weaving my way under a huge derrick that was swinging pallets of tiles onto the roof of a hotel under renovation. No question about it, this was definitely the "off-season."

I trotted past the intimidating Carlton Hotel and then past the Miramar, less foreboding but still selective. Finally arrived at the corner just this side of the Martinez. I took a left there, jogging alongside the hedge-lined patio where I had first heard the Beatles (and met Jacqueline). It would be a short few blocks up to the train station from here. Checked my watch— still about fifteen minutes till Paulette's train is due to arrive. Cursed under my breath as I felt my armpits begin to wetten. I was working up a sweat in spite of the cold damp weather. It was a small station. Only one track with a bordering (completely deserted) concrete platform about a hundred feet long. There must have been one of those municipal beautification programs not too long ago, since a long line of young elms were growing up out of round holes in the cement, and still being held upright by wire cables. Their foliage provided a continuous leafy half-canopy the length of the platform. There was a wooden bench about every 25 feet and another two or three under a pole-supported, roofed area (to protect travelers in the case of just this kind of weather). The light but persistent drizzle was now soaking into my clothes and matting my hair.

One good thing: since the station was so small it would be difficult to miss someone you were here to meet. Outside on the platform (in Cannes there is no *inside*), on a green metal lightpost I spied a framed timetable under a piece of discoloring acrylic. It confirmed a 15:58 arrival from Lyons, which should be Paulette's train. It would have been neat to have some flowers for her, but no shops nearby. Across the narrow street were a couple newsstands, a pastry shop, two standup bars, and a "Restaurant Vietnamien," but no place to buy any flowers. I was more than a little anxious.

I GUESS I JUST WASN'T THINKING

Two minutes to four and the train was right on time. What a railroad! In spite of the rushing around of other thoughts I was still able to feel a gratefulness to this rail system—not making me wait, bringing her to me right on time. I was very nervous now, trying to visualize what she would look like. Originally thought there would be no problem in recognizing her (but I'd already started towards two women who weren't Paulette). Maybe she changed her hair or something. *Keep looking.* My heart thumped. I think I spied her. And it *was* her—getting off the first or second car, way up the other end of the station. She won't see me from where she is. Gotta run up there, don't want her to worry. Round this post. Oops, "S'cuse me." *Damn toilet kit.* "Paulette, here!"

She looked smaller than I remembered, even in a bulky wine-colored winter coat, with big pom-pom buttons. Her calves and ankles were thinner than I remembered. But up close, her short blonde hair, hesitant smile, thin lips, tight white skin across sharp cheeks, and gray eyes were just the same. She appeared relieved to spy me. I thought she was going to cry, but she just dropped her suitcase and gave me a big hug. I could hardly believe all this had come to pass, and it appeared she was having the same thoughts. I spoke first. "How was your trip, how long were you on the train?"

"*Pas long temps, jusque...* No a time long, only *quatre heures. Pas un problem.*"

"Oh I'm so glad you could get here. We can have a nice visit together. Here, let me take that." I wasn't exactly sure how I was going to take her suitcase. Had to relegate my damned toilet kit to the index finger of my right hand, which had been supporting the clothing bag over my shoulder. Shifted it to the remaining three fingers, took her suitcase in my now free left hand. Wished I would have had a third arm to hold her hand. We started navigating our way down the same sidewalk I had just a few minutes ago pounded up. Past not-glamorous store fronts, behind fat ladies walking little dogs, and dodging aproned young men rushing around us carrying those long loaves of bread wrapped in newspaper. No Jaguars full of celebrities cruising around here today, that's for sure.

I was content to be silent, and she too—at least for now. We'd have time to talk soon. Rounding the corner at La Croisette, I was hoping to make the hotel selection and check-in as quick and painless as possible. It's not one of my strong points, this kind of decision making—picking a hotel or a restaurant. You can almost go without eating or sleeping when traveling with me. I'm a true Libra, and while I might be able to make life-or-death aviation decisions okay, selecting a restaurant or deciding on a hotel (or *worse*—choosing between two almost identical pairs of shoes), well that's another thing.

With jaws set and a knot in my stomach, two buildings past the Martinez, I made a quick turn into the drive of a possibly acceptable establishment—the Las Palmas (only two buildings before the one that Erica's brother had been staying in). From the street it looked okay (sort of) and not too expensive, but once inside I had second thoughts. Up close and inside it didn't look near as spiffy as it had from the street. I gave some thought to doing a quick "U" turn and trying another place. *Too late.* Paulette's right here with me. Might as well go through with it and hope for the best. There was no problem registering, though I'm sure I screwed up: *Can you believe I got two rooms.* (But at least adjoining rooms.) *Shit!* Don't know why. Who was I trying to fool. I was nervous. I wasn't sure what was expected here. The concierge (without a hint of a smile) took both passports, spoke a few words to Paulette in French, and had me pay in advance (about 45 US dollars) which was okay I guess. As with almost every French hotel I'd been in, the caged elevator was designed to carry one person with a not-so-big suitcase, or two small people. We were jammed in it. My legs were shaking. I pulled the squeaking metal gate shut across the opening, and waited for the outside door to swing shut. It did, bounced twice and finally came to rest on the switch which would allow us to motorize. We started up with a jerk. I had butterflies. I didn't know— even remotely, what would be happening next.

The room was like the whole day, a plain cream-colored chamber of mediocrity. Not disreputable, but certainly not giving the impression that money was no object to me. And my intention was *not* to low-ball it this time. Didn't know it would be this unspectacular when I chose to enter the drive. *I* felt off-season. Didn't know what to do. It was too early for supper. *Talk,* that's what I said we'd do, *talk.* Maybe go down to the lounge for a Cinzano and talk. Relax! *(Like that was possible.)* Just hangout. I think Paulette was as lost as I was for something to do right now. We passed a few minutes hanging up some clothes and freshening up. The door between our rooms was open, but no conversation. I broke the silence, "Paulette, would you like an aperitif? We can go downstairs for *un verre.*" (I'd learned that the French refer to a "drink" as a "glass"—thus: *un verre.*)

"Oui, yes Roger, that to be *parfait.*"

I was hoping things would somehow go smoother soon. *Maybe after a drink.* In answer to her next question, I replied, "..nothing special, just wear something comfortable." A few moments later she stood in the doorway for my approval. She looked like a school girl, in a green plaid dress with wide shoulder straps, over a white turtle-neck sweater. I later learned that the French elite snobbishly say (and particularly about Americans) that *only clowns wear plaid.* My heart went out to her. Downstairs, to further test my resolve for the day, I was informed that the Las Palmas had no lounge. A momentary *Ugh.* Need a plan "B." Knew the Martinez had a bar—in fact two of em. Can't miss. We'll go there.

We passed over an hour in the more comfortable lounge of the Martinez, but felt a little strange in such a storied location that was now all but deserted. It wasn't the Carlton, but it sure beat the Las Palmas. Sitting there, for the first time I had an unhurried opportunity to really observe her. While her smallness initially suggested it, she wasn't frail. Up close I saw strength in her hands and wrists, and sensed a woman with her share of backbone. It was just that she appeared so unsure and vulnerable. Made me want to be protective of her, and do or say things that would make her happy. The skin on her temples was almost transparent, I could see the small veins underneath. Her eyes were searching, wanting to light up. Her short blonde hair was in tight curls. I noticed her shoes were well-worn and not expensive. She wore almost no jewelry, and what she had was modest and tiny, and losing its luster, resembling the skimpy type of bracelet and charm a girl gets from her first boyfriend. I suspected now, though I didn't realize it on the *Leonardo,* Paulette was on a budget.

From the conversation, I gathered that Paulette might be concerned about her single status—of being thirty and not yet married. What comments she made, hinted at that. As best I could translate, she had been engaged to a local guy in town, but blew that arrangement when she took that job in the states. She was living with her parents now, secluded in a small apartment on the fourteenth floor of a low cost high-rise. She had those working girl blues; was employed as a technician in a state laboratory, putting in lots of hours, trying to save, and hoping that earning her own keep was one way to live up to the expectations of her parents. This European woman—for one, was not so different from many young American women.

Back to the Las Palmas, and it was time for dinner, or close enough— almost seven. There was no heat in the room and cold damp air was tumbling in through the top of one permanently jammed-open window. The skies, the wind, the Las Palmas—none were helping me to feel comfortable. The weekend was not taking on the festive or carefree mood of previous trysts. Something was not natural. It was too mechanical. It was a constant effort constructing and holding up this rendezvous, minute by minute. Like if I stopped talking or moving, rigor mortis would set in; there would be no more movement or sound, and Paulette would evaporate. *It was not going easy.* All the elements were warning me. But we're here and this thing is going to have to play out. I'd planned on it. I suspected Paulette had planned on it.

We passed about thirty minutes getting ready for dinner. The adjoining door was open but still not much communicating going on. I think we were both nervous. Sooner or later we would be in bed together. I had the feeling, not just to enjoy it, but to carry it out knowing it was the only thing left that could salvage the weekend, and perhaps even suggest longer range events. *Whew—not too much pressure.* One good thing, I knew where I could take her for dinner: Le Bistro, the place Major Burnham had taken the pilots that first night. As I remembered it—a warm and friendly establishment with a large fireplace (which would come in damn handy now). Who knows, with a couple glasses of Bordeaux I might feel a little more at ease, and the up till now lacking activities and mood might improve. (It usually did, but I never felt like I needed it more than now.)

Finding it was not as easy as it might have been, but I finally succeeded. And at first glance I deemed it a positive move. It had more people in it than any place we had seen all afternoon. Inside, it was warm and smoky, with lots of laughing diners. *Please God.* Once seated and a little more relaxed, I had the fleeting (hopeful) impression that things might get better. If anything could do it this place should. I'd never been to a restaurant like this in the states. Primitive, with an uneven floor of warped boards stretching between roughly mortared walls, and a ceiling questionably supported by hand hewn and bent timbers. And as I had remembered, one corner of the room did have a stone hearth, in which currently (and fortunately) was a blazing fire. That would surely add to the ambiance, which was sorely needed at the present time. Major Burnham had told us the restaurant was over a hundred years old; not a recent restoration to just pull in tourists.

Thankfully I was hungry. If I would have plopped down and then realized I had no appetite, that would have done it. I knew right away what to order—suggested it, and Paulette was more than glad to go along with it: Chateaubriand for two. While waiting for our flamed, table-sliced entree, Paulette introduced me to one of the continent's most popular libations, a Sandeman Porto. (We had it before the meal although I was to later learn it is actually an after dinner drink.) Never mind, it helped noticeably. My blood was beginning to warm. A good start. The Porto was a beginning, but I still had a long way to go. The worst type of conversation evolved, in that Paulette continued to ask me about me, and *my* life. I was in the same boat again; babbling vagaries—which if they sounded as imprecise to Paulette as they did to me, she would have thought she was with a conversational dimwit. Other than that tack, I would have had to outright lie (which I did to some extent, but did not enjoy). She it turned out, wanted to learn as much about me, as I did about her. Only trouble is, you already know enough about me to realize there is nothing admirable to relate. I recognized that in the long run, to confess a little bit, would be best.

When it seemed an appropriate time, I tested the waters by casually mentioning that I *had been* married. (I could just visualize my wife overhearing this little bit of news!) Paulette didn't even flinch. Could it be divorce is as common in France as in the United States? Evidently, or she was not going to let minor details discourage her from any possible scenarios she may have considered. I stumbled through, implying whenever I got the chance to squeak it in, something that would indicate that ultimately I would be available. I have certainly realized this is not honorable (though it's the standard tack in a thousand supposedly "singles" bars every night).

We were arm in arm on the walk back to the Las Palmas—the best walk of the day (which is not saying a lot). It wasn't misting and it wasn't windy, and the wine had done its best. We were laughing (though not convincingly), but at least feeling well enough to make the effort. I knew it couldn't last too long, there would come the minute when I would have to go through that adjoining door and justify her weekend. Not just do well, but in this case excel and fulfill her unspoken but likely expectations for this rendezvous. *Try not to worry about that now.* Still time, we're only halfway home. Paulette was teaching me French. I could see it would not be an easy language to learn. But it passed the time and took the pressure off. (Concentrate on something else.) Sooner than I would have liked, we were in the hotel, up the tiny ascenseur, and into our rooms. She into hers, I into mine. That damned adjoining door was still open. *Would she think she had to come to my room? Was she as worried about her role? Gotta nip this in the bud.*

"Take your time Paulette, I'll freshen up and be with you in just a few minutes." Having said this (more boldly than I could have imagined), I exhaled a sigh of relief and pushed the door almost all the way closed. This would give her some privacy and let us both go about whatever preparations we saw fit. I was ready before her, I'm sure. I did everything I could think of and it only took me three minutes. I was clean everywhere (just in case). Used my Moustache cologne—a generous dose of it. Of all the things I should have packed but didn't, was a pair of sexy-looking bikini underwear. There I was in a pair of baggy (and wrinkled) striped boxer shorts. No way I'm going through that door in *these*. But can I walk in there naked? Don't think so. There has to be some show of propriety, some kind of feigned innocence. At least I think so. My upbringing was that it's not proper to just assume when you ask a girl out on a date and she accepts, that she's therefore made the decision to have sex with you. Even though in this Cannes meeting, assuming otherwise is out of the question. Tonight there is no otherwise. It's going to happen. As they say in the military, "This is no drill, we are firing for effect!"

I made a quick change, sitting now on the side of the bed in my gym shorts, which were a slight improvement—being skimpier and made of a dark colored satin material. Nothing to do but wait, and speculate about my forthcoming performance. How could I keep hoping it was just an unfortunately long streak of the wrong chemistry. I'd had the problem for as long as I could remember. If the right chemistry would ultimately prove me functional, when in the hell was it going to happen? *How many women was I going to have to go through before I find it?* Looking down now towards my almost numb key body part, I can tell you, I was certainly going to need a miracle on this, thus far, disastrous day.

My heart skipped a beat. The beam of light which had been coming through the crack of the door was now gone. Her lamp had been switched off. It was now dark in the adjoining room. She would be in bed now. Had to be. *It's now or never. Up to me now. I'll wait just a couple minutes.* Okay, *now*. Ventured in, straining to see how Paulette might be waiting. My eyes—when they were accustomed to the darkness on the other side of the door, made her out. She was in bed on her side, under just a sheet. The rest of the bed clothes were draped off the end of the bed, piled on the floor. Her eyes were closed. She was to all appearances asleep. I knew better. The incoming light from La Croisette painted one thin stripe across her shoulders. I had no idea what type of initiating procedure she might be expecting. I sat on the side of the bed a moment or two (nervous as hell). Decided to just start by stroking her hair. Went okay I guess. She didn't move or say anything. After a short time of this and when I had gained some composure, I slid under the sheet, and allowed the lengths of our bodies to touch.

The miracle I was hoping for was not forthcoming. I did not immediately get hard (or worse, even slowly get hard). In the meantime I caressed every square inch of her body, touched and kissed all the warm and private hollows and folds of her body. After about fifteen minutes of this I could imagine her saying to herself, *All right already, I'm ready. Let's get with it!* In spite of this awareness I had no choice but to persist in continuing my delaying tactics. By now the bottom sheet was pulled loose and bunching up in large uncomfortable wrinkles. My elbows had sheet burns, and we were both damp with the perspiration that comes in these ordeals. Certainly the time of her arousal had come (and perhaps—gone).

I don't know if she was aware of the reason for my deferral, but I'm afraid so, because she wrestled herself up and on top of me, gave me a long hard kiss and then began touching my stomach and legs, and elsewhere. After several minutes of this (and my own soulful pleading to the Almighty) I thought I was beginning to feel something happening. I sensed a slight increase in size and weight. *Should I wait and hope for more, or strike while the iron may be heating up.* I reached down and snuck a quick feel. Not great but maybe firm enough. And terrifyingly, *I knew it could collapse in a matter of seconds.* (Shades of Rhodes and Ingrid.) I decided to go for it before it knew what was happening and decided to sabotage me.

With the fleshy device I found myself with, entry was not going to be possible. Once again I was forced to rely on pressure and replicated moves. Besides my own well familiar depression, I knew it had to be a disappointment to her. It was about our only chance to salvage this ill-conceived reunion, but it fell miserably short. I think she was weeping. I couldn't tell for sure if she had taken her pleasure. Since I couldn't tell, it probably meant she didn't. (Maybe that's why she was crying Roger.) If she didn't, who could blame her after my performance? It was over. We lay together without speaking for fifteen or twenty minutes—certainly not because of the lasting effect of my love-making, that was for sure. Maybe just because the next step, the next interface, upright and face-to-face, with a light on, might be even more awkward (if that could be possible).

I left her bed when I knew it would not be too soon, and went to my room, through that damned adjoining door. Pushed it closed and heaved a long sigh of revulsion. In the bathroom I switched on the light, and if things had not been going badly enough, I was startled to see myself not just slightly stained, but smeared with blood. A starkly unpretty sight. I looked like an extra from *The Texas Chain Saw Massacre*. Paulette had gotten her period, and from the looks of things a heavy beginning. Surely she hadn't known. Just as I was squatting down on the bidet I heard the adjoining door swing open, and a distraught (near hysterical) Paulette was suddenly in front of me, both arms extended towards me, pouring out words in half-French, half-English.

She was distraught, pleading for my forgiveness; pitifully distressed. I don't think I'd ever seen anyone more apologetic, more embarrassed. She blurted out a few more French phrases and then gave up, head in her hands, devastated. The same damp draft was coming in the same stuck-open window. It was late. I had no choice but to take her into my arms. I was drained; completely spent, and disgusted with my activities; my life! I mustered the strength to help her back into her room, and onto her bed, which was now a bare mattress covered with a beach towel. There, laying together motionless—neither of us responsible for something more—was, under the circumstances, as comforting as anything could have been. The sad retrospection on both are parts, was only snuffed out when we drifted off to sleep.

In the morning, Paulette broke the news to me: She had only been able to get one day off from work, and had to leave at three this afternoon! I was surprised and disappointed (and at the same time—somehow relieved). When she finally blurted it out, big tears started down her cheeks, like she really wanted to stay. Maybe last night was not as bad as it seemed (my inability and then her embarrassment). As we readied ourselves to go out for a *petit dejeuner*, my interest in her only escalated. I watched her as she straightened her room and sorted her clothes. I saw a diligence—an awareness for what were the responsible things to do. I felt an increased admiration for her. But in her face I had seen before, and saw again, some unable-to-be-hidden, troubled look, just behind her eyes. One could not help, in speaking with Paulette, to sense there was some sad thing in her life; perhaps another event that she had not yet chosen to share with me.

Once again, I was at the Cannes train station in the same damp gray weather as yesterday, but we didn't speak much. I knew I should have. I wanted to. I knew I should have been reassuring her and planning our next meeting. I don't know why I wasn't. I didn't know then and I don't know now. Oh sure there were suggestions, and dates discussed, but it all seemed to be make believe to us both. Finally her train arrived. It would only be in the station four minutes. It's always until that moment, that real emotion lies blanketed. Now, the sadness welled in my heart, and much more I fear—in her heart. I felt the "thirty and alone thing." I saw it in her eyes. She was sure she had missed again. Blew it again; was throwing in the towel with me. No chance now. I wanted to say, No no Paulette, it's not your fault. It's me. I'm the misfit. I shouldn't even be here. You're okay. You're wonderful! Nothing but good things will happen for you. That's what I *wanted* to say, but I didn't say anything, except in my awkwardness, how great she looked. And though for sure she was a handsome woman, right now—at this moment, my compliment was forced. With a tear-streaked face she shook her tightly-curled blonde head and denying such a thing could ever be true, weakly responded, "Yes Roger, but I have already thirty years!"

Stammering, I foolishly blurted out, "But Paulette, you don't look it. No one would guess."

To this, in the reality of the dilemma as she perceived it, she responded with all surety, "That not matter, that ne make pas la difference, thirty year are fini." I felt the pulsing in my neck and a rush of confusion. There were some noises and movement, a hug, and she was no longer in front of me. I was alone on the platform. She was on the train, but I couldn't see her through the windows. The train was moving and in a few seconds it was out of the station. I wasn't ready to move. Just hold my own for a moment here in one place. A couple deep breaths. In fact just sit down. Use the damned bench. Sit in the drizzle. It doesn't make any difference.

Although Paulette had to go back, I still had the rest of the day and tomorrow. But who needs it. I for one had no stomach to tackle it. I was finished. I knew that something perhaps important had come and gone, and while there could have been an entirely different outcome, it was finished now. I had no energy to start something new. I wanted to be somewhere in the dark, a*lone*. It was time to try to understand what had already happened; have confidence in more important things: your family, doing your job, and your integrity. Forget creating relationships with yet more people. Got to stop inviting strangers into my life. Better to reflect, and try to learn something here. I'd tried before, so was not confident I'd be able to find any answers this time.

I decided (and this is how bad it was) to not even stay in town; go back to the ship. Regroup. Sleep. Avail myself of peanut butter pie, or a good workout with Dale, or write some letters. I could always come back ashore if the mood struck me. Plus with two weeks in port this time, there'd be lots of opportunities to frolic and explore; many more nights (if in this state of mind I would be up to them). I have to heal now. Now is the time for healing. I'd only paid one night at the Las Palmas, so I didn't have to engage in whatever it would have taken to get a refund. The Las Palmas and their staff of one had not impressed me (but then I doubt I impressed them). Was glad to be out of there. I don't think the concierge liked me from the beginning; even less when I told him we would not be staying the second night. The heck with him. To the liberty boat. One was waiting (almost like it knew I would be slinking back to it). With a complete absence of enthusiasm or any anticipation for coming events, I collapsed on the first seat I came to. Everything was over. I was tired and more confused than I had been yet. One more boat ride.

Staying Current

Yeah, you guessed it. I did find the energy to go ashore again, but not right away I can tell you. While it only took me a day to ready myself physically, two more were necessary to reset myself mentally (and not sure I made it by then). Would have been even longer were it not for—in spite of the weather, the great tales being spun by the guys coming in off liberty. The fourth day I decided to try it once again, but this time I was going to do it more safely—as part of a group! After my discouraging, thought-provoking and enervating experience with Paulette, I wasn't anxious for another personal one-on-one entanglement. This time I would just be one of the guys. And while thusly there may not be any big adventures awaiting, there was bound to be some good times and camaraderie. And there was. We played darts and dice games at an Irish pub, spent a bunch of time at the Corsican bar that Nick had discovered, and had an *All Pilot's* dinner at the now famous Le Bistro. All in all—a lot of healthy fun. A great chance for me to work myself back in the fold, and appear as less of a loner. We even started socializing with some of the navy pilots from the other squadrons on board. Turns out they were just like us, except we wore dark green and they wore dark blue. Same colleges, same home towns, same sports, same ideas.

I GUESS I JUST WASN'T THINKING

In fact we'd adopted one guy in particular—Norm Lundquist, a Crusader pilot from VF 103, the Navy fighter squadron. Nick and Earl had met him the first day ashore, and he had started to run with them. Tall, blonde and crew cut; seemed his only wardrobe ashore was gray flannels, maroon V-neck sweaters, and white tennis shoes. If ever there was an All American boy, it was Norm. A little naive and with a ready smile, he was "right off the farm," from Sioux City, Iowa. One time, having a beer with Bob Harmon (actually Bob was having the beer, Norm was having an orange juice and club soda), Bob suggested he do like he and Don Goft; pick up a Jaguar XKE over here and ship it back home. Norm said, "Hey Bob, it was almost a scandal when I left Iowa to go to Florida to be a jet pilot. If I came home with a foreign sports car, that'd do it!" We all laughed and secretly admired the small town life of a guy like Norm. Without having to worry about cat shots and night traps for a while, we were becoming more laid back (and liking it). While this in-port didn't seem like Christmas, it did start to seem like a vacation.

Saturday morning I went ashore early with Mike Ballard and Nick Cassopolis, and our new Navy friend Norm. We'd of course discovered the morning French delight—freshly baked croissants, and by nine we were at one of Cannes' more popular *boulangeries*. There, crowded around a small aluminum sidewalk table we were wolfing down more than our share of those light and flaky ten Franc apiece treats. The French eat them as is, but we were spreading ours with unsalted Danish butter and raspberry preserves from Switzerland. And the coffee—no way to describe it. You just have to taste it. Any drink the result of such noisy grinding, steaming, and finally spurting down out of such a strange looking stainless steel contraption, was bound to be exceptional.

It was going to be a great relaxing day, enjoying one of the first clear mornings since we put in. You should have seen us, stretched out, legs sprawling, heads back, feeling the warm sun on our faces. Not a bad life. That is up until two Navy Shore Patrol guys came by. "Excuse me sir. Liberty is cancelled. Everyone has to be back on the ship by noon." *By noon!?* Holy Shit, there's no war. No sign of trouble. No drills scheduled. What the hell is going on.

"Norm, maybe they just mean you—you're in the Navy, we're Marines." We gave it a try, but it wasn't a joke. *Everyone* had to be back on board. *Shit!* Some guys had hotel rooms. Some guys had rented cars. Some guys were shacked up. Some guys—well they had no idea where

204

they were. There was no time to lose. VMA 331 pilots as usual had a hotel room, and so we had all kinds of junk in it to retrieve. (Can you believe everyone was supposed to "tell at least one person" to help spread the word.) Lets see, ten past ten now. No way they'll have everybody back on board by noon. What a mess this is going to be, everybody trying to get back to the ship at once. But what can we do. Might as well go. They had put on extra boats—I could see that, but it was still a traffic jam at the dock. There were three at the landing now. One was just pulling away. A second was too full to get on, and a third was jockeying for position to tie up. As soon as it docked, Nick, Mike, Norm, and I, got in (doing our share of grumbling).

We asked every pilot we saw, if they knew what the heck was going on. I spied Larry Webber as I climbed on board. "Larry! You know why we're being called back?"

"Yeah, I heard the Captain and the Director of Flight Ops decided that two weeks was too long to go without flying—we might get stale. Gotta stay current."

"So what's that mean. What are we going to do?"

"We're going to up-anchor at 1400, steam out about thirty miles, and fly two quick launches."

What? This was hard to believe. Going flying was the last thing I was thinking about. (Or I suspected anybody was thinking about.) What a way to ruin a day. I couldn't help but think other people must feel the same way, though maybe not. The ride back to the ship (at a faster clip and even more bumpy than usual) was understandably quiet. Everyone was a little stunned. Half the guys were nodding off (as well as you could under the liberty boat buffeting). A lot needed shaves. We didn't look much like we were going to soar with eagles. (Like I said before: More like we were going to roost with turkeys.) When we reached the top of the ladder, the VMA 331 Duty Officer on the flight deck was passing the word. *All Pilot's Meeting in the Ready Room at 1300. Be there in flight gear. Everybody. All Pilot's Meeting in the Ready Room at 1300. Be there in flight gear. All Pilot's...*

When I got to our stateroom Jim had come and gone—already on his way down to the Ready Room. Took off my "civvies" and pulled on my flight suit. I passed two or three other guys on my way to the Ready Room, and was pleased to find out that I wasn't the only guy who thought this whole idea stunk. When I got to the Ready Room the Colonel was already at the podium. "Now don't bitch and moan, I know this is not what you had in mind, but Air Ops believes it's the thing to do." He had already seen enough faces to know the idea was getting a cool reception, and was softening the blow. "We'll put up a four plane division in each launch. Bob is getting the crew schedule together now. It'll be ready to check in about fifteen minutes." At 1400—right on the button, I heard the unmistakable noise of the anchor chain grinding its way up through the starboard aperture. We were on our way. Took a five minute break and went up to the flight deck where I watched my adopted Cannes shrinking in the distance. Boy what a difference some sunlight makes (remembering how dismal it looked when we pulled in this time last week). The air was cool, but the clear skies and sunshine made you *think* Spring.

Back down in the Ready Room—checking Bob's hand written crew schedule, I was surprised to notice I wasn't on the list for the first launch, and I wasn't on the list for the second launch! *Holy shit. I wasn't even going to fly.* Of course with fourteen pilots on board, plus the Skipper. Mathematically, seven guys wouldn't get to fly, and I was one of them. I almost felt guilty. (But not enough to overcome a greater feeling of relief.) I just wasn't in the mood. The guys that had lucked out (missed being on the schedule) were noticeably more carefree than those whose number had come up. We were horse-playing, perhaps being a little loud, when the first flight of four slunk away to a far corner to begin their preflight briefing.

We steamed for about an hour before I felt the big craft listing in a slow turn, which I knew would be putting us into the prevailing wind for the launch. After several minutes and a couple minor heading adjustments, the ship's speaker announced the corpen (ship's course for launch) and called for all flight deck personnel. About thirty minutes later the "Pilots man your aircraft" call came over the P.A. Our four guys: Jim Stremlow, Doug Shannon, Don Goft, and Earl "The Fox" Freeman, one by one—from various positions on the several pieces of Naugahyde furniture (where they'd been uneasily lounging since completing their briefing) struggled to an upright position. They stretched, shook out the wrinkles and began gathering up their helmets, kneeboards and other paraphernalia. We gave them a thumbs-up, or a punch in the shoulder as they paraded by (each with a look of at least obedient resignation). They filed out of the Ready Room like the gladiators of old going through the hatches to the floor of the Coliseum.

I have to tell you, observing launches or recoveries on a carrier, is no dull pastime. It never gets old. It's a heavy duty high speed kaleidoscope of huge hurtling objects. It takes exactly twelve minutes to launch twelve planes. If it's the second launch, then exactly one minute later—after they're gone—on the thirteenth minute, the first landing plane from the previous launch, slams into the deck; and eleven minutes later the last one is down. You've never seen anything this big, be this synchronized. There's so much being done by so many people—at the same time. And it's all critical "life or death" stuff. Launch personnel are continually ducking under skin-searing 1000 degree jet blasts and jumping over limb-severing cables. Even in heavy conditions of rising and falling decks and in near gale force winds, it appears to be unfolding with the precision and orchestration of a philharmonic. The ship's company assigned as flight deck crew are at high risk, constantly only yards from death or dismemberment. It's a miracle there aren't serious accidents every launch. On the contrary, amazing safety records prevail; a tribute to the reliability of the technology used, the excellence of the training conducted, and the dedication of the people involved. Unfortunately it's a statistical fact that few cruises are completed without the loss of at least one life. In fact I'm not sure one has ever come back with "all hands." (We already made our sacrifice in November, when that tug rolled off the flight deck and fell on top of the kid on the aft elevator.) But something like that seems to happen at least once each cruise.

Myself, Bob, and Ernie decided to forego the Ready Room TV and watch this launch from a safe superstructure cranny we'd found, located about twenty feet above the flight deck. After climbing up two flights of stairs (ladders) inside the superstructure, we ventured outside onto a small, balcony (referred to as the Vulture's Nest*). High and protected it was an ideal vantage point to observe the action. The prevailing wind was about fifteen knots, and the carrier was underway at about fifteen, so the combined wind across the deck was at least thirty knots. You can imagine the difficulty with which the people were walking, and steadying themselves, and trying to holler to one another. Even up in our protected area the buffeting wind was making our eyes water, chapping our lips, and smothering our conversation to one another. Bob rubbed the outside of his arms and complained about not having worn his flight jacket.

The now hot cats were steaming and oiled, ready to do their thing. There goes the test runs! Nowhere on the ship could you miss hearing the horrendous slamming and hissing of the wenches and pistons. Even up here—high above the din, it shook us. But it really got the attention of the guys walking on the deck. The screaming and thudding was just inches beneath their feet. Inspectors were now running the lengths of the shining, smooth wet slots, kicking lumps of grease back in the holes, checking for any worn spots or kinks. All the pilots were just about finished preflighting their aircraft. Some were already in the cockpits. The plane captains were stowing the ladders and scurrying around pulling the safety pins that trailed their red REMOVE BEFORE FLIGHT warning flags. The canopies were coming down.

Although the launch preparation looked as if it were being accomplished in a frenzied manner, to the ship's company personnel it was not the confusing operation it appeared to be. They had done it hundreds of times. Every man knew exactly what he was supposed to do, and how and when—to the last detail. The launch personnel (cat crews, wire crews, crash crews, ordnance crews, taxi directors, etc.) could be well proud of themselves. Once again, each group wearing their bright and uniquely colored vests to identify their flight deck functions.

As usual we would use four cats. The two forward-aligned cats, and the two angle-deck cats. You'd be shot straight off the front, or taxied to an angle deck cat, and be shot off the port bow. The tempo was picking up. Taxi directors were running this way and that, hailing planes left and right, urgently signaling them forward, jockeying them into sequential positions to be hooked to a waiting tug, and hauled onto the next vacant cat. *No delays!* You didn't know which cat you'd be launched from until the last minute. Sitting there, all strapped in and straddling a screaming jet engine like a rodeo cowboy, you'd be nervous as hell, looking in every direction for your possible signalman. Then there he'd be—your taxi director, suddenly right in front of you, frantically waving at you and signaling, forward, forward, forward! Almost snapping his arms at the elbow, urging an immediate response. *"Now. Now!"* This was *not* a slack time.

All the crews were in the aircraft. The engines were running. The deck was clear. Things were about to happen. The chief in charge gave the signal for the first aircraft to be hauled onto the number one cat. An A-4 Skyhawk like ours, but from the Navy Attack squadron was on the cat now. Two guys were on their hands and knees underneath it. They're at the nose gear now. They've got the halter attached. The blast fence right behind the readied aircraft started up. There's the run-up signal. The helmeted and goggled Cat Officer was leaning into the thirty-knot wind, his yellow sweater billowing and trouser legs flailing. He raised his hand and gave the sign—that familiar, high energy, almost frantic circular motion that meant *Power Up!* We watched in anticipation, half holding our breath—knowing so well the feeling and what was coming next.

Seeing the signal, the pilot jammed the throttle full forward and the engine responded. There was a deafening reverberation and a screaming yellow flame shot out of the exhaust pipe. Under full power the nose dropped down as the front strut was compressed under eight thousand pounds of thrust, now trying to tear the aircraft loose from the still attached harness. The salute, and *Ka-frigging-bang!* There she goes. The aircraft was propelled out of it's own image, streaking forward and off the bow. At first a scary-looking sink, then the thrust took over, a recovery, and it was climbing. One off. Number two coming. Already in position on the number three cat. *Khawham!* It was sent hurtling down the deck and clawed its way skyward. A third, on cat number four and a fourth on cat number one. Behind each of the cats a blast fence raised up automatically to deflect the powerfully dangerous jet blasts from their horizontal rearward vector, to a deflected—harmless but intimidating—straight upward direction. Just before the shot, when the aircraft was at full power, violent columns of black, boiling air would rocket skyward from these blast fences. One, two, three, four, off. The first Navy squadron was airborne.

More exciting now—our own guys. In front of our eyes and without a minute wasted, Jim, Don, Doug and Earl were being urgently signaled forward, hauled onto the cats, and hooked up. *Khawham! Whoosh!* Jim was gone. Don was next. Without ear plugs the noise could cause permanent damage. One, two, three jets turned up at full power. Six-hundred degree air roaring rearward and upward! *"Khaw-ham!"* Don and Doug were gone! Earl was next, on the number three cat. The cat crews, about finished with our flight of four, urgently signaled the taxi directors to begin moving the next flight of four onto the vacated cats. The tow tugs were moving around the aircraft like ants around lumps of candy. Now the second Navy squadron—VF 103, was being taxied up and strapped onto the vacated cats. A Crusader was being directed to the number four cat, just outside of Earl, who was now on the number three cat. Bob— who had just returned (now wearing his leather flight jacket) wasn't happy with where the Crusader was taxiing. "Geez Rog, that's dangerous. That Crusader's gonna pass right through Earl's jet blast."

I GUESS I JUST WASN'T THINKING

"Should be okay Bob. The blast fence will raise up when Earl's given the signal to power up." Right while I was answering, the launch officer started the runup signal for Earl (who had no way to see behind him). Oh no, Earl's going to full power *and the blast fence isn't coming up.* It was like watching a glass of milk tip and not being able to reach it or say or do anything—just paralyzed. It goes over right before your eyes. The swept wing Crusader, passing behind Earl, at first almost in slow motion, tilted, then tilted a little more, then its right wing came up and right main gear lifted off the deck. It began to skid to the left. In front of God and country it went sideways about ten feet to the left edge of the flight deck; was over and gone! With a hundred people watching.

Before the right wing went through vertical, thank God—we saw the ejection seat hurtling away from the tumbling aircraft, and thankfully, with a trajectory slightly above horizontal. "He's out Bob! He got out!" The guy had ejected. *He did it!* (We all secretly wondered if we would have the nerve and reflexes to get to the ejection seat handle before our aircraft rolled inverted.) In these over-the-side incidents, ejecting a half second late would be suicide, propelling you downward into the sea. This guy had done it. He had the presence of mind to do it! We watched the hurtling object—half-man, half-metal, arc out and away from his aircraft. We all watched for the separation, when an air bladder inside the seat automatically inflates and pushes the pilot out of the seat. This separation is what triggers the mechanism to deploy the pilot's parachute and decelerate the human projectile. No seat separation, no parachute.

But the pilot remained in the seat! Speechless we watched the guy and the seat together, at a high velocity hit the surface. There was a huge spray and he ricocheted into the air again. This time he fell back with only a small splash—not a hundred yards off the port. By now the crash alarm was going full blast and the ship was already heeling hard in a turn. The inaction and lack of animation that occurred when the plane was going over the side was short-lived. The deck was electrified now. Accelerated activity everywhere. People were running and pointing and shouting. Binoculars were out. Commands were booming over the loud speakers. A light skiff and three rubber rafts were put over the side. The rescue helicopter was launched. The crash alarm continued howling.

The ship circled for thirty minutes, while the boats and chopper frantically crisscrossed the impact area, apparently without success. Divers went in two or three times, also with no luck. The chopper repeatedly

210

dipped down to within five feet of the water, but nothing sighted. The edge of the flight deck was lined with observers. In a couple minutes I could no longer be sure I was looking at the right spot. I'd lost track of where I thought he went in. But even when I had the spot, I never saw him come back up to the surface. Never saw him after the second hit. Not a good sign. We waited topside throughout the whole search—about an hour. Had to abort the search now. Had to turn into the wind to recover the first six aircraft. Geez. Makes you feel sick. I was pretty sure I'd seen a man die. He had ejected in time, and even if he hadn't, *why the hell didn't he separate from the seat?* That didn't compute. He was in the air for at least three seconds, he should have separated from the seat, and then the parachute would have deployed. Maybe something didn't function right. I felt a little ill. Decided to go down to the wardroom; have a glass of milk. *Shit!*

When I got to the wardroom, several of the guys were already there, and looked as if they felt as bad as I did. I sat down next to Nick, who looked like he was taking it bad. "Did you see it Nick? Bob and I were up in the nest. We saw the whole damn thing from the flight deck."

"No. I was in my stateroom. One of the guys from VF103 phoned me up. That's how I learned it was Norm."

"Lundquist?!"

"Yeah."

Earl was sick, knowing it was his jet blast that blew our new Navy friend Norm over the side. Of course it wasn't his fault. The blast fence timer malfunctioned. Norm's body was recovered the next morning, and the carrier made its way back into the Cannes harbor, everyone conjecturing with "what ifs" and "whys."

Why He Stayed in the Seat

The rest of the inport stay at Cannes (in comparison), was uneventful. Regards the accident; five days of re-thinking the whole thing. When they had recovered Norm, he was still strapped in the seat. This being the case, a thorough maintenance investigation was ordered, to find out why he had not been pushed out from the seat. Too late for Norm, but a very important, critical oversight was discovered. There is an HMI (*Handbook of Maintenance Instructions*) for every type of aircraft. It covers the removal and replacement of every piece of equipment on it. When periodic safety inspections are performed on the ejection seat (every fifty flights) the maintenance technicians use this manual, step-by-step—like a Bible. Nothing is done from memory. Everything must be done "by the numbers."

In the manual used for Norm's seat, the disassembly of the seat was spelled out okay, but on the instructions for the reassembly, *there was a step left out.* The manual had shown a piece being removed for cleaning and inspection, but failed to list its replacement during the reassembly process. So if the guy who put the seat back together was not the same guy who took it apart, he would not know about the missing piece. The piece—a small brass bushing, was necessary to guide a pointed shaft that punctures the nitrogen bottle. The escaping gases inflate the bladder, pushing the pilot out of the seat. This bushing was not around the shaft in Norm's seat. Without it the pin had jammed in its track and never reached the nitrogen bottle. Therefore, the bottle never released its pressure to inflate the bladder, so Norm was never pushed free of the seat. What's worse, after checking all the other Crusader HMI's on the ship, it was discovered that the omission was in every one of the manuals. In another month, this bushing could have been left out of more seats. All the Crusaders in the fleet were grounded until all the seats were inspected to make sure the bushing was there, and a reprint was published to that page in the HMI.

A Real Man of Mystery

Last day in port I finished up all my chores early and was ashore by noon. Had my fill by 5 p.m. and decided to call it a day. Get back in time for the evening meal. Back to the ship one last time. I jumped down into the liberty boat, somewhat worse for the wear from this stay in Cannes. Made myself comfortable on the driest bench seat I could find, and began mentally preparing myself for the forthcoming fifteen days of flight ops. While waiting for the boat to depart I became aware of a slight commotion on the pier alongside the boat. One of those Shore Patrol guys was engaged in a conversation with a couple of civilians—an older couple. Straining to hear, I think they were asking if they could have a tour of the ship. (Which is not uncommon.) We usually had at least one Visitor's Day during each inport stay, though today was not that day. In fact we never had one during this Cannes mooring.

I was trying to hear if they were American or not—didn't look it. I'd say they were in their late fifties or early sixties. He was a nice looking man, about five feet ten, in a long and smart-looking top coat. At this point in my life I didn't know much about custom tailoring or camels hair, but could easily tell that his coat was not of the inexpensive variety. He had just enough frame remaining to suggest he had been a reasonably strong younger man. His hair had a serious thinning problem, but there were just enough dark strands, combed straight back, to disqualify a description as bald. His wife was a tiny thing. Several inches less than five feet, with jet black hair, parted in the middle and down to her shoulders as straight as rain. Couldn't tell her nationality. She was quiet as a mouse, content to patiently wait while her husband did the talking. With eyes turned optimistically upward, you could see that she had grown to know a confidence in his handling of these kind of things.

I again directed my attention to the well dressed gentleman. He appeared to be a capably persuasive person, with an easy smile and infectious mannerisms; obviously difficult to argue with and I suspect not accustomed to coming out second best. His voice had a pleasant timbre and he was being very respectful to the Shore Patrol guy, considering he was old enough to have been his father (and could just as well have been the local mayor or a prime minister). From the expressive way he used his hands while he talked, he could have been Italian or French. But wait, nope—I think he's American. Now, hearing his English more clearly I would have bet on it. (Though I'd been fooled before.) When he had finished making his case, he shrugged his shoulders and clasped his hands together. With his head cocked interestingly to one side, and wearing a smile of anticipation, he waited for the verdict. I raised up to hear the chief's response, which I already knew would be negative based on his grim expression. "No sir, we're not having a Visitors Day on this in-port. You'd have to come on board as someone's guest."

I had become sufficiently interested in the new stranger to momentarily forget my fatigue and depressed state. "Chief! Over here, I'll sign for em." Rather than continue shouting I hopped up out of the boat and went the few steps over to where they stood. The chief didn't mind at all to have this rescue occur. Even as his combatant, it was impossible not to wish the stranger well.

"Good Afternoon. My name is Roger Yahnke, I'm a pilot on the *Forrestal,* and I'd be glad to show you around."

His never having wavered smile suddenly broadened, and he glanced down at his wife as if to say, *See honey, I told you everything would be all right.* Her loving look upward indicated that in her mind, the outcome was never in doubt. He enthusiastically introduced himself. "Leo. Yes, Leo Lippe. And this is my wife Winona. This is very kind of you. Very kind.

We were really looking forward to visiting the ship. We're Americans you know—originally from California. Thank you so much. Thank you." I jumped down into the boat and then offered a hand up to Leo. He lowered himself into the boat and immediately turned to help his diminutive spouse off the edge of the pier. As they walked towards the seating area their excitement for the forthcoming afternoon radiated from their faces. At the turn of a key the well-tuned inboard came vigorously alive, and I was once again listening to the deep rumbling song I'd heard so many times. The boat lurched suddenly away from the pier and Leo and Winona had to scramble for the safety of a nearby bench.

Underway I smiled, seeing them huddled side by side beneath the dripping canvas canopy. He was holding one of her hands in both of his, in an affectionate and protective manner. (I could see now, I'd met at least one proper husband.) I respected him for his actions and wondered what it would be like to feel an honest love towards one woman. I envied his state of mind and heart. I guessed it was not at all complicated to him. He knew just what he should be doing with and for his wife. Above the noise of the engine, the wind, and flapping canvas, in a raised voice, Leo began a conversation. "We live in Milano now, I have a business in Italy. We were over visiting some friends in Nice, and they told us about the ship being in. Gosh, we sure are glad you happened along.

"It's my pleasure, Leo."

Leo explained their motivation: "A month or so ago Winona and I saw that movie "Flight Deck," and ever since then we've been saying we gotta get over to the coast and visit one of those US Navy flat tops." He looked down at Winona, as if to encourage her to corroborate their mutual desire to visit the big American craft. And he got it like always—the cutest and coyest smile which transmitted, *"Certainly love."* But still not a word out of this tiny lady. "You know Roger I have some good friends in Germany—in the optical business. The family has been grinding lenses for three generations. Their stuff is used on special cameras in the satellites. Their name is Yahnkel also." (That's what I get for trying to make it sound like two syllables.) I repeated my name—like Gramps pronounced it. He apologized more than necessary and continued, "So tell us, what do you do on the *Forrestal*?"

"I'm a pilot. A Marine Corps pilot."

"A Marine Winona. He's in the Marine Corps! That's wonderful, isn't it. And how exactly do you Marines fit in on the carrier?"

"The carrier has five tactical squadrons—you know, fighters and bombers. Four are Navy squadrons, and one—sort of visiting, is a Marine Squadron; either an attack or a fighter squadron. My squadron is VMA 331. We're an attack squadron. Attack means we don't shoot other airplanes, we go for targets on the ground, with bombs, rockets and missiles. Hate to admit it Leo, but our squadron is called the "Fighting Bumblebees." Leo laughed at our moniker. Not to make fun, but because he knew it was expected to rouse a chuckle. I continued to field comparatively interesting questions from Leo, about life aboard a carrier and about flight operations, and sort of—what our mission consisted of here in the Mediterranean Sea. (I didn't tell him about using church steeples to begin pull-ups to drop a nuclear weapon.)

Soon enough we were bobbing alongside the great steel hull of the ship, like a tiny cork at the water's edge of a stream. As something of a "how to" demonstration, I preceded Leo and Winona with the "total commitment" leap—from the rising and falling liberty boat onto the lowest rung of the nearby unsteady ship's ladder. I was gratified to see the liberty boat personnel being extra courteous and going out of their way to help Leo and Winona as they negotiated this often tricky chasm. (More than one guy had ended up in the water between the liberty boat and the ladder.) We commenced the vertical ascent up the liberty ladder to the flight deck. I would learn later that Leo was a true patriot, but my first indication of this was seeing how noticeably taken he was when I performed the sea-going tradition of saluting the Colors (the American flag flying at the stern) as I stepped on board. As soon as he got on the flight deck he asked if he too, might do the same. I signaled an okay. He rendered such a dignified salute I was embarrassed at my perfunctory compliance (and vowed to take this step more seriously in the future).

Regarding Leo and the tour which took place. I've noticed that many people seem embarrassed to show that they have been impressed, often acting "above it all." Perhaps in an attempt to elevate their own status. Leo was not at all like that. He was one of those rare people whose status is never in doubt from the minute you lay eyes on him, and who gains further respect and admiration through his humility and eagerness to learn. I was beginning to have the feeling that this was a man I would want to learn more about. On the trip out to the ship I hadn't been able to pick up a single detail of his life, and so far, not much during this tour of the ship. Instead, the time was filled with his *oohs* and *aahs*. He had a way of making everyone feel like their job was special and difficult. And although I sensed he was a man of large accomplishments and varied experiences, I don't think it was a just polite act. I think he really was very interested in the young men and their tasks aboard the *Forrestal*. I took him everywhere, including the high slanted forecastle where my Olympic weight set was once stored. Seeing this (and meeting Dale in the middle of a set of heavy bench presses) he reiterated to Winona, how the US Marines always stayed in shape. (Never mind Dale was in the Navy.)

About one hour into the tour I discovered that Winona could speak, but her sentences were very short and so subdued as to make understanding her very difficult. I leaned over each time, with a most interested expression on my face, to encourage her to offer more. I think Leo appreciated this. He was more like a father to her than a husband, never failing to lend her a guiding hand, or assistance with a door, or chair, or whatever. Perfect chivalry. I was—as you might guess, observing this devotion with some measure of guilt. The turning point of the tour was when we ran into the Skipper, Colonel Cunningham. He suggested I invite Leo and Winona to dinner on board. *We could eat in the wardroom. We'd take the evening meal in the Officer's Mess!* Wow, talk about finishing up on a high note. The immaculately clean and formal environs of the Officer's Mess was good at creating a special mood. Leo and Winona got their own sterling silver "Honored Guest" napkin holders. I had always made a habit of being extra polite with the mess staff (those huge brown Filipinos and Polynesians who run the US Navy galleys). I would always ask them about their families (waiting for them on remote pacific islands) and when they would next get a leave to see them. Perhaps in return for this show of concern (or in sensing the same stature and presence in Leo that I did), the cooks and waiters showered him with attention. The food couldn't have been better. It went just great.

Mike Ballard and Nick Cassopolis ate with us and were just as polite as could be. (Gotta thank them later.) And Leo—who it was obvious could offer a lot to any conversation, was an accomplished listener. He offered up his complete attention to whomever was speaking to him. This being the case everyone was thrilled to meet him, and his presence on board as my guest turned out to be a real hit. Everyone loved Winona too, the tiny silent partner by his side. She followed every action and sound, but never interrupted the flow. The meal went better than I could have hoped for, and would you believe—for desert they served their now famous, peanut butter pie. Today Leo had gotten all he had bargained for on his visit to a US Navy "flat top."

I accompanied them back to shore of course, and on the same liberty boat we'd come in on. Leo repeatedly and very enthusiastically extended me an invitation to visit him and Winona at their home in Milan. I told him the ship would be back in Italy in a little over a month—at Genoa, and I might be able to get a couple days off then. He was very excited about this possibility, and from then on acted as if it was a foregone event. He told me Milan was only an hour or so train ride from Genoa (and there were lots of trains). He said I just had to see Milano. It was Italy's commerce center and one of the fashion capitals of the world; see the opera, and even the place Mussolini had been hung. He made sure I had his address and phone number, jotting them down on a piece of paper from a well-worn, but handsome looking leather note book he had whisked from an inner pocket. (Using the attached, miniature gold pen.) As I read the address, I noticed the paper was monogrammed *InterContinental Arms.*

After the trip ashore—during a long parting conversation, I was finally able to learn a little bit about Leo. He indeed was someone of far reaching accomplishments, which will come out later. He told me that now, he was the head of an American company manufacturing small arms in Italy; *replica* small arms—for sportsmen and collectors. Almost all of the manufacturing was done in the little village of Brescia, about 50 miles east of Milan, on the north edge of the Plains of Lombardia. Must be quite a place. He described it almost reverently; an expansive, flat, fertile area nestled right up against the southern cliffs of the Swiss Alps. He continued, "Certainly you've heard of Stoeger's *Shooter's Bible?"*

Though I didn't think I had, I knew it was wisest to indicate I had. "Yeah, sure, I've heard of it."

"Well we're in it—four pages. "Intercontinental Arms." We have a black powder Navy Colt and a new 41-magnum, single-six—just like the famed Colt Peacemaker. Except ours is called the Dakota. And we've got two long rifle models: our 44-inch Kentucky Long Rifle, and another with an even longer barrel called the Super Kentucky Long. We have a whole line—all hand crafted, and I mean hand crafted by these old guys. True artisans. Just wait, you'll see. You'll really be surprised." Earlier, in another conversation (one of the few Winona had entered into) I had learned that during World War II, Leo had been a high ranking member of the OSS (the Office of Strategic Services), the forerunner of today's CIA. Could it be that his background and now his position with this Italian-based gun company, had something in common. (I would learn later, it did!)

"How come you chose Italy? Why there?" I asked. Though he never answered the Italy question satisfactorily, he did tell me all about why he chose the town of Bresica. For over 100 years this town had been the sole producer of the world famous Beretta pistol. Here, generations had been weaned on the firearm business, sitting around their house, cutting and polishing triggers, hammers and cylinders. There was an abundance of skilled firearm craftsmen (and women) here. Leo said that because of crazy Italian tax laws, he didn't have any large and modern factories, or even one documentable factory.

"You see, in Italy there are huge taxes on employers with over seven employees. So we just sign up six-member families, to work over small vices on kitchen tables and desks, right in their own houses. Believe it or not, that's how we put out a whole line of replica small arms."

I was a little excited now about the prospect of visiting Leo and seeing this operation first hand. I probably could work it out. We all were a little sad to see the day come to an end, but finally we bade each other a good night and God's Speed. Leo made sure I knew that he was marking his calendar for February when I would visit them. And I was sure—if not then, I would certainly see this gentleman again. Evidently even Winona was looking forward to my visit. In her most animated gesture of the day, she extended one small hand to my sleeve, and gave me one of the sweetest *we're counting on you* smiles I've ever seen. Then she left me with a puzzling one, saying she just couldn't wait for me to meet their Flipper. Whatever or whoever that might be. (I would find out, but that's another story.)

Chapter Eighteen
A TRIP TO THE BLACK SEA

Nothing Special About the First Hour

The at-sea period—from Cannes to our next in-port, was—thankfully, uneventful. Seemed it was over before it started. (Well it was only seven days and that may have helped.) We were back in Istanbul and as you might imagine I was anxious to see Belkis and experience whatever this visit would provide. She had said she would have a wonderful surprise for me next time I arrived in her grand Turkish city. Still well remembering my last visit—and *that* surprise, I was certainly excited about what might be awaiting me this time.

Had to stay onboard till late afternoon. Caught the 1700 liberty boat. A little past seven now. No longer dusk. Dark. Once again I was a reluctant passenger in one of those austere, black Istanbul taxis, on my way to Belkis' apartment. She lived in what they called the "Old Section," which was neatly tucked away just behind the modern and fashionable financial district. Only two blocks off the grand Avenue of Banks the clocks were turned back. Suddenly you were in an eerie, hundreds-year-old, crude and adobe-walled barrio. Tonight, there wasn't a creature in sight—the place was deserted. Infrequently placed dim street lamps were doing their best to illuminate grime-laden bulwarks of dirty brown mortar. Evidently the driver was not a stranger to these parts, skillfully guiding his vehicle through the maze of sharp turns. Three streets deeper and I still hadn't seen a living soul. Vague and mysterious in their own shadows the walls seemed to be looming menacingly closer on either side. Now down another alley, even more narrow than the previous. Didn't see how it could have ever been originally intended for motor vehicles. No curbs or walkways on either side. Squeaking through, I was just waiting to hear the screech of metal against stone. I could have reached out either side of the cab and snatched flowers off the window sills.

Based on how he exploded around one blind corner after another, the cab driver was consistently making the risky assumption that there would be no oncoming traffic. And thank God—so far he had been right. For a Saturday evening, the place was especially abandoned. It was as if the whole neighborhood was out of town and this route was not an otherwise approved thoroughfare. I felt as if I was in a very secret place. For reassurement I fingered the fifty dollars (mostly borrowed) in my trouser pocket. Not much, but maybe I wouldn't need any. (As a safety net I had my American Express card.) Suddenly we were into an area that had been obviously renovated to include more upscale residential dwellings.

Belkis met me at the door with her usual flourish. I was invited in (but not for long). As soon as she had gathered up her purse and stole, she had me turned on a heel and back out the door. It was as if she didn't like it in there herself. And from what short glimpse I had of the apartment, I could understand that. Not well lit. Hard wood flooring so dark it looked almost black. Sparsely furnished; a couple brocade settees and two or three chairs—all tightly upholstered and stiff looking. It didn't strike me as a comfy place. As soon as we stepped out she began chattering, asking me questions about my activities since our memorable night in jail six weeks ago. She didn't tell me a thing about where we were going, or what we were going to do. I was hoping whatever it was, it wouldn't be too expensive.

Bound For Parts Unknown

On our way, but not in the cab I had taken to her apartment. She ushered it away, having arranged for one of her own. The driver appeared to know her and be elated to have her as his fare. (Understandable, since it would not turn out to be a short trip.) Without any hint of a destination we were on our way. I was being whisked away like a prisoner under transport, across nighttime Istanbul. First through gaudy downtown, then a darkened industrial area, then past some tiny markets on the outskirts of the city, then a questionably populated residential area, then out the north side and into a farming community (as best I could see in the dark), and finally into flat, open and barren countryside. Combined with the mystique of an unknown destination, the threatening escape from the city was exciting. I was exhilarated—felt like someone in the midst of something sinister.

Right up my alley. The evening was at least commencing in a memorable fashion. We must have driven (and driven quite fast) for over an hour. Belkis still didn't give a hint—nary a word. We were now in a sparsely inhabited, in fact not inhabited at all—remote area. Only occasionally could I make out the silhouette of some isolated structure. No towns, no lights, no other cars. No activity. There was no moon and the starlight was dim; an especially dark night—which added to the suspense (and my feeling of being at a location not known to anyone).

We've Arrived!

Finally from out of nowhere we were "someplace." We rounded a bend (on a gravel road that we'd been on for twenty minutes) and *Bingo!* we were in front of what I guess was a hotel (or at least it looked like a hotel). There were no signs or lights out front to announce it, and the entrance was completely darkened. Only one or two rooms on the upper floors emitted any light. It looked like a resort hotel at the height of the off-season; dormant—perhaps housing only a skeleton staff, waiting for next year's big crowd. And in fact that's exactly what it was. The driver couldn't get out of the cab fast enough, committed to assisting Belkis in each and every way. Finally when he was sure there was absolutely nothing else he could do, he accepted a big hug and was on his way. A member of the hotel staff (who had been in wait while this parting took place) collected our luggage—mostly Belkis's. I only had one piece, closely resembling a gym bag. (I vowed—as soon as I could I was going to get one of those neat Italian calf skin bags with lots of straps.) Up the steps and into the reception area, which did little to change my mind about the status of the establishment. Belkis approached the counter with her usual disarming manner, flashing her smile and inquiring about our reservations. Needless to say I was a follower here, having no idea of the plan.

The concierge acknowledged that both the rooms were ready. *Both? Two rooms?* Evidently this was what she had reserved. But ah-ha, as I listened further I learned the two rooms were *communicado*. That's the word the concierge used to describe what I guessed meant adjoining rooms. He then said, eyeing Belkis with an intimidating look, "And Madame, I'm sure you won't be wanting the key for the door between them."

Oh, I thought to myself, that son of a bitch putting her on the spot like that. What can she say now? Belkis looked him dead in the eye, smiled mischievously, and replied unashamedly, "More than anything in my life."

Holy Shit! Did she tell him, or what. I had never ever had a woman so boldly express a desire for me—even in private, let alone to announce it like that! I was now sure that tonight was going to be the night.

The hotel *was* empty—evidently entirely empty. We didn't pass or even *see* another person in the lobby, on the way up the steps, or in the second floor hall. I was now ready to believe the place was actually closed, not yet officially open for business. Belkis had an arrangement or used her clout, and we would have the only occupied room! When we arrived in the room, which was certainly not extravagant, in fact at best only modestly furnished, I understood what it was I had thought I smelled in the air when we got out of the cab. *The sea!* Open water—near, that's what. A row of vertical, hinged casement windows that extended from waist height to the ten foot ceiling were unlatched and wide open. Through them a strong damp wind was blustering in, billowing the sheer curtains inwards and upwards, doing its best to pin them to the ceiling. Leaning on the wet sill, probing the blackness, the wind bringing tears to my eyes, I couldn't make out a thing. But I could hear, and now feel, the crashing of waves against the old hotel's stone foundation, straight down, maybe fifty feet beneath our window!

Where *were* we? Belkis explained. We were at the edge of the Bosporus; the turbulent passageway through which the Black Sea makes its escape towards the Sea of Marmara (and then the Aegean and the Mediterranean.) To me—the dark sky, the gusting wind, and the force of the sea, suggested a rebellious wildness about this place. I could smell adventure here. Belkis was in and out between the rooms, trying on several outfits (although she had told me there was no reason to dress up tonight). I still didn't know what our plans were. We had a couple glasses of Turkish wine. She sat on my lap while we relaxed from the road trip up. I was conscious of the soft backs of her legs against my thighs. (This was as close as we had gotten to date.)

A "Dinner Out" to Remember

Finally dressed, she indicated it was time to be off for the next surprise. To the lobby. The previously-stung concierge had evidently been tamed, since only a movement of Belkis' finger had him obediently off to get us our transportation. Waiting outside, one could feel the isolation of our location. (The stars were the closest things I could see.) The cab arrived and we were on our way. From inside our speeding metal capsule I could see nothing except the headlights reflecting on the gravel road ahead. Still surrounded by nothingness. After about fifteen minutes we made a sharp turn and slowed down. *Wow, what's this.* From what I could make out (which was damned little) we had arrived in what appeared to be an old and long abandoned village. A ghost town with small wooden front structures; like a Hollywood set from an old western. Not a solitary light in the town. Not one! Not a single car or person in sight. Not a sound or movement. This *was* a ghost town. Where on earth could we possibly be?

From the sound of the conversation (all in Turkish) between Belkis and the driver, I gathered she was telling him to go slower (though we were already at a crawl). She strained to see through the darkness. It was obvious she was trying to orient our position—searching for a familiar landmark. I couldn't help, but I strained as well. A little further, and then suddenly she let out a cry of success and I knew we'd arrived. She had found whatever it was she was looking for. The driver stopped. We were out and he was gone. With no cab to protect us, we were forsaken, abandoned in a dark and desolate night space. I had no idea what was going to happen next, though I would see in a moment.

Standing there alone on the narrow sidewalk, like statues in a petrified village, I was beginning to get a little nervous. Still not a sound or movement. No life anywhere. Belkis went a few steps in one direction, then turned and came back and past me, continuing slowly in the other direction. Finally, apparently satisfied she stopped and stamped her foot on what sounded like wood? I thought the walkway we were on was cement (which was surprising in itself, since the street we came in on was dirt). Heard the sound of rusted hinges and creaking wood. A large trap door swung up from the walk. A flood of soft light, voices, smells, and immediate ambiance escaped upward towards us. The black night was suddenly aglow.

Silhouetted in the reflected light I made out a short but stocky figure bounding up the steps towards us. A dynamo of energy with a great mustache. On his hairy torso hung a sweaty undershirt. A leather apron masked his hips and legs. He took Belkis up in his arms and swung her around. A great exchange of salutations and repeated hugs before I was introduced. Not sure how I was introduced. It was all in Turkish. (Even if in English, I'm sure I would have been hard pressed to know who she was describing.) He shook my hand (pulverizing it), wrapped me in his huge bare arms, and I think, gave testimony to his privilege in meeting me. A joyous occasion I can tell you. He led us down the stone steps, into the warmest, most inviting, firelit space I had ever seen.

Just one room; one very large, heavily beamed, low ceilinged room, with crudely plastered walls. Oddly, it stretched uncluttered from wall to wall; not a single stick of furniture. *Not a table or chair in the place.* A low, open hearth was blazing away in a far corner, sending a glow across the expanse of a plain old concrete floor. Directly in front of us, spanning the room's rear wall were two long glass display cases filled with all manner of fish, fowl, and meats. The space between the inner ends of the two cases was centered on an open arch through which the help (the owner's wife and two daughters) entered and left the kitchen.

The only seating was a line of crude and bulky, wooden booths on each of the two side walls. Behind us—on the wall we'd just come through, was nothing. No tables, no booths, no shelves, no paintings hanging (not even a calendar on a nail). Midway across the room, several gnarled posts having long lost their straightness, supported warped and dust-covered joists. Hanging from these was an assortment of earthenware jugs, pots, egg baskets, and other farmhouse paraphernalia. The flickering light illuminated shocks of straw and mud sticking out from the unpainted mortar above the rafters.

Found out that in Turkey, the patrons are supposed to inspect the kitchen. That's part of the protocol here. If you don't, the chef is insulted. We did and it was first class. There were meats, vegetables, soups and sauces, and juicy-looking entrees in various stages of preparation. Brass, copper and iron cookware hanging everywhere. Huge skillets with long handles. Old stuff like out of the last century, all evidencing years of use. Enough to put your appetite in high gear. The next few minutes were a scene—"theater" to me. (Remember that in Cannes?) But actually happening. There were five of the aforementioned high-backed booths on each side of the room. Each was identical, with hard unpadded bench seats. (All equally uncomfortable.) Belkis set about checking them out, sampling their perspective and mood-setting location and seeing how she fit. Like a housecat testing the cushions, she would settle herself down on a selected bench, squirm a moment or two, evaluate, then shake her head disapprovingly and move on to another. After three tries in several locations, finally: "Ah yes darling, this one will do."

We were paid respectful and touching visits by the owner's wife and both daughters, and the only other two diners in the place; one at a time, extending the warmest possible greetings to Belkis. (I still had not heard a word of English.) I just sat there reveling in the atmosphere and sipping what Belkis told me was the best farm wine in all of Turkey. The owner had brought out a bottle specially for us. Actually a small clay jug with no opening at the top. No lid, no cork—completely sealed. With a wooden ruler he whacked the neck of it, shattering away the top inch or so, and we were ready to pour.

While we were waiting for our meal, which we didn't order, but rather let the owner choose for us and then keep a secret, I found myself reading the graffiti scratched in the soot-stained plaster wall alongside the table in our booth. Some in English, some in French, there's Italian, and of course, what I guess was Turkish. I'll admit I may be overly sentimental, too nostalgic, but this particular night, on this wall, I read a commemoration which I have never forgotten, and have often reflected upon; trying to visualize a young, dark-eyed girl, with stars in her eyes, who knew exactly what she wanted, and etched these words:

> *Tonight I am more happy than*
> *I have ever been, because*
> *I am with the one I truly love.*

To be *able* to love—that's it. Not to *be* loved, but to love. To be one of those few people who have that gift and can know that happiness. I would like to think whoever etched this did have that capability (and I hoped the referred to relationship would be forever). A woman in love. Nothing more beautiful, nothing more prized. However, I was beginning to think, based on an awareness of my own shortcomings and infidelity, if I was any example we would soon be in short supply of this kind of woman.

The evening was a wonderful experience. In addition to a great, savory home cooked meal (roast duck I think, aubergine casserole, and baked apple with fresh cream) there was incredible conversation (and I mean *incredible*). I was engaged in a deep and prolonged colloquy with the owner, who spoke no English! I don't know if our apparent success was the result of intense personal efforts or (and much more likely) two and a half of those ceramic pitchers of wine. Neither the owner nor I considered for one moment that we were not communicating flawlessly; our gazes locked, nodding, interrupting each other, and then agreeing wholeheartedly. I have to laugh now thinking that he and I were able to spend all that time in never-never land, without realizing it.

Finally—time to go. Belkis and the owner had a short conversation in hushed tones. I paid the bill. Still have no idea how much it was. I knew in Lira it was about half of what I had. Could have been only about $25. If so, that would've been a helluva deal. (I could use the credit card at the hotel.) The owner was back at our table, excited and whispering to Belkis. Lots of good-byes, more hugs and kisses, and we were on our way up the steps to the bizarre soundless world above. It was as windy and black as before. I surfaced on the stone walkway behind Belkis, who was behind the owner. Initially, couldn't see a damn thing. As my eyes adjusted to the darkness, *what's this?* I was aware of some shapes, heard some noises, and then was able to make out a two-horse drawn carriage in the street in front of us. I recognized then the smell of heated animals, and the treated leather of the carriage compartment. The owner helped Belkis in and I stepped up behind her. *Who's gonna believe this!?* Some serious good byes, a couple shouts, a crack of the whip, and the carriage jerked forward with the thudding of hoofs on the packed dirt roadway. We were on our way.

The trip back to the hotel was excitingly different. And we took it at a good clip too, maybe too fast. Those horses were moving out, and on a narrow, rock-strewn road carved out of the cliffs high above the crashing waves below. Not at all safe! The shades in the carriage were up, and peering down out of the fringed windows, I had a view similar to the one out of our hotel room. What a journey. It was my first time in a such a vehicle and I was captive to the creaking, the smell of leather and the rocking of the suspension. What a trip. Belkis was pleased at herself to see me so impressed (and I *was*, I can't deny it).

It's Gotta Be Tonight

Back at the hotel and still reeling from the effects of Belkis' evening, I was sure that this was going to be the night. Belkis must have decided in advance that I had finally qualified. Of course after everything that had happened already this evening, making love might almost be anticlimatic. (Which for me would not be something different.) But let me tell you, this woman was going to do it right! When I entered my room it was lit only by well placed candles. Two snifters of brandy awaited our taking on the small glass table at the foot of the bed. After what I guess was a reasonable time to make a gentleman wait, Belkis appeared (in a most slinking and provocative way) at the adjoining door, wearing a see-through long black lace gown and high heels! And I suppose now is as good a time as any to make a confession. I could have told you this sooner, but guess I was embarrassed. Remember when I first spied her in the Hilton, and described her as being striking, but probably in her late *forties?* Since then and certainly now, I could say her early fifties. In spite of this—whatever her age, she acted the perfect seductress with all the right moves. I was sitting on the end of the bed, next to the small table, brandy in hand, waiting, wondering, and worrying. After pausing a calculated sufficient time, leaning (like Marlene Dietrich) against the side of the doorway, she walked straight over to me, and stopped—her smooth white abdomen not fifteen inches in front of my face. There, she pulled her shoulders back, put her hands on her hips, and plopped one foot up on the coffee table (affording me an exciting close-up of the inside of her shapely thigh). *Whew.*

My expectations in having initiated (and now continuing) this relationship with Belkis, were and still are—a mystery to me. From day one I knew she could never be that one woman I was searching for! I was at a loss. Soon enough we were in bed and I was a bit taken back. For such a strong willed and commanding personality otherwise, holding her now— there was nothing to her. She was tiny, her legs and arms were thin and soft. Her skin was warm and smooth, but loose. Her hair seemed a bit dry and stiff. Her perfume was very strong. In view of this strangely new and bizarre female offering, what inclinations I might have had to conform to her plan were substantially curtailed. But I felt like I owed her something and I *did* want things to come out the way she must be envisioning. (I didn't want to "rain on her parade," especially after the evening's magnificently designed buildup.) I knew nothing could ever be more disastrous than my reunion with Paulette, but this bedroom encounter was going to be more alien and not in accord with my objective on this cruise.

I think I did those things which would be expected of me. (If they gave points for good intentions I would be an accomplished lover.) Fortunately, mercifully, after not too long—thank God, I think maybe; *yeah just maybe.* A quick feel. This might work. Praying to the Gods of love-making and with manual assistance, I tried to enter her, and this time, managed! (To some extent anyway.) A scarce and hugely appreciated occurrence. I was shocked at how easy what little of me made it in. I'd never been in bed with a woman this old. Her opening was spacious—yawning. (I'd almost "fallen" into her.) Certainly not an entry that required rigidity. With the slightest movement, a violation that any woman could have avoided. And in my all too familiar inauspicious state, I was sure I wasn't exerting adequate pressure anywhere, and to avoid an extrication I had to forego any thrusting movements. While she must have felt my insufficiency, she gave no indication of such and when it was over she surprisingly appeared to be well satisfied.

We had a fresh (windy) breakfast on what would have been a picturesque terrace in another season. The checkout and ride back to Istanbul was quite enjoyable. Inside the city we stopped at the Political Club (to be seen), and then the Hilton lounge for tea. At the Political Club she introduced me to the Poet Laureate of Turkey, whose last name phonetically sounded like mine. Big joke there. I got an autographed copy of a book of his poems (in English). Belkis was showing me off again, which I have to admit was damn flattering. I'd never been shown off before (and deservedly so). It was late afternoon and the Hilton crowd began thinning, I was tired, and I could see that recent activities had taken a toll on Belkis. Although we gave a lot of lip service to "next times," *and her visiting me in the states!* I think we both knew there was little chance of any of this. I had a feeling when we said good-bye, that I would not see Belkis again. Sadly, but perhaps realistically, I have to consider I may have been the object of a familiar drill for Belkis. I had served her purpose and she gave me another confounding escapade to reflect on.

On the way back to the ship and reflecting on my time in bed with Belkis, I had become more worried, thinking back to some heartfelt advice I had once received. A guy who was very popular with the ladies had once told me in all seriousness: *Don't start sleeping with older women, it'll destroy you!* Wasn't sure exactly what that "destroy" thing would be, but I had an idea, and in view of my existing problems I sure didn't need to do anything that would make things worse. If I was at all concerned about one day validating myself in the rack (and you, and God knows—I was) it was not going to be with the likes of Jacqueline (that first night ashore in Cannes) and now Belkis. These women were not the type of lithe and teasing young female creatures who would be in possession of what I would need to entreat and excite me; who would finally turn the key. Early on I had sorrowfully discovered it wasn't Connie, or my wife. I had no alternative except to cling to the belief that somewhere out there, that one magical woman *did* await me.

Chapter Nineteen
A REAL SCARE

Did you ever build a sun-deck in July, perfecting your tan, watching a Yankee game and having your girlfriend bring you a cold Michelob. Not bad right? But try the same thing in January, ears stinging in the wind, fingertips so numb you can't get the nails out of the pouch (and nobody willing to stand outside and watch). No fun. And now, plowing through steely gray winter seas, and struggling across the flight deck in blowing sleet—no fun either. And of all the frightening things, after having made a night landing, let me tell you about trying to taxi forward on an ice-glazed deck, on a listing ship, into ethereal darkness. Well that's an act that solicits prayers and beseeching.

We were returning from a night formation flight—a *late* night formation flight. We were the second launch and hadn't launched until midnight. I was the Section Leader—the head of a flight of two aircraft. In the daytime we not only launched as a flight of four, but flew the whole flight that way. At night we usually broke off into two, two-plane formations. Tonight it was me and my good buddy Tripp. And in the middle of the Mediterranean. Talk about dark! Back home, strolling around at night you're usually within fifty feet of a lit house, or a hundred feet of a street lamp, or a mile from a shopping center, or 5 miles from town. Well that's cheating. You have no idea how much light is emitted from these sources—reflected back from the clouds and indefinitely trapped within the lower atmosphere. Here in the middle of the Med, there is no reflected light. It's black-black! (As I've told you before, *like being inside an ink bottle, inside a coat pocket, in a closet at night.*) You can't see anything outside of the cockpit. Not one friggin thing. You could be right-side up, sideways or upside down. No moon, no stars, no water, no horizon, No nothing. Wall to wall blackness.

And if you'd even try to look out, it'd be through a five millimeter plastic visor on your helmet, then through a solid inch of stressed acrylic canopy. Together they'd be reflecting hundreds of double images of dots and lines and circles, and your own gawking head. Forget that, *get your eyes back inside!* Everything has to be done "on the instruments." You must have absolute trust in your interpretation of the myriad of red-lit gauges, rotating and bobbing dials, needles, and flashing LED readouts crammed across your instrument panel. There's just no outside reference whatsoever. You're in your own little thirty by forty inch cozy warm world. (In fact—sweating in it.) And not good to dwell on the fact that just eight inches outside each of your elbows, was the most harsh and hostile foreign night environment. A screaming loud, sub zero, lip ripping wind, that would tear your arms out of the sockets. I'm even scaring myself. Back inside. Don't think about that.

As usual, it was a twelve-plane launch (three, four-plane divisions). Before launch, all the pilots were given two times: the exact time of the first recovery, and their own, individual, specific, "do or die," "hit the deck," "to the second" time! Tactical military aircraft do not have a large fuel capacity. You went out on "one-point-fivers" (a one and a half hour flight) with two hours and fifteen minutes of fuel. Before launch, Air Ops gives a time check over the radio for all pilots to listen to and set their aircraft clocks. And it is not just a to the minute time check, it's a to-the-second time-hack—hand at the twelve or six o'clock position. My "hit the deck" time (also called "trap time") was 0115 exactly. Not 0114 or 0116 mind you, but 0115 on the button! Tripp, my wingman, would have a time exactly sixty seconds later: 0116. Not 0115—*mine*; or 0117—the *next guy's,* but 0116! The one minute in time reserved in advance for his landing. Can you imagine getting back to the ship with the gas gauge hitting the big "E," and then having a thirty minute delay over the ship while a dozen planes try to sort out who's next? No fuel for that.

The way this sequencing is made to work, is through the use of a designated jumping-off point before you get to the ship. A spot in space where a whole stack of returning planes orbit, awaiting their assigned time to start their approach. This spot in space (called "Oscar" for aircraft returning to the *Forrestal*) was a DME (Distance Measuring Equipment) fix, exactly three miles behind the ship. At normal approach speed, from Oscar it would take you exactly sixty seconds flying-time to reach the ship. (So I'd have to depart Oscar at 0114 in order to catch a wire at my assigned time of 0115.) *Getting complicated, eh what?* And just as I was leaving Oscar, the guy before me would be hitting the deck, having his ass yanked out the back of the plane and his visor plastered against the windscreen. All the aircraft had to be at Oscar and set up in their orbit, no less than one minute before the first recovery. From beginning to end, this whole operation was one of *very* precise timing.

Arriving at Oscar and entering the stack, the old adrenaline starts flowing. Certainly all twelve aircraft couldn't be circling this same spot at any old altitude, that'd be a recipe for a sure midair collision. So not only was each pilot assigned a "Trap time," and an Oscar "Entry time," but also, based on his numerical sequence—an Oscar "Entry altitude." Tonight, my landing sequence dictated that I would enter the stack at 9,000 feet AMSL (above mean sea level), and Tripp who was next in line to land after me, would enter 1,000 feet above me—at 10,000 feet. Grinding around in the sky, we'd all listen to—not *talk* on—a common radio channel, on which the ship continually broadcast the exact time. *...In ten seconds it will be Four-Seven. Ten, nine, eight, seven, six, five, four, three, two, one... Time, Four-Seven.* If your clock wasn't already precisely correct, you'd adjust it to the exact time. And I don't mean to the minute, I mean to the *second!*

The bottom of the stack was always 2,000 feet MSL. So coming in at 9,000 feet, I knew there were seven guys beneath me. I'd be eighth to land, barring any special priorities or emergencies. (And the whole thing was only a second or two away from a real emergency the entire time.) Above me would be another four guys, hoping like hell that none of us below them would crash on the deck, or break a wire, or do something that would delay their scheduled time. The worst thing you could do was make a bum approach and end up getting "waved-off" (denied landing by the LSO). Then you'd have to "go around," pouring the coal to it, making a turn to a visual downwind, keeping the carrier in sight, and try it again from close in (without going back our to Oscar.)

This meant that instead of using your one-minute slot, you used four or five, and that's no way to make friends in the middle of the night, I can tell you that. The rest of the pilots in the stack are measuring their fuel in minutes. Delaying your buddy can mean the end of a long friendship. (Pilots have requested a change of roommates over this.) Each minute, when the bottom guy slipped out of the stack and started towards the ship, everyone else in the stack would start their descent to the next lower altitude. So each minute I slipped another thousand feet lower. *Four thousand feet now.*

I GUESS I JUST WASN'T THINKING

At launch time, when we left, the wind across the deck had been 30 mph, and it was sleeting. Sure, there's a non-skid surface on the flight deck, but it was a couple degrees below freezing, and the damn moisture was turning to ice. In fact before my cat shot, I had seen flight deck personnel taking short runs and then purposefully sliding fifteen feet through the slush. I knew that this deck condition wouldn't affect the approach or the actual landing, but, *after landing*—trying to taxi forward, that'd be another thing. *Whew*. At night, with no visual reference and the ship heaving and listing, a slippery deck could easily spell a skid and disaster.

Even at noon on a clear day, when you had all kinds of outside references, traversing this area—moving forward to the parking area after catching a wire, was not an easy task. The way the ship was usually pitching and rolling, it felt like any minute the damn airplane was going to tip. Plus, you knew they were going to make you taxi right up to within a few feet of the edge before they'd signal you a turn to straighten it out. In my A-4 Skyhawk I was eleven feet in the air, atop two, long, spindly main gear struts, and an even longer wobbling nose gear strut. And to make things worse, airplane tires are small, and have a different tread than car tires. They have the same failing as motorcycle tires—the actual area in contact with the ground is small. About the size of a playing card at best. Not much surface to grip, and there'd be a poor coefficient of friction tonight to boot. Real easy to skid. After a night landing, the taxiing forward part, was dreaded by one and all.

Another minute gone by. There's the call. *Clock's right*. I'm on my way down to three thousand. One more minute.

Things got even more hectic after you had caught the wire. After having been yanked to a shoulder-dislocating stop, you had about five seconds allotted to you to go through the quick, complex maneuvers necessary to free yourself from the wire, then shove the throttle up and shoot forward fifty feet or so. You had to clear the touchdown area as quickly as possible, so the next guy could land. But if you were too anxious and added the power too soon, the wire wouldn't slip off the hook. You'd be stuck and there'd be hell to pay. Once out of the wire and moving, you'd frantically search ahead, into a black abyss, straining and squinting to pick up two tiny faint white dots. These barely discernible, dancing pinpoints of light, smeared and distorted through the rain-streaked windscreen, were actually two Lucite wands (flashlights) held aloft by a taxi director. They did not appear as shapes or forms, or parts of the ship, they were just two dim sparkles at an indeterminate distance. You'd see them, or *think* you saw them, then they'd be gone; only to (thankfully) reappear again, another place, from the next guy to direct you. 0113: Right on. On my way down to two thousand feet. *One more minute.*

The taxi directors were the guys stationed at various points on the bow (way in front of where you landed) who would—through those barely discernable light signals, direct you safely (hopefully) to the forward parking area. All this being done on an undulating surface, while tons of aircraft were slamming onto the deck just behind you, and giant loud turbine driven wenches were rewinding the wires. And remember, guiding you forward was not a *person*—at least not to you. You never saw a man, no form, not even an outline (for that matter, no deck, or even a horizon), *just two bouncing white specks.* It would require three directors—three pairs of these lights to ultimately get you to your designated tie down area. (And you could never make out more than one set of these lights at a time.) Suddenly the dots you were hoping were really flashlights would turn into thin white circles, and you knew the invisible ghost holding them would be frantically waving his arms motioning you forward. *Next guy's coming in, get up here! Hurry up!* Easy for him to say. He's standing there with gum-soled shoes, and has been out there for thirty minutes. His eyes are accustomed to the dark. And *he* knows where he is.

For the pilots, following the directions was very difficult. Real easy to get vertigo, since besides the two white lights there was nothing, absolutely nothing visible to use as a reference. You would add power, waiting for it to take hold and the aircraft to start moving. Sometimes it would, but inside—to you, it would appear as if it were still stationary, and it was the flashlights that were moving. But you knew they couldn't be. The rule was, *the taxi directors never moved.* It was well known how this would disorient the pilot—if the director was walking to the left while signaling you to go to the right. These guys had to be good. For us, following them was mainly an act of blind faith.

Only a minute with this first guy and you'd see a new motion, a new signal. You'd know he was passing you to the second guy, who would motion you over to the side; the scary part—over to the side. (Hopefully not *over* the side!) If the ship listed and you started to slide sideways, there was only a four-inch high scupper drain, that could maybe catch the wheel of the aircraft, and save you from a sixty-five foot plummet to the water and almost certain death. In every case where an aircraft had gone over the side of a carrier, it had made a one half roll and smacked the water exactly upside down. The speed and weight of this impact could implode the canopy, crushing and suffocating the pilot in a deluge of icy gray water. Not a pretty picture. If a pilot could be sure he was going over the side (that the aircraft wouldn't get hungup on the edge of the flight deck), then—*before he tipped more than halfway*, he would eject! (Shades of Norm Lundquist.) Unfortunately if the pilot was a half second late in making the decision to eject, the trajectory of the rocket seat would not be up; maybe not even horizontal. It could actually fire him out *down!* Hitting the water head first, still strapped in his seat, he'd break every bone in his body and be dead before he had a chance to drown, and before ten tons of metal crashed in on top of him!

Finally you'd be passed to the third guy who would signal you straight forward to the bow parking area. This guy would be standing at the very forward edge of the flight deck, leaning back against a half-inch vinyl rope, strung through 36 inch-high stanchions. He was only three or four feet from his own sixty-five foot plunge. And after he hit the water— not that it would matter, he'd be run over and churned up by the carrier plowing right over him.

0113:58 *Two more seconds*. 0114! The second hand is going by the 12. *Now!* This is it, *I'm on my way in*. Gear coming down. Flaps going to full. Adding some power. Trimmed up pretty good, almost "hands-off." Airspeed stabilized, and the angle of attack is right on. 800 feet per minute descent. *So far, so good*. At least I'm in good shape at this point. But it was never hard to be in good shape here—this far out with nothing to go by. (Not crucial yet.) God willing, this rate of descent will have me at the right altitude a mile out, to pick up the "meat-ball." A three-colored, mirror-reflected light that would tell the pilot if he were above, on, or below the ideal glidepath. If it appeared orange, that would mean I was right on the glidepath. If, when I first saw it, it was yellow, or white, it would mean that I was too high. If it was deep orange, or worse, *red*, it would mean I was too low. Definitely *not* a good place to be.

At two and a half miles I couldn't see the ship, but that was normal. During night operations every white light on the ship is extinguished. (Not that there's many anyway.) And the few small red lights marking overheads, hatches and passageways, are not there to illuminate the ship. They're just to help the sailors navigate the passageways without bumping heads or skinning shins. Can't see any of them.

Part Two: The French Riviera, Leo, June, and Big Trouble

Might make a good one this time. Everything holding up so far. Must've got the power right the first time. Airspeed is holding right on. Still 800 feet per minute down. *Looking good.* Two miles out. Got it! Not the ship itself. (Not even a hint of an outline.) No shape—nothing. But I can make out the glow that's going to turn into the meatball. The color is muddy now. Can't tell whether I'm high or low yet, but know for this distance I should be reading about 1,200 feet above the water. And the radio altimeter was at 1,190. *Things are computing.* Time to make a transmission: "FastFleet 504, Meatball!" *Called it.* Now the LSO will know I'm on it. (In fact he'd know even if I didn't call it.) That's his job; can't trust us pilots to tell the truth. And your eyes and mind, and mouth, did play tricks on you. Closer in, getting tense now.

A mile and a half and on the meatball. *On the meatball!* A mile, about twenty seconds out. Looks orange—is orange. *Isn't orange!* Damn thing going yellow. Shit. *White!* I'm going high! Off with a couple percent power, drop the nose a hair, wait. Wait. Yeah, it's turning yellower, going towards orange. Coming down. I'm down on the glidepath (number three wire height). So far so good. Fifteen seconds out. *Shit!* Turning deeper orange, on the way to red. Shit. Took off too much power. Now I'm going low. Back up with the power! Little back pressure, nose up a hair, a hair more. There it is—Orange! I'm on it, a hundred yards out. Five seconds. Still on it. Five knots fast. Squeak off a hair of power. Just a hair! Good. Hold it, hold it.

Flash! Bright! Past! Dark! Ka-bang! Lurch! Added the full power I would need in case I didn't catch a wire. Great! Being slowed. I had gotten a wire. Power back. I'm Stopped. Now being pulled back. Wait for the wire to go slack, and listen for the hook to drop free. Shit, it's turning me. Getting sideways. No problem. There it is, hook's free. Pour the power to it, get outa here! Start looking. *No white dots.* Where's those friggin flashlights? *Got em!* Got the first set. Straight ahead, a little to the left. Can't see one solitary object or outline besides those two lights. Like a blind man following the harness of his seeing-eye dog. Power up a little. *Moving.* I'm moving now, can feel it. He's signaling a slight right turn. Right pedal. The pair of lights seemed to be getting a little closer and slipping a little left. That makes sense. Christ! I could feel the wind buffeting the airplane, causing the rudder to flail and the pedals to bang my feet. Just then there was the vibration of the following aircraft (Tripp) slamming into the deck behind me.

I GUESS I JUST WASN'T THINKING

There's the hand-off signal. I'm over to guy number two. Shit, further right. Clear of the angle. Barely can see these lights. Besides the rain outside, the windshield was fogged over on the inside. *You want me to go still more to the right?* Shit. Getting nervous now. Gotta be almost directly ahead of the super structure. Getting close to the right edge now. Real close to the starboard gunnel. *What the hell is this!?* The two lights were moving to the right! If I was moving to the right, the lights should appear to be moving to the left! I knew that. That just happened with the first guy. Maybe I'm sliding, could be turning. *Shit!* Could I be slipping? Could he be walking to his left (my right)? No way, *they know they're not supposed to move!*

Stabilized now, still coming ahead. I felt the ship list heavy to the starboard (the right) side. Now the lights were moving to the left! Oh no! *I think it's happening.* I *am* sliding! Brakes locked! Oh shit! I could be going over the side! *Eject?!* In a micro second—many thoughts. If I eject I could end up drowning or never being found. Definitely don't want to eject unnecessarily! Stop! *Please God.* The lights were still drifting further to my left. He was walking to his right now, or I was sliding right. Couldn't tell. Get ready! If it's going to go I have to eject before it starts to tip upside down. Can't wait till it's gone all the way over.

You're probably going to have to do it. It may be now or never. And then *it started over!* The right wing started downward. *Do it now! Can't wait!* But struggling with conflicting thoughts *I was frozen in fatal inaction.* Two seconds after it started over, at the same time I knew I'd missed my chance and was a "goner," there was a hard lurch and no more motion. I was saved. *The aircraft was hung up on something.* Before I knew it there were ten pairs of lights coming at me. There was noise on the airplane. Flight deck personnel were clambering up the left side of the fuselage and I could hear cables and hooks banging against the main gear. A woosh, and the canopy was gone. I was in the wet wind and sweet-smelling cold air. Hands were all over me and buckles were unsnapping. Straps were flying. Strong, gloved hands were under my armpits, hauling me up and out. Everyone was shouting. Things were happening. I don't know how the hell they got me down the side of that plane so fast. Never felt anything. Like a cheerleader being passed down the stadium crowd. What a crew. What action. Was being slapped on the back. Shaking my head. Meanwhile, the aft end of the ship was alive and well with the slamming and banging of the remaining aircraft recovering. (None of them the least bit aware of my near-disaster up here.)

Part Two: The French Riviera, Leo, June, and Big Trouble

With the soles of my feet on the solid metal of the flight deck, and then my butt on the padded seat of the tug, I was overcome by a wonderful, warm and tingling feeling of sheer relief. Peering through the darkness towards my plane, I could see the left wing pointing to the sky, the right one hidden over the side. The aircraft was perched precariously on the edge, the left main gear caught on something on the edge of the deck, the right one completely over the side. I'd made it. But *not* through my own skill or decisiveness, that was for sure. As far as I was concerned, me—for my part, I had failed, miserably, potentially fatally. I should have ejected. For the first one or two seconds, I *did* believe I was going over the edge, and I had "choked." I didn't do a damn thing! *Had the aircraft not gotten hung up I would have been in the cockpit when it hit the water.*

This lack of action ("choke") on my part, exposed to me again (and believe me other times are coming) that while I would go on to seek out high risk employment (for sad reasons and to prove what perhaps cannot be proven), it may not have been the road I was meant to take. In the future I would put myself in harm's way repeatedly; suggesting an aptitude and ability to come up with what it would take. Deep down inside I feared I might only be acting; fortunately able to sound and look the part, while likely lacking the born mental and physical mettle. In the years to come I would appear to be hanging right in there with the best of them, but secretly believing if push came to shove, I really wasn't one of them. (Jim Stremlow was definitely one of "them.") I don't think as long as it ran, anyone ever guessed I wasn't.

Oh, regarding the incident on the night deck: In my defense, the taxi director signaling me when I slid was relieved of duties and sent back for more training. He *had* started walking with his lights still on (the big "No-No," almost guaranteed to disorient the pilot—cause him to think *he's* the one moving), which had undoubtedly caused me to punch the brake and start the slide.

Chapter Twenty
NAPLES TO MUNICH TO NAPLES

We had put into Naples again. Since there still had not been much good coming out of Naples, I had a plan—do the same thing I did last time we docked here: *Leave—quick!* Yup, in a few hours I'd be on my way to Munich to see the home of the famous "Octoberfest!" I knew I couldn't justify buying an airline ticket, but as a Marine I could take advantage of "Space Available" travel on any U.S. military aircraft. And here in Naples there was a U.S. air base: Naval Air Station Capodichino. *My ticket out.* The guys told me there were U.S. Air Force transports in there everyday, and a lot of them flying to Germany. In fact, moored only three miles off shore, just yesterday I'd been able to see several Air Force planes circling in the traffic pattern. For sure I'd be able to get on something. Three days leave—*official* leave. Not a bunch, but enough. For once I wasn't swapping duty days to go ashore. (For once I wouldn't be corralling Trip and trying to swap duty days.) I'd hitch a ride from the naval air station up to the U.S. Air Force base at Frankfurt, then catch a train to Munich, spend two full days, and have a full day for the train ride back to Naples. (No way to catch a military flight out of Munich. No U.S. air base there.)

Waiting at the air station I was having some second thoughts, like maybe I should've worn my uniform. I sure hope you don't need a uniform to get on an Air Force plane. (I did have my ID card.) And I might've been going a little overboard with the "Continental look." I was wearing my black cashmere sweater—the one from Piazza d'Espagna, and more recently—Rhodes and Istanbul. Getting my money's worth out of this baby. (It would be another month before I put it in a dryer and ended up with a permanent size 3 for a souvenir.) Was also wearing the silk ascot I had bought when I bought the sweater. Gotta admit, I didn't look very military, that's for sure. Probably should have waited till I got to my destination to go "Continental." (And my hair was about as long as you can let it get as a Marine officer.) Yeah, good thing I got my ID card. If I'm ever gonna need it, it'll be today.

Found the terminal. Not much of a terminal and only one airplane on the ramp. *Where's all those Air Force transports?* And I think I brought too much stuff. Only four days and I've got this mammoth suitcase. Should've weighed it. I might be overweight and sometimes those Air Force loadmasters can be sticklers. It was cold and bleak, and windy too; wished I had a coat. I'd seen the European guys in these neat-looking, hip-length coats ("Macs" they called them). That'd be sharp. Maybe I'll buy one in Germany. I became more worried, because for a big naval air station there wasn't much activity. I was counting on getting a flight by noon; two-thirty now and still nothing. Sat on the curb. Threw little pieces of gravel at big pieces. Read all the signs. Not a single arrival or departure. The way it's going I'm going to spend half my vacation right here on the ramp. I'll check with Operations one more time. I think I can ask one more time without pissing them off too much. I did, and good news! Would you believe? Finally. An A C-130 is supposed to be land in about an hour, from Athens, going to *Rhine Mein, Germany!*

True enough, forty minutes later there it was on short final. A large four-engine turboprop. Bound to have at least one empty sea. *Please God, don't let it be full.* Another five minutes and the aircraft was taxiing onto the ramp in front of the terminal. I watched nervously as the people began stumbling out onto the ramp, kicking their legs and waving their arms, trying to shake out the kinks and brush off the wrinkles. They were wandering around with brown bags and paper plates, looking for trash barrels. I was counting and praying; one.., two.., three.., four. Only four guys, and I think they're the crew. Maybe there's *no* passengers. Holy Shit, the plane's empty. *Thank you Lord.*

Gotta ask. Not going to get on otherwise. Nothing ventured, nothing gained. I'll wait till they get into Operations, give them time to take a leak and get a cup of coffee. Let's see, one Major, a Captain, and two enlisted crew members. The Major's probably the PIC (Pilot in Command). I'll ask him. Followed him into Meteorology where he was going over some weather facsimile charts and station reports for his next flight. "Excuse me Major. My name is Captain Yahnke, I'm a pilot officer off the *Forrestal* out there, I'm trying to catch a ride to Frankfurt. Any chance you guys are headed that way?"

"Yeah we are, but I'm only the navigator, you'll have to check with Captain Stiddle over there, he's the PIC." The major kind've pursed his lips in a not-too-encouraging way as he nodded towards the captain. I thanked him and walked over to the captain. He didn't look like a very amiable guy to me. (As we used to say in the service, "he appeared to be spring-loaded to the pissed-off position.")

"Captain....how ya doing?"

Only a nod. Things are not looking good. I can see we're not hitting it off. *Sure wish I was in my uniform.*

"My name is Roger Yahnke, I'm a Marine Captain. A Skyhawk pilot off the *Forrestal*. Sure would like to hitch a ride with you up to Frankfurt."

He didn't answer immediately, but the look on his face was one of pain and discomfort. This was *not* the kind of thing he wanted to deal with. Finally:

"Got your ID card?"

"Oh yeah. Got it, no sweat there."

"Lemmee check a couple things first, we're not leaving right away any way."

He was gone. But I was sure—not so much to take care of things, as to slink away and think of reasons to cancel me out. I could feel it in my blood. I went back to talk to the major, at least he was friendly and I needed some positive input. He spied me approaching and asked,

"How'd it go?"

"Not great. He's checking."

"On what?"

"Dunno, that's just what he said." You know when things aren't working out. This time I knew even before they got worse. The captain came back.

"No problem I hope."

"Can't do it."

"Why?"

"Regs."

Sometimes you know that it's time to fall back and re-group. I wasn't going to do any good to challenge him right now, so just backed away looking real hurt and disappointed. Hoped he'd feel sorry for me. *Time to think.* Decided to shoot the shit with the two staff sergeants who were out by the candy machine. Turns out Captain Stiddle is a real prick. I knew the major wasn't keen on him, and these guys were downright hostile. Checked Ops again, for the last time too—could see I'd worn out my welcome with those guys. No luck. Absolutely nothing inbound, at least until midnight. *Midnight?* Are you kidding? Holy Shit. Now I've got to get on this C-130! It's it or nothing. Back to the crew and the good captain in particular. Struck up another conversation again. Got things going good. Asked if he could reconsider, and got a helluva reason that he couldn't take me:

Say what? I need a parachute? "Captain, are you sure?" He was sure. I knew he was bull-shitting. In a multi-engine aircraft you don't need to have a parachute for every passenger. But that's what he said. *I'm screwed.* (And I'll bet anything there's already more than four parachutes on the aircraft.) Talked to the Major again. He shook his head and mumbled something about the Captain. But wait a minute, if that's what it takes, I'll *get* a parachute. For sure I can sign one out from my Navy brothers here on the base, what with being off the *Forrestal* and all.

"Major, when you leaving?"

"1600....forty-five minutes."

I was outa there. Stowed my suitcase behind the Ops desk. I'd seen the Flight Equipment Parachute Loft when I came in; only two blocks from where I was. I'd hit up the Officer-in-Charge for a loaner. Get that mother and tear-ass back here. I'd be able to return the chute when I came back through in three more days. No sweat. Ran the whole way, watching my breath vaporize in front of me and then running through the cloud. Puffed my way through the door and in.

"Is the lieutenant in?"

"No sir, he's gone for the day."

The red-faced petty officer was at a long table doing some periodic inflation checks on bright yellow two-man dinghies. I was going to have to deal with him. No time to wait. Might be even easier, these chiefs always bent over backwards to help. Our conversation was punctuated by the loud gushing of dry nitrogen as he relieved each cell of its test load. Knew I didn't have much time, but I didn't rush. I made small talk first. Got a good rapport going. We were hitting it off. So far, so good. Made sure he knew I was off the *Forrestal*—only going on a few day "R&R" (*Rest and Recuperation* in the military) and would definitely be coming back right through here, in just three days. The time was right, I sprung the question.

I GUESS I JUST WASN'T THINKING

Oh no. Big trouble. The guy actually winced when I made my request; looked like he'd been shot. I could tell he would have rather had me say anything than that. He put down the air hose, let out a long breath and slumped into a chair. Boy this was going to take some kind of convincing, I could see that now. He spoke: "Captain—my dog, my Mustang, my fishing rod, anything, but please, not a parachute. You can't believe the trouble I've had. I *never* get em back—no matter what."

I rushed to reassure him. "I'll sign for it, I'll check it out officially. I'll take full responsibility."

"I don't care about you signing for it. I got a dozen signature cards in the drawer now. What I *don't* have, is parachutes! People just don't bring em back."

"Chief, you've never lent one to me before, don't blame me for those other guys. Gimmee a chance."

I could see he would have liked to lend me one, but he had obviously gotten burned so many times, heard so many stories, that nothing was going to convince him. I had brought up the subject most painful to him, but I had to keep trying. The way I saw it, my whole leave depended on catching this C-130, and now only twenty minutes to go. I poured it on him; *guaranteed* him I would be back here in Naples on Tuesday—so no problem in returning it. *Please!* Ten minutes of begging. I stayed with it. I think I was convincing him (or wearing him down). Finally, like a beaten man he sighed and glanced over his shoulder towards the chute rack. Looked to me like he was weakening. Might be on the verge of a breakthrough. I continued my barrage of promises and the details of how I would return it (feeling if I slacked off even a bit, he'd lose his nerve). *No, don't tell me.* I think he just decided to do it! He got up shaking his head and looking at the floor, and shuffled over to the chutes. He's taking one down. I'm in! What a guy.

"No, no, never mind the signature Captain, I don't need another card, just bring the damn chute back. Please." I swore my commitment to make sure he'd get it. I poured out my thanks and told him not to worry. (Hopefully when I returned it his faith in mankind would be restored.) Two minutes later I was running towards the terminal, the long chute slung over my shoulder, banging into the backs of my legs with each stride. The discomfort was a pleasure. (These WWII chutes are a lot bigger and heavier than the sky diving models you see on TV.)

You should have seen the look on the captain's face when I strode in there carrying that chute. He'd lost and he knew it. No smile I can tell you, but he nodded me out onto the ramp toward the aircraft. The major winked at me, and one of the staff sergeants gave me a quick thumbs up. It was four-thirty and I was all but on my way. The flight was almost four hours. Four uncomfortable hours on a canvas fold down seat—the sole passenger. Me and one grimy light bulb in a huge metal tunnel—for a too-long time. Military aircraft have no interiors, no linings, no sound-proofing, no insulation. You can watch the aircraft skin wrinkling under the stresses of the air loads (and hear the ribs and stringers creaking and popping). I could have reached out and touched all manner of cables, wires, hydraulic actuators, etc. Definitely not first class (but the price was right).

In addition to the other negatives on the flight, by the time we got to altitude, the cargo area (where I was on a fold-down canvas seat) the temperature had fallen to somewhere near zero, and stayed that way the whole flight. You can heat the cockpit without heating the cabin, and I'll bet that's how the good Captain got back at me for "one up-ing" him. I'd been forced to go into my suitcase three times and ended up wearing almost everything I'd packed. It was dark when we landed at Rhine Mein. My feet were frozen. There was no way I could have jumped down the three feet to the ramp; had to lower myself gently—one foot at a time. Couldn't take a step for thirty seconds. Waited till I had feeling in my ankles, then walked away like I was 90 years old.

Was able to hitch a ride to the gate and get a cab downtown. Fifteen minutes to the station. Ticket window layout easy to figure out. Got mine. Changed some money and *Bingo*, I was on my way to Munich at nine forty-five. Felt tired. Didn't feel too excited. Was dragging my too big suitcase and the damn parachute (which was beginning to weigh a ton). So far I wasn't too impressed with Germany—at least Frankfurt. Everybody looked American to me. Loud too. People shouting, pushing and shoving— just like New York. Didn't feel like I was in a foreign country. *Lots* of American soldiers. They were everywhere. At least here—around the train station, it didn't come anywhere near having the ambiance of the Mediterranean cities I was now learning to love. Maybe it was just me. (When it's drizzling, or cold and windy, no place looks nice.)

Arrived in Munich a little after midnight and even at this hour there was a lot of activity. Plus, the people here were looking and acting a little more European. Lots of neat smells; old beer, sausage, pastry. Good! Yeah, this looked like a place they could have an Oktoberfest. Got to find a hotel. Just get a good night's sleep and be ready to make the most of my 72-hour Munich vacation.

I would like to tell you otherwise (especially after this long preamble), but in all honesty, my couple days in Munich were a letdown. By now I was ready to believe that each new trip ashore owed me some intense encounter. I had discovered myself to be strangely energized by my previous worldly, free-wheeling in-port escapades. Think I had a beer and bratwurst at every eatery in Munich. Memorized a hundred store window displays. Not a great time, and the weather had turned even worse—sleet and wet snow. Spent a lot of time dashing across slushy streets between icy, wheezing, windshield wiper-snapping vehicles. Mostly just wasting time.

This whole time I had been carrying around Ingrid's phone number, and the last day I decided to give her a call. She said if I could stay one more day we could do something together. That would be Tuesday, the day I'd reserved for the eight hour train ride back to Naples. If I stayed, I would have to *fly* back—on an airline. (Big bucks.) But maybe that one more day would change the complexion of this whole visit. Maybe just maybe. *Hell I'll do it.* I'll stay an extra day and just bite the bullet—buy an airline ticket. I'd still make it back in time that way.

Probably shouldn't have stayed the extra day. My meeting with Ingrid turned out to be a non-event; a far cry from our time together in Rhodes. Guess I'll have to give more credit to the hypnotic effect of the hot summer sun and the vacation commitment in stripping away a working girl's inhibitions. In any case there was no magic here, that was for sure. I have to admit, I think she was just hosting me politely. So much for this one. Take a breath, think about getting back to Naples. Having wasted the extra time (no question about it now) I *had* to fly back. I could catch an afternoon flight and still be in Naples by supper.

I was a little nervous on the cab ride to the airport. I didn't have any reservations. Schwartz had shown me the airline schedule in the hotel. (An old issue.) There was supposed to be two flights this afternoon, an Alitalia and a Lufthansa—direct to Naples. An hour and a half. Boy, here's hoping. Patted my American Express card. The weather was terrible, as it had been for three days. Gray-gray and either snow or drizzle. Could see my breath inside the cab. God this parachute was heavy. Laid across my legs it was shutting off the blood to my feet. I was beginning to hate Captain Stiddle for forcing this extra baggage on me. (And I sure hadn't needed the heavy three-suiter Samsonite.)

The airport was not very large—was even worried about being in the wrong airport. Hope it's the main airport, not just a satellite airport for domestic flights. Yeah, guess I'm okay, there's a sign for Alitalia, so it's gotta be international. But still, it's awfully small and rustic—almost like a hunting lodge. Lots of wood. A nice place, but just one medium-sized room. Only one ticket counter in the whole place. Found the Alitalia agent. Asked about the Naples flight. *Great.* 13:30. Direct to Naples. I'm in. 11:45 now. *Perfect.* Waited in line. Only a small line. Not hearing any English though. That'll make it a little more difficult. My turn. Things going good. She's writing my ticket. The price hurts but I'll charge it. I won't think about it now, I'll cross that bridge when I come to it. Slid my AMEX card to her. *What's this?* Seems to be a problem. She's shaking her head. I can't believe what I'm thinking: *She's not going to take my card.* But why—what's wrong? Geez, I could be in trouble here. Whew. How much? "Ninety Marks?!" *Whoa.* Into my pocket, fumbling, out, counting. I can do it, but it's going to leave me with practically nothing. Still, maybe I won't need anything other than cab fare when I arrive back in Naples (and I got some Lire in my toilet kit). *I'm covered.* Guess I can do it. I'll pay cash. Wow.

Time to give her my baggage. Shove my luggage across the scale. (A lot to shove, I can tell you.) And then something I'd never thought of. *I'm overweight!* And not just a little either. The damned three-suiter itself used all my allowance. Now I'm really in trouble. With the chute on the scale I was 12 kilos overweight. "How much? Thirty Marks?!" Impossible, that's one third of the cost of the flight! I'm sure there must be a mistake. I ask again. I'm being real polite. Trying not to irritate her (or the people behind me in the line). Don't have thirty marks. That's what it's going to be, no doubt about it. No mistake. What the hell am I going to do. "Uh, yeah, take the suitcase." I grab the parachute off the scale, hoist it over one shoulder, grab my ticket and step away from the counter to try to come up with some sort of plan. Shit. I knew this vacation wasn't going good from the minute it started.

The weather stayed bad. The flight was posted as an "indefinite delay." *Great.* Now I might be late returning from my leave on top of everything else. And I have to make a stop at that naval air station in Naples. Got to return this chute before I head out to the boat! I hadn't forgotten the concern of the Navy chief who had signed it out to me. (Absolutely *cannot* let him down!) I wandered around, most the time dragging the chute behind me, sometimes propping it up against the wall. Finally—on the counter right by where I bought my ticket, I spy a little black plastic sign. It reads: "ITEMS ALLOWED ON BOARD AS CARRY-ONS: PURSES, BOOKS, MEDICATIONS, PROSTHETICS, OR ITEMS OBVIOUSLY DESIGNED FOR PERSONAL WEAR." Wow, according to this I can bring it on board with me; *a parachute is obviously designed for personal wear.* It fits the criteria.

A pre-boarding call. Maybe we're going. I line up (with the chute slung kinda casual over my shoulder). I'm telling you, I had no idea any agent could get so excited. It was a full minute before he said a single word in English. But he didn't have to—I knew what he meant. This was decades before any high-jackings or terrorist's acts had even been thought of, but there was no way I was going to get on that airplane carrying a parachute, whether it was designed for personal wear or not. I was screwed.

But a miracle, right in the middle of this there is another announcement, that the flight's delayed again. Until when? 14:30. A new scheduled departure time. I've got over an hour and an idea—a way to get this chute back to the chief. I was out of there. Into a cab. Into town. To the post office (which was one half of the train station). I'd seen it when I came in. I pay the cab and hustle myself in. Nothing written in English. A little trouble finding the international window. There it is. But first I gotta *wrap* this damn thing. Outside again, in the freezing drizzle, searching for a dumpster. Find one. Pull out some paper. *Yuk.* More rummaging, found some twine, lots of knots, but it'll work. The paper's strong. This'll be good. I'll wrap it double and tight. Tie it good. Once long ways and two times crossways around the middle. Got the clean side of the paper outside. The old writing is underneath. Looks clean enough.

Into the post office again. Now, try to find a big felt tip pen to address it. Don't buy one, just borrow one. Found a magazine store. Got one; take my time—write large and legible. *Absolutely positively have to make sure there is no chance this parachute gets lost!* I address it to the chief himself, in care of the Flight Equipment Department, at the Naval Air Station Capodichino, Naples, Italy. Even had the clerk check his Italy reference book, and found out Naples was in the province of Campania— and wrote that on the package too. Also wrote Naples twice; once in Italian (Napoli). Double checked it. This is real important. It absolutely has to get delivered. Okay—that's good enough. To the window. So far so good. The guy takes it. It's pretty big, but he doesn't seem concerned. He looks at the address, checks another dog-eared booklet. Hits a mechanical calculator, starts to tell me the cost, and then *I can see there is a problem.* He shoves the package back to me telling me he can't take it without a return address. He turns and begins talking to the guy behind him while he guesses I'm adding the return address that I just forgot to put on. "Excuse me. Excuse me. I don't have a return address in Germany, I'm just passing through."

But this guy knew the rules. *No return address, no shipping through this post office.* My mind raced. What could I do? It's only a formality. Probably anything would work. But I didn't have an address in Germany. *Wait! Ingrid's address!* I had it. I could use it. Nice and clear. Print it smaller than the destination address. Looks good. Finished. Shove the package back to him. I pat it, look him square in the eye with my most earnest expression and tell him it's *very* important. I wanted the process, starting right here with him, to commence as the critical journey it truly was. It's *got* to get there. He smiles a "don't worry" smile. Eight Marks and I'm outa there, with enough left for cab fare. In my pocket—eleven American dollars and a few Italian Lire.

Back at the airport and thirty minutes to flight time. Great. The weather is still terrible, visibility almost "zero-zero", but the flight is finally called, and a gaggle of straggling, worse-for-the-wear travelers filed out on to the icy ramp for boarding. I'm almost sure it was an old French Caravelle airliner (sort of like a small DC-9). On board, a few minutes, small amounts of confusion, and we're moving. Light snow now. Never flew Alitalia before. Doesn't look like it's going to be too bad. Stewardesses not the best looking girls I'd ever seen, but they seemed to know their jobs.

Normal Take-off. Two 360 degree circles to gain altitude before starting southbound over the Alps. Finally, above the clouds, the sun shining in the right-hand side of the airplane. We're southbound on course. My Munich trip is over. Much ado about nothing. Regroup. Gain strength for the next adventure. While I'm sinking further into the seat, feeling poorly about my life, wondering what in the hell my wife and kids would think if they knew of my shenanigans, I notice the shadows begin to move across the interior, and the sun slipping from window to window towards the rear of the aircraft, then the shadow of the wing. We stay in a bank until the sun is now shining in the windows on the left side of the airplane. *We've reversed course.* We stay on this northerly course and I'm wondering what the hell is going on. This is not a good sign. I grab the next stewardess that passes. She speaks good English and tells me we're going back. *Going back!?* Of course I ask why, and seeing I'm not going to let her go, she reluctantly tells me that *one of the pilots doesn't like the sound of one of the engines.*

On the ground, back at my log cabin airport. Into the terminal. People shuffling around in wet galoshes and wool scarves, obviously not in control of their destiny; waiting, wondering, making phone calls, whispering to one another. Christ, I gotta be on my way soon! Ten minutes later they call the flight and we're herded back out to the plane. On board, fired up, and on our way again. The same two 360 degree circles to gain altitude. The same level off on our southerly course. I'm sitting there wondering what they could have done to the engine in ten minutes. I latched onto the same stewardess as before.

"You couldn't possibly have changed an engine in ten minutes."

"No, we changed pilots."

Other than being late the engine must have been okay because the flight was uneventful. Caught a cab. My few Lire were enough to get me within a half mile of the dock. Jogged the rest of the way. It was a little after six when I caught the gray liberty boat, on the gray water, back to my huge gray ship. I felt beat. I felt blah. But I would always remember this Munich trip—for another reason, that I will share with you soon.

Chapter Twenty-One
VISITING LEO

An Exciting Reunion

A week later than I thought we'd be here, but we're here—Genoa, again. And coming ashore, the same sights and same non-inspiring place it had been the last time. In the foreground, the same sorry array of rusted tankers. Behind them, a series of worse-for-the-wear wharves, upon which battered trucks spewing diesel smoke were racing past rows of shipping containers, leaning stacks of split open crates and scrambled piles of discarded metal strapping. Closer now. Grease and debris floating on the surface. But I didn't care, I'd be on my way outa here *toute suite.* (I'm now studying French, and that means "right away.") I didn't have time to receive a response from Leo, but I had mailed him a letter three weeks ago, with the new dates for this week. Remember Leo and his wife? I gave them that ship's tour in Cannes? I was a little reluctant to take leave again, after just having been to Munich a couple weeks ago, but needed at least an extra day.

Knew I'd better start concentrating on Sara's letters, her life, the kid's activities, and things going on at the house. *Less than three months left on the cruise.* I've got to start thinking about my return. Visualize my real situation—how I'm going to fit back in. Try to picture myself in the kitchen with the family, or making a run downtown on a Saturday morning. *Whew.* Not easy. (In fact almost impossible.) I could imagine myself doing those things—going through the motions, but with a terrible hollowness; a sickening feeling in my stomach. Sara was so damned good and involved, spending so much time making sure I was filled in on everything, while I was spending so much time planning my head-shaking activities. Kevin was only one year old when I left. I hadn't had the chance to get to know him as a baby, and now I don't know him as a little person. How can I appreciate these things she's trying to explain.

But this trip (at last) everything was going to be "above board." No searching for femmes fatales, just visit Leo. Should be interesting. Don't have to feel ashamed (for once). Nothing wrong this time. In fact was a little proud of myself, finally doing something normal. And Leo had been right. There were a bunch of trains from Genoa to Milan. I was on one twenty minutes after I arrived at the station. Not a *Rapido*, but the commuter would do it in an hour and a half. No sweat. Arrived in Milan about noon. The train station there was a uniquely architectured, cavernous building. Stepping off and onto the platform, one's eyes were immediately drawn to the high-domed roof with its large, arched translucent panels. The bustling travelers below were being bathed in a comforting muted light as they scurried across the worn marble floors. It wasn't hectic— like the Rome station in the summer (with ten thousand *Europe on Five Dollars A Day* college kids). At this time of year only authentic Milanese, all of whom were well dressed and professional-appearing. Lots of smart-looking women in wide-brimmed hats, colorful scarves and alligator bags, and businessmen in gray and tan worsteds (and those smart camel hair topcoats). Surprisingly, the workers—even those I took as bound for manual labor jobs, were still wearing hats and ties, and moving ahead in a serious manner.

Not a bad day, but a little cloudy for me, and only forty degrees. At first (and important to me) the city looked organized. Not intimidating. Respectable. Directly in front of the station was a large tree-lined square, surrounded with all kinds of neat looking shops. One good thing about these European cities, the railroad station was rarely more than two blocks from the original town center. Today I couldn't tell which direction that might be, but it didn't matter. I had Leo's address and nothing to do but hop a cab. *Wait a minute,* before doing that I was going to do something proper: Give him a call first, instead of just popping in. And (I'm learning) I should arrive with a gift—any kind of gift. Not too important what, it's the idea. I did both things. For the gift, I bought something for the house; a metal vase encased in antelope skin that was embossed with vines and flowers. Really good looking and only cost about six dollars. Leo answered the phone and was thrilled. *C'mon right over. Any questions? You got the map?* I had everything.

Maybe it was just the route the cab driver took, but it was appearing that outside of the city, Milan was nothing but drab, high-rise concrete habitats. Scenery like this was bringing me to the conclusion that no place has the single-family homes of the good ol' USA. Maybe not enough land in Europe to go around. Very expensive to buy a piece of property and build your own place; thus all these middle income ten-story projects. (We take "your own spread" for granted. Based on what I was now seeing, it might better be called a luxury.) Twenty minutes later and a little nervous, we arrived at Leo's address, which was just another one of those ten-story apartment buildings. I had just assumed Leo was well-off. He had never said as much, but his presence suggested a successful international businessman. If this were the case (and it may well have been) he didn't flaunt it with his domicile.

Leo went overboard with his handshakes and hugs. I was sure I didn't deserve as much. Winona as usual stood back watching silently, with that same soft smile. The apartment was Spartan. The living room (you stepped through the door and you were in the middle of it) was large with well-polished parquet floors. But it was sparsely furnished with only a few traditional items of furniture. In the center of the room was a stiff brocade couch with a dark hard-wood coffee table and two stuffed chairs. Against one wall, a small game table and a well-stocked bookcase. Against the other, a long buffet. Cutting off part of the room was an ornately carved room divider, serving to give some privacy to a dining area just behind it. Through it I could see a lacquered dining table and four rigid chairs. Having no idea of what normal or average would be in Italy, and the costs of these types of apartments, I could well have been in one of the top-of-the-line units.

Flipper!

Leo took my things and showed me the tiny guest room where I would be sleeping. Back in the living room he gestured to Winona about something from the kitchen. Winona's attitude and expression hinted she was barely able to conceal her delight about some forthcoming event. Finally, after the tea was brought out, some cookies spread on a tray, and Leo and I seated side by side on the couch; it was time. Winona scurried out of the room, and reappeared momentarily with some sort of large black leatherette hat box (or so it initially appeared). She plopped down on the floor at my feet, and plunked the hat box on the coffee table in front of me. Up close

I could see it was more than a hat box. It was an expensive custom made carrying case. She undid two straps, flung open the lid, reached in, and with unrestrained joy—produced *Flipper!*

Holding it pridefully aloft in both hands, eye level to me, she gazed lovingly upon a shiny, bluish-gray ceramic model of a seal!? Of course I didn't know what to say. It was a nice piece of art, that was for sure. But I sensed that this was only a small part—if any, of the attention to be given Flipper. I gave a big "Ooh," and reached for it (at the same time looking to Leo for some guidance). His smiling countenance suggested I was a grown man, and would know how to deal with these things. I got only a small recounting of their vacation to the Virgin Islands several years ago, when they had bought Flipper. Winona was now cooing to it like it was a six-month old baby. Leo helped her a bit, telling me about their travels together; the many places they had visited and the good times the *three* of them had had together. On their vacations she actually bought a third ticket so Flipper would have his own seat on the plane. I felt a little awkward as I reluctantly concluded that to Winona this was not just a ceramic seal, it was a living member of the family; as much as if it would have been one of their own offspring (they had none), and would be accorded every privilege thereof.

Leo just smiled lovingly at Winona as she caressed the seal and looked to me for approval and affection. *Whew, this poor woman.* I did my best to pay the proper homage and respond in a way that would indicate as far as I was concerned, it was a living, thinking, member of the family. From time to time in this conversation, I felt especially foolish, as it occurred to me that perhaps Winona did not really think this ceramic seal was a person—that she wasn't out of her head, that it was just a game. And if it was a game, then I was the one acting crazy. I was the duped newcomer. If so, seeing what I was taking her for, she could have been insulted. I guess there was a standard time allotted for Flipper's introduction. After three or four minutes of this Leo gave Winona a loving nod, which she acknowledged. That was it. She promptly reinstalled Flipper in his container and as quickly as she had appeared with Flipper, made off to some back room with him. I felt a little relieved, but still did not have a firm idea about Flipper's place in the household.

Alone, Leo then turned to me full face, and asked me excitedly, to tell him all about the activities aboard the *Forrestal* since they had visited. I went on to tell him what exciting things I could remember about my flights and shipboard life in general. I did it, but it didn't seem too interesting to me. Of greater interest to me, was getting started on a tour of his gun factories, and learning more about this mysterious man and the extent of his arms dealing. But Leo was determined to use the rest of the afternoon to show me his city. *Tomorrow?*—tomorrow we'd leave early for the drive to Brescia to see the firearms business first hand. *That* was what I was looking forward to. I'd go on his tour today, but my heart wasn't in it.

A Little More About Leo

At this point in my life (embarrassedly) I had no appreciation for the annals and architecture of these historied European cities. For me—at least for the past six months, they were just magnificent settings; strange new arenas in which I acted out my own agenda, hardly taking note of the things of real value. During tea I was able to get Leo talking about his life and how he and Winona had met. He started at the beginning: Since he was a boy, his expertise and satisfaction were in designing, operating, and repairing small, complex, geared machinery—particularly cameras, and especially moving picture cameras. (We're talking long before video tapes and laser discs.) He "lit" in the Hollywood area, and through the skill of his hands and infectious charm, went on to become the first—the very first Director of Paramount Pictures in Hollywood. (Actually at that time it I don't think it was Hollywood.)

Evidently in those days, the director wasn't so much a conceptual artist (like nowadays), rather he was the guy who knew how to keep the cameras running. Leo was the director of Paramount's first talkie. Back then almost every film was a western. He met Winona on the set of one of these cowboy movies when she was playing the part of the Indian maiden. And I could well imagine that. (Especially if the maiden spoke no English.) They had needed a real short girl since the hero was only five-foot six. He said it was love at first sight and they had been together ever since. Although I got Leo to relate several stories he had not forgotten about the afternoon's schedule. He checked his watch and rose to his feet, and I knew further tales would not be forthcoming. I was about to get introduced to the grand city of Milano. We were going to leave Winona here, which pained me a little. She appeared completely dependent on Leo, with apparently no other connection to the outside world. I didn't want to see her left alone, but that was how it would be. On exiting Leo fawned over her, repeatedly asking if there were anything he could pick up for her, and if she was sure she would be all right. Just before going through the door, he stooped over, and with one hand held tenderly against the side of her face, kissed the top of her head. Outside the building, if I would have been in position to see, I'm sure I could have looked back up and seen her peering down through a parted curtain.

Leo's car was kept in the building's underground parking garage. A facility I was finding to be quite common in Europe. There was very little undeveloped property in these old cities; no land not already supporting worthy structures. Parking lots as we know them are few and far between. The basic trappings of Leo's parking garage suited the building perfectly. All the necessities were met, but no frills. There was no automatic circuitry to open the garage door. Ninety percent of the cars were black. Up the ramp and onto the street. We were on our way. In the traffic—in this mini car, I felt a little less protected than I would have liked. Other than that, his not new not old Fiat with its dried and dusty interior leather and wood (like the parking garage and the apartment) met all actual requirements. I was impressed by this emphasis on function, without an apparent need to "keep up with the Jones." No superficiality anywhere so far. We would commence our tour from the piazza right in front of the train station, and it would turn out to be one helluva tour.

A Guided Tour of Milan

Leo parked nearby and we walked up to, around, and into Milan's Gothic Cathedral. Leo said—the third largest church in Europe, behind St. Peter's and the Cathedral of Seville. The thing was all made out of a white carrara marble and had a foundation footprint in the shape of a Latin cross. It was pretty well stained and covered with soot by now. The project was started in 1385, but not finished until the mid 1800's by Napoleon I. I was impressed (mostly with how much Leo knew). Across from the Cathedral was the Galleria Vittorio Emanuelle II, a large, glass-roofed building with its share of neat shops and well attended restaurants. The arched *vetro* overhead was framed in black wrought iron, with curly-cues and angles. Leo said the Milanese referred to it as the "living room of Milan." We visited La Scala—one of Europe's leading opera houses, and then he took me to where Mussolini and his mistress were hung upside down at the end of world war II. (4 pm already. I could see Leo was not in the habit of giving short tours.)

In the car again. Another "must see," the Ambrosia Library—a million rare books and ancient manuscripts. Spent more time there than we needed. Next the Brera Art Gallery; and after that, in the car again bound for the

Monastery of Santa Marie delle Grazie. It was on a wall of this monastery that Leonardo Da Vinci painted *The Last Supper.* (Wow.) Unfortunately it was closed so we couldn't get in. (By now I was a little tired, and getting hungry.) He told me the city was first founded by the Celts in 400 BC, at this strategic location near a pass in the Alps. Then the Romans took over about 200 BC, and ruled it for five hundred years. After that and until about 1400 AD it was ruled by Milanese nobles. The people are almost all Roman Catholics, and according to Leo have always had a reputation for ambition and skill in business. He said finance and manufacturing have always been the major commercial activities. In the 1950's there was great industrial growth and tens of thousands of people from southern Italy came here to work. A severe housing shortage resulted, and thus—all the apartment buildings I had noticed during my cab ride to Leo's. They were built to accommodate that immigrating work force. Leo was an expert on Milan and a great talker. As he spoke and gestured artistically with his hands, I couldn't help noticing his watch; or more accurately—the way he wore his watch. Leo purposely had the woven gold band too large. The watch hung loosely on his wrist, the face was sometimes on top and sometimes under. When his arm was lowered, it slid down the back of his hand towards his knuckles. He wore it like a big bracelet. (As I do now, mine. In memory of Leo.)

Six-thirty. The tour's finished. Had started to rain. Leo said we hadn't seen the half of it, but I felt like we had. Hungry too—only tea and cookies since seven this morning. Still hadn't learned anything more about Leo, he was too busy performing his duties as the "tour guide from hell." I was surprised to find that we were not going to return to the apartment to eat. We were going to eat in town, without Winona. Rain really coming down now, people scurrying every which way. Streets shining. There's something comforting or exciting about a crowded big city in the rain. (Makes you feel like you're encapsulated "where the action is.") Leo took me into one of the strangest-appearing metropolitan areas I'd ever seen. In the middle of a very crowded section of the city, we suddenly came upon an incongruous, vastly-open space. A long city block had been turned into a park; like some King Kong creature had reached down and scooped out all the buildings in the center of this otherwise wall-to-wall barrio. On the other sides of each of the four streets bordering this bright green quadrangle were wall-to-wall, ultra modern and tall, apparently new buildings. (Just across the street could have been Dallas.) The area must have been freshly created, because there were no mature trees. In fact hardly any trees at all. Right in the middle of what had years ago been a congested tenement house ghetto, was an extravagantly spacious rectangle of table-flat, unmarred green grass.

On one end of the long park was a small man-made pond. On the other end was a man-made hill—a mound that rose maybe twenty feet above street level. Atop it was a real misfit: a tall, space age building built entirely of clear glass (and I mean *all* of it—the walls, from the floor to the ceiling, and the whole roof as well.) The glass was framed and supported by the required shiny metal framing. You could look completely through the building from any direction. It housed a restaurant on the top floor, and anyone eating there would certainly be on display. A really weird design. I suspected it would be some sort of trip to eat there, and I would soon find out. The rain was pelting now and we dashed the 100 yards from the car (leaking car) to a corner at the high end of the park. A narrow red brick walkway curved upward to a sheltered landing just outside the building entrance. Unfortunately, once on this ramp we were forced to a slow walk behind a not-to-be-rushed group, apparently unsure of their footing on the wet bricks. Under the flailing canopy outside the La Torretta di Vetro ground floor entrance we waited our turn to file in, while the standard activity of shaking umbrellas and stomping of feet was taking place. Our turn came and we entered. I couldn't help reflecting on some Disney World attraction or a set from *Star Wars*. The place just didn't fit.

Dinner in Town

I saw an elevator in the center of the building, but for some reason Leo chose to take the stairs (a bunch of them). The restaurant occupied the whole top floor—one huge room from wall to wall to wall. Inside (except the clear glass exterior walls), everything was silver or gray or black, and shining; including the floor which was dark marble. Interesting, but not warm and cozy. The kitchen was a squared island in the center of the room; completely open and bordered by a polished counter. The tables lined all four exterior walls; every table thus being a window seat. I don't think it was a swank place; appeared recently opened and at least for now— an "in" place. An American look-alike. Sitting here on the fourth or fifth floor, looking straight outward there was nothing but reflected dark gloom. Pressing my forehead against the glass so as to better peer straight down I scanned the deserted bright green rain-drenched park below. Bordering it on our side was a still-busy intersection with bumper to bumper traffic crawling along its shining wet streets. The traffic lights would change, and the windshield wiper-snapping cars would move ahead, being on guard to avoid the too-frequent police cars recklessly streaking by with sirens wailing. To me, in spite of the comforting rain, it was a little hyper out there. A tempo which made me feel uneasy. *Guess I'm safe up here in my high glass fort.*

When asked what I would like, I remembered the cannelloni from Captain Neilsen's restaurant in Genoa, and threw that out there like I knew what I was talking about. Leo looked satisfied and said it would be "out of this world." (Precisely where I was at the moment; electrified to be so far away, with such an interesting person and in such a bizarre location.) *Not a soul in the world besides Leo, knew where I was at this time.* While waiting for what has since become my now favorite Italian dish to arrive, I again asked Leo about himself, hoping to find out more regarding his day to day role in the gun business and any other activities. As had been the case previously, he again was vague on what he did with most his time. I continued to suspect there was more to it than he had said thus far. Maybe not. Maybe just my imagination working overtime. Although on the ship, he had mentioned that during WWII he was a director in our Office of Strategic Services in Europe—the forerunner to our present CIA.

I did get one neat tidbit from him during our wait. He had gone with Admiral Byrd on his second (or maybe third) expedition to the South Pole. The previous expedition had been plagued with malfunctioning cameras. The film they brought back had been less than desired. Leo, only a young man but already building a reputation as a master cameraman, had been asked to critique the film and offer suggestions. He did, and as a result of his input was invited along. Once down under "on the ice," Leo set about completely dismantling all the cameras—every piece, each bearing and gear; then washed them in alcohol and wiped them dry. He then reassembled them (much to everyone's dismay) dry as a bone, *devoid of any oil.* He explained to me, what he had told them. The problem with their cameras had been that because of the super low temperatures, the oil was congealing and slowing the camera speed. As cold as it was, heat buildup in the cameras was not a problem. And with the temperature always below freezing there was no moisture in the air, which voided the necessity of the standard protective film of oil. So why use any? And true enough, without any lubrication, the cameras functioned perfectly and Leo was a hero. As interesting as this was, I kept pushing for what he was *really* doing over here, and if all his guns were sporting pieces, or if he also manufactured or purchased other types of weapons. The intrigue I was seeking or had been imagining in my previous escapades, allowed me to fantasize full force now, with regards to Leo. He smiled, and I hoped that meant that soon enough I would know. The food arrived; my cannelloni and a mixed seafood pasta for Leo, which looked every bit as enticing as my plate.

"Look Roger, a *white* sauce—that's the way cannelloni should come; not buried in tomato sauce!" I was starved, and like I'd learned they say in France: *Hunger is the best sauce.* Without further conversation we both leaned forward and "dug in." Any doubts I had about the caliber of the food were squelched. Throughout, the rain continued to beat against the glass and the traffic below was still hectic. While bent over, debating whether or not to wipe my plate with a piece of bread, there was an alarmingly sharp sound, like a piece of gravel hitting your car windshield. For a sixty year-old guy Leo was damned agile. In an instant he was up and around the table, right by my chair. I was taken back by his concern and sudden movement. "Leo, did you hear that? What was that Leo!?" Other people had heard the sound too, and now someone was pointing at a hole and crack in the glass, *about three feet above our table!*

Leo at first appeared startled, but I could see he quickly considered it over. His expression was more one of apology for the inconvenience rather than fright or anger. He spoke Italian to the staff, who said something about another cursed ragamuffin throwing a rock. Leo nodded in agreement and said something shakily humorous like*, just tough to have a quiet meal out anymore.* He paid the bill and we left—a little hurriedly perhaps, but more or less like nothing had happened. On the way to the car I asked him again. "Leo, as high as we were, I don't think that could've been a rock. And did you see that hole? It was almost perfectly round. Could that have been a stray bullet that went through there?" I think he thought so (maybe *knew* so). He never admitted to it though. The ride back to the apartment was quiet, but I couldn't let it lay. I asked Leo one more time, what the heck he thought about whatever had come hit the glass. He finally said that it sure could have been a stray bullet, based on the shape of the hole. *But what if it was on purpose? Could someone have actually been shooting at Leo.* And if so—why? To this day when I recreate the incident, I still don't know. (Could be that's why he's not in the habit of taking Winona out to dinner.)

At Last, the Gun Business

After a special omelet that Leo took great pride in preparing, we were on our way. It would be about a one hour drive north, through the flat and fertile Plains of Lombardia, to the small town of Brescia. During this ride I got Leo to tell me a couple stories about his work as a member of the OSS. (I was still trying to make things fit my wistful thinking.) He had worked with the French underground, and behind the lines in German held territory; mostly on technical projects that involved filming (and sabotaging trains). He told me he once was called to Washington to give a confidential briefing to President Roosevelt. Before entering the Oval Office an aid cautioned him not to refer to FDR's illness as "Infantile Paralysis" (its original name). This would upset the President. "Polio" would be okay, but not "Infantile Paralysis." Wow, Leo *did* have a helluva background. My inklings that he may have been not just an accomplished person, but a connected individual, were at last being reinforced. He was no ordinary individual, that was for sure. And I still wondered about his supposedly, above board gun business here in Europe. Why live here? Why not just hire a manager and ship the stuff to the states? Could it just be a front? He previously had mentioned he didn't own the business alone. His partner was a man named Samuel Cummins. (This *did* excite me because I had recently seen an article about Mr. Cummins—"the man with the alligator briefcase" who had supposedly bought more guns than the US Army!) Well, I'll know more soon enough, ten o'clock now and we should be in Brescia in about ten minutes.

I could see high mountains to the north—rising up steeply, almost vertically, like a gigantic charcoal colored wall. Probably further, but looked like they were only ten or twenty miles away. Lots of snow on the tops. Leo said they were the Italian Alps. Just on the other side of the peaks—the downward slopes were inside the Swiss border. Leo had been saying Brescia, but that's not what he meant. He meant a village *near* Brescia. Observing it now—to my way of thinking, it couldn't even be called a village. It was a collection of about a fifty, small, crowded-together adobe cottages, plopped in the middle of a couple thousand acres of flat cultivated mud. We're talking rural here—*very* rural. And while it certainly wasn't a hotbed of agricultural advancement, it appeared farming was what made this place tick, although I couldn't imagine how they were growing much of anything this time of year. There was no town center, not a single major intersection, no stores, not even any power lines. Just a bunch of narrow and winding streets—*none* paved. I was anxious to see how the family gun-making business (or any business) flourished in this town. I was guessing it (rather than the farming) may well have been what kept the village alive.

We followed beat-up old trucks, fenders hanging, and splattered with mud. Many had homemade nets across the backs of the beds to restrain melons and gourds and other strange products of the vicinity. Lots of roadside stands selling potatoes and I think turnips or onions. Don't know who in the hell they could have been selling to. Everyone I'd seen, lived here and was a farmer himself. Lots of thick-boarded wooden carts with stalks of some kind of crop spilling out over both sides. All the men were in knee-high black rubber boots, baggy pants, suspenders, and pipes. Every guy had a mustache. Most people walking, in fact everybody walking. No cars, although here and there I saw a skeletal bicycle propped up against a fence. Scanning the village I only saw a few structure that were two stories high. There was not an apartment building or other commercial building, just those small half-clay, half-wood cottages. Behind each one was a couple hundred square foot cultivated field. None of the cottages had a front yard. The front walls were right up against the edges of the rutted roads. Passerbys on the road were only three feet from the dwelling. I could still see my breath, but things were thawing now, making the roads no more than slightly straight areas of wet black bogs. Leo made one turn after another. Even though it was a small settlement, the many turns had me wondering if he was lost. Maybe the route was necessary to stay on roads where we wouldn't sink in.

We came to an abrupt stop on an ordinary street, in front of one of those now dirt-caked, previously white-washed cottages. The same carts propped up against the walls, the same old men watching suspiciously. (No factories around here that I could see.) Leo got out and went up to the front door, which I could have reached out the car window and touched. The door swung open and Leo was welcomed mightily, or as mightily as you can be greeted by a guy with one arm (and judging by the patch—one eye). They spoke in Italian. Leo motioned to me to join him, and I was introduced to Pietro (and humbled by the enthusiasm that he displayed in meeting me) saying I guess—whatever they say in Italy. He extended his left arm, hand rolled over to facilitate a right-handed shake by me.

He was a charming-looking guy—about thirty-five, with a quick smile and a neatly trimmed mustache. His one faded blue eye was sparkling. He appeared to me to be more of Polish descent than Italian. A large square forehead and too much thick wavy hair brushed straight back, with much of it still standing up. His cheeks were permanently reddened from the cold winds here in northern Italy. He was wearing an old gray wool topcoat. Either he was expecting us and ready to leave, or there was no heat in the house. I think both were true. He was a type A personality and Leo's general manager, overseeing the whole Brescia operation. My impression was that he was a competent guy and probably a valuable friend to Leo.

The doorway greeting completed, it was to the car and on the road again. Pietro spoke pretty good English. Leo of course, told him I was a Marine pilot—off the *Forrestal!* (Boy would it be neat if everybody thought being a carrier pilot was such a great thing.) Pietro was fairly westernized, had a good sense of humor and knew a lot of American expressions. He kidded with Leo. Leo kidded him back. I could see they trusted each other completely. In addition to being the head of the day-to-day operations, evidently Pietro was a master gunsmith and loved his trade. Leo said that instead of a woman, Pietro took a nine-millimeter to bed. Also that he was the world champion in two, small-caliber handgun categories, and had been Italy's representative in this competition in the last two Olympics. (Guess you only need one arm and one eye to shoot.) It was his right arm and his right eye that were missing. I would find out later that he had lost them to a buried World War II artillery shell when he was only thirteen years old.

It wasn't a mile to the "factories," and *some* factories these were; just another cluster of small dirty cottages working under contract to the mysterious Intercontinental Arms. (Finally heard Pietro say it, and now remember having seen that heading on Leo's note pad in Cannes.) But now—at last, I would get to see the pistols and rifles being assembled. Leo started the narrative: "Roger, in these houses—these five, six houses, the Super Dakotas are made. Later maybe we'll go to another area where the Navy Black Powder Colts are assembled. This area only does Dakotas; the main pieces: the frame, cylinders, triggers, trigger guards, grip and hammers. We buy all the pins and screws from a supplier in Torino. I'll show you later where everything gets put together." He swung up his arm and pointed ahead, "This house here only does cylinders. They've been doing them for us for over five years, and before that they did cylinders for a manufacturer a little north of here. In fact Carlo's father did Berettas. Now he does the rough grinding for me—on *our* guns. His wife Anna does the filing, the son does sanding, and the daughter polishes. You can't believe the job they do. They work about two to three hours every day, seven days a week—just on cylinders. C'mon!"

Leo bustled up to an old planked door, the bottom quarter of which was badly rotted. He raised his hand to knock and at the same time it was swung open by what had to be the two heads of the household, who went on to greet Leo and Pietro with great enthusiasm (tempered by their obvious respect for the two strange businessmen). It couldn't have been a warmer encounter if they were blood relatives back in town after a long absence; full embraces, back slapping, broad grins and lots of questions. Two kids—a boy and a girl about ten or twelve, stood by dutifully, as if they'd seen this routine before and knew their role. This time I wasn't introduced (which was okay with me). The father looked like every one of the other men I'd seen walking through the streets. The woman was large and robust, with fair skin, rosy cheeks, and two teeth missing. Her thick graying brown hair was pulled back tightly. She was wearing an aproned outfit of multiple colors and patterns, resembling a quilt pattern. She busied herself right away, making a quick trip to an old wood stove to get a kettle of something. Everybody got a cup (albeit a different size and shape cup). They all spoke Italian of course, so I had no idea of the conversation. I smiled the whole time and tried to appear interested.

Though I hadn't thought about it, the room we had stepped into was the kitchen, and must have comprised 50 percent of the area of the whole cottage. The floor was hard-packed dirt. The kitchen table was handmade (likely by the man of the house) with thick irregular boards. In contrast to its worn and faded wood there was a strip of lime green Formica glued across both ends. A single shaded light hung over the center of the table, and a brightly enameled clamp-on lamp was on each end. Two vices on the sides of the table. It was easy to see that eating at this table was just an incidental pastime. This was a work-bench!

"Roger, c'mere!" Leo patted the man on the shoulder and stepped by him, motioning me to follow. He went over to a sideboard against one wall. On it were several tomato crate-type wood boxes. "Look here. This is Carlo's box. See these pieces, they're only rough-cut and drilled at this time. Carlo will grind these babies perfect." He picked up one of the cylinder pieces and dropped it into my open palm (which got under the falling object just in time). I looked at it in as educated a manner as I could muster. It was kind of crude. "Now, Roger, no, put it back in there. This

262

box here is Anna's. See how the cylinder looks when she gets it. Go ahead compare the two. Take one of hers then, here—one of the first ones." Leo took me down the buffet. There was a box for each family member. The cylinders started with Dad, and ended up in the daughter's box at the end. And to tell you the truth, the cylinders in her box were perfect. If they had been machine made they couldn't have been cleaner, or rounder, or smoother, or brighter.

Leo asked Carlo something in Italian. I recognized one word, *template.* "Roger, take this thing here, and try to pass one of Gina's cylinders through it; either way—front to back or backwards." I did. It was tight, but a perfect match. In fact it could stick, halfway through. "Whataya think of that!" The last step was wrapping them in a brown, oiled paper, and packing them, twelve to a box in a cardboard container. "Here, look at this, this is what Pietro picks up each Monday." Leo looked at me and winked, "Sometimes we get *two* boxes a week." The box was heavier than I suspected. If you saw the box (without taking this little tour) you'd think it was from some first rate automated factory line. "And believe it or not Roger, I pay em about a buck a cylinder!"

House number one had been the cylinder house. House number two was a two-piece house—triggers and trigger guards. We went through the same ritual. Next, a house for the hammer, and the hammer spring. Then the safety, and lock. Two more, doing small complex pieces, and then the frame house, where the main frame was prepared. This neighborhood was the Super Dakota factory. "I'll tell you Roger, every one of these houses is critical. Every piece has to be precisely to specs. You can't have any variance." I nodded my agreement, and checked my watch. It was quarter to two, and the early morning omelet had long since worn off. Each family was as pleased as the first to see Leo and Pietro. I wondered what in the heck they could be doing to earn such respect and affection. Certainly it wasn't the high wages they were paying. And maybe money isn't everything, or in this neck of the woods there wasn't a lot of it to go around and people were damned careful about protecting any source they had.

Back in the car we drove about five minutes, to what looked like an old barn or giant storage shed. Yeah, I think it had been an old barn—now made over into something else. We entered the ground floor from a narrow side door. Inside, it bore no resemblance to a barn. Lots of activity. It was here that the final assembly, inspection, test-firing, and packaging of the Super Dakota took place. I could see (and hear) that even before the explanation. Lots of bins and boxes. There was a twenty-foot long table in the middle of the room. About six guys at it, all handling the guns as they were passed down the line. While I was surveying all this—*Blam!* There was a hellacious boom from the end of the room. "C'mere Roger, over here." At the rear end of the building there was a guy behind a four-foot high, stoutly beamed barricade, who had just fired a *heavy load* into a bin of sand. "We do this for every gun. Hold your ears! There'll be five more. These 41 Magnums are real cannons. See this round here; it's special. It's a test round, got almost twice the kick of retail ammunition. And every one of our Dakotas gets six of these through it before it leaves. After the firing, the cylinder is inspected. It comes out and goes through this machine here. Look at this. Look in this window. It's the same type X-ray machine they use to inspect engine parts on commercial jets. The cylinder's gotta come through perfect. And they always do." I noticed the guy doing the firing, had no gloves, no goggles, and no protective vest. (He did have tissue stuffed in his ears.)

Leo took me back to the table, spieling a short explanation at each station. The damned gun was beautiful. The bluing had already been done another place. It was a work of art, no doubt about it. At one station a guy was installing the polished wood hand grips. Leo picked up a set and handed them to me. They were finished like jewelry, with marbleized grain lines, smooth as glass and hard as metal. You couldn't come close to denting them with your fingernail. "And listen to this." He leaned forward and dropped one of the wooden grips on the table. It hit and rang like a piece of steel. "That's Yugoslav walnut—the best you can get. I got one guy that goes there each spring, just to buy a tree. The kind of tree we use grows in a swamp. Look here, see these burled grain lines, that's because of where it grows. The damned roots are under water." Pietro said something to Leo in Italian. They both laughed. Leo answered "Yeah, I remember...

"Roger, listen to this: The damned Yugos were running out of wet trees, and a week before our guy went there last time, they uprooted one from off the bank, drug it over to the bayou, and replanted the sonuvabitch. Can you believe that, they tried to hoodwink us. Well, while cruising the swamp, the boat they're in accidentally bumps into that tree, and the damn thing goes over. Our guy said we shoulda seen the look on their faces when it hit the water." I could see that the grips were Leo's pride and joy. He took me to a kiln, where they cured the blocks of wood before they were cut and sized for the grips. In fact, he fondled one lovingly for a couple minutes—the whole big hard cube, and then *gave it to me*. "Here, this is yours. You can keep it." (Had to just carry it, too big to stuff into any of my pockets.)

The ground floor all explained we exited the building, only to go around back and start up a flight of exposed, not-too-sturdy, exterior steps, leading to a second floor. They didn't look safe to me, and were covered with about an inch of snow. From the top landing I could see that most of the back side of the second floor was glass, like an artist's loft. Inside (where you could see your breath), the whole second floor was a single open room. In addition to all the windows there were two huge skylights. In this dedicated space were the engravers. It was here that the Kentucky Long Rifles would get the final touch—their custom etching. Centered in the space was a narrow, four-foot high workbench that spanned the entire length of the room. Three or four guys were positioned on each side; each at his own personalized work station. These locations were marked by an old fashioned leather-wrapped vice (at chin level) with a small spot light mounted above it. The counter in front of each worker was cluttered with papers and rags, and an assortment of specialized chisels. These guys were the artisans Leo had told me about, tasked with engraving the intricate custom designs on the nickel housings of the Kentucky Long Rifles.

I'd never seen any engraving of this type going on, so I had no idea about the techniques used. (And I still don't think it's normally done like it was being done here.) Instead of guiding the chisel at arm's length with the dexterity of their hands, its accurate path was being controlled by small, gentle movements of their head. The chisel was gripped tightly in their left hand, the back of that hand across their mouth and the index knuckle buried under their right cheek bone. In fact, later I noticed that all the engravers, as a result of this method, had a noticeable callus on that side of their face. The hammer—held in their right hand, was striking the butt of the chisel, only a half-inch from their temples. The relationship of the eye to the chisel point never changed—what a marksman would call, a perfect "sight picture." To guide the chisel point, all that was necessary was to make small contractions of the neck muscles. This created ever so slight movements of the head and thus the chisel point, as it was an extension of their face.

They were using small upholstery hammers, that seemed to never stop chattering. Not hard hits, but fast—a real fast tempo. Even when they craned their head back, pulling the chisel point off the metal, their hammer arm kept up its motion, like some unstoppable machine. They were using a variety of hammers, individually weighted or modified to the preference of the engraver. One had a bunch of steel brads driven into the handle up near the head. One had thin strips of lead taped to handle; another wrapped in wire. Each rifle was receiving a custom-ordered engraving. Scraps of paper detailing the desired artwork were strewn all along the counter—penciled drawings and photos, and even one framed watercolor. Leo grabbed some of them and showed me; mostly intricate woodland scenes: a deer drinking from a pond, a multi-peaked mountain landscape, a guy fly fishing in a stream. Each a delicate piece of artwork.

On the way out (flipping my four-inch walnut cube) I asked Leo about the seven-guy rule that he had told me about on the ship—*if an Italian factory has more than seven workers, it undergoes heavily increased taxation*. He said, "Yeah, so..."

I said "Well unless I was mistaken, there were four or five guys on the ground floor of that place, and six or seven more up in the loft doing the engraving."

"Ah, I'm proud of you. And right you are. Twelve today. But, and this is what saves us: the building is *two* factories. Remember, we couldn't get to the upstairs from inside? Had to go outside and use the steps. Officially, it's two different places; has two different addresses."

It was a long day, and while everything was very interesting I was tired from trying to pay due attention for the past four hours. Kind've wore myself out listening, and trying to ask intelligent questions. Pietro let Leo do most of the tour, content to just add colorful asides. One conversation ended in a comment by Leo that caused my heart to skip a beat, and allowed me more "what ifs." I had just answered up showing unusual enthusiasm, and Leo responded, "Well when you get out of the Marine Corps, maybe you'd like to come work for me at Intercontinental Arms." With increasing doubts about what would transpire when I returned to the states, while this offer was a real long shot, *it was a breathtaking thought.*

It was after four when we dropped Pietro off. A sincere good-bye, with assurances that we'd see each other again soon. I dozed in the car on the way back. Leo let me rest. Working out all the time I may have been in good shape, but I just couldn't survive a full day face to face; constantly required to pay close attention and ask reasonable questions, without a single break. "Social fatigue." If I could have escaped for just twenty minutes—anywhere, in the middle of the day, to lay down and close my eyes, I could have made it. But with no reprieve today, I was now totally ground down. On the drive back I couldn't avoid allowing my head to fall back on what the Fiat company calls a headrest. From time to time through a heavy curtain, I heard Leo announce we were passing a worthy landmark. I was finally roused as we went over the hump into the parking garage.

Winona was as bright and upbeat as when I had last seen her, which made me happy (and seemed like a week ago). Our arrival must have been well coordinated, because once inside the front door I could smell great stuff already simmering in the kitchen. Leo told me to take a few minutes and freshen up (and did I need it); collapsed on the bed in the guest room with a damp towel across my eyes. Got a much needed twenty minutes prone. Felt a lot better. Dinner was great: baked chicken and vermicelli with chopped tomatoes, onions, and lots of garlic. I drank the coffee but was thinking I probably shouldn't have; might be difficult to sleep on the train. I had scheduled myself for the 10 p.m. train—to hopefully make the midnight boat back to the ship. There was another train at 0200, but that would mean talking myself on board one of those Shore Patrol boats or waiting on the dock for that 0600 married officer's boat. In any case, in a matter of hours I would be on my way. Returning to my other life.

A Valuable Gift and Taking My Leave

When we got up from the dinner table, I tried to help clear up a bit. Winona would have none of it. Leo guided me over to the couch, sat me down and said, "Wait right here." He disappeared behind the room divider for only two seconds. Before I knew it, he was standing in front of me holding a familiar box—the shape and weight of which I had already seen and felt many times today. My conclusion was correct. No doubt about it. *I was being made a gift of a 41 Magnum Super Dakota!* "It's a custom job Roger; adjustable sights, 7 inch barrel, inlaid grips, double bluing. And it's yours. A gift from Pietro and I." Boy was I flabbergasted. Even having been through all the factories it never crossed my mind to ask for a souvenir. (The four inch Yugoslav walnut cube would have been enough.) I was not expecting this at all. It was beautiful, and huge! A real *Dirty Harry* piece (although with my small hand barely supporting it I didn't think I bore much resemblance to Clint Eastwood). Holding it I was surprised at how little I felt on the other end of it. I beamed my thanks to

Leo; wanted to make him feel deservedly good for this great gesture. And truly—I was thrilled to death. My European adventures would be greatly affirmed by keepsakes such as this! This would be my first real trophy from my experiences on the Continent. *Wait, I take that back!* How could I forget the white bronze bracelet from King Constantine (on my right wrist at this moment).

"And look here." He took it back from me and flipped it over, exposing the underside of the frame. "What do you think of that?" I didn't think anything because I didn't know what he was making reference to. I studied the underside of the gun, the barrel, the frame, the trigger guard, the butt of the grip; nothing special I could see. Leo I guess, saw I was stumped, and tapped the strip of metal on the bottom of the frame. "No serial number, this gun's never been made. No record." *Wow*. I guess that really meant something (although I wasn't too sure I'd want to bring something like this back into the States). In any case it was a handsome souvenir and I was proud to have it.

The occasion of the gift served to postpone my departure and I'm glad, because sometime after ten the phone rang. Winona (surprisingly) answered it and waved excitedly to Leo, who excused himself and joined her in the hallway. I couldn't hear what he was saying, but it was very enthusiastic and obviously to a good friend on the other end. Lots of agreement and happy talk. It was over in ten minutes and Leo was back to the couch. Winona asked Leo what Harry had to say. I listened as they talked warmly and with some nostalgia about Harry. Turns out the Harry was Harry Stradling— the director of cinematography for the recent, eight-Oscar winning *My Fair Lady* motion picture, starring Rex Harrison and Audrey Hepburn. After having received the awards there was one individual Mr. Stradling wanted to notify personally: Leo, who had been the first president of the ASC (the "American Society of Cinematographers"). *Boy this Leo's done everything, knows everybody!*

It was about ten to twelve. I dropped a hint about being ready to have Leo drive me to the station. He heard me and didn't say "not yet," but sort of hemmed and hawed. I could see by her expression that Winona knew Leo had some reluctance to leaving right at this moment. I was to see why. A few minutes later Leo brought out a Zenith transoceanic radio, turned it on and leaned back in his chair to hear the end of the European *Voice of America* broadcast and their daily sign-off: "The Star Spangled Banner." Leo was reverent in his silence and I wagered that there should be no idle conversation during the time it played. When the last strain had faded away the radio was snapped off and returned to its place. Nothing in the way of my departure now. This event had claimed the evening. We commenced our "good-nighting" with hugs and kisses, and continued with vows to meet again soon. I told him we would be back in Genoa late next month. (We must be getting a discount there.) Leo smiled slyly and asked me, *if I'd ever been to the Balkans.* (At that time, the exact countries comprising the Balkans was not at all clear to me.) He said if I could get back up the last week of the month, he might have a big surprise for me. I gave Winona an especially enthusiastic hug. She hadn't said twenty words during my visit, but hadn't stopped smiling either.

A Scare on the Trip Back

In the car on the way to the train station I promised Leo I'd try to arrange some time off for a visit next month (which he had hinted might include a special trip). As the street lights and stark housing projects flew by, I found myself visualizing the blued 41 Magnum tucked inside my small gym bag; *real proof of the crowd I was running with.* It would now be even more difficult to visualize myself taking part in the contrastingly mundane stateside activities after my return—weeknight PTA meetings and Saturday morning runs to the hardware store. (And, causing me great concern, it would not be long before I would find myself in that situation.) Leo dropped me off at a small outlying station, not the downtown Centrale where I had arrived. This one was two stops past the main station, and so the times on the schedule I was referring to did not apply; the result of which was—I missed my intended train. With over an hour to kill before the next one, I collapsed on a hard wood bench, the victim of my own actions and in need of some sorting out.

There's a good chance I'll live to regret this carrier cruise—my goings-on, my flagrant experimenting. I *had* to feel guilty. Maybe not so much this trip, since I had been good this one time. But in summation, my focus had been and is—critically suspect. Somehow to me, none of what I was doing counted. It was part of a separate project—a detached, necessary, clinical quest that I had to see through to the finish (if there was one). It was not going to affect how my life would resume when I returned. Try as I might, instead of being dissuaded by my nostalgia for my wife and children, and saddened by the distance between us, I selfishly continued to ponder what still might be awaiting me. Even worse—after Leo's hint about coming to work for him, I now dared to consider the possibility of altering my professional and domestic situation after my return. A change that would allow me the freedom to continue my search.

Still forty minutes to wait. Antsy. Got up and wandered around. Not hungry, not thirsty. Took a look outside the station and observed a hub-bub of activity; sufficiently so to have me give some thought to strolling around outside. Unfortunately, to do so lugging a three-suiter and a gym bag (with the Super Dakota inside) was not going to be worth it. I knew (based on its contents) I had to keep the gym bag with me, but if I could stash the suitcase somewhere, I could take that walk. If you can believe this, I decided to just casually abandon the suitcase right in the middle of the waiting room. (This was forty years before terrorists in airports and all those public address warnings about suspicious luggage.) In such a location, anyone thinking about stealing it would know he would be in full view of the people seated on the benches that ran the perimeter of the room—any one of whom might be the owner of it. I put it down, stood by it a while, then slowly began edging further and further away from it—without giving any indication that I might be leaving the immediate area (in case a potential thief was observing me). I lingered a few minutes more, scanning the assortment of waiting passengers until I concluded there were no devious faces—no questionable characters. No one seemed to be paying any attention to me or the suitcase. Time to split (carrying the now precious gym bag).

Once outside I commenced to occupy myself observing the wide assortment of passersby; mostly well dressed, apparently successful businessmen, but including as well, more than a few attractive young women—most walking with purpose, but some strolling almost too leisurely. Not that it was at all likely, but striking up a conversation with one of those passersby would help pass the time and be more exciting than sitting in the waiting room. A couple times—going in opposite directions, the same curvaceous girl passed by me, and what I took to be much closer than necessary. She did not appear to be on her way home from a late night job. Once our eyes met, and though I had no intention to do so, I was almost positive it was an invitation to speak to her. But if she was looking for business I was not a candidate. (And if she was just late shift seamstresses on her way home, it could have been very awkward.) Not being motivated or as brazen as most guys, I remained silent. Same thing

Part Two: The French Riviera, Leo, June, and Big Trouble

I used to do at the high school dances: waste the whole evening trying to guess which girl might accept my invitation to dance. *God, I'd like to have that time over again.* Finally decided to abandon whatever if anything I had been considering while wasting this fifteen minutes.

Entering the station and rounding the corner to the waiting room, my heart almost stopped. I got the thump to end all thumps. No question about it. *My suitcase was gone!* It wasn't a vacancy you could miss—I'd left it dead center in the room. There was nothing there now. My heart was pounding. It's my own fault! I've been doing shit like this for years, and finally it's caught up with me. *Dammit!* I knew this was going to happen one day. I deserve it. I should have tried to get a locker. Maybe I should report it—for whatever good that would do. Who knows, still got fifteen minutes, why not? What else could I do? There was a small police office right in the station; still open, but not a friendly (or efficient) looking place. Upon entering, I spied two police officers (wearing what appeared to be about half their uniform) and who both needed a shave (in fact looked like they needed one yesterday and the day before). They eyed me suspiciously from behind a dilapidated desk strewn with sports and girlie magazines. The whole room was in sad need of repair. The unappealing pea green walls were shedding their paint, the wood doors and sills were split and coated with dust, and the floor a creaking trap. I was still carrying my gym bag with my new Super Dakota inside. But what if they search it? No, not likely, I'll just put it over here. I've got no choice. Here goes nothing.

I tried my best to explain the situation (in a way that would disguise how much of a jerk I had been). Throughout my narrative—all in English (which I doubted they understood one half of) they looked at me with an expression that said, *No matter what you say Signore, we know you're a stupid American.* Just as I was finishing, my heart soared. I saw my green Samsonite against a back wall (with about five other suitcases). I pointed and yelled, "There it is!" They didn't even turn their heads to see what I was pointing at. After another five minutes, when I had convinced them what I was pointing at, I discovered the real problem: They wanted some proof that it was really my suitcase. *Describe what's in it. Convince us it's yours.* Okay, I can do that—no sweat. Told em: trousers, shirts, a toilet kit... I could see their cynicism rising, as I called off items that would be in *any* suitcase. They looked at each other unimpressed. They'd heard this before. This was rapidly becoming absurd, and now I only had five minutes before my train. *C'mon you guys, be realistic here!*

271

I GUESS I JUST WASN'T THINKING

Unfortunately, my suitcase held what every suitcase would hold. How in the hell would I identify it? Right here and now I vowed never to leave another suitcase unattended (*and* to affix some permanent ID inside). These guys were being difficult and not going to give me my suitcase, unless I could convince them I owned it. This was ridiculous. Why did they think I picked out the green and cream Samsonite for Christ sakes. (Or maybe they did really think it was my suitcase, and were just being assholes.) Goddamit, this is getting serious. Just then it hit me! I got these guys. "Open it up. Go on, open it up! You'll find a four-inch cube of Yugoslav walnut in it! How many suitcases got that in em?" Out the door and on my way to the platform.

Chapter Twenty-Two
A MAIL CALL CATASTROPE

Back on board my head was still reeling from my visit with Leo. I was again faced with the real problem of being too preoccupied with my visits ashore, and not sufficiently concerned with my onboard duties. However (thankfully), once again during this at sea period things went smoothly. I guess after eight months we were bound to get the hang of it. And a good thing there were no flight operation surprises, because *I got a real surprise in the mail.*

Assigned to the ship is one propeller driven, non prestigious aircraft referred to as the COD (Carrier On-board Delivery) aircraft. It doesn't have guns and it doesn't carry bombs, but it does something much more important: It brings in the mail! It can fly to the nearest U.S. Military land base, pick up the FPO (Fleet Post Office) mail, and bring it back out to the ship. Its arrivals are anxiously anticipated. Not as much now of course— with the cruise all but over. Some days the COD makes it out and back the same day, if not, it overnights ashore and returns the next day. This day it had already made a round trip and mail call was sounded. I took my turn at the cage and waited. Usually a couple letters a week from Sara, a couple bills (and though I hate to admit it—from time to time, a letter from June). Today I was surprised to get one from Ingrid:

> *Dear Roger,*
> *I writing this in English because I knew you German not*
> *good so. I never forget our German lesson on Rhodos*
> *with the dog. I need to say to you about you visiting me. I*
> *am wanting to see you again. Can you come to Germany*
> *again. One last thing. My mother not know what to do*
> *with your parachute.*
> *Love to you, Ingrid*

I GUESS I JUST WASN'T THINKING

My parachute?! What the hell. Goddam Italian mail! They didn't deliver the parachute to the navy base where I got it. (Remember? The one I had to borrow so that asshole Air Force Captain would let me board his plane.) Somehow it ended up sent back to the return address I'd used— which was *Ingrid's!* That poor navy chief. After I promised him ten times I'd get the chute back to him, and now it didn't make it! Geez. I hate to let people down like that. He'll *never* believe anyone now!

Chapter Twenty-Three
BARCELONA

Talk About Being Impressed with a City

With less than two months to go we pulled into Barcelona. For me this would be the coup de grace, finally proof there was a place—a city in which I would be perfectly satisfied. Making my way down its wide boulevards and mingling with its elegant citizenry I felt as if I was (or could be) a respected part of an elevated society. I was captured by its ambiance; never tiring of viewing its expansive, wrought iron-fenced parks, ornate slate and copper-roofed buildings, and magnificent avenues lined with shops of distinction. And in no city—not even Rome, had I seen so many handsome and smartly dressed men and women. This was the most sophisticated city I had ever visited and I would not be able to forget it. I sensed a patriarchal, proper atmosphere, an untainted reputation, a status and way of life which humbled me. (You might imagine, comparing this perfection to my shallow activities and questionable motives caused me justifiable concern.) If the Riviera was my baptism by fire, Barcelona would seal it in blood.

It was 1400 now. We'd dropped anchor at 0800 and I'd been tingling with anticipation ever since. And why? I was going to see June and the Stafford Ballet girls again! In Valencia June had given me the name of the theater they'd be in here (the only information she had then). They had arrived here in late January, and hopefully were performing as planned at the Teatro del Sol. Had no idea about the city—no idea where they'd be living; just knew the theater, but I can tell you— that's all I needed. I'd find em. June was expecting me two weeks ago, but we had a damned in-port schedule change. I had considered going ashore earlier and just flat-ass—

somehow finding the girls, even without a daytime address. But knowing that was a long shot and that it could well be a late night I scratched the idea. Instead, I would make a good impression here on board for a couple hours, then try for a short nap and go in about six. That way I'd be at the theater when they arrived. Made my rounds like always; hit the metal shop, the hydraulic shop and the engine shop. The weather had been bad the last three days out and there were no flight ops. This being the case we'd had lots of time at sea to work on the aircraft and there were only a few small maintenance discrepancies not yet cleared. All twelve birds were up and ready for flight, which made lots of points with the Colonel (since the Navy A-4 squadrons only had eleven up most mornings). With nothing pressing I was able to sneak back up to my stateroom and get an hour nap.

1800 hours and on my way, or almost. Dale had the duty and was stuck on board, and was now giving me last minute instructions and a note for Wendy. Got it. Now—to the aft liberty boat. I took a deep breath, ducked my head, shoved one foot outside and squeezed through the hatch to the top of the ladder. Sixty-five feet up the wind was buffeting the platform and the whole apparatus was swaying. I paused there for a moment to take in the vast harbor scene. Once again—mooring right off the cargo piers, while it appeared a lot better than Genoa or Naples, it was still a familiar sight of debris-strewn breakwaters, a long pier and loading derricks. The distance between the carrier and the dock was being crisscrossed by fast and heavy water traffic (whose dangerous wakes could make our small liberty boat passage risky). The one I would take was presently bobbing like a cork at the bottom of the ladder. In spite of this the chief at wheel was urgently motioning me to get my butt down the ladder. Eager enough, I did. Two rungs at a time. Seemed I'd done this a hundred times now; each time anticipating a new and exciting adventure (and amazingly— usually not being disappointed).

Ow! Damn near turned my ankle dropping the two feet into the boat. Not that it's so far, but the darn boat is alternately rising and falling. You can't get a solid landing, it either drops out from under you or pops up to meet you with a firm smack on the soles of your feet. So far so good, none of my squadron mates in the liberty boat. Don't know why I should feel guilty. *Liberty*, that's what it's all about being in the Navy. "Hitting the Beach!" Do your work in a tough professional manner while at sea, and then when you're off, live it up. Work hard, play hard, and that's all I'm doing. And what do the damn Navy enlistment posters say? *It's not a job, it's an adventure!* And for me as you are seeing, that has turned out to be all too true.

As we lurched away from the hull a strong gust caught my arranged hair and slung it across the other side. So much for that. Hated my fine, mousy brown hair. Would've given anything for hair like Dale—thick curly shocks of hair that never needed to be combed; looked the same (great) all the time. Decided not to bring an overnight bag with me; might be a little presumptuous, not to mention the job of lugging it everywhere I went till we got a hotel—*if* we got a hotel. Maybe just a toilet kit, which would come in handy if things worked out. But do I want to run around all night with a plaid vinyl toilet kit dangling from my index finger? No. So, it's just me and the clothes on my back. Put off shaving til noon and got a close one—should last till the lights are out anyway.

As the liberty boat sped landward I got an even closer look at the rusting tankers, barges, tugs, and a swinging cranes. The water was dark and oily. *No Cannes yacht basin here.* Not the kind of setting I preferred, but this time I had a feeling it wouldn't matter—I was going to see June! I toyed with the idea of going directly to the theater—be early enough to intercept the girls when they arrived. Might even be able to have a drink or a snack with them before their performance, although June had said they usually didn't eat before a performance. (They wanted to feel light and be able to spring about unencumbered.) Up on the dock and waiting for my legs to steady, I surveyed the cityscape to get some clue as to a likely route to the city center. Squinting into the sunset haze over a rising skyline of tree tops, I drew a bead on the upper reaches of a cluster of tall buildings about a mile away, which I guessed marked the heart of the city.

Based on the minimal appearing distance I decided to just walk it. *Save my Pesetas.* I knew what the rate was. I knew I got 59 for one US dollar, but didn't have any idea how far they'd go. I'd have to find out with a small purchase. Usually in a new country my test purchase was a Coke. (Not too risky.) Knew a glass of Coke cost about fifty cents in the states, so whatever they charged me in the local money, I just worked that out in my head to see what the purchasing power of the local currency was. (At 59 Pesetas to the dollar, a Coke should cost about 30 Pesetas.) You certainly didn't want to experiment with a cab. If you weren't sure about the value of the currency and got a devious cab driver, you could be out a lot of money—quick. I've had several surprises with taxi fares in Europe. They're complicated. There's "one-way" extra charges, or "out-of-the-city-limits" extra charges, or "add-ons" for some districts, or "airport-return" penalties, or "after-hours" charges. (In Spain they're called *complimentos.*) And you can't win by arguing. It seems every cab driver is on a first-name basis with whatever cop intercedes.

In selecting a route to the city center, I chose a narrow, initially uncrowded, slightly uphill street that appeared to be pointed straight towards the taller buildings a half mile or so ahead. Not two blocks in, the activity began picking up; lots of tiny delivery trucks, and strange three-wheeled vehicles with canvas tops and browning acrylic windshields. They were snorting and wheezing, stopping and starting, double parking, and loading and unloading their boxes, baskets and tins. And it paid to be alert as these vehicles thought nothing of popping up on the sidewalk. Had to jump out into the street several times to avoid them (and several other times to avoid the spray from thick black hoses being used to give the sidewalk a good washing down).

On my side of the street, almost to the sidewalk—not six feet back, were the fronts of an unbroken row of wall-to-wall diminutive houses. Each tiny front yard was full of crude wooden shelving, overflowing with meat and foul and fish and produce. None were actually *serving* food; rather they appeared to be tiny "live-in" warehouses—mini wholesalers operating out of their own homes. Men and women in aprons, with brooms and mops and scoops and baskets of food, were hustling in and out of these places (dodging rosy-cheeked kids running in and out of the same narrow doorways). I was now traversing the shellfish section. Every doorstep and half the sidewalk was cluttered with baskets of clams and shrimp, and I think mussels. Amazingly, with all the seafood on tables and counters, and spread on newspapers, and spilling out of pails onto the sidewalk, there was no fish smell. Seemed every doorway had an occupant propping it up, and two feet away the front window supported a pair of elbows and another blank face. Everyone so far was dressed in combinations of white, gray, and black; checkered or plaid or striped, but no colors. White shirts, gray vests, black rubber aprons and boots.

While granted, I was on a fascinating street and making reasonable progress towards town, I spied a possibly better route. About a hundred yards to my right—looking down a side street, I could see what appeared to be a very chic kind of popular thoroughfare paralleling the one I was on. Turned at the next corner and cut over to it. And I was right. This was going to be a much better way to get to town. But it wasn't really a street at all, it was a wide brick promenade, beautifully lined with huge elms—just for pedestrians. By accident (my usual way) I had stumbled upon the world famous "Las Ramblas"—the public walk that inclines from the port (near where I'd just come from) all the way up to the city center. I eagerly joined the crowd of well dressed city dwellers and not so well dressed tourists.

Amidst them and energized by my new surroundings, I again began making my way towards the city. At some locations the branches of the trees on either side met and entwined overhead, forming a large but comfy-feeling tunnel. The density of this overhead canopy of foliage blocked out the sky like a roof—so much so that even at this time of day artificial light was required, which was being artfully provided by a combination of lamps atop ornately sculpted posts and colored lanterns dangling askance in the branches. Brightly decorated kiosks at frequent intervals along the walk were selling everything from newspapers and souvenirs, to rare birds in cages, to tropical fish in plastic bags. Every now and then I'd come upon a garishly clad juggler or hawker entertaining a small group of strollers. Or if not them, some young—what I would have called a harmless hippy-type guy playing a guitar or harmonica or other weird instrument for coin donations. I was finding it a unique and pleasurable first time experience. The people here seemed to have few worries. Even I here among them was gratefully aware of at least the beginnings of a strange new feeling of well-being.

Finally at the top—emerging from Las Ramblas, I was certainly not let down by the sights that befronted me. I was at the edge of a large and bustling plaza, impressively ringed with statues and grand old *edificios*. In the center—with shiny black cars racing around it, was a huge circular fountain (shades of Piazza Republica). The wide sidewalks were jammed with crowds of especially well dressed men and women, rushing towards cabs and buses at the end of the business day. I felt very much the newcomer, but warmly optimistic about getting to know this city better (and having it accept me as an equal). The signposts announced this location as Plaza Catalunya, and I had in fact stumbled into the city center. I remembered that June had said her theater was located near the Plaza del Sol. Now, how to find it?

While debating whether to buy a map or just ask a pedestrian, I found myself in front of a small but elegant, glass-fronted store. The bottom of the outside front wall and every inside wall was a deep toned and varnished mahogany, and these facades were further adorned with intricately carved cornices. It could have been an elite jewelry store or a place that sold precision instruments. A really classy establishment. I stepped closer and peered inside. The two side walls were lined with bronze framed display cases. The entire rear wall was comprised of perhaps twenty, side-by-side columns of small, porcelain-knobbed mahogany drawers, *that rose from the floor to the ceiling.* Hundreds of tiny three-inch by eight-inch lustrous repositories, obviously containing some unknown, valuable, catalogued items. Above this cabinetry and mounted to the ceiling was a long metal rod that spanned the entire wall. Attached to it (hanging from it) was a brass ladder with wheels at its base, so that it could be slid back and forth—the whole length of the wall. (A necessity to reach the upper drawers.)

Inside, was a thin, balding and bespectacled gentleman who I suspected was the respected owner (or if not, one hell of a distinguished-looking salesman). With one finger to his lips, then to his temple, he was sizing up an equally statured customer. Then with a nod he made a quick turn towards that rear wall of a hundred drawers. At it—his hand traced a line up a column of drawers, slid over to the next, down two, three. Evidently he'd found the sought after drawer. He opened it and delicately extracted the treasure. A skillful flourish momentarily suspended it in air before it dropped over the back of his hand for a privileged viewing. Only a second or two there, and then with equally artful movements, he fashioned a symmetric "Windsor" and held it against a draped fold of light blue cotton. *This was a Barcelona necktie store!* To me, all of Barcelona would be similarly refined. But enough ogling. Gotta find the Plaza del Sol.

The Teatro del Sol

I pilfered a free map in the foyer of a nearby hotel, studied it and was able to locate the Plaza del Sol. (At least if Puerta del Sol and Plaza del Sol are the same place.) Started at a jog towards the area. Not difficult to follow the map. The humanity I was now threading through—with their heads down, hat brims into the wind, hands in coat pockets, and moving at a brisk pace, were serious people. Reflecting on my own scant accomplishments and recent objectives, I felt suitably embarrassed and envious. All these honest people with a purpose and jobs and families and real destinations. *And then me*—without credentials or defensible intentions, thinking only of myself and having plans that spanned barely more than a month into the future. Sure, I was here and maybe appeared as if I was qualified to be here. But of course I knew different. I was an impostor—just temporarily on the scene. I hadn't earned the right to intermingle, to use these streets, and sample what this city had to offer.

Evidently the map was printed by the Dry Sac sherry company, since many locations were marked with a cartoon-like symbol for Dry Sac, including one over the location of the Puerta del Sol. I suspected this indicated they had some facility there. And the good news—on top of a building about five blocks ahead I saw a huge electronic sign that spelled out **Dry Sac Jerez.** *I'll bet that's it.* And sure enough, another five blocks and I was there—Puerta del Sol. Again a large fountain in the middle. But in lieu of old government buildings, this one was ringed with all kinds of neat-looking cafes and restaurants. I passed an organized taxi stand with a long row of waiting black cabs. A metal railing along the sidewalk kept the queue in perfect sequence. Patient, dignified-appearing people waiting. Narrow streets funneled up and away from the plaza on all four sides. Had to pull the map out once more and get my bearings. Gotta get it oriented to my direction. Swapped ends. Yeah that looks better. Gotta be here on this corner. So, out that street on the other side of the plaza, all the way— no, just two corners up, and then a left, and I should be in front of June's theater!

It worked and I found it. But of course—still only seven; the theater was abandoned. *What to do?* There was a chill in the air and the wind was picking up. Half to get out of it and half out of curiosity, I wandered around the side of the theater and discovered the artist's entrance. It was locked up tight. Debated about waiting there but wasn't sure when the girls would arrive. Probably around eight. Once again, almost every man with a jacket and tie, and wearing a hat. (Remember those early 1900's black and white newsreels, when every guy was wearing a fedora.) Strolled back down to the plaza. Wasted about twenty minutes there. It was dark now and the crowds from an hour ago had thinned out. No fun here and I was anxious, so made my way back to the theater. Seven-thirty. Another hour. That's a pretty long wait. Plus, she doesn't even know for sure what day I'm coming.

I had an idea. Rather than wait here and intercept them when they arrive, I'd just attend the show, and have a big bouquet delivered backstage during the performance. Started jogging again. *Not necessary Rog, lots of time, you'll find a flower shop soon enough.* Not too many streets later

I changed my mind concerning the flower idea, in favor of another and perhaps better idea. Back to the theater. Ticket window still not open. Gotta wait. Last time, in Valencia it didn't open till eight-thirty, and I guess here as well. Once again I was the first one in line when it did open. At the window (with no diagram to point at) I had a hell of a time conveying my wishes to the lady inside. Finally, success. I did it, and in lieu of the flower idea I put my Plan B in place—got three seats together, almost dead center in the fourth row. (The front row wasn't for sale and the second and third row were reserved.) I would sit in the middle seat, and have an empty seat on each side of me. June would be sure to spot me this way and be duly impressed. But two thousand one-hundred Pesetas! *Whew*. I felt a little weak in the knees after I did it. This neato impression was going to set me back about 35 bucks!

I fingered the thinness of my Peseta wad and had second thoughts about the three-seat purchase. Maybe I didn't need to make such an impression. Too late now, and the vacancies on each side of me would guarantee June spotting me. I wanted the surprise to be total and therefore resisted the temptation to run back to the artists' entrance and meet the girls going in. Just hide out till show time. Slipped into the theater a couple minutes before nine. Another magnificent theater; in fact bigger than the one in Valencia. The foyer was decorated like the lobby of a five-star hotel, with uniformed attendants, thick red carpeting, gilded furniture, and expensive-looking wall hangings. Inside, the same proper and well-dressed audience patiently waiting for the curtain to go up. It was packed. I thanked the Lord that I had decided to buy my tickets early. The only empty seats in the place may end up being the one on each side of me.

I wasn't in my seat a minute when the orchestra began and the colored lights playing on the curtains began to dim. I was really nervous now. My stomach did a couple flip flops. I didn't have much I could brag about. I knew I wasn't special, but right now—sitting here in this theater, I *felt* special—connected; part of something big and different and exciting. And soon I'd be with June. A woman who had won my admiration, and for whom I thought I might be experiencing—not what I had been searching for, but at least the beginnings of (for me, for once) a new and unselfish caring. I was relieved to sense that I *could* have honorable feelings and they were at last stirring inside me. The show was still the traveling *Tony Le Blanc Comedia*, with Tony and Lola (that same huge-bazoomed, bleached blond, whose hairdo was even more exaggerated this time). Since last seeing June I had gotten a Spanish language textbook and started my own crash course. And although I was now beginning to be able to read and write some Spanish, a quickly spoken sentence was undecipherable. Oh I caught quite a few phrases, and could tell when they were building to a punch line, but it would be a lie to say I understood much of anything. It was a bit tedious, but something I was willing to put up with.

The plot of the *Comedia*, I think—was almost the same. As far as the intermission and the Stafford Ballet, it was completely different. A whole new routine and new costumes. Even more gold and glitter than I'd seen in Valencia. This time it was a Roman street scene. The backdrop was the familiar near wall of the Coliseum. Right there on the stage, huge stone blocks (or what appeared to be stone blocks) were piled up to the cat walks. At least twenty extras in white togas were crisscrossing the set. Real donkeys were pulling wooden carts. And now, what I was waiting for. Here come the girls! Leaping and twirling and cartwheeling, they exploded onto the stage, announcing the arrival of the legion. Wow, centurions on horseback! *Real* horses. *Kheerist* what a show. I strained to find June. Once again they all looked the same; huge, strong creatures strutting this way and that. Bright colored hair pulled back tight, feathered headdresses, sequined eyes, sparkles on their skin, wide-smiling red mouths, full lithe bodies. Spectacular. Almost had to pinch myself to see if this was real.

She spied me—saw her give an elbow to the girl next to her and whip a quick point in my direction. June had me all right. A moment later when she swept across the footlights, real close, she winked and flashed one of her crazy grins. Seeing it my heart took flight. It was so exciting to have this all come together. I was afraid to speculate on the rest of the evening. When their routine was finished and the next act had started, I was tempted to sneak out of the theater and give a check of the nearby restaurants. That'd be neat, if I found em. But I might not. Better to just keep my seat (my seats).

I was a little impatient during the second act, waiting to see the girls again. But finally—another display of difficult, energy sapping movements. The girls did a four-high pyramid. I was so close I could see the veins protruding in their necks, and their knees shaking. A max effort, but it held. June was on the bottom (which with those legs I could understand why). Being this close, I was more aware of the relentless tempo and sheer physical output involved. In particular, I wondered how their feet and ankles ever stood up to it. They must've just been born with good bones and ligaments. Pounding, sliding, stamping, pushing off, skidding, jamming into the set. *Geez.* You'd imagine their feet would be a mass of blisters and calluses. (I would find out later, they were.) Hairline fractures, that's what the girls dreaded. Lose a month's pay or *worse*—get handed a ticket back to England. Soon enough the intermission was over and the last act began. Thought about leaving early. No, not in good taste, I'll stay. Finally it ended, to a standing ovation.

A Dinner Date with June

Standing just outside the artists' entrance I was only a few yards from the guard booth inside. It was manned by an elderly woman passing the time with her needlepoint. Caught her eye and gave a friendly nod. Was taken aback when she smiled and beckoned me closer. She didn't speak any English, but I knew from Valencia that the Spaniards referred to the girls as the *Inglesas.* I tried it and it worked. Again, surprisingly, she motioned me to continue in and go on down the hall. I smiled appreciatively and repeatedly nodded my thanks. Came to a flight of steps descending into what looked like a factory basement. A little eerie. I paused. Looking back she was signaling me to continue. I started down. *Boy, not much security around here.* Didn't think it would be this easy. Just a short way down the deserted, concrete-floored passageway below, I began to hear the girls' laughter. Boy were they having a good time!

I continued towards the source of all this mirth. Their dressing room was a temporary cubicle whose walls were framed by propped-up plywood partitions (that could have easily been pushed over by one person). They didn't go all the way to the ceiling, and over them I could just see the tops of the girls' headdresses, as they moved about inside. Two or three light fixtures (bare bulbs) were hanging from bent nails in the ceiling. On the walls were wooden hangers, and posters, and notes the girls had tacked up for one another. Tops of clothes-trees, piled with all manner of attire protruded above the partition. From time to time, some piece of apparel would fly up and drape on a wall hook. Twelve of them were jammed in this small area, but from the sounds of things, definitely not complaining. They were letting the good times roll.

The partition, used as a door was ajar, but I sure wasn't going to barge in. On the wall alongside it was that famous WWII poster of Uncle Sam in his top hat, pointing right at you, except instead of saying "*I want YOU!*" it said "*Did you take your PILL?*" Got my nerve and announced myself.

"June, I'm here." Tried to make it sound casual. I was sure they'd been plagued by "stage door Johnnys" and I wasn't eager to look like just another one. *Though what else was I?* June came bounding out. I should say, crashing out—almost carrying the rickety door off its hinges. I was smothered in a giant bear hug, actually squeezing the air out of my lungs. (Thought for a moment she was going to pick me up.) *Was this girl glad to see me or what!*

"Rogey, you made it did you! Ooh, look at you!"

A great big kiss on the mouth, and then one on each cheek. A new kind of kiss to me. Not sexy or passionate in the usual sense of the word. Rather; clean, hard, happy kisses, full of strength and meaning. I had never been kissed like this before (and most certainly not by my wife). It was a kiss that made me feel ten feet tall; the most wholesome and heartfelt kisses I'd ever received. In a matter of seconds half the troupe had collected in the doorway, now giggling and clapping and shaking their fingers at June. They were so happy for June—rooting for her (or me, or us). In no way did I deserve to be so appreciated. I don't think I'd ever felt more important. The memory of this scene remains indelible—and painful, to me.

June described a nearby café where she and the girls would meet me in about fifteen minutes. Once sure I had its exact location she sent me off with a slap to my backside. Back out the artists' entrance and into the night air. Found the place easily, picked a clean table and ordered a Dry Sac sherry. Quarter to one—early in comparison to other nights. Only there about twenty minutes and in they came. June, Laurie, Wendy, and young Claire, followed by a half dozen others. Wendy wanted to know, *where was Dale?* I explained he had the duty and gave her his note. (They would rendezvous tomorrow evening.) All those—well most of them, who had met me in Valencia came scampering over to our table. (There'd been a small turnover. Two girls had fallen by the wayside. Two new ones added.) They all took their turns giving me kisses on the cheek. Lots of questions, *How I'd been? Did I miss June? How long could I stay?* Each one took her turn. Claire dropped to one knee alongside my chair. "Roger. No Wendy, let me! Roger, will you take June to visit the states? Oh I know not now, but you know, after these *espanoles* have had their full of us?" While June was truly concerned about and extra protective of her youngest and newest dancer, with this she grabbed Claire's throat and feigned strangling her. Throughout all this and receiving so much attention, I felt like a celebrity and was beginning to think I might owe June something—something I was secretly hoping I would maybe someday be able to deliver on.

Time to come up with a plan for our late night (early morning) meal. Again, I wanted it to be something special for June. She put it to the girls for a vote. Le Drugstore won hands down. A new place that had just opened. This idea would screw up some of my plans, but I was going to go with the flow, that was for sure. A couple of the girls thanked me for the invitation, but bowed out for one reason or another. I was a little sorry, I would have liked to have brought the "whole catch" along. (I might have bumped into some of the guys and boy would they be envious.) Two cabs full did it. June on my lap (and not light). We were on our way for who knows what. I was buried in the back seat with about five of them, being smothered and pressed by all manner of firm thighs and round buttocks. By now I loved the sound of their lilting conversation and accented voices as they chattered non-stop. They smelled good, and their hair was brushing across my face. Now *this* is what a sailor calls "a real night ashore!"

We were there in ten minutes, though I hadn't see anything since we left—my nose having been buried in the middle of June's back the whole way. The girls piled out of the cab, and evidently Le Drugstore was *the* after hours place for all the artists in Barcelona. Halfway across the street the girls were enthusiastically met by a gaggle of other late night performers. I said "performers," but "artists" is what they really wanted to be called; whether dancers, singers, acrobats or jugglers. And from what I'd seen and what I would see, they damn well *deserved* to call themselves artists. During these greetings I couldn't understand a lot of what was being said— only half was in English. All the girls were pretty good at Spanish, having now been here more than six months. Hugs and kisses galore. Lots of good looking guys (making me feel a little less outstanding). June said they were dancers from other shows in town, and almost all gay (*whew*) but "quite nice chaps." They were always looking out for the girls and doing nice things for them. Several of them—still wearing their stage makeup, whisked the girls up in their arms and carried them in.

The interior of Le Drugstore was bizarre; ultra modern décor, all white—the walls, floor and ceiling. Nothing but Formica, stainless steel and acrylic; sterile-looking like the interior of a hospital lab. And listen to this: Halfway up the side walls, and spanning their entire length, a narrow, one-table-wide clear acrylic balcony jutted out. It may have been built too high, since it appeared that if someone was over six feet tall and chose to take their meal up there, they might have had to walk to their table, head bowed. At the far end of the room—on an expansive twenty foot high (white) rear wall—above and to both sides of the door to the kitchen, there were two apparently randomly staggered platforms for eating (each with one table and its own white enameled spiral staircase). This place may have been *called* a drugstore, but it was a neo-something eating establishment that just happened to sell a handful of cosmetics and toiletries at a front counter.

One of the male dancers stopped by our table and offered June a half an orange. "Junie, now your mum told me to make sure you got your *veetamins*, and I picked this one myself—in Valencia." She took it with a big smile. I was a little embarrassed as June happily and proudly introduced me to everyone in sight. I was being shown a respect I knew I did not deserve. The conversations between the girls and the other artists were upbeat and I was surprised at the theme of camaraderie and caring; *sincere* expressions of concern on all sides. One skinny guy with a struggling mustache (and his shirt open to his belt buckle) was showing everybody a hand-tooled leather purse he had bought for his "mum." The girls fawned over it and told him it was beautiful, and that his mother would love it, and how sweet he was to have gotten it for her. He was thrilled with their approval. These kids were all willing to spend the time to make each other feel good, feel important—feel a part of something. I could see it. *What right did I have to be here,* horning in and trying to get my kicks out of something I had no investment in. What kind of neat private society did these young working girls and guys have? Whatever it was I could see it was honorable. They were a family; a big, kind, and protective family. I felt out of place and I should have. But somehow I sensed (or hoped) that in my heart, I had the right feelings about June, and her girls, and her friends. And if time and some luck were on my side, they might know the sincerity of my affection.

It was a pleasure to watch June and the girls celebrate eating. They made it a momentous occasion, discussing each entree with much ado; at first registering concern, and then eyes lighting up as one of their specials was explained. When they finally ordered, it was with lots of instructions to the waiters. All done they would slam the menu shut, look up with an expression of absolute confidence as to the outcome, and begin the same routine of rubbing stomachs, licking lips, and kidding each other about gaining kilos, and weighing another "stone." When the food appeared I could readily see (as I would every time to come) that June had picked the most savory dish in the house. As long as I would know her, each time her plate arrived I'd wished it was in front of me. This time as it was set down in front of her, she leaned forward, reached out and encircled it with one forearm, acting like it was going to be necessary to protect it from me. Time to "dig in." The fork was in the air and down, and she was after it. This girl knew how to enjoy a meal, let me tell you. Your own worries disappeared at the sight of her. She relished the moment without being concerned with her appearance. No second thoughts. I think because she knew she was always doing what she *should* be doing. No falsehoods involved. No ulterior motives. Life for June was simple. No regrets. Tears almost came to my eyes, watching her and thinking of all the "what ifs," and "play-acting" going on in my life.

It was over. Dinner (breakfast) was over. It was after three now. *Whew,* was I going to be exhausted tomorrow. *What next?* What's going to happen now. Most the girls had left—alone or with members of another cast. June, Laurie and I were finally alone. Paid the bill (not too bad, considering) and exited Le Drugstore. Waiting for a cab on the sidewalk, June and I were holding hands. Don't know who initiated it but it was nice. Laurie and June were roomies here in Barcelona and had their own apartment. Could see that Laurie was ready to call it a night, and knew it would be a good idea not to suggest any further activities. I volunteered to ride with them back to their place. Only took about ten minutes. Out of the cab Laurie kissed us each goodnight, and was gone through a black metal gate. It had been a great night (and long). I knew I should have just tried for a goodnight kiss and caught the next Shore Patrol launch back to the ship. I was out on my feet, but couldn't bring myself to bow out just yet, especially since June had given no indication that she was ready to call it an evening. (But neither had she given any indication that she was considering having me spend the night.)

But it could be happening. I was being invited up for a coffee. No idea how it would work out. *Was I going to be invited to stay the night?* Up the stairs. A lot of stairs. Their apartment was on one of the top floors; a long hike, but worth it. I learned—with no elevator, the rents go down the higher you go. The apartment was cute as a button. They had really fixed it up nice. I got coffee—that's all I got, but I didn't mind, and could really use it about now. (There had been several times that my legs buckled under me as I dozed off on my feet.) I had time to sample June's goodness, without any tension. I met her two cats named Tony and Maria (from *Westside Story*). Laurie had hit the rack. June and I were alone. She had bought a

45 RPM record of that song we had heard together in the old seaside hotel in Valencia—the one by Cilla Black, "You're My World …every breath I take, every move I make." We listened to it again. Tomorrow night I might get to meet "Staffy." (Ms. Stafford was the lady from England who owned the ballet.) She was scheduled to be in town. June said she was a "trip."

About four o'clock I was convinced that if I didn't get horizontal quick, I was going to collapse. As I was talking I was visualizing scenes that had nothing to do with anything I was saying. While listening, I could see lips moving, but wasn't hearing any sounds. *We're talking critical fatigue.* And I was sure June must be tired too. I stood up, thanked her for the evening, got a great kiss on the lips, and pledged to do my best to be at the theater tomorrow night, same time. (But knew this might be a problem, since it would not be a liberty day for me.) She insisted it wasn't necessary to sit through another three acts, just meet her in the same café at quarter to one. I stumbled out the door, without asking her about maybe a Cinzano together before the show. Probably just as well.

It was at least twenty minutes before I got a cab. Guess I'm lucky I got one at all. Not too easy guiding him to the dock. And (small miracle) when we arrived there, a Shore Patrol boat was just cranking up for the trip out. Didn't have to wait till 0600, which could have resulted in me expiring first. As we bounced the mile out to the carrier I kept turning things over and over in my head. No time to think now, too exhausted. Almost to the ship. I was going to make it. On the ladder. Home safe. Into the forward passageway and towards my stateroom. Pitch Black. Jim's snoring. Shirt. Trousers. One, two, last sock off. I'm in the rack. *"Thank you God, again, for everything."*

Tired as I was I didn't fall asleep. I lay there awake, visualizing the girls, and June, and the guys, and Le Drugstore. I had suspected as much weeks ago, when I first saw that sunrise at Antibes, and smelt the coffee and croissants, but now I knew I would never be the same after this visit to Europe. My real life was on more and more shaky ground. It was becoming less real than the one that was rapidly taking shape. I couldn't make myself think about both lives in the same moment, though at any given time—in my defense (or perhaps to further debase my character), I was viewing this new world over my children's uplifted faces, and condemning myself for betraying my good wife's trust and my family's expectations. It was a very bad feeling, and worse—I had chosen to live with it. I sensed now, the adventures I had always fantasized about, in strange new places with exciting new people, were happening! Perhaps any day now (and it was a scary thought) I might find myself no longer just contemplating, but planning steps that would have me changing my work (and domestic) situation when I returned to the state. Resign my commission—maybe work for the airlines; be away from home more, free me up to continue my search. Changes that would effect Sara and the kids in a big way. Enough of this, especially now. Gotta get some sleep.

Evenings to Remember

Was awake at 0800, but as you might imagine, sure could have used a couple more hours. Never heard Jim get up. Did my chores; hit the shops and spent time listening to the troops. Mid afternoon got some bad news. Tripp had already swapped for someone else and couldn't swap with me, and it was too late to intercept anyone else. Almost everybody was ashore. I scoured the ship but couldn't find a squadron mate on board who had liberty. *I was screwed.* Nothing to do now. Just sit here and stew. The cruise is winding down, don't have much time left; not that many days—can't waste em. It was a bummer night I can tell you that. I spent the whole time wondering what the girls were doing—trying to visualize them coming into the cafe, remembering Le Drugstore, and conjecturing on what activities might be going on later. (Luckily, I'd found out in time to give Dale a note for June.) Passed a couple hours watching a flick in the wardroom. Had my peanut butter sandwich, milk and an orange. Went to the stateroom. Jim was ashore, which was good. I needed some solitude. Tried to write a letter to Sara. Didn't know how it would sound when she read it a week from now and far away, but now—here on my desk in front of me, it appeared a pitiful effort. *God help me.*

Wednesday—my liberty day today. But (shades of Rome) I'd made no special arrangements for "snafus" like this. No arranged rendezvous points. Could go ashore early and just hope to find her. No, that'd be tough. They usually slept till noon, then invaded a local restaurant somewhere (for a stevedore's brunch), then interviews and publicity appointments after that. I'd never be able to find em. Just waste another half a day. Knew a nap would be a good idea if I was going to have another night like the first one. Slipped up to the stateroom around 1500 and crashed. Felt like I'd been drugged when I awoke. Afternoon siestas are great until you try to stand up. At least I should have a little more sticking power tonight (if I ever wake up).

But that friggin Cinderella liberty (that I was consistently missing); one of these days I might get called in about it. I think all the other guys are actually coming back by midnight. Hard as hell for me to do when the girls don't get out of the theater until one a.m. I'll just have to keep sweet-talking the Shore Patrol guys again, or if that doesn't work—ride the 0600 boat back with the married Navy guys (who didn't seem to care). In fact maybe nobody really cares, not even the Skipper. Anyway I've been doing a good job on board and thank God, it's being noticed. Our aircraft have been up and flying like never before. *Oh!* Forgot to tell you! Get this: A couple months ago, Major Burnham went on that skiing trip (remember, the one he had Bob check on in Cannes) and, as bad luck (or luck) would have it, broke his leg and was sent back to the States. For the past ten weeks, I'd been *the* Maintenance Officer—the *head* of the department, reporting to no one, and what's more, had managed to keep our fleet of aircraft 100 percent available. The Skipper had been genuinely pleased. Not even two months now before we steam westward (out of my world). Really downhill now. It had been a successful cruise; no accidents (involving the Marine squadron anyway) and we'd be home before we knew it. The thought of this brought on a cold sweat. Wasn't sure I was going to be able to pull it off.

At the theater. (Just one seat tonight.) Decided to attend the performance in spite of June's assurances that I could just skip them. Knew I'd make points. (I'll bet her previous boyfriends would have taken her up on the "just meet me in the cafe" offer.) Same routine, same great performance. Finished at twelve fifteen. Out and into the cafe. June and the girls were there in no time. No need to go through quite as much ritual tonight. Also, June was taking over as tour director. The pressure was off me to come up with some great idea. First we were going to eat. Five of us piled in a cab. Directions were given and I was once again smothered in and amongst female-kind. Ten short minutes later, after having turned down an unlit and deserted city street, we stopped in front of what appeared to be a row of locked up darkened stores.

Time to pile out. But not so quick, the girls were listening to a great song on the radio, by a currently popular Spanish vocalist—Raphael. It was a romantic sounding ballad with evidently, moving lyrics. The girls made the driver wait for his fare until it was over. Now on the sidewalk scanning the darkened storefronts and shadowy doorways. (Reminded me a bit of Belkis' expedition to the underground restaurant in that abandoned

Turkish village.) But the girls knew where they were and had no trouble finding the entrance. Inside, we entered a dark, tunnel-like, club that could not have been more than fifteen feet wide, but fifty feet deep from front to rear. There was a bar along the first half of the left wall. It was so dark that although I was aware of some motion behind it and the blur of some light colored shirts in front of it; no faces or any reflections off the mirrors behind it. Nothing was distinguishable. The only seating in the place was one long, low, cushioned bench stretching the length of the right wall. Not a chair or table in the place. At the far end of the room against the rear wall (still only fifteen feet across) was a small stage upon which an Italian rock band was going full blast. The male vocalist was another hoarse-voiced, long-haired, macho-looking guy, with his head back and eyes closed— wailing away. The girls were about swooning over him. I'd give anything to swap places with him (at least for a week—to see how it went.) The only light in the entire club was what was reflected back from the three colored spots over the bandstand. We sat in the dark on the cushioned right-wall bench.

The place was owned by a chunky Lebanese guy the girls had met when they first arrived. He was a swarthy guy—about 45, with a cigar stuck in his mouth and pinkie rings on both hands. (To me, kind've phony-looking.) Seeing the girls he hurried over. Lots of hugs and a few kisses. I wouldn't doubt these club owners vied with each other to adopt the "Staffy girls." They knew it was damned good for business to have this lot come crashing in each night. If this guy wasn't a card-carrying member of the Middle East Mafia, nobody was. (An hour later, I'd meet Marcel!) The owner asked the girls if they wanted something to eat. They said yes, and I was to observe another eating festival. A long row of small tables were set in front of us on that low right wall bench. In twenty minutes each had its own tray, holding an assortment of pastry-wrapped "somethings;" strange bread and dips. Gotta admit it looked inviting, but I'm not big on eating things that I can't see and identify. Primarily limited my intake to the pieces of beef and chicken on skewers. Two cold beers of unknown origin later, I made a slight blunder: I told a good joke—one with a cute twist at the end; what I thought was a harmless joke, until realizing it was a racial innuendo at the end. The suddenly lowered heads and "*Oh Rogey*" comments from the girls was deservedly embarrassing. (I would learn that Europeans have a more modern view of a mixed ethnicity society than most Caucasian Americans.) Other than that one faux pas, the time in the *Boite Beirut* was fine.

We were outa there. On the sidewalk. Flagging a cab again (like it seemed I did a hundred times during these in-ports). Only four of us. Claire stayed. I could see that the other two with us now, did not approve of her attraction to the lead singer (and particularly June, who had a heart-to-heart talk with her while we were inside). I don't know what it is about singers and drummers, but geez—*do they get the girls!* I would see it time and time again. They were hot affairs while they lasted, but they never lasted, and when they fell apart, they really fell apart.

Here I was (again) jumping in another cab and racing across Barcelona at two in the morning. I didn't know what the other guys did when they were on liberty (since I never saw them), but I couldn't imagine they wouldn't have wanted to be in my shoes right now. *Who'd believe this?* We were in a section of Barcelona I hadn't seen; open, with spacious parks on both sides, and large trees lining the roads. Only a few very respectable looking—perhaps government buildings. After some time the driver turned through a pair of tall wrought iron gates, into what looked like a large and well-maintained public park or private estate. Once inside the gates we traveled about a hundred yards along a curving, soft sand drive, edged by neat little lanterns. On either side, manicured lawns and shrubs extended as far as the eye could see. The cab stopped in front of an imposing, large, swanky-looking, white brick building. Only one-story high, but deep and wide. (Possibly the only building on this property.)

Next thing I knew we were out of the cab and making our way up a half dozen shallow but fifty-foot-wide steps centered between two large pillars; then across a stone veranda and into an immaculate sitting room. The girls did this with no hesitancy, like they did it every day. Me? Not so sure. As confidently as I could, I accompanied them across the polished wood floor, past the array of overstuffed floral print furniture, and up to a large white archway. Through it I saw the dining area—a sea of tables inside a large, perfectly round *greenhouse!* The outside walls were curving, side-to-side, floor-to-domed ceiling glass panels. (A round, ground level version of Leo's high rectangular Torretta Vetro in Milan.) The black night outside caused all the lights and images from within to be reflected back inside a hundred times over. The dance floor was racetrack-shaped, encircling a white-tuxedoed orchestra in the very center. Tables with linen and candelabras ringed the circumference. Now *this* was a night club! The manager approached us. *I was about to meet Marcel.*

As usual, June was not one bit embarrassed about introducing me. I guess the word was out. We were an item—let the chips fall where they may. And once again I was proud. But this time it was different. I didn't have a good feeling about Marcel. He was one of those guys of uncertain origin. From his facial features and physical appearance, perhaps of middle eastern heritage. From his speech, perhaps French—from Marseilles or Corsica. Still, I'd bet on him being from Algeria or Lebanon. Balding at a young age, I'd say he was not much over thirty. Although he was only about five-foot ten and 175 pounds, you could see he was a powerful guy. Strong neck (and a two inch scar on his forehead). It was obvious, in spite of his overly polite—almost fawning façade, that this was one "tough cookie." He shook my hand (and one thing men know), by the excess pressure he exerted, it was a private attempt to intimidate me— to show his strength. The second I felt it occurring I tensed my hand to block the compression, as best I could with my small hand. (No matter how strong I might get lifting weights, my grip has always been terrible.) Think I stopped it. Never let myself wince. Tried to balance his pressure. With this, he was sending me a message. I think I had just met a rival for June's affection; someone who had recognized by her bubbling smile and exuberant introduction of me, that whatever chances he had, might be in jeopardy.

I was glad when the niceties were finished and we were shown to our table. If June had noticed anything she never indicated as much. Although we danced several times, I never did get comfortable in that place. The girls danced with each other most the time. Occasionally some Spanish guy would get the nerve to come over and ask for a dance. It was a swank place all right, well-appointed and in a choice location, but I had my doubts about the clientele. The bulk of the patrons looked like cast members from some Hollywood Mafia movie. Although Marcel was never in one place for more than a moment or two, each time I spied him he seemed to be looking over at our table. *Spooky.*

Observing June and listening to her, I suspected that in spite of her striking appearance, bold walk, certainty in almost every situation, and these uninhibited good times, for whatever reasons—she wasn't counting on any great things happening in her life. It was as if it weren't her place to expect any miracles. They hadn't happened for her mother or her older sister. Her birthright was hard work and being satisfied with the lot at hand: a wet newspaper, left-over foods, chapped skin, a broken purse strap. Was it possible that all this was *before she met me*. Could it be that now she was daring to hope something special was about to happen in her life? And if so, no matter how I admired her and felt towards her, I didn't deserve such a place in her life. I hadn't done anything to merit it; had lied and was at a loss as to how I could still be in the picture in another two months. But her eyes were upon me, and rightly or wrongly I suspected her hopes might be with me. Could it be I had at last met someone with whom I could be a good and true person (*for the first time*). I was almost sure of it, in spite of her sadly not being the mystic female that would be the answer to my desperate search. But how? What have I started here and where can it go. June was a person you could count on! She deserved the best and it's true I would have liked to be the one who gave it to her. But again, *how?* I didn't have the foggiest. I didn't know what was in store for her, and I sure didn't know what was in store for me.

It was almost four before the girls began to wind down. Talk about living the moment. They were celebrating life. They never ran out of things to chatter about. Except June. While she listened attentively to the girls and made appropriate comments, she mostly just sat there beaming at me. *God, I never felt so good, so important (and so undeserving).* I think she would've left in a minute if I would have suggested it. When we did leave, we said goodnight to Marcel (whose countenance told me the same thing it had upon our arrival). We took one cab. Dropped the other two girls off. They all seemed to have had a real good time and were noticeably pleased that June and I hadn't left early. But that would happen now. We continued in the cab to the Manila Hotel. A respectable but comfy-appearing old wooden hotel I had seen the first night—just off the plaza atop Las Ramblas. I was going to do it right—got one of the expensive suites. We'd earned it and had the time now to lie undisturbed in each other's arms. To share and think and wonder.

The room was first class—hardwood floors with oriental rugs, brocade silk wallpaper and ornate tables with ceramic lamps. The bed was large and comfortable (and knowing I would soon need all the help I could get, the room temperature was just fine). Alone in the suite, once again it was a most unsexy encounter. June didn't flirt or tease. She acted as I imagined she would if we'd been married ten years. *What you saw was what you got.* Fortunately she didn't conspire to arouse me. And that was good, because had she devoted some time and effort to that project, and with me failing to respond, it would have been even worse. Knowing beforehand that my chances were slim (the statistics now defying any other interpretation) I was resigned to hope for no more than the opportunity to show her the abundance of affection and tenderness she deserved. (*I think I was about to say show her how much I loved her.*) To show June affection and tenderness would (perhaps for the first time for me) not be difficult; in fact easy. Deservedly I had elevated June—above all others. My feelings for her were good, and true, and respectful—*a new experience.* And this time, in these appropriate surroundings and better known to each other, I had left a light on and was able to observe her smoothness and newness lying there next to me. My eyes settled on her most female part. It was dwarfed by the silky-white expanse of her powerful belly above her hugely muscled thighs. It was surprisingly small and innocent and closed; squeaky clean with just the slightest bit of soft fuzz, like the head of a small baby. It was what God had meant it to be, and it had that same pure fragrance.

Besides any of this I knew what I felt for June, and (minus me not being worthy of offering it) she deserved it. Why she would have any similar feelings for me was yet unexplained, but they seemed to be there. She consistently displayed a contentment to be with me. Even in a crowd she didn't hold back, just sat there beaming. All this was provoking in me a kind of feeling I'd never had before. I looked at her. She wasn't sleeping. She was lying on her side and looking straight at me. And not one of those sad or strained emotional fixations (that could well have been expected in a situation like this). Rather it was a look of ease and happiness and kindness—an *"ask me for the moon"* look, or an *"everything is going to be all right"* look. If you could imagine that, at this time and in view of my total inability to give her any assurances. This night together in bed, the best I could say—once again, would be "I managed."

Reflecting on my activities during the cruise, my other adventures, and my recent time with Leo, I felt a pain in my chest. Now laying here in the aura of June, sampling her body, her pure white skin against me, her darkly-dyed red hair across my shoulder, I could feel the tears welling in my eyes. I was probably racing headlong down a steep hill, picking up speed and thrilling to the wind in my face, while there was every chance a brick wall or giant pit awaited me at the bottom. I didn't know where I was going, or how I would get there (if I would get there at all) or what I would do when I arrived.

The whole in-port stay was like these two days and nights. A whirlwind of thrills and excitement. Not a single bad scene. A real high. Besides the established metropolis I'd seen the first day, June and the girls showed me all the fun places: castles converted into hotels, monasteries turned into restaurants, wine cellars made over into after-hours clubs, and my favorite, for a midnight trip back to the 1500's—the *Old Quarter*. It was a huge, completely unencumbered, unoccupied, empty, stone-paved square— several hundred feet across, lit by just the moonlight! All four sides were buttressed by twenty-foot-high stone walls. Nestled on the ground floor of this encompassing wall were an inviting selection of bistros, wineries, and darkened enclaves of unknown specialties. I would conclude that the joie d'vie of Barcelona and the affluence of its population were a Spanish birthright; a perfection that never wavered.

I was now going ashore alone every time—my own guy; slipping in and out of cabs, hurtling through the night, bursting into theaters and crashing down aisles. Then afterwards, riding the high-flying coattails of the Stafford Ballet. *June's guy!* Back in town out of nowhere—a force to be reckoned with. And surprisingly the girls approved of me. To my amazement and gratitude, the girls had given me a "thumbs-up." I was an invited guest everywhere. And the girls of the Stafford Ballet, they *were* "Barcelona after hours!" Where they were, was where it was happening. Where they went so went the excitement; laughing, singing, arms flying, hair tossed, long legs everywhere, band playing, dancing the night away. No pain, no strain, nothing but the good times. *They were gonna live forever!*

Sometimes I got in during the day and was with them for a newspaper interview at two, a "telly" interview at four, a snack at six, and the theater at eight-thirty. Out of the theater at quarter to one, and tearing across town—six deep, jammed in one of Barcelona's rigid black cabs. Racing by those same spacious parks and big strong government buildings behind high wrought iron fences. Giant silver trees and old iron street lamps streaking by. Speed runs full of merriment. No problems. The Beatles, Tom Jones, Stevie Wonder. They knew every word to every song on the world's Top Twenty, and sang them at the top of their lungs (especially "Hey Jude"). Roaring up and piling out at a great little, hidden-away, all-night restaurant! An hour later, on the other side of town hurtling down the steps to another after-hours club. These girls knew how to live. *And I just wished there was some sense, or reason for me to learn how.*

But what I had said earlier—about my activities and relationships ashore occurring in a "parallel universe," and not really going to affect my marriage on my return; well yes—that's what I thought then, and it *was* more than halfway true at the time. Originally they were to be no more than temporary and ultimately forgotten experiments. *Now I'm not so sure.* I'm yoked to the promise. It's become the force behind all my thoughts and actions. How could I possibly think—with all my past adventures still haunting me, and now having met sweet brave June, that I could ever return to the states, my family, and step back in as the same guy who left ten months ago? No way. For the first time, the word "divorce" crossed my mind. (Not yet my lips.) But the thought of it struck terror in my heart. *Help me God.*

Chapter Twenty-Four
THE CIA SECRET AIRLINE

D on't remember much about this at sea period; not because my mind and soul were still on shore (which of course they were), but because of something else. A couple days before putting into port we were up in the S2 (Intelligence) office, logging our mandatory time reviewing our target folders, and screwing around (since we were on the down side of the cruise and seriously doubted we'd get to bomb the Eastern Bloc). Looking through our S2 "Read and Initial" file, Don Goft found an intelligence report about a Navy pilot who was shot down near the North Vietnam border and crashed in Laos. *In Laos?* What the heck were we doing over there? What resolution? (Hard to believe, but I'd never heard a word mentioned about the now discredited "Gulf of Tonkin" incident.) *Lemmee see that story.* Reached for it—missed it. Bob got it. In a couple minutes he's "ooh-ing" and "ah-ing" as well. When he was through with it he handed it to me.

The account stated that a navy aircraft bombing the Ho Chi Minh trail (*Ho Chi Minh Trail?*) had been hit by ground fire. The pilot ejected and was on the ground okay, using his handheld radio to make frantic calls to try to get rescued before he was killed by the NVA. (We discovered—an abbreviation for the North Vietnamese Army). And whether it was them or armed civilians, they were closing in on his position. No response to his calls, but about ten minutes later an unmarked gray helicopter arrives out of nowhere. He knew it couldn't be from his carrier, and of course there was no U.S. land base within three hundred miles. His narrative made for some interesting reading.

> "...*The helicopter pilot must have had balls of steel. The ground-fire was horrendous and I knew he was taking hits. I could see the rounds cutting the limbs beneath him. The foliage*

299

was so thick he couldn't get the rescue sling down through it. I was afraid my chances for a pick-up were over. But he climbed back up a hundred feet, pulled the power back and fell to within ten or twenty feet of the tree tops. Then just as he was about to hit them, he pulled full pitch with max power. The sudden powerful rotorwash tore through the canopy, shredding leaves and snapping branches. He did this three or four times, all the while taking hits. Finally he'd made a hole big enough to get the hoist through. Down it came. I was on it and being lifted out before I knew it. What I saw as I cleared the trees and approached the chopper, was not what I expected. I almost leaped off the hook. There was an oriental on the skid, all dressed in black and wielding a Russian AK47. Before I had a chance to leap or grab my gun, he hauled me in. I fell to the floor straining to see the pilot. In the cockpit was a gray-haired, cigar smoking guy in a red Ohio State tee shirt, who offered me half of his tuna sandwich. This was my first introduction to Air America."

We were all asking ourselves, *who the hell is Air America?* None of us had ever heard of it. But the non-commissioned Officer in S2—before being assigned to our squadron, had been attached to the marine guard at the US Embassy in Saigon. He was observing us and chimed in. "Yeah, that's a secret CIA aviation operation over there in Vietnam and Cambodia and Laos. Doing all kinds of crazy stuff. And not just flying helicopters; they have lots of weird single engine aircraft. All civilian pilots. I met a bunch of them. Most of them keep their families in Bangkok or Singapore. If any of you guys are thinking of getting out and want some excitement, that's where to go. And they make big bucks—about $40,000 a year tax-free." This was 1965. I was making about $1,200 a month. $40,000 tax free was a lot of money!

Well as you might imagine, I'm thinking, *Could this be just what I'm looking for?* A way to continue my search. Not need a divorce; mercifully avoid that, but still live separate. A way to earn enough money to take great care of the family, while I lived alone in some far away place. *But was I really considering getting out of the Corps?* Real hard to imagine—resigning my commission. The thought of facing the Skipper (and the other guys) with this decision, was *not* something I wanted to dwell on. And

I didn't know anything about being a civilian—went right from college to flight training. Only spent one summer vacation as a civilian. A little scary thinking about trying civilian life now, after the unmatched security of being in the military; especially as a commissioned officer. Thought about it all day and returned to the S2 office at 1600. Wanted to talk to Staff Sergeant Walker (alone)—try to get some more info. Who knows, might not hurt to check with him. He didn't have an exact address for Air America, but assured me if I sent a letter addressed to them—in care of the US Embassy in Saigon, they'd get it. Wasn't too happy with such an inexact address, but it was the best the sergeant could do. I'd sleep on it, but was pretty sure I knew what I was going to do.

Chapter Twenty-Five
BEHIND THE IRON CURTAIN

Arriving at Leo's and the Trip There

The states and my real life were only five weeks away, and I had no idea how I was going to mesh things together. *I was in big trouble.* I knew I was the same named person who had stood on the deck in Norfolk that gray and windy day. But I'd been so many places and met so many people, how could anything look the same for me. And now, *June!* Oh I wasn't moping around wistfully longing for her. It wasn't like that. But each hour of the day I was pleasantly aware of her existence. Almost as if we were in each other's company, when of course we weren't; another person going through life with me each day. Not near to me physically, but still side by side. I was proud of her traveling from city to city, managing her life, taking control and making it work. I was gratified and surprised at the unselfish and respectful feelings I was having for her. (Maybe there is hope for me.) How could I ever close the door on this relationship. And by the same token, *how could I keep it open?*

I was under a lot of strain, constantly mulling things over—one hypothetical "what if" after another: from contemplating employment in some dangerous foreign city where the family would not be able to join me, *to outright asking for a divorce.* Yes, I'd thought about it so much I finally *said* it (though with a perfect wife and four kids, *how could I ever do it.*) One of the few things I did know, I had to keep doing a good job aboard ship. Make sure the maintenance department and everything about it was beyond reproach. *Had* to do that. At least have my bases covered here, so my livelihood and reputation wouldn't fall away underneath me. But how about after the cruise. What then? Am I going to stay in? Boy the way I feel now, I don't see how.

Part Two: The French Riviera, Leo, June, and Big Trouble

At this point in the cruise (my priorities being where they were) it seemed I was just flying to use up time between my escapades ashore. Things were routine and I was finally feeling comfortable in the aircraft, no more jitters on the way up to the flight deck. (I *ought* to be getting used to it by this time!) The flying was still more of the same—just burning up gas and punching holes in the sky; practice formation, practice navigation, practice 45 degree bombing, practice Zuni missile attacks, practice nuclear weapon loft maneuvers. *For what?* Personally, I couldn't see how we would ever be justified in flinging atomic weapons on anyone—anywhere, regardless of national or political priorities. Couldn't imagine we'd ever use the real stuff in anger. *Who in the hell would attack the USA anyway.* What on earth would have to be done to us to merit that kind of retaliation?

As far as I was concerned all this practice was for nothing. Couldn't say that to anyone of course; not sure which if any of my squadron mates shared this opinion. But don't get me wrong, in spite of my predictions for peaceful solutions in the future, I did believe the navy carrier operation represented one hell of a threat. Not only because of the hardware, but because of the people assigned. A competent and dedicated force, certainly able to perform "as advertised." We'd been at sea a week, zig-zagging our way across the northern Med, from the east coast of Spain toward the northwest coast of Italy. On our way to Genoa (again), which was not my favorite place. Although considering what I now know about these European cities, Genoa can't be as bad as I'm saying. I may have just gotten off to a bad start with that city. In any case, this time I had something real special to do that would get me out of there.

It had been a fast at-sea period, and we were once again closing in on terra firma. Almost time to hit the rack. Three more hours and they'll be dropping the anchor. Read Leo's letter again—the one that I had been carrying around with me for the last ten days. No doubt about it, if I got to Milan by the afternoon of the 25th, *I could go with him on that special trip.* And I was damned sure planning on doing just that, although I had not been able to confirm that with him while we were at sea. My plan was to go ashore first thing in the morning—packed and ready, assuming everything would still be on. I'd phone him from the train station—to check, just before I (hopefully) leaped aboard one of those Milano *Rapidos*. Laid back and tried to let my mind slow down. Must have been tired, never heard the anchor chain. The alarm was set for 0700 and I would have liked to have slept till then. As it was I woke up at 0545, which would make it a longer day and would require more sticking power.

I GUESS I JUST WASN'T THINKING

"Where in the hell you going this weekend? You look pretty pumped up." Jim was raised up on one elbow watching me from his top rack, hair tousled, one eye shut. I guess I was kind've noisy.

"No hot date Jim. Going to visit Leo in Milan again. Be back on board Tuesday night. Got two days leave." Jim took me at face value, told me to have a good time and collapsed back on his pillow. Jim never thought about doing something other than what he said, or ever had to make excuses. Like June, with Jim what you saw was what you got. (Greatly admired them both.) Mentally went through my packing checklist, touched a couple items to be sure and snapped the Samsonite closed. Hated this suitcase—marbleized green with a broad and badly soiled cream vinyl edge. It was Sara's luggage before we were married and I didn't look very goddam international toting it. (A few liberties ago I'd seen one of those neat black canvas bags trimmed with calf skin.) I had on my now-famous black sweater and ascot, and had borrowed Nick's London Fog raincoat. I was looking as much the part as I could. (I didn't exactly *feel* the part; might have looked a little phony.) The hell with it, to the liberty boat. This was going to be a first. *Bulgaria!* Leo said I wouldn't need a visa. Just bring my passport. Hard to believe. This should be some trip! Wanted to tell someone (wanted to tell *everyone*), but didn't dare.

In the train station at eight-twenty. Third booth I tried, finally—a phone with a tone, and taking the token too (and that pay phone thing, *that's* another challenge in Europe)! Got through to Leo. He sounded excited. Said he had been sure I'd make it and that up to this point everything was a "go" for tomorrow. *Tomorrow?* Shit. I thought we'd get started today. I'm one day short on leave now. Well, at least I could calm down and relax a little. Just get there by supper. (In which case I could have slept till noon.) And would you believe, the first damn time I'm not in a hurry there's two *Rapidos* leaving for Milan. Attempted breakfast in the *Caffe Termini,* but as good as Italian food is, I can tell you, American style breakfasts are not their specialty. (This is way before McDonalds hit Europe.) Was on board the second *Rapido* and out of the station at 0917—right on schedule. An hour and fifteen later—Milano. I was getting to be an old hand at these trips. Took it all the way to the second stop this time, quite a bit closer to Leo's apartment. Saved on the cab fare. (The train fare was the same to both stops.)

Leo and Winona were thrilled to see me, as if I'd been gone for a year, when in reality I'd just walked out their door a month ago. I gave especially energetic greetings to Flipper. (Could see that in so doing I was bringing some happiness into Winona's life.) Good thing my train station breakfast hadn't been too filling, because Leo had the makings for one of his omelets strewn across the kitchen counter (piles of diced onions, mushrooms, ham, and cheese). The master chef was about to go to work. During the ceremonious preparation I grilled Leo as to the details of our trip, about which—up to this point, he had only hinted. "Yeah," he said— not just matter-of-factly, but with obvious excitement himself, "We're going to Sofia!" Which I knew (now) was the capital of Bulgaria, and to me—dead center of the Cold War, the "black hole" behind the iron curtain. *The last place in the world for a USMC Captain to be!*

"And tell me again Leo, what's the deal? Why exactly are you making this trip?"

"A long story Roger, but an interesting one. Like I said, I may buy some guns. *Lots* of guns—in fact, a hundred thousand of them." (Holy Shit!) He continued, gesturing with an onion in one hand, the knife in the other; pausing only occasionally to nibble a piece of ham. "Pretty damned interesting. You probably don't remember World War II, but it was something! In 1942 and 43 the Italian 10th Army and the German *Afrika Corp* led by General Rommell—the "Desert Fox," were hard at it in North Africa and needed weapons. The high command tried to move a critical shipment of rifles down there; out of the North Sea port of Bremerhaven. To all appearances it was just a commercial tanker, but the records show it had a hold full of guns—a hundred thousand of them! It made it safely past the Netherlands and Belgium, then through the Strait of Dover, and apparently had it made; just had to skirt the "frogs" (the French) for a day. I'm sure when they passed the north border of Spain, they were sure they had pulled it off.

Leo was interrupted as Winona who had been listening attentively, brought us each a small cup of very dark Italian coffee.

"Would you believe Roger, a decommissioned Royal Navy frigate manned by a bunch of midshipmen—just college cadets on an orientation cruise off the coast of Portugal, challenged the tanker. The damn kids fired across the bow—the whole works. The ship tried to make a run for it, steamed right into two Brit Navy battleships. And of course *these* guys knew what they were doing; corralled it and ran it into port in Lisbon. Everyone knows that for fact—that the ship was quarantined in Lisbon. And it's a matter of record that the guns got unloaded. But for twenty-two years, nobody has been able to find them. They never turned up—anywhere. They just disappeared off the face of the earth."

There was a small delay again as Leo checked two different containers of cream, shook one, rejected it, poured the other into the mélange, whipped it a minute or two, and dumped it all in the fry pan. "Now, and here's the catch! These weren't just *any* guns, they were "Mausers, and moreover, the karabiner 98k—just about the best, most accurate, and most easily maintained firearm ever designed. You can't get enough sand and mud into that breech to stop it working; only nine pieces, three pins, and two springs!" Shaking his head almost reverently, he said, "I would love to have met that Paul Mauser—the guy who invented that action. In fact, our famous World War I Springfield Rifle was modeled after one of his earlier rifles. No, *more* than just modeled after it, it was an exact copy of one of Mauser's first bolt action rifles. It will always be the best. A classic, like a 41 Ford. And listen to this, all the tooling to make them was on board the ship as well. A goddam bonanza! Well, twenty-two years later, and they turn up last month—in Bulgaria."

While all this was very interesting, I wondered why in the hell Intercontinental Arms (Leo's company) would want these guns. I know I asked the question—several times. But I never received an answer. One thing I had been thinking, though he never said as much, was that Leo may have been working as an agent for the U.S. Government; maybe with a mission to just get these rifles off the open market. Sam Cummings' name came up again; the much publicized "man with the alligator briefcase" from Alexandria, Virginia (who had supposedly bought and sold more guns than the U.S. Army). Leo later showed me some invoices that indicated they were partners. After brunch Leo took a look at my passport, checked my suitcase and chuckled at all the clothes I had crammed in it. Later in the day he tossed a canvas bag into the guest room and said, "Fill it up, that's all you'll be carrying. We won't be checking any luggage. May not even stay the night." *May not stay the night?* The way I'd figured, we wouldn't even get there until late in the day. The rest of the afternoon I listened, but was not so excited, as Leo talked about a business that had tickled his fancy. *Sixteenth century armor!*

"Yeah Roger, last year, a hundred feet behind that two-story building—the barn, remember—where they were doing the engraving. Well we're digging this footing for a new kiln, and about two feet deep in some decomposed wood and mud, we hit something hard. Two weird-shaped, curved pieces of steel. One a perfect half-circle, about six inches by a foot, the other bigger and flatter. Both of them black and caked with dirt, but I could see they were hand crafted, with molded decorations on them. I had them cleaned up and took them to a guy in Milan. I thought they might be some kind of old body armor, and I was right. The small piece was a *Chamfron*, or *Champron*, a protective headpiece for up here, you know— on the forehead of a horse. The big one was a, I think he said, a *Peytal* or something like that—the breast plate. Two weeks later he calls me up and tells me he's got a buyer for em. In American money Roger, about $7,000! Can you believe that, just dug em up in the backyard. Since then I've done a lot of reading, and also made one helluva discovery!"

Whether I wanted to hear about it or not, Leo went on to tell me about the history of armor. It first appeared in the 1200's—a kind called chain mail. All those thousands of tiny rings hooked together and hinged with leather; covered a knight's whole body—completely flexible. Any of that stuff still underground is disintegrated. Worked good against swords and lances. But in the 1300's when they came out with the more powerful crossbows, the chain mail couldn't stop the arrows. So the next step was plate armor, and by the 1400's—full-body plate armor, and that was the rage for the next century. In the 1600's the weaponry became even more powerful and the armor had to be so thick, it got too heavy to wear. Armor went out of use in the mid 1600's. What I *did* learn was—if armor was a big deal then, you ought to see it now. *Big* business. Finding buyers and selling the stuff. Not much still around, but whenever a piece is found it brings big bucks. There's a huge black market in the stuff, especially in England and France. And even in the United States. I would learn tomorrow however, that Leo had an altogether new twist on the armor business.

Leo had a bunch of books on armor that he'd bought and gotten from the library—all now stuffed with note-ridden markers. He had highlighted all the sections on Gothic armor from northern Italy. According to Leo, it was regarded as the epitome of elegance and functional design. He would later give the books to me and tell me to take them back to the ship and read them. It was all very interesting, and I was sure there was a scheme in there somewhere. For the most part I found myself wishing away the afternoon, anxious for tomorrow (and doubting that I would get much sleep). Spent a lot of time watching Winona putts around the apartment; seemed busy although I could see it didn't take much to occupy her. She brushed Flipper's carrying case for about thirty minutes. We ate in. (No Torretta Vetro tonight.) I was in the rack by nine.

Big surprise—slept great. Leo poked his head in about seven, then made for the kitchen. I was hungry. Knew he wasn't planning another omelet, but this morning that was exactly what I felt like. So when he asked me what I wanted for breakfast, I told him: another one of his omelets. Glad that I did. He was thrilled and went through the whole procedure again. And it was great. Maybe it was the fresh Italian cheese or that special farm ham (*prosciutto*). I don't know, but they were the best omelets I ever ate. If I would have been less nervous, they would have tasted even better. (Took a pee when I woke up, after breakfast, and again just before we left.) Our stuff had been placed by the door. A few minutes there double-checking, a big hug, some last minute instructions for Winona and we were on our way.

"Like I said Roger, it's not real easy to get where we're going. Could have taken the train to Rome, then hope we make that direct flight to Sofia. But if we missed it we would've had to wait for the night flight. So what we'll do is catch a ten-fifteen flight from Milano to Belgrade—about an hour on the ground there, and then a short flight to Sofia. That worked great last time." *Wow, two flights, two countries—three counting Italy, all in one day!* I was getting more excited. Out of the parking garage and onto the crowded street. Crisp morning. Clear. No one in the world except Leo knew where I was. None of my friends. No one! I was far away and about to get a lot further. God, was I lucky to meet Leo that day in Cannes. How many other people are there in the world like him? Found myself shaking my head in response, as I asked myself, *could anyone return to a normal nine-to-five life after getting an idea of the intriguing people and places and situations out there?*

"How long of a flight is it to Belgrade?"

"Shouldn't be more than an hour if there's no traffic delays, and the weather's okay so it shouldn't be a problem." The airport was easy to get into and park. Check-in was simple. About an hour in the departure lounge and the flight was called. We taxied promptly (and to me—too fast) and were in the air before I knew it. No turning back now. I noticed that Leo kept a lot of records, using that same personalized pocket notebook (and miniature gold pen) he had used in Cannes. He jotted down flight numbers, times, and names. And then would stick the pad back in the inside pocket of that same great looking camel hair topcoat. (Someday I'm going to get one like that, so help me.) It wasn't a great aircraft; not new, and small, but it would not be a long flight to Belgrade. Leo passed some time flirting with the Italian stewardesses in a harmless sort of way. Maybe they didn't know that, but I did. (About the furthest thing I could imagine was Leo screwing around on Winona.) Shortly after we leveled off, he brought up the subject of armor again. And I was to learn the real scoop.

"Roger I'll tell you, it's one helluva business, this wheeling and dealing in plate armor pieces. A lot of money changing hands."

"I can believe it Leo, but got no idea of what kinds of money you're talking about."

"And there's an even better business, one with ten times the profit!"

"Yeah, and what's that?"

"Selling pieces of plate armor that people *think* are authentic!"

"What the heck are you talking about?"

"Selling them fake stuff. That's what I'm talking about."

"Shoot Leo, you'd never get away with that. I'm sure there are experts all over the place who authenticate this stuff for a living. Sooner or later one of them would tell your buyer his stuff is counterfeit."

"That's true enough, but we got one thing going for us."

"What's that?"

"Who do you think is the last guy in the world, to agree that a piece of armor is a counterfeit?" He didn't wait for me to answer. "I'll tell you who, the guy who just paid twenty thousand dollars for it, that's who!"

"But Leo, even if it could be made perfectly, to every last detail, I'm sure there's ways to tell."

"How?"

"Well I don't know so much about it, but those carbon dating tests, or something like that. Fluoroscopes. I don't know, but they do it. X-Rays. Some way."

"You're absolutely right Roger! And here my lad is where we shine. A couple months after I found those first two pieces, on the next lot, inside the walls of an old foundation we found a whole stack of sheet steel— maybe a half ton of it! A second building must have caved in on top of it. I cut off a couple pieces, brought them to Torino, and had a metallurgists run tests on them. And guess what? The stuff has been there since sometime in the 1500 or 1600's. I've already got authentic raw materials, this stuff was smelted four hundred years ago! We've got nothing to worry about regarding those new scopes and chemical dating tests!"

On the ground at Belgrade, and it looked like what I'd heard an Eastern Bloc city was supposed to look like—at least to me. And no longer was it clear and sunny; now at one-fifteen, in keeping with the mood, it was gray and windy. The airport was just another airport. Things were organized, but not a lot of color, not a lot of people smiling. A hard-working society—that's how I'd describe it. Lots of people doing mundane tasks. Lots of Middle Eastern looking people, sweepers, wipers, haulers—doing crummy work. That was my first impression as we filed down a lackluster, bare-bulbed corridor towards the immigration desk. Floors in bad shape. I was only a little nervous (since I was with Leo). Shouldn't be a problem, the Alitalia guy in Milan had checked my passport and handed it back to me. I guess Leo had been here before, he seemed to walk without any hesitation. Grabbed my ticket once, checked something, mumbled "great," then handed it back. I was a follower today—that was for sure. And if you didn't mind interfacing with people who apparently were just tolerating their jobs, going through immigration and customs was no sweat. Maybe because we were transient. We weren't going to stay in Yugoslavia (Serbia now) weren't even going to leave the airport. In fact we only stayed about forty-five minutes and never left the international lounge. Didn't catch it myself, but evidently Leo heard our flight being cancelled and was real upset. "The sonuva-bitches don't think they have enough passengers to make money, so they're gonna save us to fill up the next flight. Jesus Christ!" Leo was really bitching. "Over here they can get away with that." Finally (and fortunately) somebody overruled the cancellation and made the decision our flight would go (but about twenty minutes late). One more cup of coffee and another pee.

If the Alitalia aircraft was less than new, the *Jat* flight was even worse. A smaller size jet, but then as best I could count—only fourteen passengers. It was almost empty. The same type plane I flew out of Munich two months ago—a French Caravelle. The upholstery in this one featured elephants and giraffes and I guess—gazelles; the plane was probably bought from some African airline going broke. No female flight attendants either; all guys and not the friendly type you're used to seeing. (More like well-dressed guards.) As the flight progressed I sensed Leo was becoming a bit more serious; not nervous mind you, just more business-like. He read and reread some old correspondence and looked over two or three official-looking forms.

"Roger, no one is going to ask you anything. So don't worry. Only a couple of the big shots speak English well enough to get through a door. If anybody does ask anything, just smile and put out your hand. Don't answer at first, in fact don't answer at all. Put out your hand with a half smile and nod. If they ask, tell them you're my nephew." Then he began to mumble to himself. "If all goes well, let's see… three o'clock now. Should be on the ground shortly after four. Ought to make it without a problem. Yeah, Roger, we might be able to get the 9 p.m. return flight out of Sofia. Yeah, should be able to do it." *Geez, this guy's planning what I know is a very important deal, and only allotting suppertime to it.* Personally I would have liked to stay all night—see more. Really get the feel of things.

I was learning that Leo believed in doing what was necessary to properly educate himself (i.e., the history of armor), and was now proceeding to give me a rundown on the history of Bulgaria: overrun by the Ottoman Turks in the 1300's; ruled by the Turks for five hundred years; partially freed by the Russians in 1878—but lost a lot of land in the deal. Sort of independent in 1908. Two Balkan wars, in league with Greece, Serbia, and Montenegro, to drive out the remaining Turks and regain territory. Bad deal; lost even more land. Then made the mistake of siding with the Germans in World War II. Ended up a war trophy for the Russians in 1946. Total Communism by 1948. Say good-bye to the arts. Supervised religion. No private industry. State-run factories; mostly textiles and machinery. Leo said one out of five people in Bulgaria was employed by the government, which Leo said—*there*, included stores, restaurants, and hotels; almost everything was run by the state. (Was realizing that internationally, what I called a "country," was usually referred to as a "state.") I was anxious to see this type of society firsthand. Couldn't imagine too much going wrong as long as I was with Leo. (How the hell could I say that after my meal at that high, glass-walled Torretta Vetro where the bullet came through the window.) And I still didn't know who we were going to meet, or where, once after asking this question, I think Leo said some guy from the Russian embassy.

We're There!

Four o'clock and a bad touchdown, but we were on the ground—safe and sound (for the moment) in *Bulgaria!* The afternoon light was fading fast, could be dark in another hour. If this was the capital it must be a small country, or the airport's a long way from town. Couldn't see a city skyline. Fields with scrub pine on two sides. We walked on wet and crumbling tarmac—about fifty paces to the terminal building; a two story wood building painted a pale yellow. Sofia, Leo had said—just like the girl's name, but the sign over the balcony on the front of the terminal, in English characters, spelled out something slightly different—almost but not exactly "Sofia." Leo also told me that U.S. citizens were allowed to enter Bulgaria. I knew if he said it, it must be so, but it was definitely on the "banned" list posted on the ship, I knew that. *Whew!* Blind faith, that's what I needed now.

Sometimes a person can become so bogged down with their own affairs, they can't muster the energy to go that extra mile—especially for a disinterested employer. They're just concerned about getting through the day. That's the mood I felt was prevalent among the immigration officials here—half of them women; large, apparently well-fed, but with bad teeth and chapped skin. They had concerns enough of their own—you could just see that. Causing any trouble for us would have necessarily caused them trouble. If we got through, they got to go home. If we weren't an obvious problem, they weren't going to create a problem they might have to solve.

Leo had been here before. He told me that in most European countries, the usual procedure is for all entering foreigners to get a stamp in their passport—authorizing their stay. However on their return to the states, this record of entry could have serious consequences (like a fine, or even imprisonment) for a U.S. citizen who had visited a communist country. The Bulgarian officials, particularly the Ministry of Commerce, knowing this but needing the hard currency of U.S. and Western European businessmen, had developed an arrival procedure—a way they could control their borders and keep track of visitors, without discouraging the desired travelers. When Leo and I got to the desk, without even one question—in fact, barely a glance, the agent spied our U.S. passports and reached for a special pad of forms. Instead of permanently stamping a page in our passports, he gave us each a small piece of paper to insert in the passport. If we got stopped by any authorities during our visit, we just showed them the piece of paper. Upon departure we'd turn the paper in, and have a "clean" passport. No way to know we'd been to Bulgaria. *Cool.*

We were through and out onto the wet concrete walk in ten minutes. (No bags to claim.) Still one of my unfavorite gray and windy days. Leo hesitated just a moment under a galvanized metal awning (which was struggling against the wind to remain attached to its pipe framing). Seemed like he was sort of getting his bearings. Didn't know if we needed a cab, but I hoped not since there wasn't one in sight. In fact not a single car loading or unloading passengers. We could have easily been the only passengers, on the day's only flight. Couldn't see how we'd need a newspaper, but Leo bought one from some urchin whose whole outfit was obviously obtained piecemeal. Leo had Bulgarian currency, *and we hadn't yet changed any money.* (He even had coins). If I didn't feel it before this, which I had since Belgrade, there was no doubt I was standing on a street in a different world. Europe had already been so impressive, and now this; well I had a whole new baseline to judge my life and the world. A year ago I had never heard of St. Tropez, or Chateau Neuf du Pape, or Gunter Sachs, or the Via Veneto, or dreamed of going on a double-date with Maxmillan Schell, and now a trip to Bulgaria!

Leo was looking even more serious now, and getting philosophical. "Not real sure about this deal Roger. But I do know where this stuff will be going. I'm doing my part. Certain rules you can live by, no matter what you're doing in life. Doesn't even matter what you're doing. Lord knows I've done more than my share. How far to go? Who knows. What's right? By whose standards? You know what I say Roger?" I didn't answer. He continued. "It doesn't matter all that much where you draw the line in life, but once you've drawn it, can you stick to it? That's the question." I would have occasion to reflect on this more than once in the years to come (not to mention these past months)! We didn't spend much time in front of the terminal. Leo—now ahead of me, strode briskly across a puddled street and straight through an almost empty parking lot. Only a handful of cars. Once again all of them black and splattered with mud. Once out the other side of the lot Leo slowed to a normal gait—in fact now sort of casual, on a path that cut across a weeded lot. I was at Leo's side, *going I had no idea where.* It had been just misting, but now it was a full-fledged drizzle. (Shit, shades of my first evening on the famous Milan tour.)

In five minutes—only two hundred yards away from it, you would have never guessed there was an airport anywhere in the area. Empty wooded lots. Not a sound. Had to pee again, and noticed my teeth were clenched. Had a slight chill, even before one lone car went by too fast and too close, soaking my left trouser leg. Trudging along here now behind Leo, made me think about those great military leaders, who historians said, "the troops would follow straight through the gates of hell." That was me following Leo. He was motioning ahead, to a spot beyond a line of trees. Coming into view around a curve in the road and up a slight incline, I could see the outline of what could possibly be our destination. An old three-story wood-sided hotel; one that might have been a popular place in days gone by, but was now showing the consequences of years of inattention. "They'll be there; at least a driver. Should be. We're right on time. And I'll tell you Roger, some things work everywhere—and *being on time* is one of em goddamit." Leo was using more swear words than I had noticed before. (Sure hope he's not nervous.) Just then I felt his arm swing out across my body impeding my forward progress. "Let's make this dramatic. What time you got?" Told him my watch was showing about ten to five. "Slow up here. Turn in behind this truck. I told em 1700, and I wanna walk through that door when the minute hand is dead center on the black dot at the top!"

Down to Business

At three minutes of, we resumed our approach towards the Hotel Bryuksel; crossed the street and started up a narrow concrete walkway that led to the entrance. It was a long uphill trek, the hotel being situated atop a weedy bluff. There was a terrace in front. At least there was a cold and wet, twenty-foot by twenty-foot bare concrete slab. (No Cannes beach Carlton Hotel here I can tell you, but you had the feeling they knew it.) A peeling, white wood railing bordered the long-abandoned terrace, which looked all the more out of place in view of the gray skies and pelting rain. The once brightly paneled Campari umbrellas sticking up out of the tables, were now badly faded to a mottled pinkish-gray. Most were tied closed for obvious lack of sun and use (and to help avoid yanking the whole table over in a gust of wind).

Across the patio area now. Not level. Some sections were under water. Couldn't make it straight to the door. *Talk about an off-season resort.* Once again, no one in sight in front of the hotel or in the entrance. Almost dusk, some hard artificial illumination was spilling out from one lone chandelier just inside the foyer. I was nervous. Leo sensed it and gave me a short punch to the shoulder. It helped some. Immediately inside the unheated hotel was a well worn tiled area with a reception desk on the left, a few pieces of old furniture, and an open archway to our right. Leo almost stepped on my foot, turning in front of me towards it. I followed him into a formal but sparsely furnished sitting room. I spied two men standing against a dry fireplace on a far wall. They could not have looked more like they just popped out of a James Bond movie (indoors but still wearing low-brimmed hats and heavy coats). *Whew*. (Leo had made it; *exactly* five p.m.) Even if they did not know Leo—which I am not sure about yet, with

Leo there could be no mistaking, he was the "guy to be met."

They put down their teas (or vodka) or whatever they were sipping in small ceramic cups, and came forward to meet Leo. The small one, who I'm betting is the driver, held back just a bit behind the taller and younger guy, who I then noticed, had a thick cane, that he didn't seem to need. He spoke first.

"Mr. Lippe, I believe." (So far that part about none of them speaking English wasn't panning out; this guy spoke perfect English.)

"Yes, in person." I was anticipating a longer response by Leo. But that was it. Leo was right about the part of them not caring, or not asking about me. They didn't even look at me. Out of the corner of my eye, I could see two or three hotel employees now standing to the right of the reception desk. Their heads were lowered, but their eyebrows were raised and they were watching our every move. There were no hotel guests in sight. There was no bar or restaurant that I could see. No music. No sounds. The place was deserted. (Which considering the decor I'd observed so far, is exactly what the management should have expected.) The short guy, who was carrying a satchel in one hand, gestured with the other, to start with him towards the far side of the room. Leo did, and I with him, out a side door into a gravel parking lot.

There it was—the "getaway" car; an Al Capone, curtained, old black sedan. Since the two men appeared to be heading towards the front of the car, Leo and I steered towards the back. (I was right, the short guy was the driver.) Safely inside, Leo looked over, smiled, and clamped my leg. *Thank you very much*—the gesture was well needed about now. Any new thoughts were slung out the back of my head as the vehicle accelerated forward, then heeled left in a hard turn out of the lot. It was almost dark when we came out of the hotel, difficult to see well, and now from inside the car, with the tinted glass and curtained windows, I would have no idea whatsoever of the passing countryside. (Reminded me of the ride Belkis had taken me on to the empty hotel on the Bosporus.) Tried to imagine wooded areas streaking by, bridges or overpasses; strained to hear horns, or brakes, or other traffic. *Nothing.* In addition to being well sealed off visually, the muffled silence led me to believe we were in a sound-proofed vehicle. Of course no one spoke. Only two, maybe three stops. Must be even further in the country. Suddenly there was a marked deceleration, a turn, the gas applied, and I could feel us starting up an incline. A few seconds of this and it was all over. We were stopped. Engine off. Doors opening. Heart pounding.

As dark as it was when I climbed out of the car, it appeared almost bright in comparison to the last thirty minutes in the back seat. I stepped out onto a graveled surface, glancing quickly across the roof to see Leo's direction. *That's good, he's coming around to my side.* We were in a private drive; a curving, tree-hidden drive in front of an old house—a big, gaunt, empty-looking house with a large barren porch. No curtains or shades on any of the windows. Inside, harsh incandescent light was hitting hard on bare plaster walls. We were to the steps, then up and onto the porch, then in through the wide-open double front doors. The house appeared to be abandoned, or at least unlived in. Inside, there was a room to our right, without a stick of furniture. Scarred wood floors. Old fashioned fixtures. Exposed wiring and electric sockets like I'd never seen. And I was beginning to notice, no heat again.

Leo paused and I almost walked up his back. The two men in front of us had turned left into a ground floor room just ahead, and indicated to Leo to wait in the hallway. I could hear them talking inside, in fact arguing. No idea what language they were speaking. One guy popped his head out the doorway and motioned us in. I followed, closely. The room was about twenty feet square with a yellowed ceiling light. Once again, no curtains, no shades, no pictures on the wall. This was a vacant house, no question about it. Leo was led to a lone, straight back wooden chair, dead center in the room, and motioned to take a seat. His chair faced a long table in front of a wall with two big windows through which I could view the porch we had just come up on. Besides Leo's chair and the table, there was not another stick of furniture in the room. There were no chairs at the table, just two men standing behind it. I could only see their torsos. A pool table-type lamp with a large metal shade hung from the ceiling, shielding their faces from view. Two other guys were standing against one side wall, and two more alongside me on the wall with the door we had just come through. I don't know that I had ever been more apprehensive—more in doubt and less in control than right now.

It was not a comfortable feeling, peering into the darkness outside, knowing that anyone outside could easily see into this well-lit room. If there were any spectators outside (and you were just sure there were), we were on display. *Easy targets.* The guy behind the table offered Leo a cigarette. He waved it off politely, crossed his legs and adjusted that great camel hair topcoat. One of the guys against the side wall was motioned into the hallway. He never returned. Another moved to the table and laid a folder on it, in front of the person still standing. He never looked at it. Then he addressed Leo, without any small talk (no *How's the wife and kids?* or, *How was the flight over?)* he got right down to business. "Mr. Lippe, we have done business with you before, never any problem. As you know, we have something now, of considerable value. We are sure you will be satisfied. We have made a count you can rely on. We have inspected many pieces. Everything is exactly as we represented. There is no problem with delivery to Brindisi. We can seal this transfer without delay."

Leo spoke: "I believe you. I have no reason from our past association to expect any deviations. But, Mikael, your price is way off base; no way I can do that." There was an awkward pause after Leo finished (though I think they were familiar with Leo and were expecting he wouldn't just roll over with the first deal). Even so, they were obviously a bit perturbed. Expressions of indignation were exchanged, a couple harumphs, and some paper shuffling. Leo continued before they had a chance to speak. "Now I know what these are worth. You know what they can bring, *if* you can find someone to take the whole batch. I can and will, but at nine dollars a gun—nine greenbacks Mikael, and that's fair." The look on Mikael's face, which I could now see, convinced me he was not so sure. He did not seem at all pleased with this offer. I had no idea what price he had conveyed to Leo earlier, or any idea of what would constitute a fair price.

"Mr. Lippe you are not our first choice. We are only just making life easy for ourselves. The Chinese will give us twelve dollars a gun, and the North Vietnamese about the same. And we have two other potential customers as well. We are not in trouble here, believe me as well."

With this—and I will never forget it, while I was pinned to the wall, wide-eyed and almost peeing in my drawers, I watched and listened, as Leo from his isolated "hot seat" in the middle of the room, responded:

"Listen, would I be sitting here, 65 years old, with enough money in the bank, to write you guys a check for $900,000—that you know is good, if I spent my whole life believing shit like that?"

Kheerist! In a matter of seconds Leo had switched the mood from one of strained tolerance, to one of antagonism. One, that I didn't think we were well-placed to be involved in, let alone initiate. Leo, ten feet from anyone or anything, seated in the center of the uncarpeted, dusty wood-floored room, was a voice from an island. They had him positioned like a suspect being grilled down at the precinct. He had taken the disadvantageous seat all right, but he was not playing the part of any captive, that was for sure. Mikael pointed down at the stack of papers in front of him and said that it would please them perfectly to accept the other offers.

At this, Leo further prejudiced our well-being by replying in the most nonchalant manner: "Mikael, why don't you go down the hall, have a smoke, wash your face, change your shirt, put on a new tie, and come back down here. And I'll make believe you never said that. Nine dollars, take it or leave it. I don't need them either."

Holy Shit!

A conference ensued behind the table. From my vantage point I now could not see their faces due to the hanging lamp. Another guy strode in the room from out of nowhere. This had to be the head guy. The way I figured it, right about now we were two against at least six; at an unknown location in a communist country! The new entry paused just a second as he went past Leo's chair—I thought, to extend a greeting. And maybe that was his original intent, however he must have thought better of it, and resumed his stride straight to the table. After fifteen minutes of subdued conversations behind the table, the deal was closed. Leo didn't write a check for the whole amount, but he did give them what I guess was sufficient for an initial payment, at his proposed nine dollars a gun. No one left the room until some papers were signed. I could see it was over. There were no handshakes. There was no obvious lessening of the tension. But it was over. No ceremony. Nothing. In two minutes we were back in the car. (Actually not the same car.) Only a driver this time. We were on our way. This car had a ceiling light. It was on, and no switch to turn it off; it stayed on the whole time to the airport. Leo just looked straight ahead. Might have been something in this deal he wasn't real happy with. I would never know what. And I would never know who he had purchased the guns for. He had demonstrated his patriotism that late night at his apartment, and I was sure if not for the U.S. government, at least it would not be detrimental to the United States. He never brought it up again.

A Regret That Never Leaves You

The flights back, the airports, the drive to 16 Piscale Brescia—all uneventful. It was over. A late pasta meal (this time Winona played the chef). Heartfelt intimacies were exchanged and a silent bond was understood. The parting in the morning was with full knowledge of my shortly forthcoming departure back across the Atlantic. Leo had taken a liking to me and it was possible there could be something else coming. It was as if—in spite of all the obstacles, Leo and I could someday be a team; that we'd see each other many times in the years to come. In the meantime I'd have the Super Dakota to take out and fondle from time to time, the memories of Winona and "Flipper," the books on armor, and live to tell his stories a thousand times. But I'd never see Leo again.

Chapter Twenty-Six
PALMA DE MAJORCA

A Serious Monkey Wrench In My Plans

No question about it, this thing was just about over. The Russians hadn't called our bluff. We were all still here. (At least in body.) Still doing our formation, navigation, and special weapons training flights. Bob put up a flight schedule and we responded, albeit now in an android fashion. No way we could show the red white and blue "teeth-to-the-bit" attitude we had upon arriving. Although I'm sure that now, even in our present state of mind we would have been a lot more effective than during the first few months of the cruise (and *should* be after all this time). But it was over. No soviet ships, no impending war, no reason to bomb the Eastern Bloc into rubble. We'd done what we were supposed to do, no doubt about it. For ten months we had been the threat of horrible and instant retaliation. (If I'd been the Russians, I'd have been real worried.) We knew what we were supposed to do, we were capable of doing it, and we would've done it. But now it's time for reflection. Nostalgia time. (And I could tell; not just for me, some others had been bitten.) A lot of people were just putting in time.

Four more days of flight ops. I mean four more days before they're over *for good!* The way it stood now, we were scheduled to drop anchor off Palma, Majorca on Friday morning. Be moored there for one last 36-hour liberty *and no longer*, because on midnight Saturday we'd up-anchor and steam northward, up and around the island to the spot I first laid eyes on the European landscape. Remember? Polensa Bay. There—Sunday we'd have the famous "Change of Command" ceremony. Except this time we'd be the *Saratoga;* the old hands—the veterans, turning the task over to some new guys just arriving. That same afternoon—as soon as the ceremony was complete, it'd be over. We'd turn tail and run. One week from right now would see us steaming southward, to round the corner of Spain, steer for the Straits of Gibraltar, through them, and across the Atlantic, back home. *You think the thought of that didn't strike fear in my heart?*

Regarding our scheduled brief stop in Majorca, I had big plans, very big plans. Having known about it early enough I had set up a tentative rendezvous with June. It would be our last meeting in Europe—a goodbye; perhaps a *final* goodbye. Arriving in Palma I was going to hit the beach as soon as the anchor chain got wet, hail a cab to the airport and catch the first plane back to the mainland—a thirty minute flight to my beloved Barcelona where June was still dancing. The visit would be short, hectic, and require precise timing. (But Lord knows I'd been doing that the whole cruise.) I'd have Friday afternoon and Friday night and most of the day Saturday with June and the girls. I absolutely *had* to be back here in Palma by Saturday evening, that was for sure! It wasn't going to be much time, but at least it would be one more time together. I'd fly from Barcelona back to Palma about six Saturday evening, catch a quick cab to the dock, leap aboard my last liberty boat, thump my way out to the carrier, and drag myself aboard—ready to accept my fate. Meanwhile, keep up the good work, tour the shops, check the work orders, talk to the men; make sure I hang in there. Can't slack off now. Made it this far, just keep on plugging. I know what I'm doing when I'm on board. It's working. Can't complain.

To pull off this 36-hour whirlwind—with a round-trip airfare and first class hotel, I was going to need some extra cash. Stopped by the ship's Disbursing Office (luckily getting there two minutes before the cashier's cage was going to close). Hated to write another check—knew it had to be looking fishy back on the home front. Inside the cage was a real squared-away black guy I had see around the ship often. His name tag said Lieutenant Hal Jennings. Gave him my ID card and the check I'd written. He verified a couple things and began counting out the money. I waited, my mind more than arm's length from my body. When I glanced back into the cage, Hal was looking up at me with a real weird expression; a combination of discovery and irritation. His eyebrows came up, and pointing one finger at me he blurted out: "So, you're the guy! Now I know—*you're* the guy!" Of course I had no idea what "being the guy" meant.

"Whaddaya mean, I'm the guy?"

"That tune. That damned song you're singing."

Stopped to think for a second, and realized that while I was waiting I had been humming the melody of June's and my now favorite song, "You're My World." The one we'd heard on the TV that first night in the ram shackled seaside hotel in Valencia. The song she'd bought the 45 RPM record of in Barcelona.

"Yeah" he continued, "You're the guy that keeps walking past my stateroom at two in the morning; no—*five* in the morning, waking me up singing that damn tune. I recognize it now."

Thursday evening. Tomorrow would be the day. *God*. Could hardly taste my supper. Kept losing track of conversations. I was more than a little uptight—thinking about so many things, from what I wanted to say to June to what I'd pack to make the best impression. (Only going to get this one last chance to make one.) And more particularly, what I could do to make sure there was no screw-up in the flights I had to catch to pull this thing off. No way to get ahold of an Iberia flight schedule, just had to hope there were frequent flights from Palma on the island of Majorca, to Barcelona on the mainland. June had said they might even go every hour. I hope so, 'cause I'll need every break I can get. I can tell you, I was in some state.

The Worst Possible News

And that was *before* the captain's meeting. *Mandatory!* That's the word the speaker kept blaring out. 2000 hours, on the hangar deck—every single hand that wasn't actually keeping the ship afloat. An important announcement was going to be made by the ship's captain. Probably some "well-dones" and presentations handed out. Oh well, none of us had much to do anyway. I filed up the aft passageway with Tripp and Ernie. They were glad to see the cruise winding down. Good guys. We kidded a little bit. (Not something that was easy for me at this time.) But I hung in there. The hangar deck had been marked with colored tape to specify which units assembled where. Met Jim and the other guys in our designated area, just two areas back from a big platform that had been set up near midship.

I must say, a pretty well disciplined bunch. A couple thousand guys and only a minor din. The ship's captain was on the platform with all the ship's departmental commanders, and the tactical squadron commanders as well. Saw our skipper up there with him. (Couldn't miss him, six-foot five.) I was right. A whole bunch of statistics: number of sorties flown, flight hours, bombs dropped, etc. Then a long string of congratulations and unit awards. The ship's captain read a laudatory message that had been received from the Secretary of the Navy. Lots of good news. (No reference to the kid killed on the aft elevator, or Norm Lundquist.) Some plaques handed out. More handshakes. A brief address by the ship's captain. I'd only seen him a half dozen times the whole cruise; no reason to—he was up in his quarters or on the bridge the whole time. He didn't eat with us. (That's a joke)

I tried to pay attention. The ship's captain's few words were more of the same, and as expected—real nice. That is to say, *real nice up until the part that froze the blood in my veins!* It was our last in-port visit. (I knew that.) We had completed a whole ten month Med Cruise without losing a single hand to the temptations of the Cote d'Azur, the Greek Isles, the bazaars of Turkey, or the girls of Naples. The ship's captain was about to make a "first": *Returning home with all hands; not losing even one sailor to the temptations of the Continent.* This being the case (a perfect record up to this time), he was not about to let some guy with a latent wanderlust screw it up on our last in-port. So, during this two day stay, no one, repeat—*no one was going to be allowed to leave the city limits of Palma!*

I couldn't believe my ears. I was stunned—reeling. I felt as if the ship's captain had known the urgency of my plans, he would have never considered such a restriction. My ears were ringing. It was almost impossible for me (knowing how this decree would ruin everything for me) to comprehend the lack of concern displayed by everyone else. How come there were no screams and moans, no outrage or indignation? Guess it didn't make much difference to anyone else. (Who else would have had plans to catch a flight out of Palma?) I knew Ernie was saying something to me, but while I could see his lips moving, no sound was making its way to my brain. *Holy Shit, what now?*

I knew one thing. I better not ask the Skipper if he would grant me an exception (to leave not only the city of Palma, but the island itself), because if he didn't and I still went, *whoaa*—I'd really be asking for it: Direct disobedience. Better not say a damn thing. Don't force him to either be an accomplice or say no. Certainly not going to mention it to Jim either. I got my one day, plus Tripp's. I'm covered for both days. No bed check for officers. Won't matter if I'm not back on board until just before the up-anchor. I'm going to have to go for it. Nothing else I can do. Finish packing and hit the rack. Thought I might be a little nauseous.

Took a long time to fall asleep. In the morning, in the head doing that morning stuff, I heard the familiar deep metallic rattling of the anchor chain rumbling through the ship. Finished shaving, got my things. My heart was racing. Back to the stateroom. Small bag—not too noticeable. Down to the wardroom. A brunch—a big one. Managed to miss almost everyone, so no explanations were necessary. (Though by the harried look in my eyes, people were probably afraid to ask if I had any plans.) Back in the stateroom packing, Jim pops in and tells me we have to get down to the Ready Room right away. In addition to anchoring two hours late, we had to attend *another* mandatory meeting with our Skipper. Attended it. Mostly a waste of time. He just reiterated the Captain's message from the previous day. Then, *somebody up there hates me!* To add insult to injury, all the officers were told to schedule a meeting with their enlisted charges, and repeat the restriction to them!

It was 1345 before I got to the liberty ladder. Down it—two at a time, and into my bumping, salty escape craft. Once again, overnight bag in my hand, heart in my throat, face into the wind, I was closing in on a strange shoreline. This time the frivolity, if there ever was any—was missing. Just deadly intent this time. I was not someone to be fooled with.

A Clandestine Flight to Barcelona

I guess you can understand there was no way I could convince myself this last rendezvous with June could be cancelled. No way. But in carrying it out, I was sure going to have to cover my ass. The Captain's edict and the Colonel's reinforcement of it was going to require some serious decoying, like renting a hotel room (I wouldn't use) here in Palma, so it would *look* like I was staying in the city, and be sure my squadron knew. Ashore on the dock now—facing a long block of buildings, I spied a four or five star hotel about a half mile down the strand. Jogged the distance. Worked up a nice sweat. Time's the issue here. Gotta keep moving. Real late. More of a businessman's hotel than a resort hotel. Across the street from a municipal beach. (The good beaches were never inside the city limits.) Straight to Reception. Got a room. In the elevator. Up to room 227. One of the most inviting rooms I'd seen yet. Cheerfully decorated with rattan furniture and floral print pastel cottons. Across an expanse of polished Saltillo tiles there was a set of wooden-shuttered doors that opened onto a balcony. Soft sunlight was filtering through their louvers and adding to the luster of the terra cotta floor. This was one of the neatest hotel rooms I'd seen to date (and I wasn't even going to use it).

Now to work. Make sure it *looks* like I'm staying here! Pulled the spread down and wrinkled the sheet. Phoned the desk and left an early call for the morning. Turned on the TV—not too loud, but audible. Took some extra clothes, stuffed them in a plastic laundry bag and left it on the doorknob. Looks good. Hang a pair of swim trunks over the shower curtain. Get the hotel number, so I could call from Barcelona and check for messages from the squadron. A look around. Can't think of anything else. That's it. *I'm outta here!*

Had a cab in three minutes. In the airport parking lot ten minutes later. If I thought the terminal building in Munich was small, this one was tiny. Reminded me of a concession stand at a lake. The building was on some kind of inlet or sea water canal that ran twenty feet from it. Single story. Wood-sided. Inside it was just one large room. Searching for the "domestic" counter. Oops, *think it's all domestic.* Not much of a crowd at the counter. Got a ticket for the four o'clock flight. So far so good (but at least three hours behind schedule). The flight was called and I was out onto the ramp, on board and on my way; excited, nervous, optimistic and aware of an increasing sadness, all at the same time. The flight was uneventful.

Forty minutes later, touched down in Barcelona. Bigger airport here, but the terminal was still vintage; a long, one-storied, one-room building. Once inside, looking out through the row of small windows at the front, I could see the sidewalk, a couple buses, and the familiar row of waiting taxis. No line. Got the first one and was on my way. Unfortunately it was about five-thirty and the traffic was pretty bad. Miraculously made it downtown in less than fifteen minutes. Had him take me to the Manila hotel, where June and I had spent the night our last time together, and where I was going to register now, for tonight. *Funny how you keep coming back to places where you feel safe.* So far the Manila had been good to me. It was on a corner at the top of Las Ramblas, and built right up to the very edge of the street. It was so close to the sidewalk, walking along I could reach out and run my fingers along the faded green shingles. It was only five stories. The restaurant was on the top floor, right above where I was walking. Its roofline was uniquely architectured with spires and gables facing in all directions. Continuing along the front of the hotel, I passed a large residential style bay window, through which I observed gray suited reception clerks and white jacketed bellmen busily engaged pleasing the guests. Two steps past it—the main entrance. No larger or better marked than your front door. The hotel was moderately expensive, but not prohibitively so (at least in these times).

I GUESS I JUST WASN'T THINKING

Got a room again (two now, in the same afternoon). My American Express card was smoking. Up to the second floor. Along the dark green carpeting; 219, 217, should be a couple more. There it is. Into my home away from home for the next twenty-two hours. Dropped my gear, washed my face and hands. Took a deep breath (my first this day) and sat down at the phone. Called June's number but no answer. Geez, that doesn't make sense. They shouldn't have left for the theater yet. Tried again, no luck. Another cab. (I may have been the best thing that ever happened to the Barcelona taxi drivers.) I was at June's apartment at seven, but found the metal gate locked up tight. Hard to believe. No way to buzz the apartment, or anybody. *I'm screwed.* Such big plans, and here I am—alone in an abandoned neighborhood, standing in some dry grass by a peeling wall, collar up against the wind. The last bit of sunlight was trying to warm the stuccoed privacy wall (keeping me out). Looked at my eerie shadow altered across some mounds of trash in the weeds. *It'll get better.*

Suppose I could wait at the theater, or check out the little restaurant nearby—knew they often stopped in there before a performance. Went both places. Nothing. Made a couple trips back and forth. Still nothing. Waited till seven-forty. No luck. Wasting more valuable time. I was visualizing all sorts of catastrophes (like maybe the ballet contract had been terminated and the girls were sent back to London). No, no sense thinking that. It was more than just dusk now. It was dark, with an increasingly persistent wind. Alone and unsure, the city had turned hard and unknown. *Got an idea!* One that ended up using every minute till show time. Flagged another cab and again began my search for a flower shop. Up and down lots of streets I'd never seen before. Headlights, stop lights, newspapers blowing against the curb, coat hems turned up. Maybe because June and I were apart, things weren't looking soft or familiar. Found myself in a remote and strange section of town. Bound to find a flower shop soon. *There's one, gotta be.*

Inside, wasn't too hard to find a nice bouquet. Could have done it even quicker except for all the help I was getting. But there was something more. I had another idea; one that was going to make this floral delivery even more special. Rummaging through the back of the store I located some cardboard and aluminum foil. On the cardboard I drew a big star, as best I could. It didn't receive rave reviews. The manager of the shop, his wife, and the cabdriver all took a shot at drawing one, being most vocal when someone else was doing the outline. (Major competition developed between the cabdriver and the owner's wife; was afraid it could turn mean.) Lots of critiquing. *Man, let's go, I'm in a hurry*. Finally a star was produced that merited a 3/4 majority. *We'll go with it.* Cut it out, *stay on the lines*, make nice points. Held it up. It looked symmetric. Onto the next task: cover it in the foil. Glue didn't work, but we solved our problem with small bits of scotch tape. Then, with a purple magic marker and my growing Spanish vocabulary, I printed the inscription: *Una estrella para la estrella*. (A star for the star.)

Flower shop guy said no problem having it delivered. I handed over the Pesetas and detailed instructions on how to get to the theater (and a diagram showing the exact location of the artists' entrance). They would have it delivered real official-like. Some emotional good-byes. Into the cab. To the theater. Same identical show. Great again, but long. I was anxious, not knowing when June would actually get the flowers. (And I didn't really expect she'd dance onto the stage carrying a big sign saying, "I got them.") And she would have no idea where I was sitting tonight— couldn't give me a signal. When the curtain finally whipped closed I was a nervous wreck. Out of the seat. Out of the theater. Around the side and to the artists' entrance. The elderly lady in the guard booth (with the same knitting) had not forgotten the jerky young American who had popped in and out of this door just a few weeks ago. I was comforted to be waved in with a big smile, but I winced with both pride and worry when she referred to me as June's *novio*. In Spanish, *novio* means "fiancé." To the Spaniards—of a more serious courting tradition, *we were engaged*. And I would find, that the girls (perhaps with high hopes for their captain) were more than ready to refer to me using this term; trying it out, and hoping it could be said loudly and with assurance. As if in using it and seeing me accept its usage, the outcome would be even more likely. I could see they wanted to believe that good, true, and lasting things did happen to girls on the road, far from home. Not just another on and off, hot and cold affair.

Down to the first landing, then the second flight of steps, and into that same wide hallway (which I realized was a no longer used practice stage). In range now, I became aware of what I can best describe as "howling." The girls were laughing uproariously behind their leaning and oft-punctured privacy partition. Boy, could they have fun.

"June! It's me, Rog."

Once again she was out in two shakes, with a giant hug, and a half dozen of those kisses again. She was barely holding the tears back, but not because she was so glad to see me; rather because the night's big incident had them all laughing to the point of crying. June filled me in while the other girls added small details. Seems when the flowers arrived, the Spanish stagehands saw the silver star and the inscription, and just assumed it was for Lola. (Tony's leading lady with the huge bazooms.) The whole Comedia cast (including the Stafford ballet) was crowded around her as she admired the bouquet, and the star and the inscription. But her delight was short-lived, when surrounded by all her lady and gentlemen cast members, she opened the envelope and saw my note to June! And realized the flowers were not for her, *they were for the red-headed Inglesa!?*

At this point in our relationship, with the precious little time we had remaining, we were going to have to get some place alone—quick. There were lots of things to talk about. (Not that I was yet ready to tackle that task.) The future was something I just had no idea about. I was on shaky ground in every respect: my wife, my family, my job, the Marine Corps—the course my life would take. One thing though, I *had* heard from Air America. My letter had been received at the US Embassy in Saigon and some good soul actually got it to the Air America offices at Tan Son Nhut airport. They in turn sent it back to the Air America personnel offices on 1725 K street, NW. (About the best performance by the US Postal Service I'd seen to date.) Regarding the Air America response, I was somewhat disappointed by its non-committal nature. I don't know what I thought they'd say, especially since in my inquiry I didn't say I was planning on leaving the Corps and wanted a job; more that I was just interested in some details, and not necessarily available right now. (And from them, no reference to that fantastic pay scale I'd heard about.)

I know June and I could have done whatever we would have liked, but the girls really wanted us to join them. The smash new rock group—the "Animals" were in town as part of their European tour. (The Animals were the rage in the states with their number one song, "House of the Rising Sun.") They were going to have a party at one of the hotels tonight, and somewhere they had met the girls and invited the entire troupe to the bash. June and I considered for a moment. Quarter past one... *Yeah sure, we can make it."* At least for a little while. Two cabs chock full. Same kind of ride. Same utterly delightful chatter. These girls had some attitude. (Could liquefy them and inject the serum on a manic depressive ward.) And once again I was buried in the back with the same bodies, buttocks and legs pressed against me. Same sweet hair swishing in my face. Same scene I would remember with great nostalgia for years to come. I think in addition to my new and good feelings for June, I was infatuated with the group as a whole.

Only a short ride. Ten minutes later, in a mostly residential and uncrowded area of town, we stopped in front of a modest, wood-sided, three story hotel. I would have expected a downtown, stainless steel and glass Sheraton for these guys. Out of the cab. Onto the property. Several of the girls made a farce out of racing each other—running *backwards,* up the narrow sidewalk to the entrance. Through the lobby, out the back door and then onto the grassy area surrounding the pool. Was surprised to see a series of kid's swings and play-set. *What the heck kind of hotel is this for a rock group?* Evidently the Animals had not had a performance tonight (or it was an early one), since they were already here, strewn all over the area. Through the eyes of a USMC captain, they were one motley-looking gaggle. The clothing (what bits of it they had on) was loud and boldly striped. Long straggly hair. Heavy boots with garish buckles. But what was I expecting? However I must admit, after the introductions and just a few minutes with the group, I found them willing and able to carry on reasonable conversations.

There was a big ice bucket stuffed with San Miguel beers and another with tall bottles of Rosé wine; most the girls were availing themselves of the wine. I had noticed during previous outings, that while all the girls drank I had never seen one of them drunk. On their way maybe, but not out of hand. Seemed they really policed each other in this area (or maybe they just watched their P's and Q's in front of June). I had a beer. In spite of the temperature the girls had been instructed to bring their bathing suits along. By now I was on a friendly first name basis with most of the girls. Especially June's best two friends, Laurie and Wendy—who did come over and sit with us. Laurie was excited, she was about to return for that record deal, and Wendy had a new boyfriend. But I hadn't seen Claire.

"June, where's Claire tonight, she used to always tag along with us."

"Tell'm Captain. I told you so."

"Roger, do you remember the Lebanese club?"

"Sure."

"And that Italian band? Remember Carlo—the singer, he came over to where we were sitting?"

Yeah I remembered him all right—that hoarse-voiced, macho guy with the long hair and thick lips, with the silk shirt open to his navel, and tight trousers. (He was the guy I wanted to swap with for about a year.) "Yeah June, I remember. He was the guy Claire was sweet on, right? And she stayed after we left."

"Yes, that's him." June went on to tell me that Claire was infatuated with this guy, almost his love slave; used to embarrass the girls by describing how he made such beautiful love to her. She moved in with him. It was all the girls could do to keep her coming to practices and arriving at the theater on time. Then one night one of the girls coming home about three in the morning, passes Claire on a street corner—doing what women do on a street corner at that hour. Obviously they accosted her and brought her to their apartment. They called up June, who came right over. They had an all-night session. *What the hell was going on!?* Claire told them: *Carlo had put her out.*

I responded naively, "You mean he kicked her out, and she was afraid to come back, and had no money, and was walking the streets?"

"No Roger. *He* put her there. She was doing it for *him!* We told her that she was crazy! That this wouldn't work." With tears streaming down her cheeks Claire had told the girls it was only temporary—that they *both* were doing extra things, *Carlo was too!* This way they could build their nest egg quicker—have enough money to leave Spain. He was going to return with her to England! Of course shortly after this everything came apart—finished. Claire got worse and worse. One of the girls escorted her back to England. I didn't know then, still don't now—how a woman can love a man who asks her to prostitute herself; for *whatever* reason. But I would go on to learn, among some of the harder-pressed in these late night circles, this was *not* so uncommon.

In the middle of a conversation with the drummer about socialized medicine, I heard a big splash. One of the guys had leaped into the pool—*naked*. Uh oh, hope this doesn't catch on. Could get ugly, at least for me. (I was small enough without shrinking up further.) I got a chill just thinking of the temperature of that water. I knew I wasn't in favor of joining in any water sports, especially as a skinny-dipper. So far (thank God) the girls weren't joining in. Oops, another guy leaped in off a life guard stand. Two in now. Now they're tugging one of the girls—the Irish one. And she was in. Not naked, but just bra and panties (red and green). One more guy and another girl. Fortunately that was to be the evening's sum total of participants. (No wonder, considering the temperature.) The Animals had arranged for an outdoor barbeque, and the hotel staff did a good job of it.

I was starved and so everything tasted great. They played all their records, loud enough that if there were any kids in the hotel, they were up now. Surprisingly no one came out to tell us to shut up.

One Last Visit to the Manila Hotel

Half-past two June and I said our good-byes. Only had to wait about ten minutes for a cab. Another ten minutes and we were at the Manila. In the elevator, up, and into our room. Safe. The one fringed porcelain lamp I had purposely left on was spreading a warm glow. We were in our own soft and comfy space. June put down her things, came over, gave me a kiss and went into the bath. I plopped down in a big over-stuffed chair to wait, nervously (for a handful of reasons—the end in sight, hard explanations; the whole situation). *Just rest a few minutes while you have the chance.* I was aware of heavy complex feelings, overcome by confusion, frustration, my usual shortcoming, and an awareness of just what a mess I'd gotten myself into (not to mention June)! For the first time I could remember, it was as if I needed a good cry—like I actually might be able to do it if I let myself. I think I wanted to. But I didn't.

June was out of the bathroom, wearing the same comfy old bathrobe I'd seen before (the one she wore putting on her stage makeup). Before I could get up from the big leather chair I'd collapsed into, she dropped down on the carpet alongside me, looking up at me with the most loving and trusting look one could imagine. She had a hair brush in her hand. I don't know what possessed me. I didn't ask, I just sort of took it from her hand and began to brush that long red hair. I did it for quite a while. Not speaking. The look I was getting from her continued. A look I did not deserve, but one that tore at my soul. The warmth and hope in her eyes that moment is indelible in my mind today. But I had to get to the task at hand. A wonderful kiss and I was out of the chair and to the bathroom myself. Finished, I was afraid to come out; nervous about the coming physical intimacy and dreading the requirements of the conversation that would soon have to occur. We were in bed and I was a "basket case." Considering my condition, if there was one place I should have been, this was it—flat on my back in bed. But probably alone. I didn't know about June. I'll bet she could have stayed up all night and talked, but (maybe just to keep from putting me on the spot) she feigned exhaustion as well. She *had* to be expecting some explanations, some hint of a plan. But I offered nothing, and even I knew that's the one thing I should have been doing. I owed it to her. I had nothing of value to say. *I hated myself.* Whatever her thoughts, she didn't verbalize them. Guessed she could endure most anything with nary a word. We were together, but in silence. I couldn't bring myself to sort anything out; tell her anything, or ask her anything. I was a mute.

Once again not proud of myself. She was passively warm and yielding, accepted me in spite of my insufficiency, registered no dissatisfaction. I was equally unspectacular, as in Valencia and here a month ago. And now, the one time I would have given anything for a landmark performance— for a miracle, I failed. I was again, as almost every time I could remember, absent of lust or passion (when in my heart there was more concern, more feelings of love and respect than I'd ever had). And, a big problem: I'd previously concluded that my repeated sexual exploits were to find that one female who would excite and entreat me; finally turn the key! But here I am in this new and wonderful relationship with June, *and she is not that woman!* What would our future be? Would my inability to provide the release and pleasure she deserves, sooner or later cause sufficient disappointment and dissatisfaction to thwart the love and respect she now gives so freely. And equally important—not yet having found "that" woman, would everything else good about June be enough for me to give up on my search? I'd have to, no way I could hurt June. Really confused. For sure there was at least one tear in my eye when I slipped off into a fitful sleep.

Don't think I'd ever slept till eleven in my life. But that's what I was reading on my watch. June wasn't stirring, appeared to be still asleep. Looked like she'd just laid down five minutes ago—her head motionless on an undisturbed pillow. I watched her for a few minutes. I was startled as in the midst of my examination of her face, one eye suddenly popped open and she was staring straight into my face. She opened the other eye and a wonderful, easy and comfortable smile spread across her face. I felt her hand move under the sheet (scaring me), but she was just searching for my hand. There was no tension, no threat, no regret on her face. It was the most reassuring countenance I'd seen, and exactly what I needed. I felt a hundred pounds fly off my shoulders. *Could she ease my life or what?*

A placard in the room advertised a celebrated brunch being offered in that upstairs wood-floored, gabled restaurant. We took advantage of it. Made our selections and carried our plates to a vacant table in one of those private (six-foot across) rooftop spires. I guess the food was good. As you might imagine I couldn't taste anything. Out the circle of windows we were able to survey our city of Barcelona. My *plan* was, in view of last night's inexcusable lack of communication, to try to bring things out in the open now—right here this morning. *Be a man about it.* Have an appropriate and overdue discussion of our (my) situation. Try—at least *try*, to verbalize some possible eventualities. *What* eventualities? I knew for our relationship to have any chance at all, painful and almost unimaginable changes would have to be brought about in my life. I felt increasingly unwell in the face of the reality I was now considering. Up to this point I had brushed aside and postponed confronting it; those steps that would be involved, and what they would mean to my wife, and kids, and mother and father. My tact always was, *quick, think of something else!*

I barely have the courage to admit it, but I failed again here in this restaurant, to properly take advantage of what might be our last opportunity to get anything resolved. Oh I started several times (a lot of times) but I didn't commit to anything. I vacillated, got off on tangents, spoke in abstracts, kept finding myself off track. June watched and listened patiently. *God bless her.* Never asked any hard questions (ones she had every right to ask). Instead she just waited for me to say something that would make some sense. I don't think I ever did. As close as it came, we once talked about her starting a dance school in the states. (Leaving it not real clear *how* it would come to pass that she would be in the states.) Brunch was finished and we were back up in the room. A little past noon.

I don't know if it was the late night, too much breakfast, or the mental burden and efforts at decision-making, but I was overcome by a great weariness as soon as the door was closed behind us. June encouraged me to rest. She allowed me to escape, close my eyes (and let the real world slip by without an attempt to sort it out). She sat down on the edge of the bed, but we were both fully dressed, and I don't think either of us saw any need to try for one last solidifying union. Lying on my back exhausted and looking straight up at the ceiling, I felt as if the skin on the sides of my face was going to sag and drain off onto the pillow, till just a skull was left. June stroked my forehead for a while, then laid down beside me. I fell into a deep sleep. Don't know if June slept. I could have slept a week.

Woke from a dream, into what in a few weeks, could *itself* be no more than a dream. Checking my watch I saw that I had only an hour and forty minutes to make my flight back to Palma. *Have to get moving.* Like a punch-drunk fighter with one elbow on the canvas trying to get a knee under his weight, I struggled. I was exhausted from talking without saying anything, avoiding explaining away what truthfully had a very simple explanation (but one I was too cowardly to verbalize). For ten months I had either been keyed on my own plight, or on how all of this would effect Sara. But I never considered how it could affect anyone on this side of the Atlantic.

Whatever had been said, had been said. No more hypothesizing. And by now you know that June was not a "what if" type person. My ramblings and maybes must have been very frustrating to her. I had proven my weakness. I failed to make a commitment. Whatever I could do with my life, I'd do it. Nothing more could be accomplished now. *Whew, running out of time!* Dialed up the main desk. "Yes. Checkout? Thanks. Room 227. And I'm going to need a quick checkout. Will be down in five minutes. Please have the bill all ready. Yes, I'll use American Express. That's right. Yes I think so. One night, a dinner at the restaurant. Sounds right. And one more charge in the coffee shop? Okay, don't remember, no, that's fine. See you in five minutes."

As I moved about the room gathering my belongings, June sat erect on the bed, back upright against the headboard, not moving, not blinking. The dark green colors of her plaid slacks and an olive turtle-neck contrasted prettily with her fair skin and red hair. Her lips were drawn tight, arms folded across her chest, long legs stretched out in front of her, one ankle over the other. No doubt about it, she was a handsome young woman. Sure would have liked to know what thoughts were going through her sweet head. (Sure would have liked to have understood what thoughts were in my own head.) I had everything. Checked the bathroom one more time. *That's it.* Everything into the bag. June watched— watched every move I made, as if she was taking photos with her eyes and storing them away. No tears, no asking for promises. She was a real trooper that was for sure. I think—ready for the worst, and afraid to hope for the best. Soon as the last item was packed, we made for the door; out of our little world, in the hall, down the steps, and into the lobby. .

I was carrying my bag and the 45 RPM player I had borrowed from the concierge. At the cashier's counter I identified myself as the fellow who had just called for the quick checkout (although the pained look on my face and distracted mannerisms were probably sufficient to peg me as the one). Glanced at the bill. It looked about right: A couple lines for the room charge, there's a dinner charge, or something, and one more, I guess the coffee shop. Looks close enough. Shoved my American Express at him.

Two minutes later I was tucking the folded bill in my pocket. We stepped out onto the walk, in a now blustering wind, to hail yet one more cab; what would probably be our last cab together.

I Had Been Dreading This For Months

Of course June accompanied me to the airport, and as you might guess, the ride was void of any valuable conversation. She sat close by my side, holding one of my hands in both of hers, in her lap; from time to time patting it and giving me a courageous smile. Inside the terminal things did not get better. I was one confused young man and it showed. Don't know why it didn't upset her mightily. But even now—amazingly to me, no signs of regret or worry; not a tear—not from brave June. And maybe—just maybe, this time she was willing to believe it wasn't necessary. Perhaps because of the level of energy I'd put into this campaign from day one, maybe she was daring to think long term thoughts about this new relationship with this American guy. She never said so. Never asked for any commitment. But I think she held hope. *No one was hoping more than me.* Waiting in line to check in she stood by my side like a statue. Got a boarding pass for the five-twenty flight to Palma. We didn't have a drink or do anything worth relating, or of value: just strolled hand in hand together, sensing an unspoken, mutual, solemn pledge. At least that's how I felt.

The moment I was dreading was upon us: the flight was finally called. Time for one of those strong bear hugs and another one of those great kisses—unashamed and full of love. June's kisses were like I had often said about her, unafraid and without other motives, an example of her unconfused life and character. Not meant to be sexy, not meant to arouse. They were meant to tell you something, and they did! And none had told me as much as this one. She knew what she was all about, and now, what she wanted this kiss to show. Her kiss told you everything you would ever need to know, and after one only a fool would ever think he had reason to question her. None other could match it. All others, forever, would be no more than dutiful.

If I was feeling ill earlier, I was really sick now. For a short time we could watch each other through a glass partition. But then I was ushered into a departure area that had the main terminal floor all but masked. Squinting between two hinged room dividers, I was able to see her finally give up on catching a further glimpse of me, turn, and begin her walk away; out of the terminal, and perhaps out of my life. I lost sight of her, but knew I'd not soon forget that tall proud figure cutting a straight path towards the exit. Even from the back. With each strutting step her long red hair bounced upon the black shoulder cape she had taken to wearing in the cold weather (over her green suede vest and wool slacks). With her high-heeled boots she appeared even taller than she was. In this world, she was someone to be reckoned with. My heart hurt. Reader, it truly, truly—hurt.

The Flight Back to Palma City

Knew it wasn't over with June, or at least I was pretty sure it wasn't. But also knew it would have to be put on hold for an indefinite period. I collapsed on a smooth wood bench in the waiting area. A couple long sighs. Five o'clock straight up now. Could be back in Palma by six-fifteen. Catch a cab to my unused sacrificial Palma Hotel (where hopefully I wouldn't find any important messages). Pay my one night's bill and run to the dock. Catch the seven o'clock liberty boat and be back on board with hours to spare. Should work out okay. *I'm just not so sure the rest of my life will work out okay.*

I was beginning to wonder when they were going to board the flight. Five-fifteen came and went. Five-thirty also. I was more than a little concerned now, and way out on a limb. (Don't forget, I wasn't even supposed to have left the Palma city limits!) This is one time I absolutely positively cannot afford to be late. We were going to up-anchor at midnight, everyone was supposed to be back on the ship by nine, and I think the last liberty boat was scheduled to cast off at eight-thirty. *This was going to be close.* Five forty-five. I latched on to one of the airline reps and asked what the heck was going on. The answer I got was not good. They had cancelled the five-twenty flight! But not to worry, *everyone will get seats on the next scheduled flight.* Oh my God! When is that going to be?

As irritated as I was, I counted my blessings when they announced a Palma departure at six o'clock. Not great, but I still should make it okay, just under the wire (if I could catch a cab real quick when I arrived). My nerves were frazzled enough from the situation with June, I sure didn't need the flight cancellation. As I tread the tarmac towards the waiting aircraft, I felt part of a scenario over which I couldn't exercise any control. I was experiencing a melancholy and distressing confusion. One part of me was saying, *you shouldn't have left June like that. Everything has not been said, you're quitting on something when there might still be an opportunity to do more.* But for now, I knew I had to just concentrate on making that liberty boat. Everything real hung on that!

The plane was fully boarded but we were just sitting there. *What the hell's the delay.* Nothing's happening. The engines should be running by now. *Christ, six thirty-five already.* Forty minutes to Palma; that makes seven-twenty at the earliest. *Shit!* Even if we took off right now, it would still only leave me forty minutes for the cab ride to town, hotel checkout, and a mad dash to the dock to catch the last boat! Okay, we're taxiing. Thank God. Into position at six fifty-five. Please God give this flight a tailwind. I knew that usually the scheduled enroute time had a built-in cushion, and if on a late take-off, the captain cuts a couple corners and cheats on his airspeed, he can make up a good amount of time. Here's hoping this is one of those times, and one of those pilots!

When we were finally airborne, I breathed a sigh of relief (but not a big one). I could still be in real serious trouble. The more I thought about Iberia Airlines just up and canceling a flight, and then being late on the next one, the madder I got. I was outraged at how they could do something like that—ruin people's carefully laid plans (especially mine)! I decided to do something I never do, write a letter to the airline, that's what I would do. I'd get some stationery and dash off a real "nasty-gram" to the CEO. This kind of passenger treatment deserved a response. Ridiculous just up and canceling a flight at the last minute. This would never happen in the states. I latched onto a stewardess and got some of that complimentary stationery they have on board. It was an assorted packet of envelopes, letterheads, postcards, etc. I picked through them. There it is—a fold-up European envelope, already addressed to the President of Iberia Airlines in Madrid. *Great.* Exactly what I wanted. Not much space inside, but I wasn't going to write a whole lot. (At least not a whole lot favorable.) Used my felt tipped black pen. Did it all in bold caps. Real neat. No erasures, no scratch-outs. I'm satisfied. *That* should let em know! Creased it and licked the envelope. Sealed it.

Now, where's that stewardess? Got her, she's coming. Looked up, handed her the envelope. She checked it. Gave me a patronizing smile and asked if I had a pen. I nodded. She kept smiling. I raised my hand with the felt tip pen. She took it, and in front of my eyes—before I could move, she scratched back and forth through the airline address. I was dumbfounded. "What are you doing?!"

She responded: "Oh, you used the wrong envelope, this one goes to our company offices in Madrid. Now tell me, where did you want to send this?"

Getting Back to the Ship

Descending into Palma the aircraft was being buffeted this way and that. Lots of turbulence. Out the windows I could see the water swept with white caps. And in lieu of its famous blue, it was steely gray. One wing up, then down. *Whew*, not a good landing, but on the ground in Palma at seven thirty-three. The weather was terrible. Leaden skies and almost gale force winds. Walking to the terminal I had to lean hard into the wind to make any progress. Pieces of cardboard and rubbish were flying across the ramp, finally being plastered up against a chain link fence. Could be a bad storm is coming (and I'll bet there's a helluva sea-state). Through the gates and out into the parking area. Grabbed a cab and was on my way. Made sure the driver knew that time was the issue here. No chance for the eight o'clock boat, just pray I can make the final, eight-thirty boat. Could miss that one too! I was just hoping they had a later one laid on for guys like me. (I was pretty sure they would, since even though they had said everyone had to be back on board by nine, there were bound to be stragglers.)

Out of the cab and full speed up the hotel ramp, digging the room key out of my toilet kit. Got it. Inside. *Forget the elevator.* Only one flight, can do it quicker on foot. Two steps at a time, down the hall and into the room. A quick sweep, jammed more stuff into my already full bag. Out the door and to the desk. "Yes, checking out, right now, please. I'm in quite a hurry." They moved quickly enough. As the clerk prepared my bill, I noticed the room key I'd plunked on the counter—room 227. *227? Holy Shit!* True enough, that *was* my room number—*here!* Back in Barcelona at the Manila hotel, in my rush for a quick checkout, over the phone I'd given them *this* hotel room number. (My room number in the Manila hotel had actually been 213.) *I'd accidentally checked somebody else out of their hotel room.*

The bill was paid (American Express full time). Into the damp air and down the street. Not working up a sweat this time. Had a strange isolated feeling. *I wasn't seeing any other servicemen.* Spooky. Palma was a ghost town. Wind really whipping now. Globs of foam and spray flew at me from over the sea wall. It might be getting worse. Straining to see through the mist and low hanging clouds, I could just make out a vague outline on the horizon (which I hoped was the carrier). *Gotta be it, but it's a lot further out than I remembered.* Shifted my legs out of high gear and slowed to a jog as I pulled up onto the dock, fully expecting to see at least one boat for late arrivals. *But nothing!* Not even a Shore Patrol boat (like I'd hitched a ride on so many times). In fact, not even a Shore Patrol guy. Zero activity. Not a sole indication that the *Forrestal* had ever used this dock. It was deserted! And not only was there not a single solitary U.S. Navy (or Marine) in sight, there also was a total lack of townspeople! I turned and surveyed the area, and then realized, the entire waterfront area was deserted, and some of the shops were boarded up! I was at a loss. It wasn't like I was thirty minutes late, *it was like I was a month late!* I couldn't understand this and was beginning to get real worried. There was nothing to indicate the boats had *ever* been running, and *none* in sight now. What can I do? *Nothing was making any sense!*

Squinting into the wind, through the tears (and big droplets now pelting down), about a mile down the shoreline I saw a rock breakwater. A bunch of masts were protruding over it and a lot of small boats were anchored inside it. Perhaps it was the public docks or the Palma marina. Maybe—just maybe, I could hire some local boat owner to take me out to the carrier. No more jogging, that's out. My feet hurt and my lungs are on fire. I'm taking a cab. There was one right by the dock. Into it and around the strand. When I got there, I still had to walk about a quarter-mile out the breakwater to get to the marina buildings. A large, old white sign said, *Palma D. M. Yacht Club.* Who knows—*maybe.* Into the building. Shit, it's a restaurant. A bar (an abandoned bar). *Wrong side.* The other building. To it. Found the office.

"Good evening." My presence was acknowledged by two guys, well dressed. Looked like officers of the club.

"Good evening. I'm afraid I may need some assistance. I'm off the carrier, and I have a big problem."

One of them spoke perfect English; an old but handsome looking white haired guy in a black turtle neck sweater. (Looked like the English actor Richard Harris.) He took a pipe from his mouth and spoke congenially, "And you are here for some help?"

"Yes sir. I was hoping, you might spare a small craft to take me out to the carrier. Certainly I'm willing to pay whatever that would be."

A nervous laugh, and then, "In *this* weather? If we could—we would, but even your own boats stopped running about six. The seas were too rough."

I GUESS I JUST WASN'T THINKING

Well that explains it! That's something. Might help. There *was* no boat at eight o'clock (or even seven o'clock). *This turn of events could possibly disguise my tardiness.* (Assuming my absence earlier in the day had gone unnoticed.) Evidently nobody got out to the ship after six. But if not, where the hell are they? Hadn't seen anyone off the carrier since I arrived back in town. I could make up a story that I was on the dock by eight, and still missed a boat. Luck might be with me. But I still have the problem of getting out there now.

There was a chance the second gentleman might be considering giving it a go. He looked genuinely concerned, and asked the other guy something about— I think, *a twelve-meter craft.* They began to discuss it more earnestly and the conversation switched into Spanish. I watched. My impression was that a plan might be in the works. (If nothing else, it would give them something interesting to talk about on Monday when they went to the office.) Just then—just when it was looking good, as luck would have it (and it's said "timing is everything"), a huge gust of wind hit the side of the building, and tore the outside shutter off the window right next to us. From that moment on, second thoughts and better judgment prevailed. I was forced to leave empty-handed.

I think I'm screwed. Nine twenty-five. In real trouble now! Don't know if the carrier will up-anchor at midnight like planned. If so, Holy shit, can you imagine that, if they *left* me!? *But maybe some other guys missed the boat.* I sure hope so. (Misery likes company. I was praying I wasn't the only one.) *Had to think, had to come up with a way to get to the carrier!* For want of something else to do, I decided to go back to my unused hotel—check it out. I strode (praying) into the lobby, but saw only one member of the hotel staff. Not another soul. Deserted like the rest of the waterfront. From where I was, I could look across the foyer into the lounge. An apparently vacant lounge. From the entrance I perused a sea of unoccupied black Formica tables strewn with napkins, small plates and half-finished drinks. Looked like I had just missed a helluva party. About fifty tables—fifty *empty* tables!

There I stood, toilet kit dangling from an index finger, overnight bag tucked under my arm, and fresh out of ideas—now physically ill. This could be career serious. Scanned the empty room again. *My heart almost stopped when my glance got to a barely lit far corner.* A single table was occupied! And at that table, was a cigar smoking gray-suited American businessman with his frumpy, martini-wielding wife, and their beautiful young daughter *sitting on Nick Cassopolis's lap!* And Nick was in rare form. He had the most foolish (we say in the military—"shit-eating") grin on his face I'd ever seen. He was in his uniform—such as it was. His hat was on his head crosswise. Evidently he'd drawn today's Shore Patrol duty. I could see the tell-tale black and white arm band, although it had slid from its normal upper arm location and was now dangling around his forearm. (The big letters **SP** were not visible, twisted inside.) What a sight! He must have been the hit of the party.

He saw me! A double take, a moment of embarrassment, and then he jumped to his feet, disrupting his companions and nearly upsetting the table. Erect, he teetered for a second before reaching down to the edge of the table to steady himself. Got it now. Flashed a disarming smile to the parents, blew a kiss to Junior Miss America, and was away from the table and on his not very straight way over to me. Nick was one good-looking guy even "half in the bag." He may have been even more adorable to the American tourists. He rushed over to me and blurted out the least believable statement I ever heard: "Rog! Boy have I been worried about you!" It was a cinch that Nick Cassopolis hadn't been worrying about anything for quite some time.

"What's the skinny Nick. What the fuck is going on?" He didn't answer right away. Steadied himself with one hand on my shoulder. Started to talk, then broke into giggles. (I sure was glad to see someone familiar, and moreover, to see somebody not worrying.)

"Sea state Rog. Too rough. Cancelled boating about six. Each of the squadrons have a shore patrol detail to round up stragglers. I'm it for VMA 331."

"You mean I'm not in trouble? There's others?"

"Well maybe. So far just you, but I think there's two guys missing from the Crusader squadron. Was just talking to their Shore Patrol guy."

"What's the plan Nick, what are we supposed to do?"

"Gonna rent a taxi Rog. We're gonna drive the length of the island, up to Polensa Bay."

"Drive? Tonight?"

"Yeah, later on. Small island—will only take a few hours. We'll be there by dawn. In fact we'll beat the carrier there. When it arrives we'll be there and ready to hop a boat out. No sweat. Meteorology said this thing will blow through tonight. It'll be quiet on the north side by morning. Don't worry. We'll be out on the ship before the Change of Command ceremony even starts." For the first time (in six hours it seemed) I sat down, and let it all hang out. I was tired, mentally and physically. I hadn't needed it to end this way. Can't remember where we ate or what we ate, or who got the cab. Do remember—at about two in the morning we still didn't have the cab; just waiting under some trees by a little gazebo, in the middle of a small weedy park. Can't remember when it was we left, or how long it took. I was exhausted. We ended up with three other guys. Didn't know any of them. One guy damn near didn't go. His Spanish girlfriend was hanging on to him and pleading. One of his buddies had to talk turkey to him, to get him into the cab. (I watched, and I can tell you the Captain damn near lost one here.) I know it was real late when we left, and it was a long and uncomfortable ride. The sky was turning pink as we came into a small resort town, which we were all hoping was Pollensa. Three or four streets later we could see a beach area and what looked like a marina.

I wasn't sure what the plan would be to actually get out to the ship, and the ship was no where in sight. *Hope to hell we're in the right bay. I think there's two up here.* Out of the cab. Nick paid. (Which was good. I could barely afford my own fun times.) We sat alongside each other on a smelly sea wall, feet dangling, like a bunch of homeless bums, hungover and tired, waiting for a miracle. I was content to leave Nick in charge. I roughly knew what was going to happen. At least we were on our way back to the ship. Could have been a lot worse. Somewhere, I had lost my toilet kit. Not with me now. No big deal.

There it was. At 0900—as big as you please, the *Forrestal* came steaming around the point; cutting a handsome and wholesome figure for us to ogle (and dread the consequences of our tardy arrival). I thought the ship would have a plan for our pickup, and maybe they did. But Nick wasn't going to wait. He made his own arrangements for us, with some fishermen at the end of the pier. We were about to be brought out in style. You should have seen it; an old scow loaded with nets, oily tarpaulins, crab traps and drying fish innards. What a mess. (But probably no less than we deserved.) Five of us packed in with all the rusted and musty paraphernalia. I not only looked like death warmed over, I smelled like dead bait. I was one bedraggled-looking USMC captain. (And I looked better on the outside than I felt on the inside.)

Once again, a day late. (Shades of Marseilles and coming back off the *Leonardo Da Vinci*.) Leaned and got ahold of the wet vinyl handrails of the ladder. Up the rungs. The usual ritual (that I could have done without). We were officially piped on board. Only one squadron mate—Bob Harmon, the crew scheduler (and my last remaining confidant at this time) was waiting for me topside. Once again he had the hand-scrawled sign that said, *Bien Venido, Senor Fortunado.* (Another reference to our standing joke, me like the dashing "Mr. Lucky," miraculously surviving these in-port stays.) Scanned the rest of the flight deck, and heaved a sigh of relief when I didn't see the tall silhouette of the Colonel. No one else waiting for me. *Whew.* Rendered my salute to the Colors on the stern (thinking back to the patriotic Leo Lippe) and headed for my stateroom, tail between my legs.

Chapter Twenty-Seven
TIME TO FACE THE MUSIC

Our Tour in the Med is Officially Over

The Change of Command Ceremony went without a hitch and was over by 1500. Half the squadron was on the flight deck as the ship's Captain was "barged" back from the *Saratoga*. I took my share of good-natured ribbing regarding my tardy arrival earlier in the day. From time to time I was able to briefly and weakly impersonate a happy squadron member, joyful to be returning home. Joking and screwing around (now with no more flight ops to sweat) we could easily have been viewed as a gaggle of souls without a care in the world. The good times were awaiting us back home. *Hah!* In my head and in front of my eyes was a continuous collage of faces and scenes, alternating between the Cote d'Azur, Barcelona, Milano... and Beaufort, South Carolina. Wrestling with my situation, it appeared a futile exercise. I mulled over one course of action, one plan, one scenario after another; none seeming the slightest bit plausible. And I wasn't going to have much time to work things out. It would take more than six and a half days to get my head and heart back in order, that was for sure.

We snapped to attention as the ship's Captain was piped aboard and rendered his salute to the Colors. Thirty minutes later, there it was; that old familiar rumble and ratcheting, as the huge chain links began notching their way around the turnstile, and five thousand pounds of anchor started it's last journey up from the bottom. Without looking I could visualize the seaweed and muck being stripped from the blades as they broke the surface, and the water jetting off the links as they snapped over the gunnel. Probably the last time I'd witness this unbuckling, or feel the deep

344

vibrations as this ocean-goer stretched, yawned, and leaned forward into her harness. We were on our way.

A Dread-Filled Trip Back Across the Atlantic

Corpen: 200 degrees. Just as planned, late afternoon and steaming southward. The straight shadows of the superstructure angled further and further towards the stern. Past Valencia. Dusk now, Ibiza well behind us. Towards the point at Cartagena; the tantalizing shoreline of eastern Spain still in sight. I wandered to the fan tail, and once again marveled at the pounding, turbulent wake this monster spewed rearward. She wasn't afraid, I can tell you that—like a horse on the way back to the barn, head down, nostrils flared, it could smell the states. The sun had set long before we turned southwest, and the moon was high in the sky when we rounded the corner and aimed at Gibraltar. I feared it was going to be a short trip—much too short. I was gripped by woefully complex feelings of loss and guilt. Alone now on the forward port catwalk, hair plastered back, forehead damp from the wet salt air, I was the sole lookout—a sentinel of wariness. This gray monster had its second wind, no doubt about it. She was plowing westward under a full moon, white water leaping from her bow. For one of the last times I would see the eerie luminescence of the sparkling phosphorus-filled wake. I was a tiny flea on the back of a big dog; helpless to affect either direction or speed, in this voyage or in my life. Tired. *Lots to think about.* Tomorrow's another day. (Although I could not imagine it presenting any solutions of value.)

Monday: There were rumors circulating at breakfast, that Air Ops was going to order one last launch, this afternoon or tomorrow, while we were still within 400 miles of Naval Air Station, Rota, Spain. (A place we could use for an emergency landing in the case of a broken tail hook.) Miraculously, it got canceled. (Maybe they felt the vibes, remembering trying to keep everybody current that one afternoon in Cannes.) Don't know, but I for one was glad. So, for the rest of the crossing it would be mutual congratulations and lots of paper shuffling. Each of the OIC's had to prepare detailed turnover inventories. We'd spend our time getting things in order for our return to Beaufort. Once there, the squadron would start all over again. Phase I; training with new people. Most of us would be transferred to other squadrons, other bases. The squadron would have a new commanding officer.

I GUESS I JUST WASN'T THINKING

Tuesday: Spent the better part of the day touring my shops like I'd done a hundred times; mostly helping the guys with their next duty station requests. About 1500 I retreated to the stateroom and collapsed in the rack. Jim was at his desk working on his own "Request for Next Duty Assignment." Dreaming without sleeping I heard him speak. "Rog, what are you going to put in for?" I was stuck for an answer—still in a turmoil about whether or not a life with Sara was possible, and if it wasn't (or if in my demented state, I perceived that it wasn't), would I even stay in the Marine Corps, where among so many fellow officers and their wives, a divorce between Sara and I would be untenable—unthinkable. I was a mess.

"Not sure Jim, I know sooner or later I gotta think about the 'Boot Strap' program." (A helluva deal where the military sends officers back to college to finish their degree on campus—at no cost to the individual!) "Maybe now is as good as any. After that, one tactical tour somewhere, and then the Command and Staff College as a Major. I don't know, what do you think?"

"Yeah, I hear the Boot Strap program has the Commandant's blessings, and as a senior Captain you're right in the window."

I gave him a thumbs-up. He smiled, and I think he was satisfied, bending back over his own form. I was glad we didn't dwell on the subject, since once again (as so damned often with me) I was saying one thing and thinking another. I knew my lips were moving and I could hear apparently rational sentences coming out of my mouth, while at best, my heart wasn't in it. Or at worst, I was in the midst of weighing the merits of something entirely unconnected. And with a guy as matter-of-fact and straightforward as Jim, it was a glaring violation; in fact, downright risky. But this is what I'd been doing for the past ten months, and it was getting worse. No matter what activity or thought process I would engage in, nothing dislodged the major issues that had me so devastatingly preoccupied. The weight of it was there all the time. Felt like my brain was wearing out. As if gremlins were filing away the top of my brain, rasping off the cells, getting closer and closer to the nerve centers. I was now convinced, no matter what you eat, or how much you exercise, your health is much more determined by your state of mind. I felt a continuing, worse—*increasing* weariness as I sought to work things out; come to some conclusions and decide on a course of action. *Ten months to get in this fix, less than a week to sort it all out.*

Wednesday: I took some time alone in the stateroom and decided to start going through Sara's correspondence; from the first letter. Spent the whole morning and half the afternoon. I was a little encouraged to note a capability I didn't think was in me (and one I certainly didn't deserve). I was surprised to find myself getting involved and sensitively interested; almost *excited* when I read and re-read, and really tried. Like after taking a blow and being stunned, shaking one's head to remove the cobwebs, straining to refocus on actualities. I hazarded to think I could do it; like we'd be able to make it. Then, curses! Thirty minutes later—like an addict I would put on one of my French, or Spanish, or Italian tapes, hear the music, look at some photos of June and I, glance down at my bracelet from Rhodes, pick up my Super Dakota, *and just plain get sick!*

Miraculously, I think it was there—a welcomed, increasing positive anxiety to see the family. If not Sara (there was a real dread there, for obvious reasons), at least the kids. Continued pouring over the letters; in particular the latest ones. Also, undid the rubber band, opened the envelope full of photos, and began to thumb through them one by one. I saw personalities that just leaped off the paper. Handsome kids, white teeth, good hair, broad smiles, square foreheads, thick locks. (Sara's good polish heritage. Not from me.) Even with many recent photos, it was hard not to picture the kids in the stages they were in when I left. I missed them all and was very ashamed of myself (and deservedly so, as I need not tell you) for my months of inattention. Perhaps not blatant inattention, because I did send them lots of cards and little gifts (mostly picked up running through train stations). But certainly not the wholesome priority they deserved, that I saw being rendered by most of the other officers. I felt justifiably guilty in this area.

Thursday: We had a ship-wide volleyball tournament on the hangar deck. VMA 331 had two teams, an enlisted team and a team made up of the officers. I was on the officers' team of course—with Jim. (If you were involved in anything with Jim, winning was almost a foregone conclusion.) We won our first six or seven games and were in the finals. And, I gotta admit, there were moments—albeit brief moments, when I think for just a second I forgot my plight. In the midst of a lunge for the ball, a good save, or a successful spike, I was just "one of the guys." It felt tearfully good (but it was tearfully temporary). I had a monumental problem, and for me, exercise was not going to relieve stress.

I GUESS I JUST WASN'T THINKING

The whole day the mood was high. Mid afternoon the word was spread that the Colonel wanted all the officers to plan on taking the evening meal together. At 1830 hours sharp we'd meet in the wardroom for one of our last, special times together. The Officers Mess was a formal and proper place. Its tables, spread with white linen, looked all the more immaculate as they were contrasted by the dark wood-paneled walls. On all four walls hung colorful brass plaques boasting the emblems of previous USS *Forrestal* tactical units. One could not help but be aware of a proud heritage, and feel obligated to carry on the tradition. Here, fitting decorum was not difficult. At least I for one felt this way. I'm sure the rest did also. It was a great evening. Many good stories retold (more than one about me). Rave reviews and expressions of camaraderie. Lots of good natured joking and talk about possible next duty stations, and trying for *another cruise together,* sometime.

And thank God for small favors. In spite of my off-duty philandering and onboard preoccupation with other things, I must have put up a good front, because at the conclusion of the meal, after the Skipper finished his speech (an informal and nostalgic recap of the cruise) he commenced a "roast" of each of the officers. When he got to me, I was obviously worried, then surprised—and gratified, as the sincerity in his voice and extent of his accolades, left no doubt about him believing I had made a fine contribution to the squadron as a Flight Leader and Maintenance Officer. This included one left-handed compliment: He said that while I was only an average Assistant Officer-in-Charge, I was one of the best Officer-in-Charges he'd ever had. (Remember? I took over as the head of the Maintenance Department when Major Burnham broke his leg skiing.) This only made me think, *what in God's name would the Colonel have thought if I had really made the job a priority.* The finale and perhaps high point of the evening was the singing of the Marine Corps Hymn. There wasn't a dry eye in the place. Hard for me to imagine that life could be so straight forward, so uncomplicated, so honorable. *I would have given anything to have mine that way!*

Friday: (Two more days) I felt a little queasy each time I thought about the short time remaining. (More than a little.) *Dammit!* Everything was still up in the air. Five nights of laying in the rack hashing things over, and I was no closer to a course of action than when we left Pollensa Bay. I knew I needed to be certain, to be committed to a plan—one way or the other, *before* we arrived. I *had* to come to a decision. There couldn't be any vacillating when I arrived. If I arrived in my present state of mind it would be a disaster. I still had no idea if I was going to wrap Sara in my arms committed to our future, *or ask for a divorce*; put in for assignment to the Boot Strap program, *or hand in my resignation*. I was a wreck (and don't know how I thought I could come to some decision now—with only 48 hours to go). I was so unsettled at this time, it made me wonder how a condemned man could even think about a "favorite" dinner when he was going to the gallows at sunrise.

Truthfully (and mercifully) as the days had passed, and thoughts of Sara and the kids were more and more actual; I *think*, bit by bit, the fragrance and intensity of my adventures in Europe were fading. I've heard—we've all heard, how *time heals*. Even in this short period I now had to work with, it seemed to perhaps be the case. *But I wasn't sure if I wanted it to be the case*. Part of me knew that forgetting it would be for the best, since I saw no way that I would ever be able to recreate the lifestyle or renew the associations I had somehow managed to experience on the cruise. How could this be recreated? Where? Doing what? While perplexed and weighing the two mutually exclusive lives that could lay ahead of me, I realized going back over Sara's letters was helping. I grabbed the box full of them, and began going over them again. She'd done a great job keeping me up to date on the kids, their activities and signs of their growing up. Had the photos out too. *Stare* at those kids. Reacquaint yourself! I was making a valiant effort to re-instill within me that which had never been dislodged from my squadron mates.

Donna, our oldest—even at six was one over-achieving little girl, moving through her early life without questions. Oh—never told you this: Three or four months before her birth, the Marine Corps had sent me on a one year "Unaccompanied" tour in Japan—meaning *no family members were allowed to go with their service man to the foreign assignment!* Six months after my wedding day I was yanked away from my wife and denied any chance to learn and perfect my new role as a husband—for thirteen months! (One pilot's wife got a Japanese visa and came over to visit her husband. Soon as USMC Headquarters got wind of it, they promptly transferred him to Korea.) By the time I returned to the states, Donna was seven months old! Not only did I miss her coming into the world, but half her first year. And then I ineptly exercised my right to bring her up, discipline and encourage her, *without having read a single book on parenting or going to a single class on it.* Instead (and embarrassedly) I primarily based my tactics on those of a Marine Corps drill instructor—just raising my voice to an ear splitting level when I wanted to discourage her from some act. *Damn.* I'm so ashamed of my performance in that regard. But according to Sara, now—Donna, with no help from me (perhaps a plus), she was growing up as if it were something that each person was responsible for, on their own; without expecting too much help.

I had a bunch of photos of Mark. Oh, never told you; I had named him Mark Adrian after my pre-flight training buddy Mark Adrian Yatsko, who was killed in 58 during the Matsu Quemoy flap with Red China. I had vowed then to name my first male child after him. (I found Mark Yatsko's parent's address in McAllen, Texas, and sent them a birth announcement. They sent us a silver cup engraved *Mark Adrian.*) My favorite photo of my Mark, was one of him under an outdoor shower, in a too large soaking bathing suit, laughing heartily, his ribs showing. Now four years old Sara said he was always trying to do the right thing; intent on approval. You could just see it in his face. And, he was small—not much bigger than when I left. Like me he would be faced with the decision to ignore (not possible) or strive each day to overcome the stigma of being the "littlest guy" in almost every group. (Hated myself for giving him those genes.) According to Sara he was unusually perceptive, probably too sensitive, but able to assert himself; already seeming older than his years—already coming out with measured and unusually mature responses.

Stacy was a tiny thing, but a dynamo of energy. Only three years old when I left she was a lovable hellion. Talk about knowing your own mind! (And expressing it well when things weren't going your way.) Sara said Stacy was the little girl they wrote the poem about: "There once was a girl with curl, and when she was good she was very good, but when she was bad she was horrid." Sounded to me like if she was difficult now, it might be a real challenge as she grew into adolescence. I would abandon her again—twice; and yet, many years later see her stick up for me and by me—repeatedly, when my actions did not merit that support. She would name her first child "Rog."

And Kevin. Well from day one the whole world loved Kevin. One cute baby I can tell you that! He could flash a smile in a second, that would melt anyone's heart. Sara said if he could go on to keep that grin (and attitude) he wasn't going to have any problems. And finally (although not initially) this would turn out to be the case. I would live to deeply regret not spending this past year with him. I would learn that your absence during these early years cannot be made up for, irrespective of the intensity of your subsequent efforts. At best, you shape events later—as well as you can, to show your love and concern, but you never get this time back, never completely repair the damage.

In two days—less than 48 hours, in addition to facing their mother (the thought of which weakens my knees and turns me mute) I would have to look into these children's eyes while trying to convince myself that a human being like me could be their father. How could I think I deserved any love or respect from them. I didn't. Not by a long shot.

Saturday: The schedule and details of our forthcoming return flight to home base was in the throes of final coordination, and gaining hoopla. Tomorrow, Sunday *(tomorrow?!),* crossing 74 degrees west, two-hundred miles out of Norfolk, the USS *Forrestal* was going to shed its Marine Squadron. Our last launch, all twelve aircraft; direct to USMC Air Station, Beaufort, South Carolina. An 0915 launch would put us overhead the airfield at 1045. A gala "Welcome Home" ceremony was scheduled to kick off upon our arrival at 1100. I was shaking in my boots. Twenty-four hours to go and still no commitment, no definite course of action. I was not proud of myself. In fact, my weakness was despicable to me.

The initial briefing was held at 1300, and we were in the Ready Room, "all ears." Our return, a twelve plane fly-by, was going to be an appropriate and dramatically staged arrival. The Colonel of course, would lead it. (My first job was to make absolutely positively sure that all twelve airplanes were up and ready for the trip!) We received "Well Done" messages from the Group Commander at Beaufort, which included a diagram for the areas to which we'd taxi and park. On our old ramp (right in front of where we would park) there would be a big stage and a podium, and hundreds of chairs set up, where our family and friends would be sitting when we taxied in. My stomach was full of butterflies. I couldn't concentrate on any of this. I wasn't well. *One more day.*

Had a second briefing after supper. More details for our arrival. The Wing Commander from Cherry Point was going to be there to address the returning heroes and their families. Change One: A conflict in his schedule was going to delay the ceremony thirty minutes. Our launch time would be delayed till 0945. All the planes would be up and ready, Sergeant Baldwin was willing to bet his stripes on it. No problem. The plan was we'd come in over the field, lined up with the southeast runway, three divisions of four aircraft, do a three-second break, touchdown with short (too short) intervals (perhaps six aircraft on the runway at the same time), and taxi in. All together. Spectacular. (If I didn't throw up.)

An Inescapable Final, Return Flight

Sunday morning: This is it. No more time. The end of the cruise. The end of my ten month's exploit. Minus me the Ready Room was a joyous place. I wasn't part of anything good. All too soon for me, but what everyone else was waiting for, one last time, booming out of the squawk box it came: "Gentlemen, man your aircraft." I watched with hesitancy, as eagerly—almost mirthfully, the other assigned pilots commenced their last journey through those now familiar passageways and hatches, and up those narrow ladders, to emerge into the bright daylight of the flight deck. I hoped my nausea was at its pinnacle. We were not only in full flight gear, with all the associated paraphernalia, but duly armed as well. All the pilots were packing their military-issue 38 Special Smith and Wesson revolvers; everyone except me that was. In my shoulder holster was the 7-inch-barreled Super Dakota with adjustable sights (and no serial number). Close to my heart, a key souvenir. A memory stimulator that was good and bad at the same time. I was the Division Leader for the third division. Jim had the second, and the Colonel, of course, was leading number one.

The ship's company was particularly respectful and gave us a heartfelt send off. Lots of salutes and earnest handshakes. I was again made aware of the mutual respect and bonding of personnel (even of disassociated tasks) aboard one of these flat tops. I was experiencing a ton of emotions as I strapped in for the last time. Real tears, and I didn't care. The wind could've caused them, but it didn't. Sergeant Parker gave me a hard slap on the shoulder, said something extremely complimentary, and pulled the canopy down. Like so many times before; alone in this acrylic bubble, about to be launched into whatever—gray, blue, black, wet, cold, who cares? This is what we're trained to do. Paid for. I think I could do anything, *except what I'm going to have to do in an hour and a half.*

The launch went flawlessly. I needed the physical punishment of the cat shot to bring me back. The same helmeted and goggled Launch Officer, the same pants legs flailing in a thirty-knot wind. Readied my head, pressed it backward against the head rest. There's the windup signal. I eased the power lever forward—then full forward, hard against the stop. Wanted every last pound of thrust. Same unbridled roar. Whoaa! Pounded forward, sinking. *Rotate. Got it!* I'm goddam away again! *Catch me if you can!* I'm above everything! The rendezvous went without a hitch as well. (And it rarely did.) Set the course at 240 degrees. We'd go "feet dry" at Charleston VORTAC (a Navigational Radio Transmitter), then ten or twelve minutes due south to Beaufort. Don't know how I was able to fly.

It was in sight. MCAS Beaufort South Carolina was in sight. I could see the expanses of its concrete ramps, the nearby swamps of Parris Island Recruit Depot, the highway, could even make out our little neighborhood. We were letting down, 250 knots indicated, passing eight thousand feet. Lined up with the runway. The Colonel gave the order to drop off in trail. High speed letdown. Beaufort tower was on the air. We were heroes. *Some hero I was. I didn't even belong in the same airspace as these guys.* Overhead, in a slight bank I could see the whole arrangement. Our ramp was set up just like the messages had said; with a big stage, and the chairs (all full), making a sea of heads and bodies; wives, kids, families and friends, straining upward as we streaked in.

The pitch! The Colonel racked it over in his left break. Counted to myself, ...two, three, there goes Ken, ...two, three, there goes Nick, nice interval. So far so good. It was a perfectly timed break. I glanced over to the downwind and saw the Colonel wings level, gear coming down. Ken right behind him. Nick in about a sixty degree bank, arcing across. There goes Jim, ..two, three, Tripp's gone. One more. Last one. ..two ..three, *I'm over!* Oops, in my state I may have pulled it too hard—three "G's." Gained a little on Ernie. Shallowed out my bank a hair. That's it, looking good now. Out of the corner of my eye, acres of tarmac were visible beneath me, occupied by the expectant family members, dignitaries, and other interested personnel. We had messaged the flight order (aircraft sequence) to Beaufort Ops, so the wives would know which plane their husband was in. One of those heads craned back would be Sara, searching for her husband. For me, *I could barely voice the word husband.*

It was a pretty sight, four birds starting their taxi-back in a tight diamond parade formation; two more turning off; and five, six of us still on the runway at the same time—*not* an approved maneuver. One blown tire up front and there could be a helluva pile-up. (That was the last thing I was worried about.) As we taxied ever closer, even through my wet eyes and streaked windscreen, I could make out more detail than I wanted. Blobs and bodies were rapidly becoming faces and people. I was searching for a dark haired woman with kids. Maybe all standing, maybe one in the arms.

I GUESS I JUST WASN'T THINKING

I was ill. I'd never been this nervous—ever. Onto the ramp. Pulling into my slot. We were going to open all the canopies simultaneously on a signal from the Colonel. For just a moment more I would be protected. Still had time. Still in a world I knew. Not vulnerable. *There's the command.* I hit the latch and let the canopy swing upward.

A breeze that should have been refreshing struck me face on. I was only a hundred feet from the chairs. The hangar was draped in brightly-colored banners. I spied Major Burnham on the stage. A band was playing. Someone was testing a loudspeaker. People were hollering. I was terrified. I stood up in the cockpit. *There she was!* I spied Sara and the kids in the second or third row. Knee up. Stumbled on the canopy rail. Leg over the side. Where's the first step. Got it. Down the ladder. *Who stuck it in?* Never felt it go in. It was just there in the side of the aircraft. Don't trip. On the ground now. On my feet. Swaying. Scenery changing; things passing me; must be walking, running, but not feeling the pavement. Heart pounding and through my blurred eyes I could make out Sara waving while holding Kevin. All the guys are running. Me too I guess. Yeah I'm running. Don't fall. Oh God. *God, help me here.*

Epilogue
I GUESS I JUST WASN'T THINKING CONTINUES...

Part Three: The CIA Secret Airline and Eureka! She Exists! Standby for scarcely credible adventures, consequences, and deserved reproaches. Roger strove to become a devoted husband and father, but couldn't do it. Flashbacks of his European adventures caused his gait to falter. Lacking the courage to even mouth the word "divorce," he surprises his family and shocks his fellow pilots by resigning his military commission. This step accomplished he is able to get on with Air America— the CIA's most controversial paramilitary aviation operation in Southeast Asia. He chooses this employment because the pilots are housed in Saigon where satchel charges or grenades are going off just a half block away, so their families cannot live with them. Instead—handily, the pilots domicile them a short flight away in Bangkok or Singapore. This shadowy tour is just the beginning of an extended series of global, non-stop honest (albeit embarrassing) unanticipated raucous events and pivotal challenges (perhaps beckoning more advance-planning than Roger is gifted with). Part Three remains a revealing gender-centric struggle and will surely stand out as one of the most revealing and movingly meaningful things you will have ever read. Struggling in an ill-fitting world, he continues to seek that one magic but historically fated-to-failure union. Ashamed and embarrassed he sincerely and apologetically strives to explain to you his life-altering condition and his otherwise inexplicable behavior. *Readers will be surprised and gratified; unable not to leap to their feet and applaud an entirely unexpected but spectacular turn of events at the end of this part.*